Play On!

Thanks Larry
I enjoyed Music
appreciation
Hope you enjoy this
R.K

Play On!

60 years of music-making with
the Sydney Symphony Orchestra

PHILLIP SAMETZ

an
ABC
BOOK

Published by ABC Enterprises for the
AUSTRALIAN BROADCASTING CORPORATION
GPO Box 9994 Sydney NSW 2001

National Library of Australia
Cataloguing-in-Publication entry
Sametz, Phillip.
 Play on!: 60 years of music-making with the
 Sydney Symphony Orchestra.

 Bibliography.
 Includes index.
 ISBN 0 7333 0102 9.

 1. Sydney Symphony Orchestra—History.
 2. Symphony orchestras—New South Wales—
 Sydney—History. 3. Music—New South Wales—
 Sydney—20th century—History and criticism. 1. Title.

784.2099441

Designed by Helen Semmler
Set in 10½/13 pt Bodoni by Midland Typesetters, Victoria
Printed and bound in Australia by Southwood Press,
Marrickville NSW

2.5-3995

ENDPAPERS
 Front The SSO in Sydney Town Hall. *Conductor*:
 Sir Eugene Goossens (Photo: Max Dupain)
 Back The SSO in Carnegie Hall, New York.
 Conductor: Stuart Challender (Photo: Andrew Clarke)

For M.

Contents

Introduction

The circumstances of the SSO's existence have always been unusual. It was brave but not, as it turned out, so strange that the ABC began to run orchestras in an entrepreneurial fashion in the 1930s. The subsequent rise in the orchestras' fortunes and prestige was dramatic, and nowhere moreso than in Sydney. But in some ways the SSO's success was achieved despite the conditions under which it performed. For too many years it worked too hard and in too diverse a range of activities to achieve uniform excellence. This was because of the unique circumstances of its life: the ABC long insisted that its orchestras were broadcasting units that happened to give concerts, while the players in large part hoped to be regarded, above all, as performing musicians who lived most directly for their live audiences.

The SSO has worked with fewer great conductors than it has worked with adequate and even downright bad ones, and it suffered for at least three decades from an inadequate training system for Australian musicians. From the 1960s through to the 1980s, it was managed by the ABC with decreasing proficiency.

I emphasise these important factors in the SSO's history because of the frequency with which they have been glossed over in many of the ABC's official versions of its association with orchestral performance. They will not be neglected in this book. On the other hand, I have not sought scandal or conflict where none existed. I have been concerned, chiefly, to convey as clearly and engagingly as possible the elements that have made up the orchestra's life.

This has not been as straightforward a task as it might seem. Orchestral histories can be made boring because of the over zealous application of good intentions. Before writing this book, I read through some of the many narratives that have been published detailing the life of this or that orchestra. The exercise proved to me that it is not possible to create a compelling orchestral biography while trying to be polite to everyone who worked with the orchestra and about everything that happened to it. Such an approach is also inherently unfair. It cannot be assumed that because orchestras play music for a living, their lives are harmonious. Musicians can be territorial and temperamental, they can perform brilliantly or badly for non-musical reasons, and they can be very critical of one another.

Acknowledging these things at the outset did not make the writing of *Play On!* less of a pleasure. The SSO is the orchestra I grew up with and, like three generations of Sydney people before me, it opened my ears to a huge range of music without which I would be the poorer. To an extent, then, this book has been written out of gratitude.

It was my intention when I began writing *Play On!* to separate from the main part of the SSO story the parts of the ABC story as musical entrepreneur that did not immediately effect the Sydney orchestra. So only passing attention is paid here to the numerous resident and touring soloists who worked with the SSO. I felt that anecdotes about Lotte Lehmann's tours, or the return to Australia of Essie Ackland, would have unduly cluttered an already complex narrative. Similarly, the lives of the SSO's chief conductors were relevant only in the context of their work with the orchestra so that, for example, Goossens' last years in London and Willem van Otterloo's work in Melbourne are not chronicled. On the other hand, the changes the orchestra has experienced seemed to me to be inseparable from the different ways it has been managed, and the relevant internal ABC changes in managements and structure are discussed as aspects of the SSO story. So are the numerous changes to the fabric of Australian, and particularly Sydney, life. These cultural shifts often changed community perceptions of the SSO's importance.

It has been forgotten now that, in large degree, the ABC's creation of concert orchestras led directly to the acceptance of the performing arts as a legitimate part of urban life in Australia. As this book will detail, the orchestras helped make the arts important here. That the SSO is still doing this in the year of its 60th anniversary is one of the reasons why *Play On!* is as much a celebration as a critical history.

Phillip Sametz
Sydney, April 1992

CHAPTER ONE

"A first-class cottage piano"

There is no story of the Sydney Symphony Orchestra that is not a story of the ABC. The orchestra was brought into being by the ABC, grew up with the ABC, and now finds itself turning sixty along with the rest of the organisation. It has often been a fraught partnership: the quality of the ABC's management of its orchestras over the last sixty years has been undeniably variable, and has at times alienated musicians and audiences. But the ABC created a symphony orchestra for Sydney, and audiences to watch it take shape. The vision of these early years has had an incalculable effect on the kind of musical life Australia has now.

The decade in which the ABC started life was the 1930s, a time when there was a real yearning for the establishment of a full-time symphony orchestra in Australia. On the whole, the quality of intellectual discourse was poor. Australia's daily press was politically conservative and almost unfailingly Empire-conscious, rarely reporting international events from a non-British perspective. There were few basic reference works about the humanities as they had developed in Australia, no weekly or monthly magazines of intellectual rigour and no full-time performing arts companies.

It was only in painting that the situation had begun to improve, and for reasons that were to be heartening for the ABC when it became a concert entrepreneur: the eloquence of a group of radical painters (particularly George Bell), which knocked many arrogantly expressed conservative arguments on the head; and the obvious public interest in a broad range of painting styles, as evidenced by the huge success of Keith Murdoch's Melbourne *Herald* Show of 1939 (brought to Sydney by the *Daily Telegraph*). The difference was that where Bell was advocating an Australian understanding of modernism, the SSO was born of a benign paternal belief in the need for high culture.

Until the ABC began to give regular orchestral concerts in Sydney in 1936, the major musical entrepreneurs were the two Tait brothers, who had run J. C. Williamson's amusement operation since 1918. Since then they had brought to Australia Galli-Curci, Chaliapin, Paderewski, Moiseiwitsch, Heifetz and McCormack, and brought back Dame Nellie Melba for her final operatic seasons in 1924 and 1928. The Taits were hard nosed and tight fisted, and had no pretensions about the worth or otherwise of higher cultural values—their musical imports were glamorous money-makers.

Someone who remembers going to the Heifetz concerts in 1926 is Neville Amadio, who was to become the SSO's first principal flute. But the orchestra he heard accompanying Heifetz was essentially that of the NSW State Conservatorium of Music, conducted by the Conservatorium director Dr W. Arundel Orchard.

The Conservatorium players were used because at this time Sydney had no permanent professional orchestra. But only a few years before the Heifetz tour Sydney had been the home of perhaps the finest of the pre-ABC permanent groups in Australia. This had been called the NSW State Orchestra, and had been the brainchild of the Belgian Henri Verbrugghen, who came to Australia in 1915 as the first director of the State Conservatorium. He was probably the best orchestral trainer to have worked here until that time, and a terrific organiser. Joseph Post later remembered that he was 'persuasive to a degree, a regular dynamo, and the sort of man of whom you had to take notice the moment he entered the room'.

Once he'd set up the orchestra and it had given two seasons of successful concerts, Verbrugghen persuaded the NSW government to fund it as a full-time body under his direction. In essence it was a mixture of the best available professional musicians and the best Conservatorium teachers and students, and had more than seventy regular players. The orchestra gave many concerts in Sydney, Melbourne, Adelaide and even New Zealand (two tours, in 1919 and 1921) but it disbanded after Verbrugghen departed for his post as Chief Conductor of the Minneapolis Symphony Orchestra in 1922. Verbrugghen—not the orchestra—was the drawcard for the NSW government and the backers in the other centres.

The previous professional orchestra to have had any permanency in Sydney was the first Sydney Symphony Orchestra, which lived from 1908 to 1914, giving about six concerts a year and rehearsing above a fish shop in George Street near Circular Quay. Guest conductors included Alfred Hill and Melbourne's G.W.L. Marshall Hall, but playing standards were variable. It was from one of this group's organisers, George Plummer, that Charles Moses bought the ABC the title Sydney Symphony Orchestra in 1937 for £10.

Sydney's orchestral life during the 1920s, then, revolved around theatre and cinema groups, some of symphonic size, and the Conservatorium orchestra under Dr Orchard. The theatre orchestras rarely gave public concerts, although they did broadcast for Australia's fledgling radio stations. The Conservatorium, on the other hand, gave eight public concerts a year, in the words of one observer, 'just managing to keep the torch of music faintly glowing'.

It was responsible for many first performances, some of repertoire written thirty years beforehand! For example, 1927 saw the Conservatorium present the first Australian performance of Dvořák's Cello Concerto, and Strauss' *Don Juan* made his first Australian appearance there in 1929. More recent works were performed, of course, but, for logistical reasons as much as anything else, the Conservatorium could not provide sustained exposure to the breadth of the orchestral repertoire. One major problem— and one that only reinforced the perception that our indigenous musical culture was inferior to that of the 'old' world—was that Australian composers had few opportunities to hear their orchestral music played properly unless, like Percy Grainger, they worked overseas.

'You also have to remember that the big events of Sydney's local music-making then were choral concerts', recalls Ken Tribe, for many years chairman of Musica Viva. 'The tradition of massed

Henri Verbrugghen (top) and Bernard Heinze in the early 1930s.

choral singing was still very strong in the twenties, and there were regular concerts by the Philharmonic Society and their orchestra. But that orchestra didn't play so well. The coming of a properly established symphony orchestra eventually put the choral scene in retreat. Once orchestral performance in Sydney became professional the cult of the voice began to wane. There are fashions in music, after all, and the voice went out of fashion. During the thirties orchestral music became the thing.'

But to find the beginnings of the current SSO we need to stay in the 1920s, in Melbourne. In 1924, shortly after his return from more than a decade of study and war service in Europe, the sounds of Furtwängler and the Berlin Philharmonic ringing in his ears, Bernard Heinze was taken to the Melbourne Town Hall to hear the University Conservatorium's symphony orchestra (USO). Not only was the hall nearly empty, but Heinze later recalled that the standard of playing was 'frankly amateur'.

Amateur the group may have been, but Melbourne—a wealthy and glamorous city because of the gold boom and land speculation—could claim a much more diverse and consistent orchestral history than Sydney. The International Centennial Exhibition, held in Melbourne's grand Royal Exhibition building in 1888, brought with it the English composer/conductor Sir Frederick Hymen Cowen and a group of fifteen 'nucleus' musicians. These players joined a local orchestral strength of fifty-eight.

Cowen gave 263 concerts in six months (for which he was paid 'the not contemptible remuneration of over £800 per month', according to Percy Scholes). His presence and achievements stirred Melbourne enthusiasm, and Marshall Hall, the first Ormond Professor of Music at Melbourne University, was able to found a largely professional orchestra only four years later, giving subscription series annually until 1912. This group, much altered, was to become the USO Heinze heard in 1924.

In the early 1920s Melbourne was still a grander city than Sydney, and was proud of its musical achievements. It was also the Commonwealth's capital city: Canberra's Parliament House was not completed until 1927.

But Heinze was not a native Melburnian. He was born in Ballarat, a town with a distinguished musical history of its own, and won prizes for violin playing in the annual music competitions there known as the South Street competitions. He later won scholarships which took him to Melbourne, then London's Royal College of Music, where his teachers included Sir Charles Stanford. After the war he spent two years in Paris, where he studied with Vincent d'Indy at the Schola Cantorum. He was very much the goldenhaired boy on his return to Victoria and had on his side charm, tenacity and political nous. He would need all three in the decade ahead.

In the mid-1920s Heinze was nurturing three ambitions: to become a major player in music broadcasting (he had long been fascinated by radio); to oversee the formation of—and possibly himself conduct—a national symphony orchestra; and, inspired by the work of Walter Damrosch in New York, to begin a special series of concerts for children.

The children's concerts, with the USO and Conservatorium funding, happened first, in October 1924, and they were an immediate success, serving as models for the schools' concerts Heinze was later to introduce at the ABC. With his appointment as Ormond Professor of Music at Melbourne University in 1925, Heinze then began to work towards an amalgamation of the USO with Melbourne's other orchestra. This was a semi-professional body, well established and run by the Italian-born Alberto Zelman: the Melbourne Symphony Orchestra. Heinze's popularity with the press was such that the apparently good standard the MSO attained regularly did not appear to have any bearing in discussions about whether the merger should take place or not. But it did come about, though not for the expected reasons.

Zelman died in 1927. The byzantine politics of Heinze's subsequent tussles with Zelman's successor as MSO conductor, Fritz Hart, are of subsidiary interest here,[1] but in 1932 the MSO, having suffered badly in the early years of the Depression, found that it could not pay its debts. The orchestra was bailed out by the energetic, music-minded retail entrepreneur Sidney Myer, on the condition that it merged with Heinze's USO. The merged orchestra, which adopted the MSO name, again gave Melbourne a decent full-strength permanent orchestra. Sydney at this time had nothing like it.

---

[1] They are covered in detail in Therese Radic's biography of Heinze (see bibliography). Even Nellie Melba plays a part.

In any event, 1929 saw Heinze appointed to a part-time job that gave him, as it was to turn out, great influence over the future of orchestral music in every State. He became director-general of music for the new national broadcasting service.

This service was a cluster of radio stations taken over by the Australian Broadcasting Company from July 1929. The Company was the successful tenderer when the Bruce-Page government decided to have one national private company run all 'A'-class stations, taking them over from a variety of private interests. These stations were 2FC and 2BL in NSW, 3LO and 3AR in Victoria, 4QG in Queensland, 5CL in South Australia, 6WF in Perth, 7ZL in Hobart and four regional stations.[2] The Postmaster-General's department provided all technical services for them including transmission facilities and landlines.

The difference between 'A' and 'B'-class stations was that the 'A' stations earned money directly from licence fees and were not allowed to take any advertising. The 'B' stations—in Sydney then, these included 2SM, 2UE, 2GB (owned by the Theosophical Society and named after the sixteenth century martyr Giordano Bruno) and 2KY—lived by advertising revenue.

The Australian Broadcasting Company was formed in Sydney by Sir Benjamin Fuller of Fuller's theatres,[3] Stuart Doyle, cinema-owner, and Frank Albert of J. Albert and Son, music-publishing empire. Fuller's theatres and Doyle's cinemas gave the Company access to many orchestras, but the Company also started studio orchestras of its own in Sydney and Melbourne, initially of about eight to ten players, mostly to play dinner music and 'light' classics.

It may be difficult today to imagine why such groups were formed. We have become used to an orchestral broadcast as being a relay of a live performance (although studio performances are still given). But in the early years the PMG used telephone lines to broadcast 'live' events and, even though the lines were adapted to carry a wider range of frequencies than the human voice

[2] It was a complicated takeover. The Company gained control of each station only when the station's five-year licence expired. As each licence had been issued at a different time, it was not until December 1930 that the Company ran a station in each capital city.

[3] The Australian Broadcasting Commission would later broadcast Fuller's opera seasons. He would be a reassuring ally during the Tait crisis (see Chapter 2).

required, the standard of early concert broadcasts was often terrible.

Music performed in the studio was easier to control: there were only a few musicians performing, and the rooms were small and acoustically dry, presenting fewer technical problems. And there were simply not enough recordings available to provide a steady diet of lighter music. The idea of 'dinner music radio' is still with us, of course, most notably in the form of ABC-FM's five o'clock programs.

In 1929, the Australian Broadcasting Company inherited a 2FC 'house' trio in Sydney, which included violinist John Farnsworth Hall, who was later to lead the SSO and eventually become the Queensland Symphony Orchestra's chief conductor. In securing extra players to enlarge the Sydney trio into the new dinner music ensemble the Company was forming, it needed to look no further than the theatres and cinemas run by the Company's proprietors, where many of the country's best musicians worked.

One player who joined the new 2FC group at this time was cellist Osric Fyfe, who now lives in Sydney's outer west. He was playing for silent films in a trio (violin, piano, cello) at a Balgowlah cinema when he started his casual work for the Company. Many of the station's house musicians kept up similar workloads.

It was these studio groups that Heinze was to supervise in his new position but—ever the politician—he was also involved in the appointment of the Company's first Director of Programs for 3LO and 3AR. This was to be another Ballarat-born musician, also to help shape the future of Australian music, William James.

James had also studied in London, having had a more public career there than Heinze. He had appeared as pianist under Henry Wood and Sir Landon Ronald and toured as accompanist with Fritz Kreisler and Florence Austral. He also had a lot of his music performed in Britain, for he was under exclusive contract with Ricordi and Co as a composer there. He wrote more than 100 pieces for them, including operas and ballets. His *Six Australian Bush Songs*, written for Melba, date from this period.[4]

The Australian Broadcasting Company had the misfortune to

---

[4] They are referred to in the opening lines of Cole Porter's song 'Be Like the Bluebird', from *Anything Goes*: 'There's an old Australian bush song/That Melba used to sing . . .'

take up its licence in the year of the Wall Street Crash. The sudden economic slump slowed the PMG's program to build new regional transmitters, so that licence fee revenue from country areas stagnated. But money for licence fees everywhere was scarce, as many households still regarded a radio as a luxury item. The result was that the Company earned far less than it expected.

It came to the point where Fuller, Doyle and Albert felt they could not service the stations properly on the income they were getting. The partners announced their retreat from the 'A'-class field to the Scullin government in 1931 and bought 2UW a short time later. As it was, the Labor Party was committed to public ownership of broadcasting. It had the PMG draft a bill which would see a Commission set up, along the lines of the BBC, to run all the 'A'-class stations. The Bill was introduced into Parliament on the day the Scullin government fell, but it didn't matter much. It was an idea whose time had come. The worthies of Melbourne lobbied the new Lyons government very convincingly, and a similar Bill to Scullin's was passed in May 1932, stipulating that the Commission was to take over the Company's stations on 1 July of that year.

One of the things the Melbourne worthies (one of whom was barrister and state parliamentary member R.G. Menzies) argued for was that 'the cultural potentialities of the Broadcast Service be considered a matter of primary importance'. The cultural potentialities of the Sydney and Melbourne studio orchestras at this time had grown to fifteen players each. These were the groups the Commission inherited from the Company, and they were to be the basis of the future symphony orchestras in these cities. Neville Amadio, age thirteen, joined the Sydney group when the Company ran it and stayed on while completing his studies at the Conservatorium and playing in cinema and theatre orchestras.

'We were expected to play virtually everything, from salon music to reduced versions of the *1812* overture', he remembers. 'Most of it was done on one rehearsal, and that was only possible because we were all such quick readers. Most of us had played for silent films, where you were sight reading all the time.'

'Listeners-in' to 2FC in July 1932 would not have noticed much difference between the Commission's programs and those offered by the Company in June. Apart from performances by *The ABC*

Orchestra, typical musical items were an *Organ and vocal recital by Lilian Frost and Harry Schofield, from the Pitt Street Congregational Church* (next door to ABC head office at the time) or disc-based programs which were listed as *A Celebrity Recital (Recorded)*. Among the talks programs on offer were Mr R.G. McCredie speaking on a *Peep through the Keyhole of Algiers*, and *The Retreat from Mons, with Atmospheric Background, told by Major W. Kemp.*

The differences emerged once the Commission proper got down to business. The first commissioners the government put in place were chairman Charles Lloyd Jones, also chairman of David Jones (ironically Ken Myer was to be ABC chairman five decades later); Richard Orchard, who had been an actor, jeweller and federal politician, and who had served on a parliamentary Wireless Advisory Committee; Scottish-born vice-chancellor of Sydney University and one-time chief film censor Robert Wallace; May Couchman, music teacher and office holder in the Australian Women's National League; and, importantly for Bernard Heinze, vice-chairman Herbert Brookes. He and his wife Ivy, a leading light in musical Melbourne, were influential and committed Heinze supporters. Brookes was a staunch conservative, an engineer and manufacturer, and Alfred Deakin's son-in-law.

All these people were connected with the Nationalist government of the day, which may have been the only qualification they had in common. Anthony Cane has described this group as 'the motley collection of laymen appointed by Canberra'.

It was probably the Heinze/Brookes axis that had the Melbourne and Sydney studio groups increased from fifteen to twenty-four permanent players each. This happened in late 1932. But if this implied an intention on the Commission's part to gradually give each State its own permanent, decently sized ensemble, there were still many references being made to a national symphony orchestra. Indeed, in his speech on the opening day of Commission broadcasting, Lloyd Jones referred to an 'Australian national orchestra' as a 'dream that the Commission hoped to accomplish'. There was some confusion over objectives.

The ABC (Sydney) Symphony Orchestra, as the 24-piece ensemble was most usually known, did as bewilderingly varied a range of things as its 15-piece predecessor—everything from

The A.B. Commission's first studio orchestra, conducted by E.J. Roberts. Neville Amadio is second from the right in the second row.

arrangements of Mendelssohn's *Spinning Song* through to Saint-Saens' Organ symphony (with 24 players?) and Coleridge-Taylor's choral work *The Death of Minehaha* (using a chorus prepared by pianist/composer Lindley Evans, who later became Mr Melody Man on 'The Argonauts'.)[5] It even provided live incidental music for plays and split itself into chamber groups and the ABC String Orchestra.

'We used to perform Brahms symphonies with twenty-eight players—I think they got some casuals in to boost the numbers', Neville Amadio recalls. 'But you can imagine the doublings that went on! We only had one of each woodwind instrument, and I recall a second oboe part once being played by one of the violinists.'

The orchestra rehearsed in a small room in the since-demolished Arts Club building in Pitt Street, between Bathurst and Liverpool streets, and was conducted in most cases by E.J. Roberts, who may be regarded as the SSO's first permanent conductor.

Roberts came to Australia initially as a conductor of one of the numerous touring opera companies in the 1920s, and stayed put. A violinist, he had played in the Covent Garden orchestra, and then with the London Symphony Orchestra, under Richter, Beecham and Landon Ronald. He was hired because of his versatility, or as the ABC's general manager for NSW, H.G. Horner, put it: 'To conduct dinner time music, musical comedy and accompaniments to light numbers'. It transpired that he was not up to the challenges the next few years would bring.

The Sydney orchestra made very few public appearances in 1932 or 1933, and was augmented to forty or fifty players when it did so. Heinze's interest in Australian composition led to the Commission's initiating a composers' competition. Some of the prize-winning works were played in the Sydney Town Hall under Heinze, including Lindley Evans' *An Australian Symphony* and Fritz Hart's symphonic suite *The Bush*, but none made any lasting impact. The visiting British soprano Maggie Teyte sang at this concert, and the *Bulletin's* review of the evening revealed that 'her frock was entirely backless'.

Another major public event of 1933 was the Brahms-Wagner

---

[5] The ABC would later create Wireless Choruses in each State.

festival which Heinze organised through the Commissioners for Melbourne and Sydney performances (and relay on ABC stations nationally). The four Sydney concerts were failures financially— they were expensive to put on, combining as they did the Sydney and Melbourne orchestras and featuring many soloists, and the houses were poor. Dr Orchard was deeply offended at the whole endeavour, thinking that it was an attempt to belittle the Conservatorium's Brahms-Wagner celebrations of earlier in the year. But in any case Heinze had been too ambitious—the players were not ready for the difficulties of Act III of *Die Walküre* (performed in concert during the Sydney festival) and neither was there an audience ready for so thoroughly epic and serious an event. This was long before the days of such educative radio figures as Neville Cardus and Dr Floyd, and the city had been without a full-time orchestra for too long. The concert receipts, *Smith's Weekly* reported, 'would hardly have paid the cost of bringing the [orchestral] party from Melbourne'.

The whole thing was probably not really to the taste of the then general manager of the ABC anyway. The first commissioners—Lloyd Jones, Brookes and Co.—were, in the words of Dr Alan Thomas, 'all supposedly cultured, [viewing] the ABC as a public institution with a moral obligation to 'realise the taste and improve the culture of the community"'. But the general manager, Major Walter Tasman Conder, was a J.C. Williamson's protege and, as Ken Inglis has written, 'a ratings man'. He had a deep distrust of high culture.

Conder was an extraordinary character; a biography of him would make racy reading indeed. A captain of Launceston Grammar School, he was a Gallipoli veteran and had charge of venereally diseased soldiers for most of the remainder of the First World War. After the war he ran a rubber plantation in Papua before becoming governor of Pentridge jail. He then worked for JCWs which, as part-owner of 3LO before the Australian Broadcasting Company took over in 1929, made him 3LO station manager. Shortly after the Commission was founded he became organiser of Melbourne's centenary celebrations, due in 1934. He became ABC general manager after the Commission's first general manager, H.P. Williams, died in March 1933.

Conder had no interest in serious orchestral music. His

The ABC (Sydney) Symphony Orchestra, conducted by E.J. Roberts, in one of its first public appearances, a choral concert given in the Great Hall of Sydney University. Lindley Evans, who trained the choirs for this occasion, is in front of the orchestra at the right, facing the audience.

philosophy was probably best summed up by his one-time employer Nevin Tait, who wrote of JCWs:

Attractions of a high-class nature are few and far between and if, for example, Shakespeare were presented too frequently he would lose a lot of his appeal and so would other high forms of drama . . . we have to appeal to all sides of the public with our productions . . .

This attitude would cause Conder problems in the mid-1930s.

By the time of the Brahms-Wagner festival, the visit of the ABC's first 'celebrity' conductor had been announced for 1934— Sir Hamilton Harty. This was Heinze's doing, too; he suggested four conductors be invited for concerts in the near future: Sargent, Harty, Szell and Beecham. Sargent was invited to come for 1934, but cancelled when a deputy could not be found for some important engagements in Britain.

Heinze must have been immensely relieved, for the commissioners had asked Sargent to set up a national orchestra, conduct its first concerts and appoint a full-time conductor for it. In 1933 Heinze was still working for the Australian Broadcasting Commission in an unofficial capacity, doing work similar to that he had done for the Company, but he was made the Commission's official musical adviser (a part-time post on a retainer of £100 a year) by the time Harty arrived in June 1934. He wisely advised against Harty being allowed to pick the best players for any national orchestra, realising that the potential of the new national broadcasting service was such that the question of having a national orchestra at all had to be re-thought.

In 1934 the ABC and the NSW Conservatorium seem to have settled their differences. They struck an agreement whereby the best Conservatorium players (teachers and the pick of the students) would join the studio group for Harty's Sydney concerts.

The Harty visit is an absorbing episode in Australia's musical history. He relished the prospect of being a musical pioneer, but not unconditionally. His letter of agreement to Conder, written in December 1933, shows him raising an issue that was to haunt the ABC right through the 1930s and 1940s—whether or not to import overseas players. ABC management and the Musicians Union still have disputes about this. Harty wrote:

It is quite possible that I shall find some weak spots, especially in the wind and brass, which would...make it difficult...to reach a really high standard. Would [the commissioners] consider it expedient to import a small number of acknowledged first-class players to fill the gaps until Australian-born players were fitted to replace them?...I believe the question is one that should be seriously considered.

As it turned out, the orchestras Harty worked with consisted of local players entirely.

Once he arrived, Harty was given the full celebrity treatment. He was feted. He was quoted about everything ("Genial Irish Conductor Regards Jazz As A Disease", *Smith's Weekly* headlined). He mixed in all the right circles. The extraordinary publicity he generated brought much reflected glory to the ABC and its orchestras but, for the Sydney press, the success of the visit also brought into sharp focus the need for a permanent orchestra in the city.

Such an effect was heightened by Harty's eloquence off the platform. He had charm and a terrific reputation on his side, and—best of all—he was British. Australia saw its world through British eyes before the Second World War, and expected to be flattered by all guests from the heart of the Empire! As Beecham was to later write to William James:

. . . [in most of the world] Australia has a notoriety for resenting the slightest criticism passed upon its institutions, or even friendly advice coming from the well-intentioned visitor.

But Harty was not going to flatter unreservedly. He knew he was doing pioneering work and he took it seriously. His remarks about orchestral standards were quoted widely—on arrival in Sydney, after giving his Melbourne concerts, he said the Melbourne orchestra had performed well but 'perilously' for him:

They were intelligent and ready to learn but there is no one to teach them. Sometimes they surprised me by their inability to surmount even the most moderate technical difficulties. Then...they would go home and spend hours practising passages in order to make themselves perfect.

He was to write afterwards that 'the keen interest displayed by

members of the Melbourne and Sydney orchestras struck me as
a little pathetic'. We were desperate to please. We desperately
wanted to play at our best.

Harty certainly made a difference to the standard of playing.
The *Sydney Morning Herald* remarked that 'even the most
optimistic . . . had not dared hope that, in little more than a week
[of rehearsals], he could work up the Broadcasting Commission's
orchestra to performances of such genuine power'.

The five Sydney concerts were a shrewdly programmed mixture
of the high- and middle-brow repertoire: Brahms 1, *The Flight
of the Bumblebee, Death and Transfiguration, Elijah* (then a very
popular work), the *Enigma* variations, Harty's tone-poem *With
the Wild Geese*, Liadov's *The Musical Box* and Constant Lambert's
The Rio Grande (then a daring novelty)[6] were featured. There
was some press complaint that the 'novelty' items were
insufficiently serious for a conductor of Harty's stature (despite
the fact that he'd programmed them himself) and the quality of
the broadcast sound was understandably variable. But otherwise
it was rave reviews and full houses all the way. *Smith's Weekly*
even wrote a poem to celebrate Harty's arrival:

Hey diddle diddle, the flute and the fiddle,
They frolic for Hamilton Harty,
The trumpet and cello, they babble and bellow,
He's such a remarkable party.
The fiddle-bows flatten with fear at his baton,
The clarinets haste to their duty;
With energy tireless, he witches the wireless,
Enchanting the ether with beauty.

And the *Daily Telegraph* remarked that 'the famous conductor's
immaculate tailoring and his naive and modest bow immediately
made him *en rapport* with the vast and expectant throng'.

Neville Amadio remembers how exciting an experience it was
for the players to work with him. 'He was the first conductor

[6] As he had done in the 1930 recording under Lambert, Harty played the piano part
in Sydney, with Lindley Evans conducting. Publicity for this concert referred
misleadingly to Lambert as an Australian composer, but the *Listener-In* magazine was
not fooled: 'Why does the national broadcasting service persist in educating us wrongly
by asserting that [the work] is by an Australian composer? It is not!'.

Sir Hamilton Harty with the orchestra formed for his 1934 tour. This photograph was taken in the Sydney Symphony Orchestra's first rehearsal venue, the Arts Club in Pitt Street, Sydney.

of real calibre we'd ever had, and we were lucky that he had an ability to get the best out of a very mixed group of players. Ernest Llewellyn was a student then, and was brought in as an extra for these concerts. Without wishing to be disrespectful, I have to say he was probably the best violinist in that orchestra.

'You have to remember that it was quite an experience to be playing in an orchestra of that size [the Harty orchestra in Sydney had more than seventy players in it], because we were used to the sound of the smaller studio group.'

Shortly before leaving Australia at the end of June, Harty gave Conder a confidential report about playing standards and possible scenarios. This is one of the most important documents in the SSO's early history, for it forced the commissioners to plan for the future, simply by putting up so many ideas. As it was, the Harty concerts were a red rag to the newspapers, most of which were now at the ABC regularly to establish a permanent orchestra. The following remarks, from different newspapers, are representative:

'A first-class permanent orchestra is the foundation of good broadcasting, and until we have one the ABC is simply wasting time and money without getting any further . . . ' 'Paris has only three million people and Berlin four million. Surely the Australian cities should not remain, from a musical standpoint, in such a primitive state as they have done during recent years? . . . ' 'It is my personal opinion that eventually the [ABC] must become the [concert] entrepreneur of this country . . . '

Harty's report is frank and practical. 'Orchestral playing in this country is of a very indifferent standard', he begins, 'and in neither orchestra did I find more than a very few players who have any claims to be considered thoroughly efficient first-class orchestral musicians'.

Australian players were more 'familiar' with him than he was used to in Britain, although he came to enjoy their 'warmth of temperament and . . . sportsmanship'. But he discusses in the report the need for proper orchestral training and the purchase of better instruments. He found the Sydney orchestra wanting in several areas: the double basses were 'wretchedly bad', there were 'passengers' in the violins, and the trombones were 'coarse and uncertain in pitch'.

Neville Amadio agrees that there were only a few good players in this orchestra. Some were to become real strengths as the years passed—timpanist Alard Maling, who had perfect pitch; Alan Mann, here third trombone but later to become first horn; and bass clarinettist John Antill, who spent most of his working life in and around the SSO, and is best known as a composer. 'Cellist Osric Fyfe was in this orchestra, too, but was soon off to England, where he became a member of Beecham's London Philharmonic. He came back to Australia in 1939, joining the SSO and the teaching staff at the Conservatorium.

Harty's remarks about standards must be viewed from the perspective of *his* standards, and he was used to the best. That was his point, though: he saw no reason why an Australian orchestra should not play at the highest level of proficiency. As far as he was concerned, 'judging by the enthusiasm and undoubted musical appreciation shown by the large audiences at the concerts I have conducted here, there is a real hunger in the people for first-class orchestral music'. His report's main recommendations were:

That the ABC become an orchestral entrepreneur.

That the ABC hire a proper training conductor.

That there be only one orchestra nationally.

That musicians from abroad be used to fill 'short-term' gaps in this one orchestra and to train local players, a move that would lead to greater proficiency and reduced rehearsal time.

That women not be permitted to join the national orchestra.

On the last point, Harty had this to say: 'No first-rate orchestra in the world permits women in its ranks—except sometimes as harpists . . . the trouble, to my mind, is that they do not mix well with men. They have a different . . . temperament, and that is inclined to injure the general cohesion . . . of the orchestra . . . to mix them indiscriminately with men is, I think, a serious mistake. In spite of what feminists may say, men are never entirely indifferent to the question of sex . . . the average man either dislikes or (what is worse) is pleasantly interested in the woman sitting beside him, and his concentration on entirely musical problems is liable to be disturbed. I prefer an entirely male orchestra.'

❦

Harty left behind him newly enthused audiences and players, a press impatient for the ABC to act and a Commission forced to do some serious thinking about its orchestral resources. As the Brisbane *Telegraph* remarked on the twentieth anniversary of his visit, 'he made orchestras and public alike aware of what had to be done'. But it took the Commission more than a year to make the hard decisions.

'The present orchestras in Australia might be described as first-class cottage pianos', Harty wrote. 'And your people deserve a concert grand.'

CHAPTER TWO

The sounds take shape

Sydney wanted a permanent professional orchestra badly in the 1930s. It felt it deserved one. The belief that Sydney was changing, becoming a major world city, meant that a full-time cultural asset was wanted to prove that it had grown up.

Culture meant particular established Western idioms: opera, ballet and orchestral music. But it did not seem to mean theatre, as there was still no full-time professional company in Australia. Donald Horne has written of this period that 'the commercial theatre was devoted almost entirely to musical comedies; there were a few little theatres but other than a film industry given over to bush and other stock themes, just about the only Australian drama was to be found in vaudeville skits'.

The basic problem was that we had no sense of a national consciousness, indeed almost scorned the idea of one, and felt more comfortable with imported art. For example, the art form that experienced the biggest audience increase in the 1930s was ballet. Historically, the most significant event in the history of classical ballet in Australia is probably the Taits' tour of Colonel de Basil's company in 1936. This led to Helene Kirsova's staying to live in Sydney. Later, Eduard Borovansky left the company to live in Melbourne. Between them, they established professional ballet in Australia as it has come down to us in the 1990s.

Opera was more expensive to mount, and thus less attractive to commercial entrepreneurs, who knew by now that it was almost impossible to break even, let alone make a profit, presenting it. The Taits even lost money on Melba's farewell tour of 1928, after which they told the Government that regular opera performances could only be mounted with public subsidy.[1] Signs of operatic permanency were not to become evident until the early 1950s.

Painting—the only established art form with strong local roots—was being shaken up in the 1930s by a variety of forces. The Edwardian generation of painters had almost all become reactionaries and, simultaneously, members of the art establishment in the years after the First World War. They tried to keep the decadent influence of European modernism at bay. But now young artists were emerging who had studied overseas and were plainly influenced by post-impressionism, fauvism, cubism and futurism: Roland Wakelin, Grace Cossington Smith, Roy de Maistre and Margaret Preston were among them.

By the time Robert Menzies attempted to launch an Australian Academy of Art in 1937[2]—in a desire to establish a conservative hold on the visual arts once and for all—the younger artists had many supporters, including some traditional painters, and an eloquent spokesman in painter George Bell. The showdown between the radicals and the newly formed Academy gave the young painters a degree of credibility and helped arouse public curiosity. And the vigour of the painting scene in Sydney and Melbourne in the following years itself re-defined Australian perceptions of the visual arts.

But this was the first time this century that thoroughly radical figures had become taste-makers. The dominant cultural personalities in the 1920s may have been rebellious, but they were conservative too. Two people who symbolise this dichotomy most forcefully are Norman Lindsay and Percy Grainger.

Both men had enormous artistic energy as a common trait, but, as he produced all his major work in Australia, Lindsay's ethos was the more explicit to his compatriots. Although he first

---

[1] In his public speeches, Harty had reminded Australia that the same was true of orchestral music; in the end his tour lost the ABC £3238. And, as we've seen, Verbrugghen's orchestra had been heavily subsidised in its brief lifetime.

[2] 'Great art speaks a language which every intelligent person can understand. The people who call themselves modernists today talk a different language', Menzies said in launching the Academy.

became known as an illustrator (in the pages of the *Bulletin*), his later work as a painter, novelist, poet and children's writer, and his status as a great Australian 'character', gave him enormous influence. He was scathingly anti-Christian and profoundly Nietzschean, and relished and embellished his role as the romantic 'outsider' through a series of public clashes with the establishment.

His pronouncements about art were taken very seriously indeed, which makes them all the more upsetting to read now. Basically, Lindsay's message was that Australians would never create an art out of their own culture, but must instead turn to Greek mythology. 'Thus we may found a genuine Australian literature', he wrote in his journal *Vision*. 'It is a short-sighted nationalism that can be proud only of verse about shearers and horses, and measures the reality of a work by its local references.'

Lindsay hated the literature of his European contemporaries (as art gallery directors of his time hated contemporary European art), thinking it irrelevant to Australian life, and he was an appalling anti-Semite. But he was a communicator, and made at least two generations of Australians aware of societies based on ideas, of a personal morality built around a structured intellect. He was a renegade renaissance man in a provincial culture, and his influence on fellow artists and on a shocked and wowserish public was enormous.

Grainger's place as a public figure in Australia is more problematical, partly because he lived in Europe and the United States for much of his life. Australians came to regard him primarily as a concert pianist, and secondarily as a composer of sometimes bizarre music they could hardly understand. Long after he settled in the United States, he remained deeply aware of his Australianness. Even his seemingly 'un-Australian' pieces, such as his orchestral work *The Warriors*, have a sonic extravagance that is uniquely out-of-doors.

Deeper than this, though, the philosophy behind his technique of elastic scoring (a method of flexible orchestration which allows his music to be performed by many different combinations of voices and instruments) is, as Roger Covell has noted, 'part of a democratic ideal—an Australian ideal, he would have said— in which every performer is able to feel he has something important to contribute to the whole'.

Grainger and Lindsay were born only three years apart, and met one another during Grainger's lecture tour of Australia and New Zealand in 1934-35. They had political conservatism and a belief in Aryan racial superiority in common, but a major difference in their outlooks was that, where Lindsay was a cultural exclusivist, Grainger believed in studying music from all cultures, be they European or not.

Indeed, he brought music from Madagascar, China and Africa back with him for these lectures, along with European music dating back to the thirteenth century and some recent pieces which experimented with microtones (the ABC broadcast all the lectures, and he performed with the orchestras in broadcast performances, too). It has often been said that Grainger was ahead of his time, but this was a most forlorn prescience. Bringing an Empire-bound Anglo-Saxon country the art of cultures which they had barely thought worth bothering with must have been a lonely pastime indeed.

Grainger was a severe character compared to Lindsay, and despaired that his bigger, more serious pieces were often neglected at the expense of *Molly on the Shore* and *Handel in the Strand*. He was to became lonelier and less relevant as he got older, a prophet with very little honour in Australia or elsewhere. But in the 1930s his genius as a pianist and his fame in other countries— particularly Britain—made Australians proud. He symbolised international musical achievement in a country short of identity, and while he would inspire future generations of Australian composers, he had no immediate followers. He was too eccentric for his really serious work to have meaning in so complacent a place as inter-war Australia.

Ultimately, such personalities presented too many contradictions to be galvanising forces for change (J.F. Archibald is a similar example from a previous generation). They could not break the cultural drought on their own. But other factors were at work which rang in major changes with the utmost conviction.

Sydney had received one enormous modernist jolt with the opening of the Harbour Bridge in 1932. The bridge suddenly gave the city a new, large, embracingly glamorous symbol which lent itself to immediate glorification in advertisements and in painting. Sixty years later, we must try to imagine how the bridge must have captivated a Sydney that had no building taller than 150 feet—about 46 metres (this height restriction was not lifted until 1957). It was our Eiffel Tower.

It was around this time, too, that Ure Smith's magazine *The Home* began. Self-consciously chic, it was the first mass-circulation monthly to feature full-page, full-colour reproductions of Australian art. It also ran articles about international travel; interviews with celebrities from stage, screen and radio (Harty was profiled before his visit) and Australian fiction.

Then, in 1934 and 1935, Melbourne celebrated its centenary, or more precisely the centenary of John Batman's famous diary entry 'This will be the place for a village'. The festivities lasted eight months, and included a visit from the Duke of Gloucester, a National Eucharistic Congress (500 000 people gathered in Victoria Parade to receive the Blessed Sacrament), a Scout Jamboree and an event that suddenly, miraculously brought white Australia much closer to its parent culture than ever before, and gave the two largest cities—brash, fast Sydney particularly—reason to feel they would be obliged to become real international centres sooner than they expected.

The Centenary Air Race was made possible through the confectionary magnate Sir Macpherson Robertson, who put up prize money of £15 000. The race created unprecedented excitement around the country. The winners, Scott and Campbell Black, made the London to Melbourne journey in seventy-two hours, and were given a huge victory parade down Collins Street. The success of their journey led to the first Australia-UK airmail service in December 1934.

The finish of the air race and the opening of the bridge were events that symbolised the achievements of the modern era; and they were both great 'actuality' events for that definitively modern medium, radio. The impact of radio in a country of such vast distances as Australia cannot be over-estimated. By the time the Commission began there were 370 000 radio licences in Australia, and almost all radio sets would have been used in households of two people or more. The radio was cheap: you could build a crystal set for a few shillings and the licence fee worked out to about sixpence a week. For that you could hear news, talks, comedy, sports broadcasts and 'you are there' reports such as

announcer Conrad Charlton's five-hour stint for the Australian
Broadcasting Company when the bridge opened.

But radio also brought with it a lot of orchestral music from
disc. Recorded performance had been integral to Australian radio
from the earliest days, when broadcast microphones were put in
front of wind-up gramophones. Since then electric pick-ups had
made broadcasting from disc a simple matter, and it was not only
the ABC that did it. 2GB and 2UW broadcast 'serious' music
daily, and 2SM's 'An Afternoon with the Classics', broadcast on
Sundays, also became a popular program.

※

I do not want to pretend that all the implications of the events
and issues I have written about were blindingly apparent to
everyone who owned a radio or walked across the bridge the day
it opened, but they meant a lot to the man who was about to
become ABC chairman.

By 1935 the ABC had shown Sydney what was possible
orchestrally, and conjured up a vision to newspaper and radio
commentators of the new bridge-adorned Empire metropolis with
a symphony orchestra of its own. There were arguments against
the idea, of course. The most forceful case, and one that the
Commission had raised internally, was based on the difficulty of
finding enough skilled local players to put together one full-sized
orchestra nationally.

But the cases in favour of forming a full-time Sydney orchestra
of the right dimensions were now piling up. It was obvious to
the press and the radio audience (for it was of course on radio
that most people heard orchestral performance) that no one else
was going to put one together, and it was also obvious to many
that the standard reached by the Conservatorium orchestra—as
heard on ABC broadcasts—was barely adequate; at one point the
commissioners described the Conservatorium's performances as
'avowedly amateur'. As *Smith's Weekly* put it: 'The ABC has the
funds and the opportunity to become the greatest musical
entrepreneur in the Commonwealth. More, it has a duty'.

When the ABC orchestras are written about, 1935 is almost
always glossed over, but it was a year in which many crucial
events took place that would determine the course of Australian

musical life in the decades to come. These events also explain why the challenges thrown up by the Harty visit were left to lie for twelve months.

To start with Lloyd Jones retired in June 1934. He was not a young man, he was still trying to run David Jones, and he was finding it increasingly difficult to be a part-time chairman when the still-young ABC needed so much of his time. It was, after all, an organisation still trying to give itself a shape, and it thus demanded a lot more of its commissioners than the current ABC does of its Board.

One of Lloyd Jones' other major worries, though, was Conder, who was seen to be shockingly dishonest. Lloyd Jones had had him suspended at one point for charging the Commission £23 for a private 'phone call to England, and he was also accused of hiring cars for his own use and giving the ABC the bill. Conder's behaviour was given out privately as another reason for Lloyd Jones' departure.

In July 1934 the new chairman was announced. He was William James Cleary, perhaps the least appreciated of the founders of the symphony orchestras. Without his support it would have taken many more years for them to become established.

Cleary was a Sydney man through and through, and the opposite of an establishment figure. He grew up in Redfern and, at fourteen, gave up a scholarship to Sydney Boys' High to work at Tooth's brewery, so that he could earn enough money to help support his large family. He studied part-time while he worked and eventually became general manager of the brewery, also maintaining a part-time lectureship in business studies at Sydney University. Twice head of the NSW railways, his intolerance of corruption found him falling foul of right- and left-wing State governments in quick succession. He was a well-known press figure and a self-taught scholar of literature and music. The ABC audience, in his view, was to be enlightened and uplifted, and given access to the arts as comprehensively as possible. He was captivated by possibilities.

At this point Heinze was conducting four ABC children's concerts a year, two in Sydney and two in Melbourne. Cleary went with Conder to the Sydney Town Hall to hear one of these and, immediately enthused, asked for them to be given in other capital cities. This was perhaps Cleary's and Conder's first and last happy experience together. They seemed destined not to get on, and soon had a major row over a new system of talks, which Conder summed up as 'too much talking'! Cleary retorted that Conder had no vision and 'barrack-room standards'.

It was in mid-1935 that Conder was made to resign. The Commission secretary had been 'turning up lies all round', Vice-Chairman Brookes wrote in his diary. Conder was certainly no loss to music. Violinist Robert Miller, long-time SSO member (and eventually co-leader of the orchestra with Donald Hazelwood) remembers negotiating with Conder over a national six-month tour of the then recently formed Sydney String Quartet. Miller was violinist in the ensemble at the time.

'We had great problems with Mr Conder because of his lack of knowledge of musicians' requirements. He suggested we should be paid the basic Musicians' Union rate of £6 a week each on tour, and this really would hardly have covered our accommodation, to say nothing of travel. He argued that if he went to the union he would find four players who would be prepared to play for union rates. We didn't get anywhere arguing with him, so we spoke to Mr Cleary, and the whole situation changed.'

It became apparent shortly after his arrival that Cleary was going to be a full-time chairman, even though he was only earning a part-timer's salary of £500 a year. But he had many investments, and his family lived off these while he threw himself into his new job. He wanted to appoint as general manager the British-born announcer/administrator Charles Moses (planner of the disputed new talks system), and it took him four months to persuade his fellow commissioners that it was right for so young a man (Moses was not yet forty) to take up the task. Moses became the ABC's third general manager in November 1935.

Like Cleary, Moses was a music lover, but his career had so far been a non-musical one. One of the first things he did on emigrating to Australia in 1922 was to sell used cars. When the Depression took the bottom out of the used-car market he thought he might put his mellifluous voice to good use, and he became an announcer for the Australian Broadcasting Company in Melbourne. Staying with the Commission, one of his great pre-general manager triumphs was introducing in 1934 the 'synthetic' cricket relay system, which was so successful it helped increase the sale of radio licences at an astronomical rate.

And what of Conder? After his ignominious departure he started a circus, which failed, was declared bankrupt and spent a paradoxical spell in the prison of which he had once been governor. During the Second World War he organised troop entertainment in the Middle East, then settled in New Zealand, where he ran Tattersall's lottery and the 1962 Festival of Wellington. Energetic to the end, he died in 1974 aged eighty-six.

Before Moses was appointed, Cleary, Brookes, Heinze and Horner finally settled the issue of the national orchestra. In March 1935 they agreed to set up permanent studio groups, of eight to ten players each, in Adelaide, Brisbane, Hobart and Perth.

This meant in effect that the concept of a permanent national 'super' orchestra bit the dust, for it was clearly stated at the time that these groups were to accompany local artists and generally set the State's musical standards. Cleary felt strongly that the local stations in each centre needed more local input where possible.[3]

Other facets of the orchestral issue were being revealed, unwittingly, by the growth of the ABC's disc library. The large number of records now held allowed for a greater variety of recorded music to be broadcast than ever before. How long would the listeners-in be satisfied with music from records, when this was creating a hunger for live music-making?

And it was as a concert entrepreneur that the ABC had to clarify its position fairly desperately as 1935 progressed. All the management toings and froings had left the question of regular, public, ABC-generated orchestral performance unanswered. The Commission was already paying fees for broadcast to entrepreneurs such as the Taits, and existing orchestral groups such as the 'old' MSO and the NSW Conservatorium Orchestra for the right to put public concerts to air. It supplemented these groups with its own studio players occasionally, and in the organisational eventfulness of 1935 this practice passed for policy. In March

---

[3] This was largely because the audience was getting bigger and more geographically diverse. For example, there were nearly 70 000 licence holders in Queensland by mid-1935. This represented about ten per cent of the national audience.

a new Sydney orchestra was formed for a series of concerts conducted by Orchard's successor as Conservatorium director, Dr Edgar Bainton. This group used players 'chosen from the professional players of the Conservatorium Orchestra, the ABC orchestra and a few other organisations' (*Sydney Mail*). In other words, a Harty-style orchestra was flagged as the answer to Sydney's orchestral problem. The *Sydney Morning Herald* saw this, and the recent new public interest in ballet and a visiting opera company, as a sign that 'New South Wales is falling into line with civilisation'.

In reality this orchestra was something of a musical mirage. Artistic control was uncertain, and there was much organisational jealousy and intrigue, which resulted in those concerts broadcast from the Conservatorium being billed as performances by the NSW Conservatorium Orchestra, while concerts from the Sydney Town Hall were played by the NSW State Symphony Orchestra. Both were the same group. And as fine a musician as Dr Bainton was, his was not the galvanising presence of Harty. The standards reached were fairly disappointing, as The *Wireless Weekly* took some glee in pointing out. After the first two concerts, it wrote:

The Harty concerts cost a great deal, but they certainly livened up the programs; since then, we have settled down to a rock-bottom of dullness and mediocrity . . . Instead of running its own music, the Commission seems to have instituted a policy of taking only what outside concert organisations have on tap, as though a lion should let the jackals do the killing and come in afterwards for his cut.

The many issues complicating this plunge into comprehensive concert-giving began to be tackled properly when W.G. James was appointed as the first Federal Controller (later Director) of Music. He took up the job shortly after Moses became general manager. Cleary had wanted Heinze for the job, but Heinze was keen to maintain his professorship and keep up his conducting. As it was, he remained musical adviser and his retainer was increased to £250 a year.

One of the complicating issues was half-way fixed for James before becoming Controller. Once the commissioners had settled on the one-ensemble-per-State system, they examined the possibility of regular ABC-funded concert-giving in Sydney and Melbourne more seriously. In Sydney, though, there was the problem of E.J. Roberts. What the orchestra needed now, if Harty's points about standards were to be taken seriously, was a training conductor they could work with regularly. Roberts was not it.

In a confidential memo to Conder in April 1935, Horner wrote that Roberts 'is not sufficiently attentive to his duties, nor has he the flair for getting the best out of his men . . . the time devoted by him in an endeavour to improve standards is practically negligible'. Based on Horner's recommendations, Roberts was given the job of starting the Perth orchestra. Ironically, this was the sort of chamber-like ensemble he had directed for the Australian Broadcasting Company in 1929, and Roberts knew what that meant. From this time onwards until he retired in 1948, he would complain bitterly about how he had been treated by the ABC. But Horner felt strongly that Sydney needed a more serious musician. It found one in Percy Code.

Code was a quiet man, and not one to sell himself. Unlike Heinze, he was not a great 'networker', so it is not surprising that his name means so little today. But he was an important figure at the time, and, in the words of Heinze, 'an infinitely better and wider experienced musician than Mr Roberts'. In Helen Bainton's words, 'he was a conscientious workman but inexperienced in the finer points and subtleties of light and shade . . . He left much to the players and trusted them, was grateful when things went well, and was essentially a modest man regarding his own attainments'.

In 1936 Code was the resident conductor of the Melbourne orchestra, and he was brought to Sydney as Roberts' successor. The young Joseph Post succeeded him in Melbourne a short while later.

Apart from his abilities as a conductor, it is probable that Code was the best Australian trumpet player of his day. He had toured with the Besses o' the Barn Band and, later, played with the San Francisco Symphony Orchestra for six years. A winner of many competitions (including South Street, for Code was also a Victorian), he was once told by William Short, King Edward VII's trumpeter, that 'there is no player superior to you in the British Isles'. He had also studied harmony, composition and instrumentation at the Royal College of Music.

When Beecham toured Australia for the ABC in 1940, he met

Code, and later asked the SSO's concertmaster, Lionel Lawson, about Code's origins. The conversation is reported to have gone something like this:

'And what was your conductor, Mr Lawson, before he was er . . . er . . . a conductor?'

'He was a trumpet player, Sir Thomas.'

'Oh. My experience of trumpet players is that they are usually going into, or coming out of, an hotel!' Percy Code wasn't like that, as it happens, but it's another good Beecham story.

Code's arrival was an obvious boost to the Sydney orchestra's fortunes. But Moses' appointment put the finishing touches on another initiative, one of the most important in the ABC's history: after discussions with Heinze, and with crucial input from Cleary, James and Horner, Moses expanded the Sydney and Melbourne orchestras to permanent strengths of forty-five and thirty-five players respectively. In October 1935,[4] Cleary explained to the *Sydney Morning Herald* why this was such an important move:

First, being a complete symphony orchestra, [the Sydney group] will enable [the ABC] to produce from the studio symphonic works which were beyond the scope of the smaller orchestra. Secondly, when public concerts are given, and the numbers are augmented to 70 or thereabouts, the compact nucleus will represent about two-thirds, instead of a little more than one-third, as previously, thus making the augmented orchestra more of a homogenous body than before.

The formation of this orchestra . . . is evidence of the Commission's optimism as to the public taste for first-class music performed at a high artistic standard . . . we can only hope that this increased opportunity for hearing good music performed excellently will widen the circle of appreciative listeners. At any rate, the Commission is doing its part, and may fairly claim that it is anticipating, and not lagging behind, public demand.

Well, it was hardly a complete symphony orchestra, but the ABC could neither justify nor afford that, for its live music performances were not selling consistently well. There was a big difference

---

[4] A short time later the ensembles in the other states were made larger also. The Adelaide, Brisbane and Perth groups were increased to seventeen players and Hobart's to eleven.

between calling for the ABC to promote live performance and attending the result. In 1935, in addition to the Dr Bainton concerts, the Commission had promoted recitals by the Budapest Quartet, whose performances had been a source of prestige rather than financial reward to the Commission. Cleary's message here was that the enlarged orchestra would improve the quality of studio broadcasts and, it was hoped, provide a basis for larger audiences in the concert hall.

His point about reducing the body of augmenting players was important. It was not possible to maintain a high standard when so many of the players were brought in just for the big works, while the 'core' orchestra did most of the smaller studio work— dinner music, musical comedy items, etc— on its own. But what Cleary did not acknowledge publicly was that, for the most part, there were not enough rehearsals. During the Harty tour, the *Herald* put it this way:

> If playing together frequently would, in itself, make a body of instrumentalists into a good orchestra, the nucleus of the Commission's forces should some time ago have reached a splendid standard; for its members are constantly pouring forth musical comedy, and even lighter forms of entertainment, in the interim between symphony concerts. Sir Hamilton might point out . . . that more than two rehearsals are necessary in order properly to interpret a program of good music.

Heinze was well aware of the problems of inadequate rehearsal time, and suggested to Horner that the new SSO had to have three three-hour rehearsals whenever they were playing a major program.

'I realise that as the orchestra continues to gain in efficiency and in its repertoire so will less rehearsal be necessary', he wrote, 'but I am afraid that is rather further away than we imagine, for I have had ample experience in seeing how quickly the orchestras forget'. For many of the players even three rehearsals— two fewer than is standard now for the SSO—would have been insufficient.

Having decided not to approach the Conservatorium for extra musicians, partly for political reasons, the ABC auditioned the wider world for them, and Robert Miller recalls how the 45-strong orchestra was augmented for its first series of live concerts in 1936:

'The problem was to find good, experienced people to augment the orchestra to seventy players. Most of these extra players were part-time musicians; in other words they were following some other trade like butcher or baker and apart from the fact that they did play their instruments reasonably well, they were not trained in the repertoire and had probably never been called on to play with the degree of accuracy that would be required by an overseas conductor in some very difficult orchestral work. So these concerts could become quite nerve-racking experiences.'

Cleary emphasised the importance of the new orchestras to studio work for good reason. The orchestras would continue to be split into smaller groups, but *larger* smaller groups, which would have a more lustrous sound on-air. These groups soon became known in program listings as the Sydney Symphony Orchestra (for public performances and broadcasts at full strength), the Sydney Light Orchestra (thirty-one players) and the Sydney Theatre Orchestra (seventeen players). Internally, they were known simply as Orchestras A, B and C. Melbourne was given an equivalent structure.

And as it was from Sydney and Melbourne that most of the national programs were relayed, the presence of two large staff orchestras in these cities would allow the broadcast schedules to be greatly freed up. Horner suggested to Cleary how the new forces could best be used:

In both Sydney and Melbourne the A orchestra in one city shall be utilised as a complete symphonic unit one week, and provide during that week one full symphony concert on the National Relay [2FC], and one hour's performance on the alternative station [2BL], which will not be relayed [outside that State]. During the same week, all light orchestra music is to be provided from the other major State by Orchestras B and C, this to include musical comedy, support to choral work and every type of light orchestral program. By this means each State will be supplying serious music one week and lighter music the next.

'The expansion of the orchestra was very exciting at the time', Neville Amadio recalls. 'For instance, it meant that we had a pair of each of the woodwind as part of the core group, so that if we were doing a Brahms symphony from the studio we could play it without augmentation. We hadn't been in that position before.'

The first piece of work the new Sydney orchestra was given was a series of opera broadcasts conducted by Maurice de Abravanel, who was in Australia with a touring opera company brought here by Sir Benjamin Fuller. Although clearly a good conductor, Abravanel's presence proved to be ridiculously disruptive, and caused Cleary, James and Moses problems that climaxed with a press feud in July the following year. This was not the kind of diversion they needed while they were trying to see through the birth of a new orchestra.

The Abravanel saga started in mid-1935, when the Taits brought to Australia the young Yehudi Menuhin. Having organised orchestral performances for him, the ABC had Abravanel conduct Menuhin's Sydney concert and Heinze the Melbourne. The *Daily Telegraph* was about to sponsor a series of Sydney Town Hall concerts with Abravanel and a special pick-up orchestra, called the Sydney Professional Musicians for the occasion. The paper's review of Menuhin's Melbourne concert was openly insulting to Heinze's conducting, and was the start of the *Telegraph's* campaign to make the ABC give Abravanel something permanent to do. This campaign increased in hysteria after Cleary's announcement of the new orchestra.

But beyond giving Abravanel more opera broadcasts and some studio concerts to conduct, the Commission did nothing about the press agitation. The reasons are easy to guess: Abravanel was fairly temperamental and Heinze did not like him, and most likely felt threatened by him, for Abravanel was the better conductor. In the eyes of the *Telegraph* and the *Wireless Weekly*, the ABC was dithering. After all, here was a fine young conductor who had been in Australia doing a variety of things for more than a year. Why would not the ABC give him the new Sydney orchestra to run?

The affair came to a head in July 1936 when Abravanel, just before leaving the country, said that the 'dictatorship' of the Commission by a small but powerful Victorian minority (read Heinze) was responsible for his services not being retained in

Australia.[5] Cleary's swift denial followed, and Abravanel's hilarious reply followed that. This is how that parting shot was fired, according to the *Sydney Morning Herald*:

Perth, Sunday: Referring to the statement attributed to him in an interview in Adelaide on Saturday, Mr de Abravanel said tonight that it contained many mistakes, due possibly to the hurried nature of the interview, which was given while driving from the station to the aerodrome at Parafield—the interviewer driving the motor car.

The Menuhin concerts had other, long-lasting repercussions, too. It was only after great public pressure that Cleary agreed to negotiate with the Taits for Menuhin at all, for the Taits were notoriously mean. But Cleary was really shocked at the conditions asked: £1000 for one broadcast, the ABC providing the orchestra and the conductor free, the broadcast not to be advertised until twenty-four hours beforehand (to maximise box office) and the advertisement not to feature the name of the soloist. Cleary got the fee down to £500, which was still an awful lot of money. Moses felt the ABC had been 'held to ransom'. He convinced Cleary that from now on the Commission had to be its own entrepreneur, for no one but the Taits was importing artists of Menuhin's calibre and reputation.

⁂

In Australia, the press attitude to orchestral music in the 1930s was a mixture of reverence and proud ignorance. Cleary and Moses, well-informed music lovers both, realised that nothing would change unless more music could be heard more often.

For example, the following item was published by the *Telegraph* in 1934:

MUSIC WITH YOUR MEALS

Dinner-time music should be bright and cheerful, stimulating, and require

[5] This was really a lot of empty huffing and puffing, for Abravanel was leaving to take up a conductorship at the Metropolitan Opera, New York, that would pay the equivalent of £97 a week. He was earning around £35 a week with the ABC. In Australia, the average weekly wage at this time was around £2.

no special effort of mental concentration for its appreciation, says Mr Roland Foster.[6]

He suggests the following dinner music programme:

Overture: *Marriage of Figaro* (Mozart)
Ballet music: *Sylvia* (Delibes)
Pianoforte: Gluck-Brahms Gavotte, and Waltz in A Major (Levitzki)
Violin: 'Preislied' (Wagner-Wilhelmj) and the 'Slav Dance' (Dvořák-Kreisler) . . .

In arguing for one national orchestra, the *Wireless Weekly* discussed the level of organisational ability needed to run a symphony orchestra. It explained why the New York Philharmonic had such hefty running costs:

The New York orchestra sets out to be the world's best and many of its heaviest expenses are due to competing with other orchestras for celebrated conductors and solo performers and advertising. Australia would be satisfied with an orchestra on a more modest scale.[7]

Meanwhile, the *Telegraph* critic, 'Barnum's Ghost', offered his opinions on one of Percy Grainger's 1935 broadcast concerts, which evidently contained one of Grainger's *Hill Songs* and his *Tribute to Foster*. It is hard to know which of Delius' pieces is being referred to, however:

Hope I'm not speaking out of place, but I think the ABC could do with a tip or two from an old showman. Things strange, curious, extraordinary and unique are in my line, so when Percy Grainger is on the air my valves and ears are at his disposal.

. . . Perce needs firm management. His props included one grand piano, two harmoniums, a marimba, musical glasses, two orchestras, five solo singers and a choir which sang in eight parts. What did he do with them? First item was people wailing miserably; second item was people wailing still more miserably; . . . Followed Perce's idea of what a hill would sing like if it had taken lessons—it must be hell to be a hill!

---

[6] Foster was a professional singer who later wrote a popular volume of memoirs, *Come Listen to My Song*.
[7] This is especially hypocritical given this journal's vigorous campaign for establishment of a permanent orchestra.

. . . We wound up with 'Doodah Day,' which opened brightly but soon relapsed into woe. Voices crooned 'doodah, doodah' as if it were Greek for 'all hope is dead'. Sounds fondly believed by Perce to indicate the buzzing of bees permeated the middle portion, but put no sting in the mixture.

I believe Perce personally conducted all these dirges, but if he had made a mistake anywhere it probably wouldn't have been discovered until years afterwards . . .

In mid-1935 Heinze put forward a list of Celebrity Artists to be invited here in the following year, to give orchestral and recital performances.[8] This was to be Sydney's first season of what the Commission called Celebrity Concerts, and it featured Ezio Pinza and Elisabeth Rethberg (who appeared together), and expatriates Eileen Joyce and Dorothy Helmrich. Europe's increasing political instability was a great advantage to the ABC in the years immediately before and after the Second World War, for it meant that many artists were more inclined to travel the great distance required than they were during the 1960s, when the increasing power of the record industry and the relative stability of Western Europe meant that top-flight conductors and soloists were harder to attract.

The time distance was much greater then than now. The return journey to Europe by sea took twelve weeks, which meant that the cost of importing artists was much greater than it would have been for a European or North American entrepreneur (the ABC paid ship's passage, internal travel and accommodation), and some artists were not always willing to find the four to six months 'off the circuit' that the ABC required.[9]

However, the ABC paid well. When Tauber toured here in 1938 he earned £1000 a week. This was pretty much the fee Tauber would have expected wherever he worked, but it was far more

---

[8] The list is prefaced by this curious remark: 'I feel we have had such an influx of foreign Jews and Australian musical opinion is being formed by what these musicians do, that it would be a welcome change to concentrate a little on English musicians, although they may be of Jewish origin'. Heinze then goes on to recommend such prominent Jewish artists as Myra Hess, Harold Samuel and Solomon.

[9] Where the ABC usually took its artists on national tours, the Taits often presented their artists in Sydney and Melbourne only.

than the Taits would have offered. The guaranteed income from the licence fee gave the ABC short-term advantages over Williamsons that later would lead to near-disaster.

In the meantime, the *Wireless Weekly* was full of praise for the concept of a regular concert season. 'This news will be received with satisfaction by all who have been interested in the progress of broadcasting and the decline of music in Sydney during the past ten years. Indeed, the establishment of yearly symphony concerts will be the first of which we are aware in the history of Sydney in which amateurs and students will have no part.'

The guest conductor for 1936 was Dr Malcolm Sargent, who was of course to have appeared two years earlier. This visit was the beginning of an association with Australia and the ABC that would last for thirty years. Sargent died in 1968, the year after his final tour here. The audiences and critics of 1936 loved him: he was slim, handsome, well dressed and a 'showman' conductor to boot. The 'Flash Harry' techniques he became famous for were already in place: the flower in the buttonhole; the way he walked on stage just as the applause for the concertmaster rolled away; his dramatic pointing of the baton at the timpani, to signal the start of the national anthem, as he strode from stage left to the podium.

Neville Amadio remembers that he was extraordinarily conceited. 'He was always concerned about the way he looked. He also had a lot of clever pet sayings, so that you might be rehearsing a work with him years after he'd previously conducted it with you, and he would stop in exactly the same place and tell you exactly the same thing. That was a bit much sometimes.'

His 1936 repertoire was not as adventurous as Harty's had been, but it was well chosen: his performances of Elgar's *Enigma* variations would have been excellent, and he gave solid performances of Brahms' first symphony, R. Strauss' *Till Eulenspiegel*, Dvořák's *New World* symphony and the Verdi Requiem. Sargent was not impatient with local standards, and worked the orchestra hard. There were not yet many subscribers, and the ABC's obvious 'papering' of the Town Hall (giving out free tickets in order to have a decent-sized house) caused much press comment. But Moses and James knew they were leading the charge, and, with Heinze, began drumming up subscription support from Sydney's elite for a regular concert series. In any case, the praise for the quality of the music-making was almost universal.

Like Harty, Sargent wrote a report on orchestral standards, and found himself generally pleased with the Sydney performances, although, like Harty, he regarded the importation of a few 'training' players from the United Kingdom as an important possibility. Horner would have been overcome with *déjà vu* at reading Sargent's comment that 'the Double Basses have not been accustomed to look upon themselves as artists'. He noted that 'an outstanding player is, of course, Llewellyn. I could strongly recommend him as a leader, either violin or viola'. He also made this deadpan remark of the viola section in Melbourne: 'the deafness of the second player at the first desk is a disadvantage'.

He called for the formation of one national orchestra, and was to have temporary success when a National Symphony Orchestra was formed specially for his second visit, which coincided with the New South Wales sesquicentenary. The orchestra—essentially a combination of the Sydney and Melbourne players—gave three concerts.[10] The public and press enthusiasm for the 100-piece group was tremendous, and Sargent told Cleary that if this group could be kept together he would come back to conduct them every year. But, in the words of Ken Inglis, 'his hosts were flattered but not tempted; for they were comitted to a thoroughly federal policy, and they hoped that the visiting conductors would help to raise standards all round'.

The term 'Celebrity Concerts' was to prove itself a problem in quick time, partly because of its in-built elitism, partly because it implied that every artist was a celebrity. The latter was patently not true, for in Sydney Sargent appeared with two young Australian soloists who were far from being celebrities just yet: Ernest Llewellyn (Chausson's *Poeme*), who was in the orchestra's viola section at the time, and the pianist Beatrice Tange (Liszt's E flat concerto). These were the first of many ABC subscription concerts in which Australian soloists would appear with overseas conductors (and *vice versa*). The tradition continues today.

---

[10] Of the first of these, the Sydney *Truth* wrote that 'black velvet amounts almost to a uniform among a sartorially distinguished audience'.

Dr Malcolm Sargent and the National Symphony Orchestra, formed especially for his 1938 tour. The front row of violinists contains three of the most important string players to have worked in Australia. Second, third and fourth from the left, respectively, are Robert Miller, Ernest Llewellyn and Haydn Beck.

If the glamour of attending an event at which celebrities were to be the main attraction implied the ABC's interest in a certain kind of audience, Moses' directive to begin subscribers' committees confirmed it. Only Melbourne had such a committee: Heinze had started it in the 1920s, and Ivy Brookes ran it. The brief now, in other States, was to enlist the support of Government House if possible and recruit subscribers from there down. Horner did well: Lady Gordon started as the committee's patron, and the 500 subscribers of 1936 had become 1735 by 1940. (It is perhaps of interest to note that in 1936 Sydney's population was 1 267 000. 500 subscribers represented one quarter of the Town Hall's capacity for one performance.)

'Heinze believed the patronage of the social elite was very important to successful concert-giving, and that Ladies' Committees should be taken very seriously', recalls one of James' successors as Director of Music, Harold Hort. 'They were really crucial at this early stage, when subscribers had to be created from nothing.'

Although this method of audience-building was a great success, in most other respects the 1930s was a period of missed opportunities for the orchestras, largely because the Commission was trying to learn the business of putting concerts on. Sometimes too many broadcasts of a guest artist were scheduled, which kept paying audiences away; sometimes artists were given return engagements too soon after their first tours, as happened to Lotte Lehmann; tours could be too long, meaning that the number of concerts given exceeded box office demand and the interests of the radio listeners; and sometimes conductors were given too much freedom in their choice of programs. For example, one particularly indigestible Georg Schneevoigt concert looked like this:

Suite in G minor..Bach/Reger
Variations and Fugue on a theme of Mozart ....Reger
Piano Concerto No 2, *The River* ....Palmgren

Interval

Symphony No 4...Sibelius
The Silken Ladder—Overture[11] ....Rossini

[11] To be fair, concert programs in this period were longer and more freely put together than we are used to now, but the combination of works in this instance is, to say the least, unusual.

Other symptoms of the ABC's inexperience as a concert promoter were the Szell tours of 1938 and 1939. Most of the musicians interviewed for this book felt that Szell was asked to come too early in the Sydney and Melbourne orchestras' lives. But Adelaide was something else again. He said of the Adelaide orchestra that 'between the least I will expect and the best they can do lies an unbridgeable gap'. At the first rehearsal with them, Szell put his baton down at one point and sighed, 'I see I shall have to start at the beginning'. He then asked the leader if he could borrow his violin for a moment, whereupon he held it up and said, 'this is a violin' . . .

'Szell used to tell people that he knew musicians called him a bastard but he didn't care', long-time MSO leader Bertha Jorgensen recalls. 'He was a wonderful conductor but so rude to the players. And he had cold, steely blue eyes that I'll never forget.' Gretel Feher, a music lover of long standing, met Szell during his 1939 tour. 'He was charming socially, but a pig to the orchestra', she says.

Robert Miller remembers a curious incident from this tour, when Szell conducted the concerts in which Schnabel was soloist. 'We were about to finish the final rehearsal of the *Emperor* concerto. The coda of the last movement comprises a very fast series of semi-quavers, which can be played at great speed to give a brilliant finish to the work. Schnabel did this with great aplomb, stood up, bowed to the orchestra, closed the piano lid and walked off. Whereupon Szell got down from the rostrum, opened the lid of the piano and played the same, very fast passage much faster than Schnabel, closed the piano and walked off.'

Szell's second tour was also notable for the first Australian performance of Walton's first symphony (well received) and the SSO's first-ever suburban concert, given in Newtown's Majestic Theatre (now a Greek community centre). The Commission's quaint term for this exercise was 'bringing music to the industrial suburbs', and ticket prices were accordingly lower than for Town Hall concerts. This first suburban performance (soloist Haydn Beck, music by Beethoven, Stravinsky, Mozart and Glazunov) was a huge success, as this now touching story in the *Daily News* (7 July 1939) reveals. Headlined 'Musical Feast at Newtown', it reads in part:

William James with Dr Malcolm Sargent during the latter's 1938 tour (top).

Georg Szell (standing) with Artur Schnabel during a break in rehearsal in Sydney.

'I used to like Bing Crosby, but after hearing Szell I am satisfied this is the real thing. Give me Beethoven every time after this.' This was the comment of Mr Jack Robertson of Newtown after hearing . . . the ABC's first suburban concert. Mr Robertson is 22 and works in an iron foundry.

'I've never heard anything like this before, and now that I have I don't want to hear anything else', he said . . .

'I don't understand music, but this is too thrilling for words', said Miss E Thornton of Newtown. 'It makes you feel things you never quite thought of before, just like you want to throw out your chest and sing', she added.

If we want confirmation that the Town Hall concerts were not attracting many working-class people in the 1930s, the ABC's efforts to bring the orchestra to working-class suburbs is proof positive. Subsequently, concerts were given in Marrickville and Petersham town halls and the Embassy Theatre, Manly.

The problem with Szell was that he did not have the temperament to train orchestras of the SSO's then prevailing standard, and he lacked the personal warmth that would have helped create a rapport with the players. A veteran of the SSO and MSO cellos, Kathleen Tuohy, says simply that 'he had lost his humility'. Once he'd left, his influence left too, and he was not really interested in returning after the Second World War: he then became a United States citizen and spent most of his time developing his celebrated relationship with the Cleveland Orchestra.

In his report on the orchestras, Szell was typically brusque, and fairly pessimistic about the ABC's prospect of achieving reasonable playing standards in all six capitals. The Sydney double basses were 'quite bad', and the tuba 'quite impossible'. He had praise for the violins and flutes.

William James noted in a letter to Heinze: 'His personality seemed to me a little cold, likewise his interpretations'. Szell's views on music could be pretty interesting, though. He told a Brisbane reporter that 'the ultra-moderns have no followers . . . the future of music will certainly not be with atonality or anything of that sort. The fruits of these movements will be plucked by others.

'Stravinsky's position today and his position 20 years ago are very different things. We see him now in some sort of perspective.

He is no longer a leader of the moderns. By many he is considered a reactionary. And his recent work, *Jeu de cartes*, is certainly older in spirit than Strauss' *Salome*, written 40 years ago.'

Szell also made a startling suggestion for a neat solution to the problem of establishing a permanent opera company in Australia. 'All your big cities are ports. A floating opera house would be an admirable and economic idea. You could take an old ship, convert it and take it from capital to capital with a season in each city.'

Schneevoigt was a figure of much greater importance to orchestral standards in the late 1930s. Born in Finland in 1872, he had a considerable reputation by the time of his first visit in 1937: as a champion of Sibelius' music, as founder of the Oslo Philharmonic, and as conductor of the Finnish National Orchestra. It was on a visit to London in 1934 with this orchestra that he made the first ever recording of Sibelius' sixth symphony. He made two ABC tours, in 1937 and 1940, and their importance lies in their long-term impact on playing standards.

For Schneevoigt was a superb trainer. Neville Amadio believes that his work formed the technical foundation of the future SSO. 'We had never been trained better up to that time. He was the greatest, sometimes demanding up to ten rehearsals for certain pieces—that was unheard of then. He wasn't a very vivid conductor, though, and he often lacked a certain flair in the concert itself. But he was a great teacher. When he said 'With the end of the bow' to the violins, all the bows had to be in the same place, and he wouldn't start the passage until they were.'

Schneevoigt would take section rehearsals. He was very patient. And he was a character. Bertha Jorgensen remembers that he hated having women in orchestras. 'If he wanted to insult any of the men he would say "You play like voomans". One day one of the girls in the orchestra passed him in the corridor, and he handed her a broom, as if to say, "This is what you should be doing."[12]

---

[12] He was quoted in the *Daily Telegraph* as saying that 'In a country like Australia, which is crying out for a population, a woman's place should be in a home bringing up a family rather than playing a musical instrument. It would be good for music, too'. He told reporters at his first press conference that 'there is one place for the woman . . . in bed, and not all of them are good there!'

Georg Schneevoigt applauding Arthur Rubinstein after a performance with the SSO of the Brahms Piano Concerto No 2 in 1937.

'He had a strange sense of humour, too. We were playing a Strauss waltz in a suburban concert and he left the stage in the middle of it to sit in the audience.'

Isa Robson sang in the choir in Schneevoigt's SSO performance of Beethoven 9 in 1937. 'At one point in rehearsals he sent the choir and the rest of the players away to drill the cellos and basses in their recitative passage in the finale. He wanted to get it as soft as possible.'

'At the beginning of Brahms 4 he shouted to the violins for half an hour because they could not conceive how he wished the first phrase to be played', SSO veteran Helen Bainton recalled in her book *Facing the Music.* 'I don't know how many times I put up my viola ready to join in at the second half of the bar, only to put it down again because Schneevoigt was still not satisfied.'

His English was not very good—the Australian press sent his accent up mercilessly—and in announcing an encore at the end of a Sydney concert he referred to it as a piece from Sibelius' suite to *Belshazzar's 'Dinner'.* He was upset by the laughter that followed. Music historian Isabelle Moresby probably sums the man up best, in her book *Australia Makes Music*:

He was the most patient and thorough musician and one of the most exasperating individuals. It was often a tussle to know whether the players loved or hated the incorrigible old man. For his pluck and humour he was forgiven many unpardonable remarks. To work with him was to value his musical sensitivity and profound knowledge, yet he was like a wilful, naughty little boy playing up because—luckily—he held the baton.

'I began going to orchestral concerts in the late thirties, and Schneevoigt was one of my earliest experiences', says Ken Tribe. 'You must understand that I carry impressions rather than solid memories of those concerts, but I do recall a good orchestral sound, which is something we weren't used to at the time. The Con orchestra had been OK, but Schneevoigt's concerts showed us that what the Conservatorium had provided had been second rate. The new orchestral experience the ABC gave us in the thirties established for the first time this century a continuity of quality in the field.'

Schneevoigt's quest for perfection could take its toll. Robert Miller recalls the problems his demands made on the SSO. 'A lot of the extra players had developed bad habits over the years, and this resulted in much heart-burning. The rehearsals for our first Schneevoigt concert were unusually detailed, and resulted in a highly nervous performance.

'Being the great man that he was he apologised to the orchestra later, taking full responsiblity for the tension at that concert. He realised that he had put the screws on too soon, given that we were working with quite a few part-time players. But he certainly lifted the standard of that augmented orchestra to a very high level.'

Sibelius was a controversial figure in the 1930s. For example, the *Bulletin*, rarely fond of anything new and non-Anglo, remarked of Schnéevoigt's Sibelius 6 with the SSO that '[the work] would have to be given many times before the average audience could get much out of it'. But with recordings of his music thin on the ground, Sibelius had also been a great technical challenge to Australian orchestras until Schneevoigt's arrival.

'Percy Code was quite an adventurous conductor, and I can remember him reading through Sibelius 2 with us in the mid thirties,' Robert Miller says. 'This work had such a contemporary flavour that we found we couldn't get very far with it. Code felt it was beyond our comprehension and his, and we put it aside.'

Schneevoigt also gave the first Australian performance of a Mahler symphony on his first visit when he conducted the fifth with the SSO. Like Sibelius 6, it was a difficult work for the audience and for the players, few of whom would have played a bar of Mahler's music until then. The Sydney *Sun's* review was headlined 'Symphony for Undertakers'.

'The symphony was calculated to put any undertakers in the Town Hall audience last night in a good mood, since it began with a 30-minute funeral march, designed, one would imagine, to be played at the funeral of a leading pork-butcher of Vienna . . . The symphony went on to a scherzo that did not scherz . . .'

Unwittingly, Sydney was years ahead of its time in hearing this work. Only in Vienna and Amsterdam was Mahler's music heard with any frequency in the 1930s. It would take the presence of Neville Cardus in Australia to make Mahler's name familiar.

So the 1930s were to end with no chief conductor in sight and a war looming that would effectively cut Australia off from almost all European and American talent for five years. But in addition to the musical predicaments the Commission was to be left in through its own inexperience and indecision, it was to have a catastrophic legal wrangle while it dealt with a damaging rebuff from federal cabinet.

※

In January 1937 the Commission held auditions in Sydney and Melbourne for players who had not so far worked with the orchestras, and the results were alarming, particularly as some key players in the two major orchestras were known to be inadequate. Heinze and James wrote that only a small percentage of the players who presented themselves for audition in Sydney and Melbourne were worth any further consideration. 'Even among the finalists there was again only a small percentage to recommend for symphonic playing. Generally speaking the technical foundation of those who presented themselves for audition was utterly unsatisfactory.'

Heinze and James recommended that two oboists, two bassoonists and four horn players be brought from abroad, or more specifically, from London orchestras, for permanent membership of the Melbourne and Sydney groups. (In his report, Sargent had said that the playing of these instruments was causing a major lapse in overall standards.)

Moses wrote to the Postmaster-General in May with a slightly better pedigreed version of the problem: he explained that Harty, Sargent and Schneevoigt felt strongly that music in Australia 'is handicapped by the absence of competent players of certain 'key' instruments, and will continue to be so handicapped unless such players are brought from abroad. The instruments in question are the Oboe, the Bassoon and the French Horn'.

But Cabinet was not interested. In response they simply said that 'with careful selection and proper training, the material is available in Australia to meet the Commission's needs'.

It is doubtful that Cabinet was in a position to know whether this was true or not. What the ABC needed were players who were good now, not, with training, in three years' time. They had just been told they could not have them. Ironically, the Second World War and its aftermath would bring excellent musicians from Europe to live in Australia and swell the ranks of the SSO; violinists Bela Dekany and Abdrew Hoffman, principal viola Robert Pikler and principal cellist Hans George among them. Still, the question of importing British players would resurface in 1944.

Perhaps the greatest orchestral dilemma of the decade, though, was that caused by the events which began in February 1938, when J. C. Williamson Ltd took out an injunction to restrain the ABC from staging public concerts. Defeat in this would have put the SSO's future in real doubt. After all, it was being augmented to reasonable symphonic size specifically to give public concerts.

In the first place, of course, the orchestras' existence as public concert-giving units was the result of a fairly free reading of the legislation that established the Commission, the Broadcasting Act of 1932. Paragraph 23 of the Act is ambivalent enough:

The Commission shall, as far as possible, give encouragement to the development of local talent and endeavour to obviate restriction of the utilization of the services of persons who, in the opinion of the Commission, are competent to make useful contributions to broadcasting programmes.

But in comparison Paragraph 24 virtually fires the starting pistol:

The Commission shall endeavour to establish and utilize, in such manner as it thinks desirable in order to confer the greatest benefit on broadcasting, groups of musicians for the rendition of orchestral, choral and band music of high quality.

It was the ABC's definition of this latter paragraph that the Taits would bring into question, almost as soon as Harty landed.

❦

The Taits first wrote to Lloyd Jones in July 1934 after the ABC had begun negotiations with Vladimir Horowitz for an Australian tour. These negotiations were to prove unsuccessful, but that was not to become as big a problem for the ABC as the fact that, at the same time, the Taits were negotiating to bring Horowitz here too, and for a lower fee. The first Tait letter said, in part, that 'it is our business to undertake tours of this nature, and we must take exception to the ABC being permitted to compete with private enterprise in this line of business'.

But the Taits did not follow through immediately, and it is not hard to see why. After all, they had never brought a conductor to Australia, so that Harty's tour could hardly be considered threatening. The Budapest Quartet were not really in the Taits' line, either.

The conflict began in earnest when Pinza and Rethberg toured in 1936. Although the box office for their concerts built slowly, their presence attracted enormous attention, and the prestige was painful to watch. The Taits were about to tour Richard Crooks, and did not want him to seem less significant than the singers the ABC had on offer. They wrote to the Prime Minister in March lodging a formal objection to the ABC's concert activities. They claimed that as an arm of government the ABC should not compete with private entrepreneurs, and that the income from licence fees allowed the Commission to offer fees to artists far higher than the Taits could afford.

The Taits were arguing from a poor position. They were principally interested in musical comedies and hit plays, and treated the concert business as a sideline. In 1935 and 1936 they brought to Australia one concert artist per year (Menuhin and Crooks), and made sure their programs were as populist as possible and that broadcasts were few and far between. They were trying to sell tickets, and only coincidentally aiming for Cleary's goal which was, unashamedly, the improvement of public taste. Cleary knew the ABC would experience some empty houses for its pains, but the slowly increasing financial success of their concerts—the Eileen Joyce tour being a major triumph—convinced him that the ABC should stay in the concert business. The Taits never got to grips with the differences between their own intentions as concert promoters and the ABC's.

For example, the Taits suggested quite seriously that they would have no objection to the ABC bringing international artists here to perform in studio broadcasts only.[13] But is this almost purposeful

---

[13] Cleary thought this last suggestion idiotic, and the *Wireless Weekly* agreed with him. 'Is it seriously contended that the Commission should bring out international artists and keep them locked up in studios? . . . Are listeners to be deprived of the

lack of comprehension so surprising? The idea of an entrepreneurial public enterprise was new, confusing and threatening to a company that felt entitled to claim pioneer status in the history of Australian entertainment. When the press feud between the two parties began a few months later, E.J. Tait showed how little he understood the ABC's intentions when he told the *Sydney Morning Herald*: 'We claim that we have done much more than the ABC to improve the musical taste of the public, and the fact that we have had practically 100 per cent successful tours is evidence of the appreciation of the public'. Cleary argued that box-office success and long-term cultural gains were not the same thing.

During the feud many newspapers began to question the validity of the Taits' claim. Some journalists and letters-to- the-editor writers were particularly irked by the Taits' assertion that the market would only stand one visiting artist per year. A correspondent to the Labor Daily noted that:

The recent season of Richard Crooks in Sydney was a box office dream; not so the Rethberg-Pinza concerts. Where in that instance did the private firm suffer? . . . It is a sign of utter weakness to complain of just competition. The complaining should be left to the public, which has been theatrically starved. Who, other than the Commission, would bring Dr Sargent to Australia? He will direct a great number of Australian musicians, most of whom are constantly employed by the ABC. Real artists are worth big money. If, for example, the Commission brought Gigli to Australia, at enormous cost, we, as listeners, would get our value. Surely, too, we would want to see the great singer as well as hear him, and as we pay a yearly [licence] fee of one pound one shilling

---

[11] *continued*
joy of hearing these artists [in concert] because commercial entrepreneurs wish to make a profit out of one artist every twelve months?'

The kind of concert broadcast Williamson's liked their artists to give can be judged by this note from Keith Barry, the ABC's Controller of Programs, to Moses in August 1938, written while the American baritone Lawrence Tibbett was on a Williamson's tour:

The much boomed broadcast of Tibbett last night actually consisted of five songs and an item by the Theatre Royal Orchestra. The rest of the time was taken up with discussions about the number of Stations on the relay and Ardath cigarettes. The broadcast was timed for half an hour. It is also worthy of note that this singer was not permitted to broadcast until he had completed his concert tour.

we are entitled to the privilege. The public are not likely to suffer from the bringing out of these artists . . . It is far more likely to hurt the private firms, until they compete firmly with the opposition.

The *Sydney Morning Herald* did not feel the Taits' argument held water either:

They say that their management knows much more about catering successfully for public taste than the Commission does. That is a reason why they should fear the ABC less rather than more . . . If the ABC ceased to give public concerts, it is doubtful if any of the Taits' one-time competitors in the concert business would return to their former activity, as they all seem to have retired from this field. Unless they did, or unless some completely unexpected new concert agency sprang up, the Taits would remain in complete possession of the field; and, presumably, would present artists at rare intervals, when they thought the pockets of the public would stand it. That is to say, the various [State] capitals would suddenly lose their present advantage as rapidly growing centres of cosmopolitan music, and become mere local backwaters.

And the *Wirless Weekly* asked, 'what will happen to the Symphony Orchestral season if the Commission is not to be allowed to give public concerts. Would Australia ever see a conductor like Harty again?'.

On the other hand the *Telegraph* and *Smith's Weekly*, seemed to relish the conflict with *Smith's* running one story headed 'Can ABC Legally Give Concerts?/ *Smith's* Doubts It/Taits Should Bring Test Case'.

But the listeners were basically supportive and Cleary and Moses were determined not to give in. They were also encouraged by the Taits poor skills as negotiators. At one point the Taits wrote to Moses saying 'we are feeling very keenly the competition created by the Comission', which was not perhaps the most sophisticated approach they could have taken.

Heinze was scared by the whole business, and advised Moses to back off. 'On the whole, it would be infinitely wiser to try and find some basis of co-operation with the Taits. You may feel this is a display of some weakness in view of recent happenings in the press, . . . [and], of course, as a disadvantage, we have

The cover of a publicity brochure announcing the 1938 concert season

The SSO on its first tour to Newcastle in 1938. Conductor Percy Code is fifth from the left in the front row (holding hat).

the acknowledged greed of the Taits to cope with', he wrote in November 1936.

Astonishingly, the next page of this letter finds Heinze devaluing the very activity he had helped set up. 'The more I think over the question the more I feel that the ABC is going to find itself, because of its public concert activities, engaged in the maintenance and upkeep of an expensive organisation managing only the concert section of its work. And one might logically argue that concert work does not come within the province of broadcasting.' As well, he had obviously forgotten the Menuhin negotiations when he wrote, 'we could surely safeguard ourselves from exploitation by satisfactory treaty'.

Twice, in 1936 and 1937, the Taits tried to interest the ABC in permanent co-operative arrangements along the following lines: the ABC pays artists' fees and the Taits run the tours, paying hall hire costs, advertising etc. The Taits and the ABC then split the box-office receipts on a percentage basis.

But Moses and Cleary knocked them back both times. In May 1937 Moses wrote that 'it would be neither advisable nor practicable for us to hand over our concert management to these people: the experience of the past year has enabled us build up a Concert Department which is daily becoming more efficient and more effective'.

Cleary had financial objections, too. In June 1938 he told the Postmaster-General, A.J. McLachlan, that he had done an abstract of how much more the 1936 and 1937 concert seasons would have cost had the Taits' partnership arrangements been accepted. The answer: £12000 more than it actually cost us to run the concerts'.

By this time the Taits had decided to take out an injunction against the ABC, claiming that the Commission had no constitutional right to put on public concerts when it was supposed to be a broadcasting organisation. Crucially, McLachlan agreed with Cleary that 'as Williamsons are the aggressors, it is highly undesirable that anything should be done which might suggest that the Commission is afraid of the threatened test of its powers, and can be driven into a bad bargain by any vested interest which attacks it, rather than face the test'.

For the orchestras, the impending court case meant a suspension of plans for the 1939 season. Heinze was on his multi-purpose overseas trip at the time, and was suddenly forbidden to offer contracts to anyone.

But in only a month, by July 1938, the Taits were getting cold feet. Williamsons had leased its amusement business to another company, Australian and New Zealand Theatres Ltd, who, although retaining one of the Tait brothers on its board, was less interested in a court case where the outcome could be far from certain. Again, the new company's negotiating skills were not brilliant. Cleary told McLachlan:

. . . I have learnt that some of the Directors of the new Company have been making indirect approaches. For example, Mr H.S. Chambers, one of the Directors living in Melbourne, asked one of the members of our staff to lunch with him, and during the course of lunch asked whether he thought the Commission would be willing to come to terms . . . Mr Chambers then told him that if the Commission did not come to terms it was likely that the new Company would proceed with the action.

This of course is a very foolish way for the Company to embark on overtures to the Commission, although it shows they are anxious.

Another of the new directors, S.S. Crick, came to see Moses in Sydney, who told him simply that the new company had to decide whether or not it should abandon the action, without relying on the ABC to surrender any of its powers as a concert presenter. Moses delightedly reported to the commissioners:

As a parting shot I told him with a smile that we would be very surprised if experienced business men went on with such an action in any circumstances, because apart from the heavy legal costs involved in fighting the action to the highest Courts, a successful verdict could prove no more than a barren victory, as he knew there were many ways of getting round such a matter.

Williamsons dropped the action on 1 August, 1938, the price extracted from the ABC being a requirement added to the Broadcasting Act which required the ABC to broadcast all or part of any public concert for which a charge was made. This meant that schools concerts, for example, for which no admission fee was charged, were exempt from this amendment.

Clement Semmler has argued in his book *Aunt Sally and Sacred*

Cow that Williamsons were foolish to accept this as an appropriate peace offering, since the ABC went on to become one of the world's largest concert-giving organisations. But the Taits were not interested in becoming concert entrepreneurs on such a scale anyway; and the requirement did of course increase the amount of live music on air dramatically, for beforehand the ABC had broadcast part or all of *most* concerts. Now they were supposed to put virtually everything to air.

As it worked out, though, Moses was able to bend the rules a little. He began by getting the commissioners to recommend that all Celebrity Artists be engaged for the least number of concerts they were prepared to give. This meant that the number of concerts in which a conductor or soloist could give the same work or works was minimised. So far so good. But the increase in subscription concerts after the war made this an insufficient measure.

The ABC finished the decade with mixed musical fortunes. Orchestral standards were improving everywhere, but Roger Covell was largely correct when he wrote in 1963 that 'the standards achieved . . . were necessarily very erratic and would nowadays be thought shocking'.

In the medium term, the chief conductor question could not be solved largely because the war would prevent the SSO from finding one. Code and Post were good trainers (though they hardly received credit for so being), but at that time it would have seemed absurd to have appointed an Australian as a chief conductor. What the audience, the press and to an extent the musicians wanted, was a galvanising, glamorous foreigner. The Sydney press thought Sargent was chief conductor material, and the public loved him, for apart from his other attributes he knew how to flatter us; he was more the politician than Harty in this respect. The rumour was that he might be interested in a long-term appointment.

In May 1938 Heinze was in Europe conducting, talent-hunting and finding out about the latest broadcast technology. Moses cabled the BBC and asked for reports through Heinze on conductors who would be suitable for major appointments in Australia. It was only then that the ABC found out about Sargent's long-term availability, by which time he had been announced as visiting for his National Symphony concerts later that year. Schneevoigt had made his first visit the year before and Georg Szell was about to start his first rehearsals with the SSO at the beginning of his first Australian tour.

The 'favourites' from Heinze's list were Sargent, Schneevoigt and a young Englishman who had just taken over the City of Birmingham orchestra from Adrian Boult, Leslie Heward. But nothing was done. It is hard to know why, because Heinze expressed great keenness in his letters from the United Kingdom about the need for the ABC to make an appointment. It is worth noting, though, that a few months earlier Moses had raised the possibility at a Commission meeting of giving Schneevoigt a three-year contract (Schneevoigt had by this time had a successful start to his first national tour). Vice-Chairman Brookes, Heinze's great ally, got a motion through which prevented any decision being made about a chief conductor appointment until Heinze's availability to take up such a post was determined.

The minutes for this meeting also record that 'the question of a shorter-term engagement for Professor Schneevoigt—eighteen months or a year—could be raised when he was ready to discuss it'. Not very enterprising; the commissioners were not falling over themselves to make a decision, it would seem. And unfortunately, Moses and Cleary never initiated a chief conductor search in the United States or Continental Europe. In this respect, at least, they were creatures of their time.

But the war that would isolate the overseas talent would make the orchestras more valuable to their cities. It was a war long before television, long before the easy availability of complete symphonies and concertos on disc, and long before the cultural diversity Australians now take for granted. In this war live music-making was a rare source of inspiration and comfort, and as a result Sydney and its orchestra grew much closer than they had ever been in the 1930s.

CHAPTER THREE

Conflict and Renewal

The challenges that seemed so daunting to the SSO during the Second World War gradually gave the orchestra greater internal strength and a more ardent relationship with Sydney. Before the war audiences at Sydney Town Hall concerts had been heavily dominated by 'society', but this began to change as the first wave of European immigrants arrived in 1938-39. And the war gave art music a new relevance to thousands of local people who had never been to a concert before. Art in all its forms meant more to Australians during the Second World War than at any time in our history, and musical performance was perhaps the most galvanising 'artistic' experience of the day.

The two high-water marks of the ABC's war-time orchestral achievements were the Beethoven festivals in Sydney, Melbourne and Adelaide in 1943-44; and Ormandy's 1944 visit, organised through the United States Office of War Information. Both events reinforced the power of music to console and inspire in times of physical and spiritual distress. It is no accident that Moses' successful work in establishing a permanent full-strength SSO began in the last days of the war in Europe. Music had been seen to have meaning.

The first concert season of the war—1940—unwittingly prepared SSO audiences for the more vivid changes that were to come: there were no international star soloists on offer. But the Australian soloists included such outstanding musicians as violinist Dorcas

McClean and pianist Eunice Gardiner. And another pianist appearing with the SSO lived as close as Vaucluse: Ignaz Friedman.

James Methuen-Campbell has written (in *Chopin Playing*) that 'there were certain works of Chopin in which Friedman was virtually an unrivalled master'. In *The Great Pianists*, Harold Schonberg called him 'one of the most unusual and original pianists of the century'. The war had forced him out of Europe, and he lived here from 1940 until his death in 1948. He played with the SSO often, and in recital, until rheumatism made it impossible for him to perform. He was also an important teacher at the Conservatorium—his pupils there included Rachel Valler and the late Igor Hmelnitsky. But, historically, he came here too early for us to appreciate him fully, for we made no recordings of his playing, most critics took him for granted and he soon became known—almost pejoratively—as a resident artist.

The cult of the international Celebrity that Moses and Heinze had created was undoubtedly bad for local music-making. It reinforced our sense of cultural second-rateness all too well; yet two years into the war we were thrown back entirely on our own musical resources and had to like it. In a year-in-retrospect piece on Sydney's music in 1939, the *Sydney Morning Herald* used the headline 'Triumph of Celebrities', and remarked:

Local singers and instrumentalists were able to give solo recitals only on the smallest scale. Even then, these concerts were often a losing proposition. The plain fact is that the public has lost confidence in the resident musicians. The causes [of this] are obvious.

The cleavage is intensified by the ABC's drive to publicise visiting personalities at the expense of the residents. So the public becomes celebrity-minded and looks for sensationalism, rather than quiet worth. That is the case, to some extent, the world over; but in Australia the process has been carried to an extreme.

Long-time SSO subscriber Kathleen Wall confirms that the atmosphere in early concert seasons was unfriendly to local musicians. 'Australian conductors, in particular, were unpopular. You had to be a visitor to be any good.'

But the war did change these attitudes. As Therese Radic writes in her biography of Heinze, war-time isolation gave Australian performers unprecedented opportunities, 'without the European celebrity circuit to feed in soloists'. Heinze found to his surprise that, once the locals had the concert platforms to themselves, they were better than anyone had expected. 'They had simply not been taken seriously as soloists before.'

Nevertheless, the ABC would adopt an apologetic tone about its war-time concert activity. Bernard Heinze told one newspaper in 1942 that 'we should be extremely grateful that so many women have been able to fill the vacancies in the orchestras caused by the men being called up. In the SSO there are 34 women players compared with 20 in peacetime'. He went on to say that brass instruments, for physical reasons, were outside the range of 'the average woman'. This would surprise the many female Australian horn and trumpet players of the 1990s.

In a 1946 program the war years are described (probably by William James) as follows:

. . . so the orchestra carried on, severely handicapped because of manpower restrictions and depending largely on women instrumentalists and local conductors and soloists . . . From 1940 till 1944 no overseas conductors came to stimulate our interests. Yet music flourished in spite of that fact.

There was certainly no need to apologise about conductors in 1940. The Pacific war had not yet begun, and the year brought two outstanding visitors: Antal Dorati and Sir Thomas Beecham. Dorati had been here in 1938 as Music Director for Colonel de Basil's ballet company. About a year later, when the outbreak of war had made him virtually stateless, the ABC offered him a tour for the year of 1940. It was doubly welcome because it could be worked around the dates of another season Colonel de Basil had offered him for Australia.

Neville Amadio remembers Dorati as a virtuoso conductor, 'terrific for cues'. He was meticulous, too. Bertha Jorgensen, then a rank-and-file MSO player, says Dorati was the only conductor she has ever been frightened of.

There were two important works for Sydney in Dorati's SSO concerts, one of which was described by the *Daily Telegraph*:

Mahler's mind was rarely clear enough of affairs to be devoted entirely
to composition, and in consequence the dignity of his works is often
lost in a certain worldliness and triviality. The religious mysticism, which
was a feature of much of his work, was sincerely felt, but did not inspire
his finest moments.

The work in question—Mahler's fourth symphony—was about
to receive its Australian premiere under Dorati. And the above
was published as a preview of the concert![1] Dorati later referred
to this performance as 'much-disputed', which probably means
that James was reluctant to have another Mahler work played
so soon after the poor reception accorded Schneevoigt's Mahler
5. Neville Cardus began reviewing for the *Sydney Morning Herald*
in 1940,[2] and his was the only positive review of the piece:

I cannot recall many finer pieces of conducting than Mr Dorati's,
considering that he was dealing with a kind of music which is entirely
out of the common symphonic run. The orchestra (unlike one or two
of the critics present) declined to lose faith during the apparent 'dullness'
of certain sections of the work . . . Mr Dorati and the strings of the
Sydney orchestra were extraordinarily clever in getting the Mahler tensity
and colour [in the slow movement], the proper tone and almost tearful
cadence.

Given the enthusiasm of this review, it seems strange that Dorati
never became known as a Mahler conductor in his later career.
He wrote to Moses later that he would have been proud to have
presented this performance 'anywhere in the world', which says
a lot about the success of the training work Sargent and particularly
Schneevoigt had been doing with the orchestra.

The other Australian premiere performance Dorati gave with
the SSO was of Weinberger's Variations and Fugue on an English
Folk Tune (*Under the Spreading Chestnut Tree*). This work has
vanished entirely from the repertoire, but the SSO played it almost
once a year during the war. It is worth examining the reasons

---

[1] It must be remembered that Mahler's critical stocks in English-speaking countries
were very low between the wars, and that Sydney did not hear a bar of his music
until 1937.

[2] As long-time *Sydney Morning Herald* critic Lindsey Browne remarks, Cardus followed
Beecham to Australia '*à la* Boswell and Johnson'. He lived here until 1947.

for its popularity, for in many ways the piece came into the world under circumstances that symbolise the aspirations and dilemmas of the war years.

Weinberger (composer of *Schwanda the Bagpiper*) was a Jewish Czech. Some time in 1938, after the Nazis invaded Austria, he saw a newsreel in which George VI sang the folk song 'Under the Spreading Chestnut Tree' at a boy scout camp. Some people reading this will remember the elaborate pantomime that used to be integral to an effective rendition of the song, and in the newsreel the king was pointing to his 'chest' and his 'nut' along with everybody else. Weinberger was deeply moved by the 'democratic simplicity' of the newsreel footage, contrasting it as he did with the spectacle of the Nazi regime in his neighbouring countries. He felt compelled to somehow capture the spirit of what he had seen, and wrote his Variations and Fugue as a result. He left Europe after the Nazi invasion of Czechoslovakia, settling in New York.

The work, vivid in its depiction of British life, had great meaning for an audience isolated from its parent culture and now sending troops off to fight for it. Each of Weinberger's seven variations has a title that evokes a romance of Britain, such as *Her Majesty's Virginals*, *The Highlanders* and *Mr Weller Senior Discusses Widows*.[3] Weinberger's piece became so closely associated with the war that, by the 1950s, it had all but disappeared. It probably reminded people too painfully of years they were trying to forget.

Dorati's report on his 1940 tour is good humoured, honest and very musicianly. Obviously the standard of the SSO's playing had improved since Sargent's report of 1936, for Dorati noted that 'whilst the Sydney orchestra today can be called professional, the Melbourne one still has the remains of "dilettante" elements (amongst the extra players)'. He also remarked that 'the average Australian orchestral player is keen, painstaking, musical and very willing. Many of them work against great handicaps, such as lack of proper tuition, lack of steady employment [he is referring here to the 'extras'] or sufficient (or any) occasion to listen to good music.

'The spirit to combat in the players is a certain inferiority

---

[3] Sam Weller is a character from Dickens.

complex, even in your major orchestras . . . very good results came from the method of merely persuading them, in the first place, that they *are* able to do the job.'

He urged Moses to keep the augmented Sydney orchestra together for eight or nine months a year rather than for the six months of the subscription season. This would not happen until after the war. He also echoed all the visiting conductors the SSO had so far worked with in recommending that the ABC 'import, at least for a period, a few first-rate overseas players'.

While Dorati's tour was virtually free of public drama, conflict with the ABC, civic authorities and the press was common throughout Beecham's tour. Dorati was present when Beecham arrived in Melbourne, and in his autobiography recorded the following exchange between Beecham and an eager young reporter. Beecham was asked what new works he was going to perform in Australia.

He announced with an Olympian gesture: 'I have a rather interesting novelty for you. A tenth symphony by Beethoven.'

The young man was astounded. Here was his scoop. 'You have found a new symphony by Beethoven, Sir Thomas? Where did you find it? Is it genuine?'

Sir Thomas, without blinking an eyelid, replied, 'Oh yes, I found it in the British Museum. And inasmuch as it comes from the British Museum, it *must* be genuine.'

The young man wrote feverishly. 'And is this the only novelty you bring, Sir Thomas? Or are there more?'

'An eleventh, a twelfth symphony by Beethoven . . . I don't even remember . . .'

Luckily, the story was intercepted before it hit the paper, but Beecham continued to antagonise the Australian press, so they naturally felt obliged to antagonise him back. These bouts with the newspapers would remain Beecham's most hated memory of the tour. The Sydney *Telegraph* had warned its readers before Beecham's arrival that he was 'famous for his use of the great Australian adjective', but he was far more versatile than that.

His arrival at his first Sydney rehearsal set the tone for the public clashes to follow, says Robert Miller.

'A great entourage of officials arrived—people from the Music Department, reporters, cameramen and the like. Charles Moses introduced Beecham to the orchestra, whereupon Beecham placed himself on the rostrum. He was highly amused at the number of people in attendance other than the musicians. One of the cameramen then asked Beecham if he would mind taking up 'a characteristic pose'. He replied, 'What is a characteristic pose for a conductor?'.

' "Well, with your baton well in the air", the cameraman said. Whereupon Beecham said, "I make no characteristic poses for anybody, other than for the musicians". Then he paused, and said, "and in fact you now have thirty seconds to take your shots and leave the studio". He then apologised to the orchestra and the rehearsal got under way, but he seemed to have no respect for anyone but the orchestral players.'

Indeed, Beecham was already famous for being polite only to musicians; on his ABC tour, it sometimes seemed as if he were behaving as badly as he could. Of the many headlines he made throughout his four-month visit, one resulted from his telling a Sydney reporter that the Harbour Bridge was far too big and should be removed. In another celebrated incident that Neville Amadio recalls, 'he was having drinks with some of the SSO principals in his hotel, when he suddenly remembered that he was supposed to be meeting the State premier. So he apologised to us and we left. But the headlines that followed—"Beecham Keeps Premier Waiting" and so on'.

Tact was not his strong point. He was quoted as saying that the 'applause your audiences have given me has incomparably been the smallest in my experience', which was mild compared to the following broadside: 'There is a much larger percentage of illiterate, unpleasant and even vicious people here than in any other civilised country known to me. To tell me that the majority of your population is intelligent, tolerant and well-behaved in the sense we understand it in Europe is sheer nonsense'. This was not perhaps the most appropriate thing to say during a European war, nor was it the flattery we expected from distinguished visitors. The Sydney *Truth* responded with extraordinary viciousness:

We just don't get above the primordial slime in artistic expression, do we, Sir Thomas? . . . Clad in their villainous, verminous wild animal skins, simple Australians living 12 000 miles from the kernel of all European art can hardly be blamed for their ignorance of music.

We were brought up on the song of the surf, Sir Thomas, not on the crochets and quavers of temperamental virtuosi. And we love our open-air life and derive deep and ape-like peace from the lullabies of gum-leaf bands. We know this to be wrong, measured by your lofty conceptions of musical appreciation, but have pity on our immaturity.

None of this kept audiences away. Beecham's Sydney concerts were all full to overflowing but the success of his concerts did not modify his attitude to Australia (In a letter Beecham wrote to James from New York in early 1941, the conductor launched into a great tirade about our cultural backwardness and explained that Australia would need to do a lot of growing up before he would be prepared to make a return trip. 'At the moment the Australian people is ready only for flatterers and sycophants, and not for innovators and reformers; and until it evinces an honest disposition to learn, no real change is possible.'[4]).

Beecham insisted on the orchestra doing a proper warm-up before he rehearsed them, and many players got to the studio twenty minutes early. On the other hand, he was the only conductor up to that time who would let a rehearsal finish early. 'It was unheard of', Bertha Jorgensen says, 'but we realised later that he was deliberately under-rehearsing. He would rarely tell you what he wanted you to do, or talk about phrasing or anything. But on the night of the concert it was just magic—his greatness was electric. He knew that he had the power to play on an orchestra like a great soloist.

'Joseph Post [then the MSO's resident conductor] had been working with us for about a week to prepare for Beecham's concerts, and then found that many of the problems he'd had with us over phrasing and ensemble just disappeared under Beecham. He was absolutely amazed, and said "it's bloody hypnotism!". I don't know

---

[4] In terms of change, I hope someone pointed out to Beecham that if he had come to Australia ten years beforehand, he would have had no orchestras to conduct.

what it is Beecham had, but hypnotism might not be too far off the mark.'

Beecham's Sydney programs were ambitious and eccentric, but they were structured with great integrity and a feeling for complementarity and contrast. Here are two of them, the second featuring choir and soloists:

Symphony No 3 ....Boccherini
Facade, Suite No 1 ....Walton
Haffner Symphony..............................Mozart

Interval

Parsifal—Good Friday Music...................Wagner
The Golden Spinning Wheel ....Dvořák

Orchestral Suite—*The Faithful Shepherd*.....HandelBeecham
The Seasons—Part 1 (*Spring*) ....Haydn

Interval

Appalachia....................................Delius
Introduction and Cortege
(*The Golden Cockerel*) ....Rimsky-Korsakov

Beecham's description of playing standards in Sydney and Melbourne probably gives those of us too young to have heard the SSO in its early years the most vivid idea of the sound the orchestra would have made:

In the Sydney and Melbourne orchestras there are the most surprising inequalities of achievement among the players. Sitting cheek by jowl and occupying equal positions of consequence are players who, on the one hand, can take their places in the finest orchestras of the world, and others who would not find admittance to those of the third and fourth rank. To an audience which has not had the opportunity of hearing anything else, this disconcerting discrepancy of performance will not appear singular; but to the European or American ear, it would be both glaringly and uncomfortably manifest. Until a higher uniformity of execution be acquired, no one can maintain that there is a single orchestra in Australia which could hold its own in competition with the orchestras of other musical countries.

Beecham suggested that a national orchestra be formed for touring purposes only, playing in cities and major towns for a fixed time each year to show, by example, what Australia could achieve orchestrally. Of course, this idea had long died as far as ABC management was concerned, even as an experiment. The worst result of forming the so-called National Symphony for Sargent's 1938 concerts had been the need to divert the press' calls for its permanency. There was no way Cleary, James and Moses were going to open this argument again, particularly in war-time conditions. As Roger Covell has written, the touring seasons for such an orchestra in each centre could only have been brief, giving no chance to nurture the loyalties of each local audience. And it is worth noting that, after the mid-1930s, there were no local musicians urging for a national orchestra. It was our Celebrity Artists who kept pushing it.

Lost amid the bad temper that Beecham's visit engendered, there was one local response to the Great Man in which we can still take pleasure. Beecham had been quoted in the *Telegraph* as saying that people should always wear evening dress to concerts. The *Sunday Sun*'s music critic, Howard Ashton, responded as follows:

The weakness of this argument is that about 99.99 per cent of Australians do not dress for dinner. It is better to say that a good concert deserves something in ceremonial approach—a good dinner, by the way, is also in that category. I have tried music in evening dress and without, and can frankly say that it does not make a bit of difference, either in heightening my appreciation of good music or lessening my anguish and boredom at bad.

In the meantime, Heinze had returned from Europe and the United States early in 1939, and had been as busy as ever. One of his first war-time concerts with the MSO featured Marjorie Lawrence, who wanted the final scene from R. Strauss' *Salome* included in the program. But only days after the war began the press had asked 'Shall Bach be Banned?'. The ABC had received letters from listeners asking that German music no longer be played on air or in concert. But it was quickly decided that the only music to be outlawed was that for which a living German composer would receive royalties, so *Salome* had to go.

There was a problem with recitals, too. Soprano Dorothy

Helmrich told ABC Radio in 1982 that she was made to sing German lieder in English right through the war, although she was fortunate to be able to use singing translations by Sir Robert Garran, a constitutional lawyer and former Commonwealth Solicitor-General who later had published a book of lieder translations that was an international success.[5] The book included translations made especially for Helmrich.

The relationship between Heinze and the ABC changed in 1940 when James and Cleary decided to abolish the position of Music Adviser and establish in its place a Music Advisory Committee. Now that a Concert Department had been set up to take over the organisational aspects of concert-giving from James' Music Department, Cleary felt that the growing pains had been eased, 'and the Commission feels that it should now lift from its staff the shadow of the implication that it is still in swaddling clothes'. Heinze chaired the first committee, the members of which included James, NSW Conservatorium Director Dr Edgar Bainton, and Dr Keith Barry who, as the ABC's Controller of Programs, supervised the orchestras' on-air existence. The committee's main role was to make music policy recommendations to the Commission, but as the Music and Concert departments' bureaucracy became stronger post-war, the committee's importance slowly shrank, and it met infrequently. However, it survived as far as 1984. Heinze was a member until his death.

In early 1941 it became apparent that the visiting artists James had hoped to bring for the forthcoming season were not going to make the trip. Leslie Heward, the violinist Joseph Szigeti and the British duo-pianists Bartlett and Robinson all cancelled. Cleary took a typically positive view of the problem. 'In some ways it is good that we are faced with these difficulties', he told the press, 'for they will lead to greater opportunities for our own musicians'.

Heinze was immediately 'called up', not as a soldier, but as the ABC's permanent conductor. Melbourne University gave him a year's leave of absence 'as a wartime measure', to take up the post. But he was away for more than a year: he was to become the major musical personality of the war years, at least until Ormandy arrived, travelling all over the country between 1941

[5] *Schubert and Schumann: Songs and Translations* (1946).

and 1945. His workload was enormous: in less than eight months he conducted twenty-eight children's concerts and twenty choral and orchestral concerts. All the other resident conductors—Code, E.J. Roberts, Dr Bainton et al—were given less to do, which was a tribute more to Heinze's skills as politician than his abilities as conductor.

Given that the war years were those in which Heinze's national fame soared, it is worth examining his conducting credentials in some detail. I knew before I began writing this book that Heinze was never as well respected in Sydney as in Melbourne, but hardly any of the musicians I have subsequently spoken to admired him for his conducting. Someone associated with him for most of his career in Melbourne said: 'I respected him as a person enormously. I really can't say anything about him'. Another long-time Sydney colleague was more forthright:

'He was a tremendous organiser, an energetic man with lots of good ideas, but he was not a good conductor. He had a habit of rubbing players up the wrong way all the time, because he never admitted he was wrong. He would often stop after a mistake at rehearsal, look at a player, and say 'my boy, what did you do?!'. And he had no sense of humour about himself at all. I remember a schools concert when a paper aeroplane hit him on the back of his head while he was conducting. He just put his baton down and walked off the stage.

'And although he wasn't a very interesting musician to work with, he gave the best schools concerts, there's no doubt about that. You have to remember he was a very insecure man, always jealous of other Australian conductors who were better than him. But children were completely non-threatening and he just knew how to talk to them.'

Charles Buttrose, who became Director of Publicity and Concerts in 1958, agrees that Heinze was never keen to promote the virtues of other conductors. 'We used to have a saying when I was young that Melbourne barmaids always ate their young. I think it's true for Australian conductors, too, in a way. I might tell Bernard that I'd seen a wonderful SSO concert with Joe Post the other evening, and that he'd conducted so well, the orchestra responded magnificently and so on, and he would say very distantly, "yes, Joseph's a promising lad". Well, the promising lad was nearly fifty!'

The SSO's principal viola for many years, Ron Cragg, remembers Heinze being temperamental: 'We used to have hellish days with him. He would lose his temper, march out, call players into his office and dress them down. Yet later in the same day he could turn around and be so nice to you.'

'I couldn't say that I ever looked forward to playing under him', horn player Clarence Mellor says. 'I would always wonder what was going to happen next. You could not meet a better bloke off the rostrum, but he carpeted me a few times because he thought I was laughing at him. I must admit I couldn't follow his beat half the time. Yet he did so much for music in this country.'

'Every time he conducted the orchestra there was an incident of some sort', says long-time principal tuba Cliff Goodchild. 'He would get flustered or lose his place, or think a player was having a go at him.' It didn't help that the SSO often misbehaved in his presence—this was usually because he had been rude to them. The violinist Geza Bachmann would sometimes tremolando at the end of passages in rehearsal to annoy Heinze, whose ear was not good enough to pick out which player was the culprit. As SSO violinist Eva Kelly recalls: 'Heinze once thought he'd figured out who it was, and angrily sent off another of the first violins, Donald Blair'.

Kathleen Tuohy remarks of her Heinze experiences in Sydney and Melbourne: 'One had to be a tolerant sort of person to get the best out of him. He was not a good psychologist with orchestral musicians.'

The SSO's principal cellist between 1951 and 1959, Hans George, says Heinze was a curious man. 'A great organiser and a wonderful PR man, but difficult to deal with from a player's point of view. I remember a children's concert I did with the QSO in Toowoomba, where, after a rather lacklustre demonstration by the brass section Heinze said to the children, "I'm sure they can play it better than that!". The second time it was even worse.'

'I found that he was not nearly as difficult to deal with as people made out. He may not have been a great conductor, but he did an incalculable amount for music in this country, and of course always took an interest in new and unusual repertoire', Harold Hort recalls. 'I remember him saying to me once, "Dear boy, it does not matter what happens in between as long as we start and finish together". I liked him very much.'

One instance when the SSO and Heinze did not finish togther was a war-time performance of Mussorgsky's *Pictures at an Exhibition*, in which there was sufficient confusion in the finale for Heinze to stop the orchestra and begin the movement again. Cardus merely wrote that 'the Great Gate of Kiev apparently fell off its hinges'.

'I really enjoyed planning concerts with Heinze', says composer Nigel Butterley of his time in the ABC's Music Department in the 1960s. 'He regarded certain pieces as "his", and I remember his reaction when he heard that someone else was conducting my *Refractions*. He said "But, my dear, they cannot do that, it is *my* piece!".'

'He is a controversial figure', says John Matthews, SSO manager between 1970 and 1975. 'He could be an absolute pig to musicians— there's no two ways about it—but I have nothing but ninety per cent accolades for him. If it weren't for Heinze the history of music in this country would be completely different. Every orchestral player in this country should be grateful to him.'

He liked conducting contemporary scores, but sometimes found himself defeated by them. In 1946 he gave up on Walton's overture *Portsmouth Point*, saying it was too difficult for the SSO, but a short while later the young oboist Charles Mackerras gave it a complete run-through at his conducting audition. For Nadine Amadio, as for so many others, Heinze was a central figure of her youth.

'When I was studying at the Con he put on a Festival of Contemporary Music with the SSO that included Schoenberg's *Transfigured Night* and *Ode to Napoleon*. These works were beyond him, really, but he was so passionate about them. I know we used to call him "old soup pot" and "57 Varieties", his jowls would shake and we would make fun of him. But he had a sort of presence.'

His presence during the war years was tremendous, helped by his unfailing eye for spectacle, and an instinct for what would attract press attention. He had crowned his recent return from abroad with staged 'pageant' performances of Samuel Coleridge-Taylor's trilogy of Hiawatha cantatas in Melbourne's Royal

Exhibition Building. 45 000 people packed the hall during the fifteen-performance run. Now that he was (for the time being) the ABC's permanent conductor, he looked for ways to put the orchestras to work for the war effort and raise the profile of orchestral music-making while he was at it.

For example, his schools concerts (or Young People's Symphony Concerts, as they were called) went from strength to strength. In 1941, for one concert, the NSW Education Department received applications for 1500 places more than the Town Hall could hold. Extra performances were hastily arranged.

But Heinze's first war-time Sydney 'epic' was the Melba Memorial Concert of May 1941, which raised money for the Lord Mayor's Patriotic and War Fund of NSW. There had been a number of SSO fund-raising concerts given in 1940, but the Melba evening was a particularly galvanising event. First, no permanent memorial had ever been erected in Melba's honour; and, second, Melba was an active fund-raiser herself during the previous war (becoming a Dame as a result). The concert was the occasion for the unveiling of Arthur Murch's famous Melba plaque, which adorns the Northern wall of the Sydney Town Hall.[6] The SSO spent much of the night accompanying soloists, most notably (in the context of the war, at least) the pianist Una Bourne, who had been Melba's 'associate artist' in recitals in Britain.[7] A musician of some renown when she returned here in 1939, she stayed on to play as soloist under Ormandy and become the only woman on the ABC's national advisory committee.

The second major Heinze 'epic' was a showcase for music by Australian composers. The public profile of Australian composition had always been a major concern of Heinze's. He was one of the prime movers in the 1933 composers' competition and its 1935 successor. While these had been good public relations exercises for the ABC, they had not brought forth any works of lasting interest.

---

[6] The plaque was in place on the night of the concert, donated by the English baritone and Melba protege Lord Lurgan. It is positioned near the door through which Melba most frequently entered when she performed in the Town Hall.

[7] As an associate artist to Melba, Una Bourne would have been employed to play solo piano pieces between Melba's recital items. She was not Melba's accompanist.

Now, realising that patriotic feeling was running high, Heinze and James constructed two programs of Australian works for special (that is, non-subscription) concerts in October (Sydney) and November (Melbourne), 1941. The Sydney concert featured Clive Douglas' *Symphonic Fantasy*, Robert Hughes' *Estival—A Song of Summer*, Miriam Hyde's *Fantasy Romantic* for Piano and Orchestra, with the composer as soloist; Brewster Jones' *Symphonic Poem: Australia Felix*, Roy Agnew's *The Breaking of the Drought—A Poem for Orchestra and Voice*, with Dorothy Helmrich; Frank Hutchens' *Ballade for Orchestra* and Alfred Hill's *Maori Rhapsody*.

As the concert was not devised by the Music Advisory Committee, Dr Barry only had notice of it once it had been submitted for broadcast scheduling. He had some reservations:

It seems to me that if we are to do due honour to Australian composers we can do it better by including their works in the normal way in our programs rather than putting them all together for practically a whole evening's program. With these concerts we are putting up what might be regarded by some cynics as a warning sign—'Beware! These are Australian compositions!'

These turned out to be prophetic words. Tickets moved slowly, despite discounts for concert subscribers, and the critics were merciless in their derision of the works played. In the *Sydney Morning Herald*, Neville Cardus called the Sydney concert 'a deplorable mistake':

It gave the impression that no music has been heard in this country written later than 1904 . . . Oh, these symphonic and romantic fantasies! The very titles date the works bearing their names. Are these composers aware yet that a revolution occurred in music after the 1914-1918 war, and that another revolution in music is due? . . . I listened in vain all the evening for a single transition of key, a single turn of melody that was not mannered and embalmed thousands of miles away in the heyday of Edward VII.

The *Daily Telegraph* was no kinder, noting that 'even if there are no first-class composers in Australia, those who do work here should at least try to acquaint themselves with contemporary tendencies'. Both critics had faint praise for Roy Agnew's piece, and Miriam Hyde remembers that *The Breaking of the Drought* made a great impact on the audience. It was a most arresting work, in my opinion'.

The concert was a real act of bravery given that Australian music, unlike Australian painting, had found no audience. And the somewhat antiquated tone of the music would not have surprised the more tuned-in listeners present. Bernard Smith has written memorably about The Myth of Isolation in relation to painting, but musical composition in Australia has had a comparatively fitful history. While, by 1941, painting had begun to develop a strong Australian identity, there had been no musical equivalent of the Heidelberg painters to help start a school of Australian composition. Neither did the cultural climate encourage deviations from the well-defined musical norms. And one also has to ask whether the pool of talented composers was very big. As Lindsey Browne says: 'You never hear any music by Clive Douglas now, nor should you, I think'.

So it is no disgrace that none of the works in that 1941 concert is now familiar concert hall fare, but it is surprising that the Australian composers who became prominent after the war and who quietly pushed the musical boundaries forward from 'the heyday of Edward VII'—particularly Margaret Sutherland, Dorien Le Gallienne and Raymond Hanson—have fallen so completely into neglect. The history of Australian music does *not* include a giant lacuna between Grainger and Sculthorpe.

This concert of Australian music caught Sydney just before two momentous changes. Pearl Harbour was bombed in December, and in mid-1942 Singapore fell to the Japanese. The latter of these events had two immediate results: the war came closer to home, and the long and often stultifying ties of Empire slowly weakened as the influence of the United States became stronger. To the ABC's musical operations, the increasing nearness of the conflict brought much drama. Moses, First World War veteran and self-confessed war-horse, had already left for the army, joining as captain early in 1940. He would be Colonel Moses by the war's end, his ABC seat kept warm by T.W. Bearup, who had been ABC Manager for Victoria and who was a quietly competent general manager, very different to the flamboyant Moses. The SSO had lost one of its players before Pearl Harbour, too, but not to the armed forces. Neville Amadio remembers:

'We had an Italian double bass player called Ricci Bitti. He would never play the national anthem at the beginning of concerts with the rest of us. You know, he would stand but he just wouldn't play, because he was a committed Fascist. On the morning Italy announced that it was joining Germany's side in the war, four detectives marched in to the Arts Club building during rehearsal and just took him away. No "excuse me's", no nothing. He was interned straight away.'

Plans for a new ABC building in Forbes Street (on the Clapton Place corner where the old radio building stood until recently), designed to house all radio departments and the SSO, were well under way when war was declared, but the project was put on ice, never to be successfully revived. Then in late 1941 most New South Wales departments, including the SSO, moved to suburban Burwood. Many people living in harbour suburbs were selling up in fear of Japanese attack to move further inland, and the Burwood move was also a form of evacuation. The NSW Education Department gave the ABC free use of an old, fairly run down, Arts Club building on the corner of Condor and Hornsley streets which had most recently been occupied by camouflage net makers. It cost a few thousand pounds to renovate and extend the site, but it was rent-free for the rest of the war.

By mid-1942 many SSO players were on war service—Neville Amadio, Robert Miller, Alan Mann, violinist George White (who was to become leader at the war's end), Osric Fyfe, and trombonist Frank Locke among them. A lot of the positions these men occupied would be taken by women. In 1942 Linda Vogt became the first woman to join the SSO wind section.

'I'm from Melbourne originally, and played as a casual in the MSO. Heinze picked me out to be the second flute in the SSO, since Bert Anderson, the regular second flute, was taking Neville's place. So I joined the SSO when I was nineteen years old. I came to Sydney on the train, was met at Central at about 9 a.m., and was rehearsing at Burwood later the same morning. I lived in a boarding house in Wollstonecraft, and used to go in to the Town Hall by train. There were fewer cars about then, and I would see lots of passengers in evening dress going to concerts.'

1942 brought changes to the Town Hall concerts, too. Saturday evening performances were shifted to quarter past two on Saturday

A publicity shot of the newly enlarged SSO taken in Burwood Park near the rehearsal studio they were about to vacate for Kings Cross. George White is the concertmaster.

afternoons because of blackout restrictions, and the City Council moved its two big chandeliers from the auditorium to protect them in the event of enemy attack. Strangely, although one like them hangs in the building's vestibule, the two chandeliers that were removed then have never been put back.

For the players remaining in the orchestra, the war cut off supplies of many instruments, and it was even hard to buy strings. But the SSO soon found that the privations of war brought some pleasant surprises, as well. It seemed, for example, that the army wanted orchestral concerts in its camps. An army survey taken in the Eastern and Northern commands in mid-1941 showed that fifty per cent of the troops expressed an enthusiasm for orchestral music, and that thirty-seven per cent declared a moderate interest. It no doubt heartened Bearup that one-third of the soldiers said they owed their interest in music to the radio.

The SSO's first army concert was conducted by Percy Code, and given at Ingleburn camp on 11 February 1942. It was 'an unqualified success', James told Bearup. 'I admit to some fear and trembling as I arrived, seeing a crowd of 1000 to 1200 soldiers with ice creams and bottles of lemonade—and not very quiet preceding the concert.' Expecting the worst, James had sent Lindley Evans to the camp on the previous evening to give a preparatory talk about the music, and just before the concert itself Evans gave a quick summary of the instruments of the orchestra, 'in his usual breezy style'. Anyone who remembers Evans as Mr Melody Man of 'The Argonauts' knows how friendly a personality he was.

The enthusiastic responses of the enlisted men on this February evening surprised and delighted James, and he noted that 'this great Hall, on a hot night, with its doors open, gave the Troops an opportunity to enter and leave as they pleased, and I should say that not a dozen went out before the end of the Concert'.

Further successful army concerts followed, but there were mistakes. In September 1942 the MSO found itself playing to a troop concert for which attendance was compulsory. Not a good move, as the *Telegraph* reported:

Many of the men wanted to go to an annual ball, but all leave was cancelled and they were marched to the concert. After they were seated on the unpadded wooden seats, they were ordered to put out their cigarettes. They answered with 'boos' and shouted: 'This is the freedom we're fighting for'.

The crowd settled down for the second half of the concert, but as Dr Barry remarked, 'This scheme can only be successful if it is conducted on a basis of purely voluntary attendances'.

1942 also saw the SSO give its first concert in Canberra, in which the young Norah Williamson (a member of the orchestral violins through the Goossens era) was the soloist in Lalo's *Symphonie espagnole*. All the time, around the country, audiences for orchestral concerts were growing. This was partly because Heinze and James kept the programs conservative (although there was the occasional novelty, such as Stravinsky's violin concerto, with French-born Jeanne Gautier the soloist); partly because war-time restrictions meant that ABC concerts were one of the few events of city leisure-life that went on regardless; partly because many of the American servicemen on leave here took an interest in music; and partly because music itself came to be more important to the general community.

This last was due to a number of factors other than the war. One, as Ken Inglis has noted, was the impact of Walt Disney's *Fantasia* (1940), which so vividly married music and images that it remains one of the most communicative experiences of music to young people; and the other was Neville Cardus' ABC program, 'The Enjoyment of Music', which was a showcase for recordings of major works from the chamber, orchestral and operatic repertoires. As Roger Covell has written:

Any musically inclined person who grew up in Australia during those years will recall Cardus' Sunday night broadcasts with affection: the mellow, breathy, ruminating voice, with its unpredictable portamento glides from one word to another; the air of happy confidence and serenity in his judgement; above all, his ability to communicate the excitement of a change of key or a contrast of tone colour . . . Cardus may truly claim to have had a greater influence on the course of musical taste than any other single broadcaster elsewhere.

But he did not do it alone. The ABC's Education Department had broadcast an 'Adventures in Music' series in 1939, and the program-makers in Talks often featured music-based discussions,

The SSO's first army concert, given in February 1942 during World War II, at Ingleburn camp.

such as 'Australian Composers Speak' (1945). Parts of the 'Women's Session' were regularly devoted to music, too. In all, musical programs accounted for around sixty per cent of ABC air time in the early 1940s.

Nothing illustrates Australia's need for music in these years better than Heinze's Beethoven festivals. They eventually took in Sydney, Melbourne and Adelaide, but it was not planned that way. No one was prepared for the phenomenal appeal of the first festival, in Sydney, and indeed it is unlikely that it would have had such success before the war. There were seven Sydney concerts, with virtually one a week between early February and mid-March 1943. The first few were given in what is now Verbrugghen Hall at the NSW Conservatorium of Music, but all seven concerts sold out on the first morning the box office opened, with the police being called in to control the crowd. Thus the later concerts shifted to the Town Hall to cope with audience numbers, for the ABC had at one stage been obliged to erect a loudspeaker system on the lawns of the Conservatorium to handle the overflow.

The performance of the Ninth symphony was an enormous success. There was high excitement in the hall and a swag of happy correspondence afterwards to the daily papers. Cardus noted in his review that as a reading of the score it had certain uniquely Australian qualities:

In fairness to those present who do not know the music thoroughly, the fact must be stated that this was a Ninth Symphony now and again short of its metaphysic, its mystery, its reflectiveness. In a word, it was a Ninth Symphony transplanted to a country that is mainly objective and given to living externally.

Incidentally, Cardus rarely found Heinze's conducting inspiring. Charles Buttrose remembers him walking out of a concert in which Heinze was conducting a Tchaikovsky symphony. Cardus' review of the performance read, in part: 'I left after the first movement; not even I am expected to eat the whole of a bad egg'.

The success of Sydney's Beethoven season led to similar sell-out festivals in Melbourne and Adelaide in 1944. In Adelaide, the relatively small 1000-seat capacity of the Town Hall meant that Heinze conducted fourteen Beethoven concerts there instead of seven, all to capacity houses. In the more competitive post-war atmosphere of Australian music-making, Heinze would find the ABC touring a greater number of international conductors, many of whom had about them a glamorous halo Heinze could not duplicate. He would never again regain the immense adulation he received in these strange, battle-weary years. He was never again to be Australia's starry messenger of music. This was his finest hour.

Another feather in the cap of Heinze's Great Moment was the first Australian performance of Shostakovich's seventh symphony, the *Leningrad* (1941), at an SSO Red Cross benefit concert in August 1943. The work was surrounded with intrigue and excitement—how the score had been smuggled out of the Soviet Union on microfilm, how Shostakovich had been a fire-fighter during the siege of Leningrad. These things captured the extra-musical imagination of all the allied countries, and the *Leningrad* became quintessential propaganda almost immediately the score was printed. Toscanini and Stokowski had a celebrated brawl about who would give the first performance in the United States. This dragged on for so long that the work was not given there until mid-1944 (Toscanini won). In Australia, the *Leningrad* became to the second half of the war what Weinberger's variations had been to the first. For the fall of Singapore changed everything, making the British seem almost villainous as it boosted the worth of the other allies. In fact it was in 1942 and 1943 that we began—albeit unconsciously—to turn to the United States for guidance about our identity. We were slowly swapping empires.

The presence of the United States armed forces, occasioned by the Pacific war, brought massive changes in thinking about our way of life. To start with, American servicemen were, on the whole, better dressed, better fed, more widely read, more articulate and more gentlemanly than their Australian counterparts. This beguiled our women. Second, our men were beguiled by technology Australia had never encountered before, such as super-efficient agricultural machines developed here with the help of US Army food production technicians. The Americans were good for our industries, too. With so many more soldiers to feed, our canning activity expanded rapidly. One Australian company grew 1600 kilometres of asparagus for canning in 1943-

44. We began to buy Coca-Cola. Major Maynard A. Joslyn was brought here from California to start our dried vegetable industry.

Musically, the orchestral invasion began with the American composer-conductor Leith Stevens, who conducted the SSO in a concert called 'American Rhapsody' in August 1943 (music mostly by Gershwin and Ferde Grofe). But 1944 brought the Maynard A. Joslyn of music; the first *real* Celebrity Artist to touch Australian soil since 1940. As Charles Buttrose recalls: 'When Klemperer first came here in 1949 he joked about Ormandy as the Lend Lease conductor, and Charles Moses said: "Well, he might have been that, but he got a bigger fee than Beecham, and Beecham was paid the highest of any conductor's fee up to 1940".'

But Eugene Ormandy was allowed to be more than a terrific conductor who came and went. Although he is no longer thought of as such, we will see that he was made to play the role of the first advocate for the establishment of the Australian symphony orchestras as permanent concert-giving bodies.

Ormandy's Sydney concerts were received with wonder and amazement. Apart from Shostakovich 5 (a first Australian performance), he concentrated on the standard repertoire— Beethoven 5 and 9, the *'Enigma'* Variations, Brahms 2—which gave his audiences an immediate grasp of the improvements he achieved in playing standards over those of the last three years. Cardus was one of many critics who expressed amazement at the playing of the SSO under his direction: 'the customary black-and-whites were changed to vibrant colour and homogenous texture', he wrote. He found the SSO performance of Haydn's Symphony No. 102 under Ormandy so refined that it might have been played 'by an orchestra of the most finished chamber style, imported during the last few days from Europe (via Philadelphia)'. On a less eloquent note, the *Sunday Telegraph's* Roland Pullen remarked that 'for once we were able not to fidget when a difficult passage was approaching, but to sit back and enjoy ourselves'.

The only performance which was kept for posterity from the Ormandy tour was the Beethoven 9, and it reveals itself to be intensely 'finished' and shaded. Ormandy demanded and secured a wide range of dynamic colour, and Cardus' remark about 'the customary black-and-whites' clearly refers to the sudden expansion of the Sydney orchestra's capabilities. Unfortunately, previous conductors' comments about the quality of the oboe playing bear themselves out painfully in much of this performance, but the overall corporate standards are remarkably high.

Ormandy should only take ninety per cent of the credit, however, for he was on a deluxe ride indeed. His contract insisted on there being 100 musicians in every orchestra he conducted in Australia. And of course he wanted the finest players. This meant that he took a select group of the best principals with him to each orchestra he conducted, be it in Sydney, Melbourne or Brisbane. Appropriately, there was an air of the self- consciously messianic about him.

'He was meticulous about everything', the ABC's Victorian manager of the day, Douglas MacLean, recalled in 1982. 'He once delayed the start of a rehearsal to make sure there were 100 musicians on stage. He found there were ninety-nine, and wouldn't continue! I think the ABC had to bring a viola player down from Sydney who could barely hold her instrument, just to make up the numbers.'

Among Ormandy's band of strolling players were John Robertson, Neville Amadio and Haydn Beck, who travelled as his concertmaster. Although barely a name today, Beck was undoubtedly one of Australia's finest violinists. Born in New Zealand, he had been in Verbrugghen's orchestra, subsequently played in trios in Farmers department store and—a piece of corporate crossover unthinkable today—in ensembles for 2FC when it was owned by Farmer and Co. He 'guest'-led the SSO from time to time in the 1930s, also appearing occasionally as soloist, and was leader of the *Ballets Russes* orchestra under Dorati in 1939. When that season finished, he toured with Colonel de Basil's company to New Zealand.

His success with Ormandy resulted in a row with the ABC about his salary, which they refused to increase when he felt that Ormandy had made him worth more money. He went on to teach at the Conservatorium and lead the orchestra on 2GB's 'Music Hath Charms' program. He also ran a Marrickville-based group called the Civic Symphony Orchestra which made some records in 1952. Beck left Australia to play in London's Philharmonia orchestra for two seasons (1953-54), then went to live in Portugal,

Eugene Ormandy (right) with the concertmaster for his Australian tour, Haydn Beck.

playing viola in the opera orchestra there until he died in 1983. Bertha Jorgensen remembers him well: 'He was a very fine fiddler, but a bit of a tough character. When the ABC refused to give him more money, he threatened to resign. Of course they accepted his resignation': A portrait of him hangs in the Wanganui art gallery.

Bertha Jorgensen was Beck's deputy leader for Ormandy's Melbourne concerts, and her memories of the conductor remain vivid. 'There was a lot of tension under him. He had the back desks in tears sometimes because he was so unforgiving. He would fix them with his cold stare and say: "Why are you playing in that position?". Two fiddlers from the ABC's Melbourne dance band came in as extras for his concerts but he chewed them up in two days, and they were gone after that. But his sadistic streak— and I think he was a bit sadistic—was part of the electric effect he had on the orchestra. We finished one concert with a Strauss waltz, and one of the people in the audience told me that during the performance the whole orchestra swayed like snakes in three-four time!

'But, you know, he could lay it on a bit. He told me that I was the best concert mistress he'd ever had, and his wife said "You've never had one before!". He also—very cruelly I think— told three or four of the key players that they were so wonderful they had to come to America and join the Philadelphia Orchestra.'

Many people who were in their teens and twenties during the Ormandy tour still speak of his concerts as some of their first great musical experiences (there were seven Sydney concerts in all). Pianist Rachel Valler, the critic Fred Blanks and the late composer and administrator Werner Baer remember them as being intensely exciting. But Ormandy attracted widespread popular attention, too, with major profiles appearing in newspapers and women's magazines. He was even the subject of an argument between the Potts in Jim Russell's comic strip!

To bombardier Neville Amadio, Ormandy was more than a great name. William James wrote to Amadio suggesting he apply for leave to play in the Ormandy tour. His leave application was refused, but Amadio's commanding officer told him to go absent without leave to play the concerts. The officer told him that 'if I got picked up he would come and get me'. Amadio played all his concerts in uniform, and the army left him alone. But for those orchestral servicemen unable to make the Ormandy concerts, they were a sad omission. 'That I didn't work with him is something I'll always regret', Robert Miller says.

The important long-term effects of Ormandy's visit began when he followed Harty, Sargent, Szell, Dorati and Beecham in writing a report on the standards of orchestral playing in Australia. Those earlier reports, as we've seen, were written at the ABC's invitation, and recommendations in them were either acted upon, put on hold indefinitely—for quite practical reasons, like union difficulties or money—or ignored because they conflicted with policy.

Unlike those reports, though, Ormandy's was addressed not to Moses or James but to the Minister for the Army and Deputy Prime Minister in the Curtin government, Frank Forde. This in itself might not have made an earth-shattering difference to the report's effect, but Forde released it to the press within a month of receiving it, thus giving it threefold currency: as a document the Government was happy to have in circulation (this could hardly have been said about Beecham's report, for example); as a number of issues worth public discussion; and, tacitly, as possibilities the ABC needed to pursue.

Ormandy's was to be the last report written by a visiting conductor, and it was to be the most far-thinking of them all.

For example, he recommended the building of 'an appropriate hall in each city for symphony concerts, drama, opera and ballet'. In these halls, 'the development of television should also be considered in the design. Proper heating and air- conditioning should be installed, not only for the comfort of audiences and players, but as a necessary condition in maintaining proper intonation in orchestral performance.' We would soon contemplate seriously the building of such venues.

The crux of the report was Ormandy's advocacy for the foundation of permanent symphony orchestras in each State: 85-member bodies in Sydney and Melbourne first, and the other capitals following, on the understanding that certain key players would be imported from overseas. Importantly, though, the report's first sentence addresses Forde as follows:

Ever since I had the pleasure of meeting you, at which time you requested that I send you my recommendations for the establishment of permanent symphony orchestras in every capital city in Australia . . .

In other words, Ormandy had been asked to prepare a much braver document that any of his visiting predecessors. It was a great tactical move: the Americans wanted our 'hearts and minds', we wanted a musical saviour who was glamorous and foreign, and the Australian government wanted to show us that we had more to learn from the Americans than we thought.

Among Ormandy's other major conclusions were that players who had been arriving in Australia from Europe since the late 1930s should be encouraged to audition for the orchestras. Neither the ABC nor the Musicians' Union had so far done much encouraging. Most importantly, Ormandy recognised (no doubt with James' advice) that 'the present economic provision for music in Australia has extended the Commission's resources to their limit. I am convinced that the ABC should be joined in the financial support and control of [the State orchestras] . . . by State and Municipal Governments'. It is something of a mystery that the issue of separate, supplementary, civic funding had not become an issue before this.

The report's success was virtually assured, for, as in his press interviews, Ormandy was a great salesman for our possibilities. 'I am convinced that this great country is on the threshold of musical and artistic developments which few Australians dare even visualise', he wrote. 'The desire for growth is evident in the enthusiastic responses your audiences accord great music.' And on returning to Philadelphia, he lost no time in telling the American press about Australia's potential.

Moses served in the army for three years before Curtin asked him to come back to his old job. He hit the desk in March 1943, and was well on top of things by the time Ormandy wrote his report in July of the following year. In fact by then Moses had already instigated a major front-office re-shuffle and, to accommodate special new forces programs, a re-shaping of the radio schedule. He made sure that the ABC's response to the Ormandy report was swift and decisive. This time there was no dithering.

By late August 1944, Moses had received detailed briefings on the Ormandy report by James and Barry. Both men were positive about its conclusions—James, after all, had been a major architect of the orchestras' expansion to date—but saw a number of problems, namely:

1. Even if all the players then on war service returned to the orchestras immediately, and all available 'extras' were employed full-time, there would still be big gaps. The SSO, for example, would have been 18 players short of Ormandy's suggested 85-member band. And there would have to be tough negotiations with the Musicians' Union: principal players of the oboe, horn, bassoon and double bass would have to be imported from abroad.

2. Because of the size of the 'gaps', the likelihood of full-size, full-time orchestras being established outside Sydney and Melbourne was remote. This 'gap' problem was aggravated by the fact that the orchestras in cities outside Sydney and Melbourne were then relatively small; the cost difference between maintaining them and maintaining the nominal 85-strength orchestras in their place was thought to be too great.

3. If Sydney and Melbourne did get full-time orchestras, they would each need 'a full-time conductor of standing' (Moses' description). James bravely wrote: 'This does not mean that we have not in Australia conducting talent which, with the necessary guidance and experience, could eventually take its place in charge of such orchestras'. As well as a chief conductor, James called for permanent assistant conductors to take studio performances.

For Sydney, the issues fell into place almost immediately, when Moses attended a meeting organised by the Minister for Education, R.J. Heffron, on 5 October. There, Heffron spoke of the forthcoming retirement of Edgar Bainton as director of the State Conservatorium, and A.W. Hicks, of the Public Service Board, suggested that the next director of the Conservatorium could also be the new SSO's first chief conductor.

Later in the meeting Roy Hendy, the Town Clerk, said he intended to recommend that the City Council provide a £10 000 pound annual subsidy for the proposed 'new' orchestra, in return for a guaranteed number of free concerts each year; and Heffron spoke also of the State government providing a 'substantial' annual subsidy. Moses had to do some tap-dancing here, for there was as yet no notional operating budget for the large 'new' orchestra. He said simply that the ABC had no more money to spend on full-time augmentation. Soon, though, he and Keith Barry got to work figuring how many free concerts the SSO could afford to give. This wound up being twenty-six for schools (Sydney and regional areas) and twelve for the general public (Sydney only). Everyone agreed that the ABC should retain full control of the orchestra, but that an advisory board, representing the interests of all three funding bodies, should be formed to meet regularly.

In November, Moses and Bearup (who was now assistant general manager) began negotiations with the Musicians' Union over an increase in the SSO musicians' working week from twenty-one hours to thirty-three. At the same time, Heinze, James and Code were trying to determine how the SSO could be reconstructed and expanded. They decided the magic number of eighty-five players could be whittled down to eighty-two, as most of the then-standard repertory could be played at that strength. They also decided that a permanent symphony orchestra of that size needed a dedicated orchestra manager—someone to set out players' rosters, engage extras, arrange country tours and so on. Such a position had not existed to date.

While the war in Europe might have been over, the Pacific war was not, and many key musicians were still soldiering. Heinze, James and Code recommended that, at the war's end, places in the new orchestra should be widely advertised, and that a number of players should re-audition for their positions. They mentioned the woodwinds particularly:

So long as this section is hampered with such weak and faulty double-reed players, there is little hope of improving the general standard of the orchestra. The biting criticism that has been levelled so frequently at the wind section has been, unfortunately, only too well earned.

Inherent in this re-audition process were terrible problems of player morale, and ABC management did not quite avoid them all. But, as Moses put it, 'we are not interested in merely getting 82 players. We want 82 players who are not merely capable, but good players'.

The union was not ready to talk Moses' language for a few months yet. In late 1944, the union's secretary side-stepped the 'quality' issue by telling the *Daily Telegraph* that 'if the ABC offered year-round employment for full orchestras in each State there would soon be a supply of players to meet the demand'.

By January 1945, the ABC's Concert Department had worked out what the real running cost of the new orchestra. This turned out to be £60 000, as opposed to the £30 000 the 'old' orchestra had cost in 1944. The £60 000 included chief conductor (£3000); assistant conductor; orchestra manager; librarian; leader (concertmaster); and music hire. If the ABC put up £30 000 pounds toward the running of the new orchestra, and the City Council £10 000, this left the State government to find the other £20 000.

As far as the State was concerned, it wanted fairly specific benefits for its investment, including more country touring; orchestral availability for performances of opera and ballet, if and when there were any; the availability of the best players to teach at the Conservatorium; and higher playing standards, *ergo* greater civic pride in the orchestra.

In May 1945 the whole scheme was put on hold as different aspects of it began to fall over. The ABC could not reach agreement with the Musicians' Union about the length of the working week, rates of overtime payment or the importation of the crucial four players; the recently increased licence fee of one pound—vital to the ABC's ability to contribute the £30 000 to the SSO it had promised—was not yet guaranteed to be maintained; and Cleary had resigned in February.

Moses' departure for the army in 1940 had temporarily stalled a growing rift between the two men, which grew to real animosity once Moses resumed the general managership. To put it bluntly, Cleary and Moses had grown jealous of one another, Cleary eventually accusing Moses of disloyalty. On his departure the chairmanship was offered to Commissioner Richard Boyer, who was in London at the time at a British Commonwealth Relations Conference. His absence stalled any consultations with the Commission about the SSO for the time being. Although Boyer was supportive of the plans for orchestral expansion, from now on Moses would handle most orchestral negotiations himself.

Cleary's particular energy and cultural ambitions would not be duplicated in any of the ABC's future chairmen.

In September Moses and the union finally reached agreement for a thirty-hour week with a basic weekly rank-and-file salary of £11.5s (players were then earning £7 12s for a twenty-one-hour week). The ABC was also allowed to import its four players for two years only, after which time these players' positions would be reviewed in case any likely Australian talent could take their place. The union's rule on this issue remains the same today.

With the State government subsidy now guaranteed, the orchestra's working week was initially divided up (December 1945) as follows:

1. Symphony Orchestra of 72-82 players . . . . 15 hours
2. Studio Orchestra of approx. 45 players . . . . 15 hours
3. String Ensemble of remaining string players . . . . 15 hours

The war years had seen a dramatic reduction in the amount of time the orchestras had available for studio work, as the ABC relied more closely on non-salaried 'extra' players to fill orchestral positions, and because the good permanent players not in the armed services were too busy, some of them travelling interstate regularly to 'plug holes' in other orchestras. And several freelance ensembles had been engaged to fill program slots—among them those of Montague Brearley, Isador Goodman, Fred Hartley and saxophonist Clive Amadio, brother of Neville. It is doubtful whether the fifteen-hour divisions were ever fully adhered to.

The complexities of the new orchestra's setup are made clear in the following plain-speaking Moses note to Barry and James, written just before the auditions took place. He is explaining the workings of the interim establishment of the orchestra, to take effect from 15 January, 1946:

Some of the extra players should be engaged on a strictly temporary basis, ie: a definite indication that we cannot guarantee them a continuity of employment. This will give you an opportunity in the meantime to investigate fully the availability of other players of talent, and also to hold places in the orchestra for (a) players returning from defence leave; (b) four overseas players whom it is hoped to engage . . .

The auditions were a week long and the new SSO, the first orchestra that resembled the SSO we know today, came into being on 21 January. Some of the 'old' orchestra's original players were made to leave, resulting in such new faces as the freshly-appointed first oboe, Charles Mackerras. Some of these 'superseded' players were sent interstate to the smaller ABC orchestras, while Moses encouraged his State managers to invite their musicians to apply for the better-paid SSO jobs.

In early February, the orchestra moved into refurbished studio premises at 50-52 Darlinghurst Road, Kings Cross (these are the studios, much altered, which later became the headquarters of the Australian Chamber Orchestra). James felt that the Burwood Studios were too far from the Town Hall to make for a fully productive thirty-hour week. The players were not sorry to leave Burwood, either, for the studios were neither comfortable nor designed for orchestral broadcasts and rehearsals.

'The studio attendant at Burwood was an ex-vaudeville comedian called 'Titch' Irvine', Neville Amadio recalls. 'He was a real character. Now, one of the early international soloists to come here for the ABC was the saxophonist Sigurd Rascher [1938]. Titch was setting up for a broadcast by Clive's ensemble, and had put the chairs in the wrong formation. Anyway, he and Clive had a heated argument about the arrangement of the chairs, which finished with Titch telling Clive: 'You may bring home the bacon, but you'll never be a Rascher.'

∗

'Australia now has its first full-time symphony orchestra', Moses told the commissioners. Well, historically, this was not true, and even the new SSO would spend some time in the studio playing in its smaller formations. But there is no doubt that, within the framework the ABC had devised, the SSO was now on earth mainly to play live concerts. Dorati's vision of a concert orchestra 'kept together for eight or nine months a year' was real indeed.

The new SSO and the acclaim that greeted its birth was one of a number of important cultural shifts that made the last days of the war special. As Geoffrey Serle has noted, 'a quickening, an alertness, a revival of utopian hope and a resurgence of national idealism were clearly discernible'. The New Theatre movement was born, as was Australian New Writing. Attendance at art galleries increased and the demand for books grew as the war progressed. At war's end, a National Film Board was talked about. And in 1944 James founded the ABC's Concerto and Vocal Competition, dedicated to the discovery of Australia's young instrumental talent. This annual event continues today as the Young Performers Awards.

But the next SSO problem Moses had to worry about was summarised for him by the *Sydney Morning Herald*, in brutally materialist terms, only a few weeks after the new orchestra was formed:

The SSO must have a first-class, permanent conductor with the least possible delay. Any continued neglect of such an appointment will prevent taxpayers and ratepayers from getting full musical value from the 20 000 pounds and 10 000 pounds that the Government and the council have experimentally paid out on their behalf.

CHAPTER FOUR

The Goossens era

'I *do not* want to listen to works I don't know!', an SSO subscriber yelled at music critic Curt Prerauer one concert evening during Goossens' reign as the orchestra's chief conductor. But the period in which Goossens had control of the orchestra was all about new experiences: there were more visiting conductors and soloists, more new and neglected works on concert programs, a new evening concert series designed for young people, and the altogether exhilarating sensation of having an outstanding international musician living here for most of the year to run the city's new full-strength symphony orchestra. It is no wonder that so many people still talk of the SSO under Goossens as one of the great partnerships in the history of Australian music.

In the best and broadest sense, Goossens helped Australian culture grow up, and in particular he helped create the notion of Sydney as a major world city. Luckily, he was here during a period of great social flux, in which his reformist zeal was more welcome than it would have been even ten years beforehand. In Australia, as in other Western countries in the post-war period, an impulse to broaden the range of cultural experiences took hold, and our blinkers were slowly coming off. Between 1946 and 1955 Australia saw tours by the Ballet Rambert, the Old Vic company (headliners Olivier and Vivian Leigh), the Stratford Memorial Theatre Company (Anthony Quayle) and the Boyd Neel String Orchestra. Musica Viva gave its first concerts; Sumner Locke-

Elliot's play *Rusty Bugles* was produced by Doris Fitton's company; Patrick White's novel *The Aunt's Story* was published; the Elizabethan Theatre Trust was established (and would be the wet-nurse to The Australian Opera and The Australian Ballet); and groups were formed with a view to establishing Australian operatic permanence: Clarice Lorenz's National Opera of Australia (Sydney) and Gertrude Johnson's National Theatre Company (Melbourne).

Goossens' strange and sinister departure for Europe in 1956 seemed to many commentators at the time to violate this spirit of cultural inquisitiveness. It remains one of the great Australian puzzles, and it is discussed in detail in the next chapter. The important thing to stress here is that while some people felt that, after all, Goossens had done what he could in Sydney and would not have enhanced his or the orchestra's reputation any further by staying, we can hardly say how he would have developed as an artist in the light of the changes that took place shortly after he left, or how he might have altered their course: the arrival of television, the beginnings of a national opera company, the building of the Sydney Opera House.

For people who saw and heard Goossens' work with the SSO, his personality seems to have coloured all kinds of experiences of Sydney at the time. And that was what he wanted. But in reality this post-war decade belonged to William James too. He had always been a terrific talent hunter, and he now exploited the new convenience of international air travel and the general European disorder to bring to Australia an incredible array of great performers: Otto Klemperer, Paul Kletzki, Rafael Kubelik, Solomon, Georges Thill, Claudio Arrau, Ginette Neveu, Witold Malcuzynski, Alfredo Campoli (under shared management), John Barbirolli, Walter Gieseking, Louis Kentner, William Kapell, Irmgard Seefried, Elisabeth Schwarzkopf, Wolfgang Schneiderhan, Hans Schmidt-Isserstedt, Suzanne Danco, Anton Dermota and Hans Hotter are only some of the artists who appeared for the ABC during the Goossens years. As James' successor Herbert Cannon recalled for ABC Radio:

'The great artists of the day were receiving less than their normal quota of engagements in a Europe still recovering from war, and indeed some performers were virtually displaced persons. For example, the reason Otto Klemperer toured here in both 1949 and 1950 is that he simply wanted somewhere to perform while his residency status was so uncertain.'

Another reason for the huge increase in the number of touring artists was the orchestras' rapidly increasing national audience. In Sydney, the subscription concerts that came to be called the Red Series were established in 1936. A second, repeat series of concerts was added to cope with the bigger war-time audiences in 1942. The influx of post-war migrants from Europe and the return home of servicemen and women helped boost audience numbers still further, and the year in which Goossens took up the chief conductor post, 1947, saw the introduction of a third series. By 1954 the SSO's main subscription concerts were being given five times each, or rather one program was played twice (Wednesday and Thursday) and the other three times (Saturday, Monday and Tuesday).[1] And the Youth Concerts started in 1947. Adding schools concerts, country tours and studio broadcasts, the SSO was easily one of the busiest orchestras in the world.

⁂

The 1945 season brought the 'old' SSO's first post-Ormandy visitors. With the European war over transport problems were eased somewhat. This was the year William Kapell made his first visit, offering a new piece that was a huge audience hit, Khachaturian's piano concerto. The tragic, gifted expatriate Australian pianist Noel Mewton-Wood[2] was also featured as soloist, in Stravinsky's *Capriccio* for piano and orchestra, and Haydn Beck gave the first Australian performance of Busoni's strange violin concerto. The two guest conductors were the Canadian Sir Ernest MacMillan and the returning Sargent.

MacMillan's French National Day concert was made more eventful by the appearance on stage of a drunk, who somehow got into the Town Hall during the performance of the Debussy *Nocturnes*, eventually finding a seat amid the double basses. He took a bow with the rest of the players at the end of the piece.

[1] Sometimes the new series' concerts were a repeat of the Wednesday and Thursday program.

[2] Born in Melbourne, Mewton-Wood studied at London's Royal Academy of Music and with Artur Schnabel, and made frequent trips back to Australia to perform. Regarded as one of the great pianists of his time, he committed suicide in 1953.

More seriously, Sargent had the Embarrassing Moment of 1945 at a Burwood rehearsal when the SSO's third trumpet player, Arthur Stender, realising suddenly that he had left his music on the train, read along with the second trumpet part instead. It was not until the end of the three-hour rehearsal, when Sargent asked the trumpets to play a passage on their own, that Stender owned up. Until then, Sargent had not noticed the difference. Dark looks all round.

The 'new' SSO's debut season, 1946, got off to a tentative start. Moses and the ABC publicists had sold the newness of the orchestra perhaps too well, for a first concert by a new combination is bound to be less than perfect. Cardus noted that 'so far the progress made is naturally of a kind that is more readily discerned arithmetically than aesthetically'. He praised Percy Code's handling of Sibelius' first symphony, but said that the playing was 'much as usual, no better, no worse'. Things improved as the year went on, until Cardus could describe Walter Susskind's performance of Mahler 4 with the SSO and soprano Thea Phillips as 'remarkably sensitive'.

Goossens made his debut with the orchestra during his 1946 tour as an ABC guest conductor. His repertoire included his own Concertino for Double String Orchestra, the suite from Walter Piston's ballet score *The Incredible Flutist*, and the first Australian performance of *The Rite of Spring*.[3] He made an immediate and profound impact on audiences, critics and orchestra. Neville Cardus remarked of the first concert that 'Goossens is a master conductor who has no need to bounce or flounce for effect . . . he is absolutely free of that consciousness of audience which marks the contemporary second-rater. The orchestra has seldom played so genuinely or with so much absorption in the music for nothing but music's sake'.

Neville Amadio: 'Our first impression was of a man of great dignity. He commanded respect because he gave respect.'

Perhaps Goossens' most perceptive gesture during this guest appearance was his performance of excerpts from John Antill's ballet *Corroboree*. This came about after Goossens asked James if there were any Australian scores he could perform. James showed

---

[3] He had conducted the first British concert performance of the work in 1921.

him a number of pieces, but Goossens did not find any to interest him. Antill, then an ABC control engineer, had not sent *Corroboree* in for consideration. As Harold Hort, one of James' successors as Director of Music, explained: 'John Antill was so self-effacing it was difficult to get him to do anything about promoting his own music'. The score was found at Burwood in the clean-up that occurred before the move to the Kings Cross studios. It had been presented to Sargent for his perusal in 1945, but was not performed. When Antill, after much persuasion, took the music to Goossens, the conductor was genuinely excited by it. 'He danced around the table', Antill recalled many years later. 'He said "I'll take this page and this page and that section, and make a suite out of it". This suite was what he played in the Town Hall a week later.' It received an eight-minute ovation, and Goossens later conducted it in Cincinatti (where he had been chief conductor before coming to Sydney) and London, and the SSO/Goossens partnership recorded it for HMV in 1950. It was a sensation. As Roger Covell has said, *Corroboree* made 'the public at large realise that music truly belonging to the twentieth century was being written in Australia'.

To Moses, Goossens' international renown and musical adventurousness, and his rapport with the SSO and its audience, made him the ideal candidate for the chief conductorship of the ABC's first permanent full-strength symphony orchestra. But Goossens declined the offer. The war was over at last, and after all his years working in the United States he wanted to conduct in Europe again. And besides, how could we match the fee he had been getting in Cincinatti? Moses thought over the problem. Dr Bainton was now retiring from the Conservatorium directorship. Two years before, the Public Service Board's A. W. Hicks had suggested that the SSO's first chief conductor might also run the Conservatorium, and Moses now worked out a financial package that combined the two positions. This gave Goossens a basic conductor's salary, part of it as untaxable allowance, and a director's salary at the Conservatorium of £1500. To this was added £100 for every concert he conducted for the ABC outside New South Wales (fifteen of these concerts per year guaranteed), and a £250 allowance as Conservatorium director. This meant that Goossens' annual income would be around £5000—more than the Prime Minister was earning at the time. Goossens accepted the offer. He made it a condition of his contract that he could spend some time in Europe at the end of each SSO concert season; he did not want to drop from the rest of the world's gaze altogether.

If it seems hard to imagine that one conductor could be worth so much trouble, the prestige Goossens brought with him should not be underestimated. He was born into one of Europe's most distinguished musical families, for not only had his father and grandfather been conductors of some standing, but his brother Leon was one of the world's leading oboists, and his sister Sidonie is still making guest appearances with the BBC Symphony. She was the orchestra's principal harpist between 1930 and 1980. Eugene began his professional career playing violin in restaurants and cinemas, before joining Sir Henry Wood's New Queen's Hall orchestra. Then in 1915 he became Beecham's assistant at the Beecham opera seasons staged at Covent Garden. Between 1921 and 1926 he conducted Diaghilev's *Ballets Russes* in its London seasons, each of which featured new music commissioned by the company.

All this time Goossens had been composing, and his works were getting performances. As conductor and composer, his reputation in the 1920s was that of a young radical, for he conducted memorable seasons of recent Russian and British orchestral music and caused frequent stirs with his own sophisticated, highly-coloured scores. His tone poem *The Eternal Rhythm* (1921) was sufficiently advanced in idiom to be praised by the young Arthur Bliss. In 1929 his opera *Judith* was performed successfully at Covent Garden, and 1937 saw his other opera, *Don Juan de Manara*, performed there with Lawrence Tibbett in the title role. Both works were written to libretti by Arnold Bennett.

Goossens first went to the United States in 1923 at the behest of George Eastman, the founder of Kodak, who had set up his own orchestra in Rochester, New York (he was getting his Eastman School of Music going at the same time). Then in 1931 he was appointed principal conductor of the Cincinnati Symphony. He was adventurous there too, making many important gramophone records, including the Walton violin concerto with Heifetz, Tchaikovsky's then rarely heard *Little Russian* symphony, and Stravinsky's ballet *The Nightingale*. He also appeared with many of the other United States orchestras. Goossens was considered a fine and important conductor by the time of his 1946 trip.

He arrived in Sydney as the SSO's permanent conductor in July 1947. At the ceremony to welcome him, held in the Kings Cross studios, Goossens made a speech in which he said, in part: 'Last year, the SSO gave a performance of *The Rite of Spring* after only three three-hour rehearsals that was as good as any I have heard in any part of the world. The fame and glamour they attained at that performance is known throughout all the places I have since been. I have said, and I repeat, that I will put this orchestra among the six best in the world. That is not a dream. I believe I can bring it about. I want to feel that when the time comes there will be in this city a group of genuine music-lovers sufficiently numerous and sufficiently enthusiastic to make all my dreams come true . . . It will take time to bring about all these things, but it must become a *fait accompli*'.

'Among the six best in the world' . . . that phrase resounded through the national press, and through the orchestra itself. The bravado of it, the air of glamorous transatlantic certainty, caught everyone's imagination. Was it really possible? As Goossens' influence took hold, it seemed less and less farfetched. He perhaps went a bit far when he told the press a year later that he looked forward to a time 'when members of the SSO will be as well-known to the public as the Bradmans and Darbys are today— a time when people will point and say "That's Bill Jones the bassoonist", just as today they say "That's Ray Neville the jockey" '. (*Smith's Weekly* sent the idea up mightily in a cartoon feature called *Prelude to Popularity*.) But there is no doubt that the orchestra played better and was better run under Goossens than it had been at any time since 1932.

Indeed, the Goossens years were also the best of the SSO's years for some time to come, for his sense of style and daring helped give the orchestra an identity that the Sydney of the day found captivating. There were few cultural figures of his eloquence and presence around, and Sydney saw him in almost messianic light. In short, the city took to bathing in his reflected glory. Goossens' daughter Renee recalls the kind of impact he made on post-war Sydney:

'In father, Australia had a musician from the real Europe, the

Eugene Goossens (second from left) pictured shortly after his arrival as SSO Chief Conductor, with wife Marjorie, Charles Moses (left) and William James (right).

real world. He was bringing culture and feeling, he had worked with Diaghilev, with great musicians that Australians had heard of, and he had a regal personal bearing. Yet he also had such a dynamic approach to his work here, and, with a great deal of energy, opened up a whole new world of repertoire.'

乄

Before discussing the extraordinary public impact of Goossens' leadership, it is important to stress that one of the main reasons the SSO became so significant an organisation in the decade after the Second World War was that many great players joined the orchestra during Goossens' years as chief conductor. The huge strides forward achieved in these years could not have occurred without the working symbiosis of Goossens' expertise and a better band of instrumentalists being in place. Some of these players joined as a result of migrating to Australia, some were headhunted by Goossens. Either way, they were as integral to the success of the 'new' SSO as Goossens himself, and deserve as much recognition.

The first of the new breed to arrive was the British oboist Horace ('Jimmy') Green. In late 1946 Charles Mackerras left the SSO to work in Europe and Green was his replacement. He had played in the London Philharmonic and London Symphony, and turned down an offer from Beecham to lead the oboes in the Royal Philharmonic so that he could emigrate to Australia with his family. The first of the 'principal imports' and an outstanding musician, he was a pupil of Goossens' brother Leon, and the first member of the orchestra whom Goossens addressed by his first name. This irked many of the other players.[4] But he was a great artist. Ron Cragg remembers: 'I studied oboe with Ian Wilson [then the SSO's principal cor anglais] for a while. I was inspired to do so by hearing Llewellyn in the Brahms concerto under Goossens, and I thought Horace Green's playing of the oboe solo in the slow movement was the most wonderful thing I had ever heard!'. Green also became a teacher of oboe at the Conservatorium.

Another exciting arrival was that of John Kennedy. His father

[4] Green was not appointed by Goossens. Discussions had been held with him for more than a year before Goossens took up his post.

and mother were the cellist and pianist team of Lauri and Dorothy Kennedy, both of whom had settled in Australia from the United Kingdom and made substantial careers here. John Kennedy had been appointed first cello in the Liverpool Philharmonic Orchestra in 1946 at the age of twenty-four, and thus became the youngest orchestral principal in the United Kingdom. He joined the SSO as principal in 1949, and was a great audience favourite because of his superb musicianship and flamboyance on the platform. To the rest of the orchestra he could be alternately hilarious and disturbing. Neville Amadio: 'We were rehearsing a work with Klemperer that had long passages of cello tremolando, and suddenly John stopped doing the tremolando with the bow and began moving his cello madly from side to side instead. We killed ourselves laughing, but Klemperer wasn't very impressed.' Ron Cragg recalls that Kennedy would sometimes 'do a whirly' with his cello during a performance, but that he played so well that he was never reprimanded.

Kennedy also gave solo performances with the orchestra, and made a memorable Sydney concerto debut under Kubelik in the Elgar concerto in 1949. 'That was one of the great concerts for me', Nadine Amadio says. 'A group of us went to supper at a friend's place in Kings Cross afterwards, and John got very drunk. As we all left we made a lot of noise in the street singing bits of the Elgar, and a policeman stopped us and asked John what was in his cello case. Unfortunately, he said "a machine gun", and the policeman gave him a bit of trouble.'

Kennedy stayed in the SSO for two years and taught cello at the Conservatorium as well, but he resigned from the orchestra in 1951 because 'the strain of attempting to combine with my orchestral duties any serious efforts at solo work, chamber music or teaching, is beginning to impair my health', he told Moses. He then played with Musica Viva for a few months, before going back to the United Kingdom to take up the principal cello chair at Covent Garden. He came back to Australia in 1959 as senior cello lecturer at the Melbourne university conservatorium. Always a boisterous personality, he developed an alcohol problem, and never played publicly again. He was the father of the British violinist Nigel Kennedy.

Kennedy's successor was another fine musician from overseas.

Hungarian-born, Hans George came to Australia by a fairly hair-raising route. 'I was a Dutch citizen, living in Java and playing in the radio orchestra there when war began. I joined the Dutch underground and was caught and imprisoned by the Japanese. After the war I worked for Dutch intelligence, as I was able to identify so many of the Japanese military they wanted.

'I arrived here in 1951, and was warned that I might get a job the next day or the next year. I guess I was very lucky because Goossens heard me and I joined the SSO as rank-and-file cello. Goossens had said to me 'Have you got time to wait?' but John Kennedy resigned soon after I arrived. John had a fantastic sense of humour. When he was told that he had to sign the attendance book at the Con every day, he went to the book and signed himself up for the whole year at once!'

One import who did not work was Charles Gregory. This British horn player had been recommended by Dorati in 1940 as one of the select musicians the ABC should bring to Australia. By the time he arrived in 1948, the horn section was being led by Alan Mann, whose career has been described as 'possibly the most significant and influential of any Australian brass player'.[5] Under Harty, Mann played third trombone, but he became the orchestra's second horn in 1936. In 1937 an Italian player, Guido Gervasoni, joined the SSO, and took Mann's position. Gervasoni had played under Toscanini, and came to Australia with an Italian opera company in 1900. He stayed in the SSO, a great veteran, until 1948.

With Gervasoni in the orchestra, Mann was promoted to third horn (which, in the structure of an orchestral horn section, is the second principal position), where he stayed until he was enrolled for military service. He came back from the war as principal horn, and took up a teaching post at the Conservatorium, where his pupils included Barry Tuckwell, Clarence Mellor and Robert Johnson. Unfortunately, he and his new third horn, Alf Hooper, did not get on, and Hooper appears to have been interested in

---

[5] He is so described in Richard Montz's historical survey of the SSO brass section, an important document for anyone interested in the life of the orchestra (see bibliography).

securing the principal's position for himself.[6] When Hooper went on two years' study leave in 1948, Gregory arrived to replace him, and another power struggle ensued.

Gregory's credentials were impeccable. He had been Chairman of the Board of Directors of the London Philharmonic, Professor of Horn at Trinity College and the Royal College of Music, and first horn at Covent Garden. Goossens knew him from London, and although he respected Mann's playing, he was interested to see what Gregory might make of the principal's position. He found out when Alan Mann took six months' sick leave in 1949. Neville Amadio: 'Well, Gregory was supposed to be so wonderful, but you couldn't hear him! And he had a terrible toffee-nosed attitude. That rubbed a number of us up the wrong way.' ABC management were not impressed with his playing either, and Gregory resigned early in 1950. Alan Mann returned shortly afterwards and signed a contract for first horn position. He was one of the few principals on contract at the time. Most were salaried ABC employees.

The only other brass player on contract was John Robertson. Although he has been mentioned in previous chapters, he did not join the SSO as first trumpet until 1948. Until then he had played for silent films, as principal trumpet with the Toronto Symphony, as soloist with the St Hilda Colliery Band, and with Jack Payne's dance orchestra in London. He had also played with Frank Coughlan's band at the Sydney Trocadero, but immediately before his SSO appointment he was the MSO's first trumpet. Like Kennedy, he was a flamboyant player and was featured frequently as soloist. In 1949 he played the obbligato part in the *Allelulia* from Bach's Cantata No 51 for soloist Elisabeth Schwarzkopf, who was on her first ABC tour. Sydney musical identity Peter Sainthill takes up the story.

'Schwarzkopf was incredibly beautiful on this tour, and when Robertson got to the front of the stage to take a bow with her he was completely mesmerised by her decolletage. He was asked later what colour her eyes were, and he said dreamily "Pink . . . both of 'em".'

---

[6] The conflict may have arisen in part because of their very different styles of playing. Mann was trained as an orchestral musician, and felt that the brass band background from which Hooper had come did not breed good orchestral horn players.

SSO horn players of 1950: from left, Douglas Hanscombe, Clarence Mellor, Claude Katz, principal horn Alan Mann and Barry Tuckwell. Mann was teaching all four players at the time and all four were under twenty-one.

Robertson made news when he had a piccolo trumpet imported in 1949 for a performance of Bach's second Brandenburg Concerto. Few orchestral players used the instrument at that time.

'Previously, I always played the Brandenburg part an octave lower, because on an ordinary trumpet you can't go high enough', he told the *Sunday Sun*. 'I *could* play the right octave on the conventional trumpet, but it sounds completely wrong. Besides, I would just about have to bust my boiler.'

Looking at his new piccolo instrument, he said that 'most players would run a mile rather than play the thing'.

For all his jokiness, Robertson could tackle a very wide repertoire with great skill. In 1952, he gave the world premiere with Bernard Heinze of Raymond Hanson's trumpet concerto which, like almost all of Hanson's music, has suffered a neglect that has sent it into a musical Twilight Zone. The *Music Maker* magazine wrote of its 'indigenous idiom':

On hearing it one is nostalgic for this aged continent of ours, the deep purple-brown-red distances; the atmosphere surrounding places of the Centre, the world of ancient wisdom that pervades the silent bush. The work is very surprising in its newness and the desire to hear it again is strong.

In characteristic fashion, Robertson summed up his attitude to orchestral brass playing thus in 1972: 'You have to have cast iron nerve, ability and youth. It's the devil's own job to keep awake during a performance after a day of practice, rehearsal and golf'. Sadly, illness robbed him of retirement, and he died at the age of sixty-six, only a year after he left the SSO in 1973.

Any discussion of the Sydney Symphony's particular qualities during the Goossens years must give prominence to Ernest Llewellyn, who succeeded George White as concertmaster in May 1949. While he had played in the orchestra in the 1930s (as violist and violinist) and appeared as soloist with it, Llewellyn had spent most of his time since his release from war service leading the Queensland State String Quartet, a group funded by the Queensland Labor Government. They gave something like 500 children's concerts and fifty public recitals a year, so he was kept pretty busy. He did maintain some solo engagements, though, and one of these was Walton's violin concerto with the SSO under

Four great SSO string players photographed in 1951: from left, violist Max Cooke and violinists Ron Ryder, Ernest Llewellyn (concertmaster) and Donald Blair.

Paul Kletzki in 1948. Goossens was at every rehearsal, and after the run of performances asked him to become the orchestra's concertmaster. Apart from a year's absence on scholarship, he led the SSO from 1949 until 1964, the year before he started the Canberra School of Music. He remained a major figure in the ACT's musical life until his death in 1982.

He was an outstanding musician, with fine leadership qualities, and he won great respect from conductors. He developed a long-time friendship with Isaac Stern, who became a regular visitor to Australia in the 1940s and 1950s. It was said that in their performance together of the Bach double concerto with the SSO you could not tell the two players apart. 'He was a wonderful man, naturally musical, much loved by the players', Cliff Goodchild recalls. 'You know, he was so excited about Klemperer's conducting of Mahler 2 that, after the first performance, he rang Hephzibah Menuhin, who was in Melbourne at the time, and insisted that she and her husband fly to Sydney to hear it on the next night.'

Goodchild himself is a product of the Goossens period, having joined the orchestra full-time in 1951 at Goossens' invitation. The family name is carried on in the SSO by Cliff's son Paul, who at the time of writing is the orchestra's associate principal trumpet.

'In 1945 I won what were then called the Australian Championships', Cliff remembers. 'One of the newspapers came and took a photo of me. Someone else's photo appeared in the paper over a caption that said "Cliff Goodchild, who hopes one day to play in the SSO". I'd never heard of the SSO! Until then I'd played at school—the Sisters of St Joseph at Kincumber—and as soloist in various brass band competitions. I joined the RAAF band towards the end of the war, then the ABC helped me get a discharge so that I could join the ABC Military Band.

'The SSO borrowed me from the band from time to time, and my first performance with them was during Klemperer's first tour here in 1949. I was a casual in Bruckner 7, which requires Wagner tubas. There was not one in Sydney then, so we used euphoniums and bass tubas instead. Joseph Post[7] worked flat out to get us in tune. I remember my audition for this concert. I could not

---

[7] Post became the SSO's associate conductor in 1947 and was, in effect, Code's successor.

even read bass clef then, so I played a cornet solo called *Fatherland* on the tuba!

'My immediate predecessor was a Borstal boy called Frank Lomas. He had a nasty disposition and very few friends, it seems.[8] Dooley Ward was the tuba player before him, an old Irishman. I never met him, but he got a glorious sound out of an amazing old instrument that he had patched up with tape. Beecham said to him once, "What is it made of, cardboard?".

When Goodchild gave the first Australian performance of Vaughan Williams' tuba concerto, he received a lot of help in learning it from, surprisingly, the orchestra's principal viola, Robert Pikler. 'He helped me understand the shape of the piece, he turned it into music for me. What a player he was . . . I even remember how he played "Three Blind Mice" at schools' concerts.'

Pikler was another post-war arrival to the SSO's ranks. Originally from Budapest, he had travelled widely before being interned by the Japanese in Java, as Hans George had been. He came to Australia on his release in 1946, and played first violin in the Musica Viva quartet until 1952, when the quartet broke up and he joined the SSO in the first viola chair. Ron Cragg:

'I was working for the instrument makers A.E. Smith in the late forties, and this man walked in and asked, in quite a thick foreign accent, to see some violins. Well, I showed him some and he started to play them. I was so impressed I arranged for him to meet Smith himself. He always remembered our first meeting with affection, and it was quite an honour to follow him in the principal's chair in the SSO.'

Ken Tribe remembers that Pikler joined the orchestra reluctantly at first. 'He was naturally a chamber musician, but in 1952 Musica Viva was running out of money and couldn't support the quartet any more, and the group also had a number of internal problems. John Kennedy, for example, who joined after he left the SSO, was a much slower sight reader than the other players, and this caused a lot of tension. Basically Robert joined the SSO because of the security it offered him.'

The name Neville Amadio has appeared frequently in this book,

---

[8] Many conductors had complained about Lomas' playing, and after he walked out of a rehearsal in 1948 the ABC fired him. He committed suicide soon after.

and it is important that his presence not be taken for granted. He was first flute in the SSO before there ever was an SSO (he joined the 2FC orchestra in the days of the Australian Broadcasting Company) but really came into his own when the orchestra was enlarged to full strength, and he was able to play works for larger orchestra that featured more interesting flute parts. His playing in Goossens' performances of Ravel's *Daphnis and Chloe* and Debussy's *Prelude to the Afternoon of a Faun* were highlights of the era, and he made many solo appearances with the orchestra. Szell, Beecham and Ormandy all invited him to become principal flute in their orchestras overseas, but, for family reasons, he was not able to accept. Under Goossens he was one of many fine players, whereas previously he had been one of a handful. He also led a very happy section that included the husband and wife team of Linda Vogt and Colin Evans.

The standard of the SSO's double-bass playing had been a regular target in conductors' reports and the first major step forward was the appointment of Charles Gray as principal double bass in 1947. An Englishman, Gray had toured Australia with the Boyd Neel String Orchestra early in that year, and decided to stay. Like Horace Green he was one of Beecham's favourite players, and like Green he left a busy United Kingdom career to bring his family here. He led the SSO basses until his retirement in 1966.

At time of writing the longest-serving member of the SSO is Clarence Mellor. He joined as fourth horn in November 1948, became principal on Alan Mann's retirement in 1963 and is still playing in the section. Apart from his long service, he can also claim 'old boy' status, as his father was the orchestra's first trumpet from the mid-1930s until 1946.

'I come from a family of musicians', Mellor says. 'My grandfather was a leader of brass bands and named my father Thomas Meyerbeer Mellor. And my uncle was George Strauss Mellor. If you were born into a musical family in those days you were inevitably named after a composer. It was the fashion'. Mellor and his father were in the SSO together only in the year young Mellor joined.

'I took up the horn when I was eleven, and first played with this orchestra under Kubelik, when I was fourteen. The Conservatorium High School gave me three days off to do it. But I never imagined I'd be in the section! In fact, I used to dodge practice whenever I could.' In 1950, Mellor was in a horn section that was loaded with Alan Mann pupils. Mellor, Barry Tuckwell (who left the section in July of that year for the United Kingdom), Claude Katz and Douglas Hanscombe had all studied with Mann, and were all permanent members, even though Hanscombe, at twenty-one, was the oldest of the four! The Sydney *Sun* described young Mellor in flattering terms: '[He] is one of the youngest and heaviest men in the orchestra. He weighs 17 stone, 7 pounds [111 kilos]'.

Some of the players I've written about here were called New Australians when they arrived in this country, and there were other European musicians who joined the orchestra just after the war, while they were trying to set up a new life for themselves: violinists Geza Bachmann, Peter Ashley and (briefly) Bela Dekany and double bass player (and sometime composer) George Kraus were among them. Not all the 'old' players made them welcome. There was a certain amount of anti-Semitism and anti-'Wogism' in the Goossens SSO that made the orchestra a less unified group than it appeared to be on the Town Hall stage. Peter Sainthill:

'There were too many factions in it at the time, and that had a bad effect on *esprit de corps*. It was when Goossens collapsed in rehearsal in 1955 that the players were brought to a "whole" feeling. They then realised what they would lose if he went. After that, I think they played better than ever.'

One musician remembers a particularly unpleasant experience that led to the orchestra's players' committee having Horace Green sacked.

'It was the first time we had worked with Rudolf Pekarek, a Jewish conductor from Czechoslovakia, and nominally the QSO's chief conductor. Pekarek began his first rehearsal by saying how honoured he was to be conducting such a fine group of players, how much he was looking forward to working with us and so on. Anyway, we started playing and Horace Green had an important solo near the beginning of the piece, which was I think a Rossini overture. He was a bar into his solo and he started to make mistakes. So Pekarek stopped and said, "Ah Mr Green I must have cued you incorrectly, we will start again".

'Well, then I heard Green say in a sort of loud undertone something about "Bloody Jews" and I went over to him and told

him quietly that he couldn't speak like that. Anyway, whenever
we got to the spot in the overture where this oboe solo came
up Green would make mistakes, and Pekarek finally realised what
was going on and became very upset. He said "Why do you do
this to me? I love this country so much, and I am so looking
forward to making music with you". So during the rehearsal break
the players' committee met and asked that Green be sacked.'

One of the most important new 'members' of the orchestra
was Joseph Post, who became the SSO's associate conductor in
1947. Due to ill-health, Percy Code had asked to be transferred
back to his family town of Melbourne, where he again became
the MSO's resident conductor. Post's career was already
distinguished when he was offered the SSO job, and he did not
like the term 'resident'. He accepted the title 'associate conductor'
and was given a more rewarding role than Code had, partly because
the SSO itself was now a full-strength group, and therefore offered
the second-in-command more challenges; and also because, good
though Code was, Post was far and away the better conductor.

His career was a mixture of great success and almost unbearable
frustration. Appointed professor of piano and oboe at the New
South Wales Conservatorium at the age of eighteen, he went on
to become one of the best conductors of opera in Australia, and
was one of the prime movers behind the National Opera Season
in Melbourne in 1948. He later became Musical Director for the
Elizabethan Trust Opera Company in its first seasons and, after
William James' retirement, the ABC's Associate Director of Music.
He also took over the directorship of the New South Wales
Conservatorium when Heinze retired in 1966. He remained there
until his untimely death in 1972.

Most musicians who worked with Post retain a high regard for
his abilities as a conductor. Indeed, there is little dispute that
he was the best resident conductor until the advent of Stuart
Challender. But his career never seemed to develop as it should
have. This is partly because Post made a name for himself in
the 1930s, after Heinze had already established political supremacy
in the orchestral field, and partly because Post's was a somewhat
contrary personality. He had a short fuse, and Donald Hazelwood,
now the SSO's co-concertmaster, remembers with amusement his
brusqueness with children at schools' concerts. 'I can still hear

An open air event: June Bronhill sings with the SSO under Joseph Post in the Sydney Domain in December 1951.

him saying 'Sit up straight! No Talking!' to them in that clipped tone he had.

He worked closely with the Music Department on the development of the Youth Concerts (work which went largely uncredited), and had his shining moment in 1951, when he came back from a year at the BBC, on exchange with Charles Groves. While he was away he conducted the Halle Orchestra and a BBC Symphony Prom concert at the Royal Albert Hall. But he never achieved the chief conductorship of an Australian orchestra, and relinquished the Musical Directorship of the Elizabethan Trust Opera Company after only two seasons. He was someone who, in Charles Buttrose's phrase, 'never got a go'. As Ron Cragg puts it, 'He was always the bridesmaid'.

Violinist Eva Kelly: 'Post was underestimated all his career, yet his conducting was so clear to play under. I suppose he was not a great politician, because he was always very honest! He would never go behind your back. Heinze had a lot of bluff on the podium, but Post was wonderful'.

Colin Evans, principal piccolo in the orchestra for many years, thinks the sad curve of Post's career was caused not just by bad luck. 'If only he had relaxed a bit more I often think he might have had a greater career than he did. He could be very tense, and he suffered badly from migraine.'

'I think the cussedness in him came partly from his frustration at not having been able to achieve greater things', Ken Tribe suggests. 'If his career had taken off, he would most likely have been a less bitter person.'

Harold Hort disagrees with most of these judgements about Post. 'He was a tremendous technician, and one of our greatest conductors of opera. But he would not push himself, he had no ambition. He wanted to play bowls and tend his garden. When he was on exchange with Groves he could not get home quick enough.'

Whatever the reasons for the proscribed scope of Post's career, Sir Charles Mackerras believes he deserved better. 'I have never really understood why Joe did not become the greatest and most influential musician in Australia', he says. 'I suppose he was a bit rough in manner at times, what we would now call "ocker". This wouldn't be a problem now, but it was not quite "right" then. He had no airs, and rather scorned people whom he thought too precious. He could say things like "Whacko, cellos!" after they'd rehearsed a passage well. Heinze was virtually his opposite. He was very suave, spoke beautifully, and mixed in the right circles, but he was not an outstanding conductor at all.'

'There is no question but that Post was the finest Australian conductor of his day', says *Sydney Morning Herald* critic Roger Covell. 'But he was at his best when there was a lot going on, when he needed to be very alert and on top of everything. That was one of the reasons he was such a good conductor of opera. At orchestral rehearsals, as I understand it, there wasn't much he could do with a piece once the notes had been got right. He didn't have burning ideas about music that he wanted to get across, yet he was an inquisitive musician in terms of repertoire. For example, towards the end of his career he gave the first performance in this country of Richard Meale's *Homage to Garcia Lorca*.'

As it is, Sydney concertgoers probably remember him best for the times he took concerts over at a moment's notice. There were a number of hair-raising occasions when he had to learn repertoire overnight. One of these was a 1955 subscription concert with the violinist Max Rostal as soloist. On the first night, during the second movement of the Bartok violin concerto, Goossens collapsed on the podium and was taken immediately to hospital. The following night Post was there conducting a very difficult program, which also included Florent Schmitt's large and complex *fin de siècle* tone poem *The Tragedy of Salome*. Lindsey Browne was full of praise:

There is something about these sudden musical emergencies . . . that shocks everybody concerned into a music-making power of higher voltage than usual . . . Joseph Post is one of Australia's most vital, vigilant and resourceful musicians.

Yet for all these capabilities, his unglamorousness and bluff ways— and perhaps his desire for a comfortable life above all—combined to deprive him of the fame and attention he seemed to deserve. SSO percussionist Colin Piper remembers one of Post's last concerts.

'Post never encouraged the percussion section, he always told us to keep it down. Well, in 1972 he was given the Percussions of Strasbourg concert to conduct, and I think of it now as a kind of sign from God that it was time to hang up his baton.'

❦

The first year of Goossens' permanency, 1947, also brought Rafael Kubelik, who gave invaluable lessons to the orchestra in the styles of playing required for Czech music, in this instance works by Novák, Suk and Dvořák (he returned for more concerts in 1949). Linda Vogt has great memories of Kubelik: 'The first moments of his first concert were amazing. As he raised his arms his face lit up, and before a note of music was played he transported us into the world of the piece we were about to do. He was on another wavelength and he easily took us all there with him'.

James and Goossens programmed Czech pieces regularly in each season, so that the work Kubelik had done with the orchestra was well exploited. In fact, Goossens conducted Smetana's tone poem *Richard III* in that 1947 season. Like so much of the music played in these years, it was followed in printed programs by the description: 'First performance in Australia'. Goossens actively encouraged visiting conductors to bring new or rarely heard works to Sydney, and there were perhaps more premieres per year between 1947 and 1955 than at any time in the orchestra's subsequent history. The following is a list of *some* of the first Australian performances given by Goossens and the SSO during this period:

Don Banks: Four pieces for orchestra
Barber: Music for a Scene from Shelley
Bartok: Music for Strings, Percussion and Celeste
Bax: Symphony No 4
Brahms/Rubbra: Variations on a theme of Handel
Britten: Suite from the opera *Gloriana; Mont Juic*
Bruckner: Symphony No 1; Symphony No 9
Copland: *Billy the Kid*
Paul Creston: Two Choric Dances
Debussy: *Jeux*
Franck (orch. Pierne): *Prelude, Chorale and Fugue*
R. Harris: Symphony No 3
Hindemith: Philharmonic Concerto; Symphony in E flat
Ibert: *Ports of Call*

Kabalevsky: Symphony No 2

Liszt: A Faust Symphony

Mahler: Symphony No 1; Symphony No 7, Symphony No 8;
   Das lied von der Erde

Martin: Petite Symphonie Concertante

Martinu: Symphony No 5

Milhaud: *Suite provençale*

Nielsen: Symphony No 5

Prokofiev: Symphony No 5 (three years after its world
   premiere); *Scythian Suite; Romeo and Juliet*—Suite

Rachmaninov: Symphony No 3

Ravel: *Valses Nobles et Sentimentales; Rapsodie Espagnole*

Alan Rawsthorne: Violin Concerto

Scriabin: *Prometheus—The Poem of Fire*

Shostakovich: Symphony No 6

R. Strauss: *Metamorphosen; Symphonia domestica; An Alpine Symphony;*
   concert performances of *Salome* and *Elektra*

Stravinsky: *Apollo Musagetes*; Symphony in Three Movements; Symphony
   in C

Margaret Sutherland: *Haunted Hills* (world premiere)

Tchaikovsky: *Manfred* Symphony

Tippett: Concerto for Double String Orchestra

Vaughan Williams: Symphony No 4; *Sinfonia Antarctica* (given in the
   year of its world premiere); Tuba concerto

Villa-Lobos: *Bachianas Brasileiras* No 2

The many other Australian premieres given by other conductors
include Klemperer's Shostakovich ninth symphony (written in
1945) in 1949; and Kubelik's 1949 performance of Vaughan
Williams 6, which took place just over a year after the world
premiere.[9] Although Heinze was jealous of Goossens' success in
Sydney, he also maintained his interest in new music, and
conducted many first performances in Sydney during this period,
too, including Honneger's third and fourth symphonies, and
Britten's violin concerto (with soloist Thomas Matthews). Nadine

---

[9] The *Catholic Weekly*'s 1949 review of the Shostakovich now makes strange reading.
'This composer is a curiously uneven workman', it opines. 'There is little doubt that
if the circumstances permitted, and his own personal character was a little more self-
disciplined, he would be one of the greatest composers of our time.'

Amadio explains the differences she perceived between the two conductors when she was a young music student.

'Goossens opened so many musical doors. Heinze loved music passionately and he did try to present new works, but suddenly along came a man who was an excellent conductor, who wanted to open up the repertoire. I was sick with excitement! I went to as many concerts as I could.'

Of course this view was not shared by all the subscribers, particularly those who had been going to concerts since the pre-war days, when there were few novelties and lots of standard repertoire. But, as Clarrie Mellor recalls, 'Goossens was able to have all those amazing things played because he programmed them very cleverly. He would put them in every so often, and break the audience into the newer idioms'.[10]

'There was one dear old lady who used to sit about six rows from the front in the stalls. She was absolutely huge, and we called her the Battleship', says Tempe Merewether, who has been a SSO subscriber since 1936. 'She always wore long sleeves and in any modern-sounding work she would pull her sleeves up and ostentatiously put her fingers in her ears. She would then sit like that for the rest of the piece.'

Goossens had his way of dealing with the Battleships. One correspondent to the *Sydney Morning Herald* complained about the amount of new music in SSO programs, and Goossens responded with the mixture of loftiness, flattery and confidence that so characterised his public utterances. 'An intelligent community such as this one must be kept in touch with significant contemporary musical expression', he wrote.

Just as we first ascertain whether new paintings, books and plays are to our taste by seeing, reading and hearing them so must important unfamiliar music be heard at our concerts. A conductor, therefore, either pays his audience the compliment of sampling it, or goes down to posterity (with the community) as culpably reactionary. I bluntly state that the lee-way to be made up in this respect in Australia is considerable.

[10] As a *Sydney Morning Herald* columnist wrote of audiences in 1948: 'Listeners to symphony concerts are divided into Athenians, who delight only to hear some new thing, and descendants of Lot's wife, who indulged to the point of excess in the backward look'.

No orchestra in the world can ring yearly changes on a constant repertory of the same popular symphonies and still present vital concerts of general interest. For one listener demanding strictly conservative fare, there are today 50 who rightly demand a more variegated diet. This, I venture to say, will be found at our concerts with (I modestly hope) the mutual bond of confidence and self-esteem between performers and audience which alone is the secret of a happily progressive community of music-lovers.

It takes all kinds to make a world, particularly one with a *Wozzeck* in it . . .

Audiences were also encouraged by some of the important critics to be open minded about new and rarely played music. The most eloquent advocate for Goossens' new programming policy was Lindsey Browne of the *Sydney Morning Herald*. Browne succeeded Neville Cardus as the paper's main critic on Cardus' return to the United Kingdom in 1947. (Previous to that he had been Cardus' deputy.) On the first anniversary of Goossens' chief conductorship of the SSO, Browne wrote a piece entitled 'Goossens Lights A Candle', in which he said that 'The all-round quality of the orchestra's performances over the last 12 months, and the adventurous eclecticism of its programs have given liberal evidence that Goossens is the right man in the right job'. He also gave a useful picture of Goossens' conducting style:

He can relish caviar without sympathising with the sturgeon. He is a hedonist. Music for him is a matter of sound and of taste and of pleasure; he will give a clear and direct account of it without subscribing to the romantic notion that the conductor's soul should obtrude itself between composer and audience.

Browne was one of a number of new generation Sydney critics—including Curt Prerauer, Martin Long and Wolfgang Wagner—who were more articulate and knew more about the repertoire than many of their predecessors. They were all broadly supportive of Goossens and helped educate the audience into enjoying a wider range of musical styles. Indeed, in 1948 Curt Prerauer used Goossens as a stick with which to beat Heinze:

'Our musical life, before the arrival of Goossens, contained many a profiteer from mediocrity. Many of them are still there, but they can be relied upon for being afraid of someone better than they. As a matter-of-fact, this is the old reason why our standards are what they are.'

It also encouraged the more progressive members of the audience that the space given to ABC concerts in the social pages shrank as the critics' columns got longer. Lindsey Browne remembers the slow but sure shift: 'The pre-war audiences were socialites for the most part, doing the right thing by being at a concert. They were not really responsive, and this only changed with the arrival of European refugees into the Town Hall audience. They were used to really listening to a performance, and that helped bring about a change in audience behaviour, and indeed, in the make-up of the audiences.'

Gretel Feher arrived in Sydney from Vienna in 1938. She remembers the first ABC concerts she attended and her astonishment at the behaviour of the audience. 'To start with people were very well dressed, but there were not as many men as there were women, which I thought was odd coming from a city where music was important to everybody. And many of the women, during the concert, were knitting! I had never seen anything like it before, and I remember writing about this in letters at the time.'

Cardus had also been puzzled by the dominance of women in concert audiences, and wrote in his parting article for the *Sydney Morning Herald* (May 1947) that 'Australian women are much more interesting, better read, and wittier than the men . . . I am frankly puzzled why Australian women don't do something to educate their men'.

As much as audiences had become, on the whole, more broad-minded and responsive, there were still problems. During one of Walter Gieseking's Town Hall recitals in 1952, a young woman sitting in the organ gallery—Miss Geraldine Hutchins, 24, of Randwick—got bored, took out her gold compact mirror and began doing 'a full repair job', as the *Sunday Sun* put it. The light reflected from the compact by the stage lights was a major distraction for the audience in the body of the hall, and a woman told Miss Hutchins off at interval. The culprit was unrepentant.

'Mr Gieseking played some very boring music', she told a reporter. 'If he took my advice he'd play more popular music. Semi-classics, I mean, like Tchaikovsky, Chopin, Debussy, Grieg and Bach. If I don't like the type of music they play I wipe them, but I think Mr Gieseking has talent.'

Nadine Amadio remembers the Town Hall organ gallery of her student days as a home for a colourful cast of characters. 'They were the only seats in the hall we could afford, and it was where all the eccentrics used to sit, too; people who read the paper, or ate Sao biscuits through everything. One woman once sang along through a whole Mozart symphony, and I tapped her on the shoulder and said, 'You are to be admired for knowing the work so well, but I wish you would shut up so I can enjoy the performance'.

There was also the problem of people leaving the hall during music they did not like. In 1954, fifteen years after its first Sydney performance, Walton's first symphony got some people out of their seats before its conclusion. Eunice Gardiner explained in her *Telegraph* review that this was no reflection of the fine performance given by the SSO under Joseph Post. The crowds headed for the exits during Goossens' performance of Vaughan-Williams fourth symphony too, and as the *Catholic Weekly* reported: 'Almost as soon as the work concluded there was a rush for the doors, with scarcely a thought of rewarding applause for either the conductor or the orchestra'. As late as 1960, one printed program, under the listing of *The Rite of Spring*, added: 'Concert-goers are requested not to leave the hall during the performance of a work'.

Another problem that has not gone away is that of audience coughing, although it would seem that Sydney audiences behave themselves a lot better in this regard than they used to. In a 1952 piece called 'Our Rudest Audiences Ever?', Lindsey Browne had the coughers for breakfast:

On many occasions, audiences could hardly have been more destructive of all that is good in music and theatre if they had gone to their entertainment armed with peashooters, water pistols, postman's whistles, bags to 'bust', bullroarers and Richard Strauss' wind-machine . . .

We have coughed alone. We have coughed in duets. We have coughed in full chorus. We have announced little themes of coughs and developed them steadily throughout a concert in strict sonata form. We have imitated the peevish Pekinese. We have bayed forth so loud and strong from the hollow caverns of our bronchitis that even the Hound of the Baskervilles would surely run off in terror yelping from us.

According to Alan Ziegler, Goossens got to know about the quirks of each subscription audience fairly quickly. 'He used to say that you could tell what night of the week it was by the kind of applause you got as you walked onto the platform. The Monday night concerts were new then and had a more enthusiastic audience than the Wednesday night series, which had many subscribers who went right back to the first subscription concerts in 1936.'

'In the months leading up to my graduation from the Conservatorium in 1955 Goossens would ask me what I wanted to do for a living', violinist Jenny James remembers. 'I said "Well, I'd like to play in the orchestra" and he said, "You must practise your sight reading". He told a lot of up-and-coming players that.'

Clarrie Mellor: 'Many visiting conductors who worked with us in the Goossens period were surprised at the variety of the works we were playing, and we began to get a reputation as a great sight-reading orchestra. We would come back from our Christmas holidays with a clear two or three weeks before any public concerts, and there would be a thick folder of music on each of our stands, all new things, and we would sight read through it all. You could get back into form on the job.'

Goossens' programs were not only adventurous, they were long. Most of his 8 p.m. concerts finished at 10.30, and some later than that. It would not be possible to program concerts this way any more since our concentration spans have been shortened by television, but a look at BBC Proms programs of the period show that Goossens was following the British fashion of the day, at least in terms of length. His choice of repertoire was idiosyncratically expansive. Here are a few 'Goossens specials':

Overture: *Abduction from the Seraglio*.....................Mozart
Pohjola's Daughter: A Symphonic Fantasy.............Sibelius
Symphony No 3...Brahms

Interval

The Song of the Earth ....Mahler
(first performance in Australia)
Soloists: Florence Taylor and Max Worthley

❧

Symphony No 4 ....Schumann
Violin Concerto ....Dvořák
Soloist: Eugene Prokop

Interval

Scenes and Dances from Part 1—*The Three
Cornered Hat*..Falla
The Rite of Spring..Stravinsky

❧

Overture: *News of the Day*............................Hindemith
Symphonic Suite: *Spring* ....Debussy
Impressions from Nature, Part Two ....Malipiero
(first performance in Australia)
'All Hail Thou Dwelling', from *Faust* ....Gounod
'The Dream', from *Manon* ....Massenet
Soloist: Gino Mattera

Interval

Symphony: *Romeo and Juliet* ....Berlioz
(omitting choral fragments, except Finale)

❧

Two Roumanian Folk Dances ....Bartok
Three Fragments from *Wozzeck* ....Berg
(first performance in Australia)
Sprechstimme: Elsa Haas
Piano Concerto..Rawsthorne
(first performance in Australia)
Soloist: Paul Badura-Skoda

Interval

Symphony No 9 (*From the New World*) ....Dvorak

Don Juan ....R. Strauss
The Four Seasons, for Violin and Orchestra ....Vivaldi
Soloist: Maurice Clare

Interval

Symphony No 3, *Ilya Mourometz* ....Glière
(first performance in Australia)[11]

For all Goossens' advocacy, and the enthusiasm of some critics, it is still an object of wonder that so many new and then-obscure works (such as Berlioz's *Romeo and Juliet*) were introduced to Sydney concert audiences before the breadth of the orchestral repertoire was available on disc, before indeed audiences were all that familiar with the orchestral music of the first twenty years of the century. Part of the answer lay in the amount of cultural 'catching up' most Western countries felt they needed post-1945; in Sydney the need was particularly acute, as the pre-war orchestra would have been unlikely to have been able to play much of Goossens' repertoire convincingly; and as we've seen in previous chapters, it needed a Cardus to convince Sydney that Mahler, for example, was worth their time.

Now concert audiences were ethnically diverse. The increasing number of Jewish Europeans not only taught the Anglo music lovers of Sydney how to respond enthusiastically to a good performance, they also brought with them a better knowledge of the orchestral repertoire. And these re-energised, distinctly post-war audiences had, with the general press, given Goossens a mandate to broaden Sydney's musical experience, so that there was less ducking for cover in the face of new music than there is in the 1990s.

But the phenomenon also had a lot to do with the kind of repertoire that was new in the late 1940s. Ken Tribe:

---

11 *The Four Seasons* was still regarded as fringe repertoire when this concert was given in 1954. At some ninety minutes, *Ilya Mourometz* is the longest purely instrumental symphony in the repertoire, although it may have been performed on this occasion with cuts.

'It is all about idiom. The idiom of a new piece in the forties—a Vaughan Williams or Shostakovich symphony, or one of the Britten concertos—was such that you could feel familiar with the music after only two or three hearings. At the time, many people looked forward to performances of such works for this reason. The gap between composer and audience widened considerably in the sixties, to an extent that audiences are still put off new pieces today.'

By virtue of Cardus' recent departure, the SSO achieved an overseas reputation very quickly. Cardus was disappointed on returning to London to find standards there so mixed. He wrote in the *Manchester Guardian* in 1948 that the quality of London performances, and, in some quarters, standards of knowledge among audiences 'are not above those of Sydney and Melbourne, to say the least':

Eugene Goossens and the Sydney orchestra, like Barbirolli and the Halle, prove once again that in a compact community, and with constant orchestral rehearsals under the same conductor, musical culture and the technical presentation of music are likely to develop more intensively and more genuinely than in a cosmopolis.

If the orchestra's profile at home was also high, it reached new heights in 1953, when a batch of commercial recordings by the SSO under Goossens' direction was released by EMI, first for the domestic market and then internationally. This was a real first, and made enormous news. It also made the cover of *Gramophone* magazine, which caused many Australian eyes to boggle.

The SSO had made commercial discs before, but not with the same impact. During the war a Parliamentary Standing Committee recommended that Australian compositions be recorded, and as a result a 45-piece SSO recorded Frank Hutchens' *Phantasie-Concerto* for two pianos and orchestra, and Lindley Evans' *Idyll* for two pianos and orchestra, both with Hutchens and Evans at the keyboards and Dr Bainton conducting. There had also been war-time recordings by the ABC Light Orchestra (the 31-piece version of the SSO) under Heinze which included music from William James' long-ago ballet *By Candlelight*. All these discs were

Eugene Goossens gesturing to the soloists after the first concert performance given in Australia of R. Strauss' Elektra. Soloists include Phyllis Rogers (second from left) Allan Ferris and Marjorie Lawrence (holding bouquet).

On a larger stage, the Goossens/SSO recordings of 1952 make front page news in the UK.

made for the Columbia label, and were sold on the local market only. They are now quite rare.

The SSO's first post-war recordings were made, like the Hutchens and Evans pieces, in the less-than-ideal conditions of Ashfield Town Hall. In 1950, for EMI, Goossens conducted there the two suites he had extracted from Antill's *Corroboree* and, as one observer wrote at the time, 'the almost constant accompaniment of high-powered truck engines, car horns and yelling children outside the hall did little to improve the collective tempers of Mr Goossens, the orchestra or the recording engineers'. The acoustics of the hall resulted in a fairly foggy recording, but the performance still sounds pretty lively. The *Corroboree* recording was popular as both a 78 rpm set and as an LP in Australia.[12]

On his annual trips to Europe, Goossens would tell virtually anyone who would listen that the SSO should become one of the great recording orchestras of the world. His advocacy bore fruit in early 1951, when Moses was in London and persuaded EMI's general manager Sir Ernest Fisk that the SSO should make recordings that EMI would market and distribute internationally. The next London visitor was James, who went to Europe on a talent-scouting trip in the northern summer of 1951. He sorted through much of the detail of how the recordings were to be made, and secured an agreement that EMI would send to Australia one of its senior engineers, Arthur Clarke, to supervise the sessions and work with EMI's local technicians. Clarke's involvement with EMI's HMV label went back to 1907, and he had made Gigli's first records in Milan just after the First World War.

Clarke's major task was finding an appropriate recording venue that sounded like a real concert hall but had a sufficiently short reverberation time to make recording on the relatively unsophisticated equipment of the day straightforward. Goossens had already dismissed the Kings Cross studio because of its 'shooting gallery' acoustic. Clarke decided that the Sydney Town Hall 'did not absorb enough sound' and that the Conservatorium acoustic was 'like dead mutton'. He eventually settled on the Great Hall at Sydney University which, while imperfect, came closest to the conditions he wanted. He thought it a safe distance from

---

[12] In the early 1950s EMI released its classical recordings in both formats.

the noise of Parramatta Road, and not too big. Still, he had special carpets laid on the floor and heavy drapes hung on the walls to dampen down the fairly lively acoustic.

Goossens and EMI planned to record Beethoven's second symphony, Saint-Saens' *Danse macabre*, Turina's *Sinfonia Sevillana*, Mahler's seventh symphony, Massenet's *Scènes pittoresques*, Mendelssohn's *Scotch* Symphony, Butterworth's rhapsody *A Shropshire Lad*, the Polka and Fugue from Weinberger's opera *Schwanda the Bagpiper*, the *Shepherd's Fennel Dance* by Balfour Gardiner, and Grainger's arrangement of the *Londonderry Air*. This was perhaps too ambitious a list for an orchestra unused to recording conditions, and it transpired that EMI had been a bit ambitious, too: it underestimated the number of 78 rpm sides the works would occupy. For example, only two sides had been allowed for the Butterworth, which actually needed three, and four sides for the Turina, which really needed six. This physical expansion of the material recorded during the sessions led to the abandonment of the Mahler symphony, which is unfortunate given that the work was performed for the first time in Australia by Goossens and the SSO in 1949. The Balfour Gardiner may have been recorded, but if so it was rejected for release.

The sessions were not trouble free. The orchestra soon tired of performing in the four-and-a-half minute chunks required in the dying days of 78 rpm, and noise from trams, aircraft and pigeons delayed the sessions. Nevertheless, the records were a great success not only in Australia but, as Goossens had hoped, on the international market. The recordings of the Turina, Massenet and Weinberger were, for many years, the only versions available, and the Beethoven received a famous accolade from the authors of the *Record Guide:* 'If this is the general standard there, then the citizens of Sydney are indeed fortunate'. In *The Gramophone*, Andrew Porter wrote that the Mendelssohn recording 'confirms the high reports we have received of this Australian orchestra. They play with an altogether admirable precision and attack'.

Goossens began lobbying for an overseas tour for the orchestra in 1951, and hoped the success of these discs would help get the SSO to Europe, but the ABC baulked at the expense and the logistics. Here Goossens was looking to the future, for it was not quite yet the age of international orchestral touring, and the SSO would not travel overseas until 1965.

The EMI recordings were one of the SSO's many firsts under Goossens, and outdoor concerts were another. Having worked for so many years in the United States, Goossens had first-hand experience of such permanent outdoor concert venues as the Hollywood Bowl, New York's Lewisohn Stadium and Philadelphia's Robin Hood Dell. He was puzzled that Sydney's summer climate had not already led to the building of a permanent outdoor music shell, and set about proving that the city should have one by starting a series of free outdoor concerts, scheduled for the summer of 1949-50.

The first concert was given in the Botanic Gardens, near the Conservatorium, and attracted around 20 000 people. Pleased as he was by the success of this first concert, Goossens at this stage was only experimenting.

He wanted a site that was good enough acoustically to warrant the building of a permanent shell. The natural acoustic properties he was looking for needed a landscape in which 'a sloping terrain leads down towards another slight inclination which automatically forms a second sounding board'. After the first few concerts, held in the summer of 1949-50, he tried another part of the gardens, near Farm Cove, then Cooper Park, St Leonards Park, and, in a celebrated failure, Centennial Park.

The demountable Centennial Park stage was erected at the bottom of a natural amphitheatre near the park's Ocean Street entrance, between the reservoir and the bus depot. The cannon of the Royal Australian Artillery were engaged to join the SSO in the finale of Tchaikovsky's 1812 overture, and they made a spectacular visual and aural contribution to the event. Unfortunately it had started to rain by this part of the concert, and the water running off the surrounding slopes quickly turned the audience area into uncomfortable slush. The cannon also set all the neighbourhood dogs barking. And it was May, not the warmest month for outdoor events in Sydney. *Smith's Weekly* thought the cannon were hilarious, and promptly published a cartoon feature which included a depiction of a poster, hanging outside the Conservatorium, which proclaimed 'Goossens Get Your Gun, 5th Week'.

The concerts demanded great patience from the orchestra. The temporary stages the SSO used were not well insulated from nature's vagaries; wind frequently blew music off stands, sun often shone on instruments. Players had to compete with aircraft noise and cicadas. One double bass player returned from an outdoor concert to find Argentinian ants taking a tour of his instrument. The quality of amplification was also erratic. But the concerts proved to be hugely popular, regularly attracting crowds of 25 000 or more. Once these events had created their own momentum Goossens conducted fewer of them and Code, Heinze, Post, Clive Douglas, Henry Krips and even Otto Klemperer conducted subsequent concerts. They were given every year until the summer of 1956-57.

The ABC scored a coup by getting Cinesound and Movietone newsreels to attend some of these concerts, and the Cinesound Review clip of the first Botanic Gardens venture was highly supportive. 'An audience of 25 000 acclaim this innovation', the narrator enthused. 'The people want good music and from a properly constructed permanent music shell. Let there be no rest for authority until open air symphony becomes a regular part of our lives.' By the time of the 'cannonic' *1812* in Centennial Park a few months later Fox Movietone could call the concerts 'a regular feature of Sydney's cultural life'.

They may have been regular, but no one was offering to build the shell Goossens wanted. He decided that Cooper Park was the best spot of all the ones he had tried, but he could not get Woollahra Council interested. He soon ran out of the time and energy needed to keep the project on the boil, and after he left Sydney the concept of regular open-air orchestral concerts quietly died. When the SSO and the Festival of Sydney started them again in the 1980s a temporary stage had to be erected every year. Such a stage is still in use in 1992. It has to be raised before and folded up after the events it is used for, at great expense, just like the stages on which Goossens and the SSO performed. Despite the many political promises to the contrary, Sydney's permanent outdoor stage seems as far away as it did in 1949.

The lack of civic interest in this project and the frustrated SSO tour were two of many sore points that tempered the gratifying adulation Goossens enjoyed in Sydney. He and the ABC parted

The Age of Experiment: Goossens introduces Sydney to outdoor orchestral concerts. This photograph was taken in Cooper Park in 1950.

company over a lot of things, particularly publicity for the
orchestra. On one of his first country tours an advertisement
for an SSO performance appeared in the local paper the day after
the concert! He made quite a noise about that. He was also annoyed
that the first major country tour of 1948 occurred 'at the opening
of the season, the orchestra being permitted to slink out of Sydney
with no publicity or photographers present to record its departure.
Sydney can't be reminded too often that it has an orchestra'.
So there were no laughs when, outside a regional cinema where
the SSO was to perform, he found a poster which announced,
within a heavy black border: 'The Management deeply regrets
that no pictures can be shown tonight owing to the visit by the
Sydney Symphony Orchestra'.

Above all, Goossens wanted his first years with the SSO to
involve only a few guest conductors, so that he could be,
unashamedly, the dominant influence on the young orchestra.
But he found himself one of nine conductors scheduled to stand
in front of the SSO in 1947, and told Moses of his frustration.
'The free hand I had hoped for is constantly being tied by petty
frustrations. The orchestra is again faced with a season shared
by a number of different conductors, a policy highly detrimental
to its present development.' At Goossens' insistence, Moses and
James did reorganise the 1948 and 1949 seasons, so that Goossens
conducted the bulk of the public concerts. Indeed, in 1948 Paul
Kletzki was the only overseas guest conductor to work with the
orchestra.

But, despite efforts to do so, Goossens could not dislodge Post,
whose blunt manner was at complete odds with his own. Post
was replaced by the composer/conductor Clive Douglas as the
SSO's resident conductor in 1952, but, as Cliff Goodchild and
Colin Evans remember, Goossens took a big stick to him just
over a year after his appointment.

'We were doing a studio broadcast of *Daphnis and Chloe* from
Kings Cross, and Douglas wanted to make some cuts. These were
not clear to everyone, and everything fell in a heap, with finally
the bass clarinet playing away by himself. Goossens was listening
to this broadcast, and two weeks later Douglas was the permanent
conductor in Tasmania!'

For all his forcefulness, Goossens did not have the time to

be the detailed administrator the Conservatorium needed, and many critics and musicians have since commented on how the SSO got the better end of Goossens' interest and energy. In the late 1940s, though, criticism of his Conservatorium directorship was hardly voiced publicly, and his honeymoon with Sydney seemed infinitely extendable. It was not only through his SSO performances that the relationship developed; one of the issues that kept their love alive was Goossens' immortal phrase, 'Sydney must have an opera house'.

He first talked about a new home for the SSO in 1947, to the disinterest of the State government. Moses was not interested either, and explained that he was in the business of broadcasting, not building. But Goossens was a great urger and would not let the issue drop. He felt that the Town Hall's capacity of around 2000 seats was restrictive at a time when the SSO's audience was growing every year.

His first preference was for a new multi-purpose hall that would accommodate opera, ballet and orchestral music. He wrote an article for the *Sydney Morning Herald* in 1949 in which he blithely remarked that 'Sydney's future opera house will be chiefly concerned with housing the SSO. Since the concert shell in which the orchestra will perform is a removable unit, there will be no undue interference with scenery and properties which might be currently in use by an Opera or Ballet Company'.

The article, 'How Long Before Our Opera House Dream Comes True?', was a clear indication that the needs of the orchestra were uppermost in his mind. However, as he got to know Sydney's theatres, and began to stage operas with the Conservatorium opera school in the Conservatorium's main hall, he realised that conditions for opera performance were pretty terrible.

The world premiere of *Corroboree* as a ballet took place at Sydney's Tivoli Theatre. The pit was far too small for the SSO, and some players had to be put in boxes on either side of the stage. The orchestra's timpanist Alard Maling was perched in a box with an excellent view of the stage and appeared to be enjoying the show hugely when he was not playing. The then Professor of Music at Sydney University, Donald Peart, said that such conditions 'would not even have done justice to a make-believe jazz band'.

Goossens had begun to strike a common chord with the Australian temperament, for by continuing to irritate the State government and ABC management with his Opera House, he made Sydney itself more excited about the project. Speculation about the building appeared in the press regularly, particularly the question of where it would be located. Goossens' first choice was Bennelong Point, on which had stood historic Fort Macquarie, but which at this point was a home for Sydney's trams. Goossens was most likely led to this choice by two people: the architect Professor Leslie Wilkinson, who used often to say that the best site in Sydney was used as a tram depot, and the consultant planner to the Cumberland City Council, Dr K. Langer, who had included it in his proposals for architectural additions to Sydney.

The State government would not commit itself to the project or to the release of the Bennelong Point site. The then Minister for Transport said that Fort Macquarie was a very important depot and could not be moved. Goossens was resoundingly offended.

'Had the authorities chosen to make available the fine harbour site at Fort Macquarie, at present occupied by a castellated brick tram-shed, Sydney might now boast the proudest music theatre in the world', he wrote soon after the decision was taken. 'My chagrin at this failure to remove Sydney's greatest obstacle to further musical development is patent and undeniable. I do not mince words in saying that it not only definitely hampers, but threatens to set a term to both my practical and advisory work and usefulness on behalf of the city's music . . . Parochialism is an ever-present danger.'

Goossens and his supporters, who included the theatre designer William Constable and the architect Hugo Stossel, began looking elsewhere. The sites speculated upon included Wynyard Ramp, on the site of the Menzies Hotel; the Domain, between the Art Gallery of NSW and St Mary's Cathedral (this site was given provisional approval); the City Bowling Club (behind Hyde Park); the Capitol Theatre, and Chippendale, behind Sydney University.

This last option was the favourite of the Parks and Playgrounds Movement of New South Wales, the honorary secretary of whom charitably told the *Sydney Morning Herald*: 'The city area will have to expand and we should like to see this as the first move.

The slums of Chippendale should be pulled down and in their place a cultural centre should be built.'

The turnaround in this first stage of the Opera House saga came with the State government elections of 1952. The new premier, J.J. Cahill, met Goossens and expressed enthusiasm for the Opera House project. Two years later Bennelong Point was secured and Goossens was appointed to a committee to advise the State government on how to build an opera house. It was this committee which, in 1955, established the architectural competition that attracted Jorn Utzon's winning design. Goossens' involvement in the project finished there because he left the country for good in May 1956.

Geoffrey Serle has suggested that 'taking into account all considerations of prestige, the decision to build an Opera House on Sydney Harbour reflected the growing respect for the arts in the period'. An awakening, articulate curiosity about our cultural identity gives the immediate post-war years a particular flavour. It was this curiosity that gave momentum to the Opera House idea. But our pubs still closed at six o'clock. It is not too far-fetched a suggestion that Goossens left Australia because our pubs closed at six o'clock.

꽃

One important event of the Goossens period, the Youth Concerts, hailed as 'the idea of the decade' by the Melbourne *Herald*'s John Sinclair, was not directly Goossens' doing. Part of the new SSO's agreement with the City Council stipulated the provision of 'a minimum of 12 public concerts at popular prices in the City of Sydney'. For some time Heinze had been nurturing the vision of an evening concert series developed especially for young people, and they began in 1947—one series of six concerts—with the stipulation that they were to be attended only by people twenty-five and under.

The popularity of the series was enormous, partly because the adult subscription concerts were becoming so hard to subscribe to, partly because the Youth Concerts were cheaper (sixteen shillings for a season ticket), and partly because the forward-looking aura of Goossens' leadership gave the SSO an energy to which young people responded. In 1949 the ABC introduced a second series of six concerts. To meet the increasing clamour for tickets, a third series opened in 1951, and that sold out, too. Youth Concert subscriptions were not renewable, and season tickets could only be bought from the ABC box office in February each year.[13] The annual line-up for tickets became one of the great photo opportunities of the era. Here is the *Daily Telegraph's* report of the scenes at the 1952 opening of the box office:

Box plans for the 1952 Youth Concerts series open at 8am today. By 4pm yesterday more than 30 young men and women were in the queue. Last night more than 400 people settled down with rugs, sleeping-bags and deck chairs to wait for the doors to open this morning. The ABC concert manager (Mr Eric Burnett) arrived at 11pm and stayed all night, ready to make arrangements in case of rain.

The Youth Concerts were an idea whose time had come. Whether Heinze intended it or not, they were one of the first pieces of target marketing in the history of the arts in Australia. Young people responded to the concept of a special series devoted to their interests, and a Youth Concerts committee, formed in early 1947 (before the concerts had begun) and representing a variety of Sydney's youth clubs and organisations, kept the momentum going.

Lindsey Browne called this audience 'the most exhilarating concert company in Sydney'. The 'age 25' ceiling promoted a kind of club atmosphere that also worked in the series' favour, but it did not stop older people trying to get in. As *Smiths' Weekly* reported of the box office queues: 'Adults adopted what they imagined to be youthful, innocent expressions and got in the line ready to swear they were not a day over 25'.

The heartening thing to observe from some forty years distance about the early Youth Concerts is that the adventurous spirit which characterised the main subscription programs of the period is evident here as well. Not surprisingly, some of the most

---

[13] Between 1947 and 1951 concert staff and the Sydney concert box office were located in the basement of the ABC building at 264 Pitt Street. A special Youth Concert box office was set up in the lower Town Hall for 1952, and then in 1953 the box office moved with the State and Federal concert departments to Broadcast House in Elizabeth Street, staying there until the mid 1980s.

A Goossens epic: Mahler's Symphony No 8, Symphony of a Thousand, given in the Sydney Town Hall in October 1951. Soloists included Elizabeth Allen (left) and Florence Taylor (second from left). The choirs pictured are the Hurlstone Choral Society (now Sydney Philharmonia Choir), the New South Wales Conservatorium of Music choir and a combined choir from metropolitan high schools.

interesting music turns up in Joseph Post's concerts. He was much more inquisitive musically than his posthumous reputation would imply, and he was a great believer in the Youth Concerts concept. 'I preach the gospel of these concerts very strongly', he told the *Daily Telegraph* in 1950. 'I think they are mainly responsible for the big audiences Australian concerts get now.'

Some of the works Post conducted at the Sydney Youth Concerts were Bloch's Concerto Symphonique (with pianist Jascha Spivakovsky), Chausson's symphony, English composer Maurice Jacobson's Theme and Variations and the *Rondes des Printemps* from Debussy's *Images.* John Farnsworth Hall introduced Arthur Bliss' Music for Strings, Walter Susskind offered Vaughan Williams' *A London Symphony*, and Goossens conducted three of Schoenberg's *Five Orchestral Pieces*, a set Goossens referred to as 'the Rosetta Stone of all atonal music'. Post and William James made sure that artists of the same quality as were heard in the adults' series performed in Youth Concerts, and although this was not always achievable the early Youth series featured such pianists as Richard Farrell, Moura Lympany and Paul Badura-Skoda; violinist Michael Rabin; and soprano Suzanne Danco. It was also an occasional forum for young Australian soloists, many of whom had been winners or finalists in the Concerto and Vocal Competition; and for soloists from the orchestra, including Neville Amadio, Cliff Goodchild, Robert Pikler, Ian Wilson (the SSO's principal oboe after Horace Green's departure) and John Robertson.

The SSO/Sydney love affair that made the Youth Concerts such a hit also gave the ABC box office major headaches. There simply were not enough SSO performances in the year to satisfy demand, and the free concerts the orchestra now gave regularly in the Town Hall often attracted more people than the hall could hold. In 1950 *Smith's Weekly* could write that

Australians are turning into lovers of high-class music so fast that if the trend of the past five years is maintained there won't be a genuine be-bop fan left in the Commonwealth within a generation, and the bobby-soxers will be yelling for Beethoven instead of the old Bing boy.

Subscription renewals were the most stressful time of year for Burnett and his staff, because there were always more potential new subscribers than there were spare seats, as Tom Mead explained in the *Daily Telegraph* in 1952:

Several couples have been 'estranged' at the concerts for two and three years, parting as they go in and meeting afterwards outside because their seats are on opposite sides of the Town Hall.

Others want separate seats because they have been divorced since they booked last year. 'I just couldn't bear having to sit alongside him', Mrs X will confide.

Tickets were left in wills, and it could be a major issue if a divorced wife kept a pair of concert tickets in her name. Angry calls to the box office from irate ex-husbands were not uncommon. The great demand for subscriptions was complicated by the fact that all tickets were written out by hand until 1952.

'You can imagine how wide the margin for error was in a system like that', says Alan Ziegler. 'A subscriber might get a Red I ticket instead of a Red II, or Body of the Hall F instead of Gallery F. The box office would stay open all weekend after the bookings had closed to clean up the mess. It really was all weekend, too, from early Saturday morning to early Sunday evening. You know, you would go through all the paperwork and realise that you'd put someone in on the wrong night, so you would have to ring them up and say, "Excuse me, but would you mind checking your tickets to see if they are indeed for Wednesday evening?" and so on. It was a silly system, but Eric Burnett had grown up with it and did not want anything different. I finally persuaded him that manual ticketing was not up to the demands of an ever-expanding concert season, and he agreed to have the tickets printed, for the first time, in 1953. We sailed through the processing that year.'

∗

Imperfect though they were, the workings of the concert-giving organisation Goossens met at the ABC were much more sophisticated than those which had greeted Szell, Schneevoigt and Co. And as each of the Goossens years passed Moses' belief in the prestige value of orchestral performance grew mightily, with the result that the ABC continued to become better at putting concerts on. In the late 1940s the ABC spent £220 000 on running the orchestras nationally. (There was also a subsidy of around £9000 which was used against box office losses.) This represented about one-fifth of the total ABC budget of the day, and it goes some way toward explaining how James was able to lure leading international artists here: he had a lot of money to spend relative to the ABC Concerts budget of 1992.

When it was set up in 1932 the Australian Broadcasting Commission had inherited William James from the Australian Broadcasting Company, so that a music department was virtually in place before the Commission had even gone to air. James' quietly efficient manner commanded much respect, and he came to wield a lot of power, as it was his department that worked with conductors, soloists and Keith Barry's Program Department on the music to be played in orchestral concerts.

But the Music Department did not actually put the concerts on. That was the job of the Concert Department, which was established in 1936 under one of the ABC's most talented administrators, Robert McCall. He was Federal Concert Manager for two years, and eventually became the ABC's assistant general manager before leaving Australia in 1946 for a long and distinguished career at the BBC.

McCall's successor was Roy Lamb, the second and last person to be Federal Concert Manager. He had the job from 1938 until his retirement in 1958, when Charles Buttrose took over and became Director of Publicity and Concerts. It was in Lamb's time that the Concert and Music departments developed such a low regard for one another. On the one hand, although he was a member of senior management, Lamb was paid a lower wage than any of his counterparts, and had a staff of two concert assistants to plan all the tours of every ABC artist (orchestral concerts and recitals) and every orchestral tour, nationally, and make sure that travel and accommodation were organised for each centre. On the other hand, the Music Department often thought of its colleagues in Concerts as mere clerks, with no musical brains.

While the federal concert office planned the tours, a concert manager in each State, and his concert officers, made all the hall bookings, organised the publicity, and looked after the artists. The NSW concert manager, and the SSO's principal contact within the Concert Department, was Eric Burnett. He was born Eric Burnett Moses, but Moses Charles thought it was too confusing that two people with such a distinctive surname should work in the same city for the same organisation. So Eric Burnett he became. True, his was not a great musical mind, but it did not have to be, since his job was not to conduct the concerts, but rather to make sure the concerts (and recitals) happened. Alan Ziegler came into Burnett's department as an ABC cadet in 1950, the year in which regional subscription series began. Until then the SSO's regional concerts had been the only ABC events in any given town, but now country people could subscribe to a number of different performances each year. Ziegler remembers the horrendous workload of his superiors:

'The country subscription series were usually a mixture of recitals and orchestral concerts. Let's say there was some advance work to do for a forthcoming recital in Horsham. During the time I worked for the concert department in Melbourne it was not unusual for a concert officer to get on the Overland at 8 p.m., and arrive at Horsham at one in the morning. You'd prepare for the Horsham recital then get an early train back to Melbourne, be in the office at nine and probably have a Town Hall concert that night. That was standard procedure. There was no paid overtime, and you were not encouraged to travel in ABC time. It was not until the 1960s that paid overtime became the norm.'

Lamb, Burnett and their Concert colleagues were constantly pushed by the sheer increase in orchestral and recital activity that occurred in all the years of the immediate post-war period. For example, the agreement with State and local funding authorities that had given the SSO permanence included clauses specifying more and bigger country tours. The 'old' SSO went to Newcastle twice a year (in most years) and had been to Katoomba, Bathurst, Wollongong and Canberra, but did not otherwise play in regional centres regularly. Just after the 'new' SSO was formed Keith Barry had a survey conducted throughout New South Wales to find out about the standard of facilities for orchestral performance in New South Wales country towns, and the orchestra soon began regular and extensive country tours. In 1949 alone the SSO gave schools concerts and evening performances in Canberra, Goulburn, Wagga, Albury, Young, Wollongong, Armidale, Tamworth,

Newcastle, Maitland, Orange, Bathurst, Lithgow, Murwillumbah,
Kempsey, Taree, Lismore and Grafton.

'This expanded country activity led to the creation of an assistant
concert manager position', recalls Rex Ellis, who was the first
person to take up the job, in 1951. 'In the 1950s the SSO gave
around twenty-four concerts a year in the country, and we shared
the organisation of the different regional centres up between a
small New South Wales concert staff. It was a lot of work.'

Larger audiences in the capital cities were leading to more
performances in the major venues, too. The number of ABC
concerts grew dramatically, and the SSO's ninety-four
performances of 1946 became 147 in 1951. The 1735 Sydney
subscribers of 1940 had become 13 531 by 1951, a year in which
there were more than 30 000 subscribers around the country.
The concert-giving mechanism had been forced to become more
complex as a result of this growth, but the programming and
planning power remained always in Sydney. In the years to come
this centralist form of control became more elaborately
bureaucratic, and stifled any attempt at regional autonomy. The
system was to grow more confusing and intractable as more of
the orchestras gained permanency. After Sydney, and based on
the model of the SSO's establishment, the orchestras of
Queensland, Tasmania, Victoria, South Australia and Western
Australia were enlarged under agreements with city councils and
State governments. By March 1951 all six orchestras were playing
as enlarged, full-time bodies.

In the meantime, as James had recommended, the SSO now
had an orchestra manager. The first of them was Ken Lawson.
He worked in the Music Department but, necessarily, *with* the
Concert Department, and as he was on a higher salary scale than
his Concert colleagues his relationship with them was not always
cordial. But he is a legend amongst the SSO players who worked
with him, and his brilliance as an organiser was very much part
and parcel of the Goossens era. Neville Amadio remembers:

'Ken Lawson was a genius, with a fantastic memory for detail
both financial and logistical. In fact, he knew the birthday of
every member of the orchestra, and he'd ring each of us up on
the right morning, too.' John Matthews: 'Ken was a fabulous
organiser. He knew the business side of everything, and maintained

Rex Ellis renames a train on an SSO country tour (top)

Humour in adversity: SSO members Eva Kelly, violin (standing), and Jessie Mankey, cello, entertain themselves and others on Central Station at the start of a country tour in October 1950 as their train is delayed by a rail strike. Neville Amadio (standing, centre) watches.

an enormous interest in the orchestra even though he did not have a musical background.'

Cliff Goodchild also remembers him with affection. 'He was the one who got me into the SSO. He was always on the lookout for players, and he heard me in the ABC Military Band at the time. He said to me "When are you going to quit playing *Alpine Echoes* and *Annie Get Your Gun* and play some real music?". That was in 1951. He cried when Goossens left.'

CHAPTER FIVE

Expansion and after

The relative financial comfort of the ABC Music Department just after the war gave the whole organisation more international musical clout than it has enjoyed since. And with a larger national audience feeding in more revenue than could have been imagined even in 1940, there was real impetus to expand the range and size of ABC concert activity.

As we have seen, this impetus manifested itself in the setting up of regional subscription series, the expansion of the SSO's Sydney performance schedule (which meant a concomitant drop in the time the orchestra spent playing for studio broadcasts) and a hugely increased number of guest conductors and soloists. The SSO now had large captive audiences aged anywhere from the ten-year-olds of the schools concerts to the veterans who had been subscribing since 1936. Often the most challenging things attracted full houses, such as Goossens' 1951 concert performances of *Salome* and *Elektra* with Marjorie Lawrence. Such works were absolute novelties at the time.

But the enormous growth in audience, activity and prestige the orchestra experienced in these years was obviously not going to last forever. The 1950s would bring the revelation of an Australian drama that touched a wide audience, in particular the breakthroughs of Ray Lawler's *Summer of the Seventeenth Doll* and Alan Seymour's *The One Day of the Year*; a revitalised Musica Viva which, after its reorganisation in 1954, began to operate as a full-time chamber music entrepreneur, offering a mixture of local and overseas groups; a reasonable stability for the national opera and ballet companies; and a more diverse and publicly recognised group of contemporary Australian artists. By the late 1950s there was, in Geoffrey Serle's phrase, 'a recognition that the arts *mattered*'.

This meant that the ABC began to taste some real competition, and therefore faced a new set of challenges. But by the end of the decade the ABC's Music and Concert divisions were not in a great shape to be challenged by the emergence of a marketplace for the arts. Significant management changes had taken place, and they ushered in an era characterised by too much self-satisfaction and too little thinking about how to reconcile the demands of new and changing audiences with the requirements of an organisation that, in part, still saw its orchestras as providers of broadcast material.

And while the orchestras received Moses' full support until his retirement in 1964, the business of music-making became outranked on the ABC's chain of being from 1956 when, coincidentally, Goossens left Australia and the ABC began television transmission. Television necessarily took up a lot of the ABC's time and energy, and quickly replaced concert-giving as the major recipient of ABC resources. As well, orchestral management soon realised that in Moses' successor, Talbot Duckmanton, the Commission had a leader avowedly disinterested in music. As we shall see, these were some of the factors that came to make the SSO an often stodgy participant in the new diversity of Sydney's arts activity in the 1960s and 1970s.

In the early 1950s, though, no one saw anything stodgy about the SSO. If anything, its performances seemed to offer some of the most sophisticated pleasures of Sydney life. Richard Bonynge remembers his experience of the concerts as a student, when he was studying in Goossens' diploma class at the Conservatorium. 'Goossens had really electrified the atmosphere, and we all felt that he was making marvellous things happen to Sydney's music. I mean, the SSO was a superb orchestra in the late forties. Goossens' whole manner—that slightly aloof glamour—had shaken us up, because Sydney was a bit of a country town at the time, and still fairly complacent. Well, Goossens hardly stood still for a minute and we were really in awe of him. And in opening up the orchestral repertoire as he did he introduced a lot of French music, which was really something for me, as you can imagine.'

It was an age of great soloists, one of whom was a young Viennese musician who made an impressive Sydney debut in 1952, on his first concert tour outside Europe: Paul Badura-Skoda.

'William James was on one of his regular European trips to discover young talent, and in every city he called on the leading music personalities to find out who was worth his attention', Badura-Skoda recalls. 'I met him in Vienna when I was twenty-three years old, and I played a special audition for him of the *Waldstein* sonata. He seemed to be very impressed, and he asked me to come to Australia. I brought Alan Rawsthorne's piano concerto with me on this first tour because I had the impression that Australia was then still quite British, and that the piece would be well received for this reason. In fact, Sydney did remind me then of a provincial English city like Liverpool or Birmingham.'

Our provincial Englishness was emphasised for Badura-Skoda by the need to play the National Anthem at the beginning of all his ABC performances, including recitals (this ruling held sway until 1974). He recalls an embarrassing incident.

'In one recital I forgot to play it—"God Save the King"—it was on my first tour, and I launched straight into a Mozart fantasy. I saw then that everyone was standing up, and I thought that the audience must have been very impressed with my playing to give me a standing ovation at the start of the recital.'

Among the parade of great guest conductors during the Goossens years, none made a greater impact than Otto Klemperer. Indeed, his four performances of Mahler's *Resurrection* symphony with the SSO have been described as some of the greatest orchestral concerts in Australian history. But he had already suffered with poor health by this time, an operation for a brain tumour in the 1930s leaving one side of his face permanently scarred. He was a strange and often difficult man to work with, as Bertha Jorgensen remembers:

'By the time the ABC toured Klemperer here in 1949—the first of his two tours—I was leading the MSO, or the Victorian Symphony as it temporarily became. I was told that one of the first things Klemperer had said to Bill James on arriving here

One of the greatest conductors to have worked with the SSO, Otto Klemperer was pressed into service for open air concerts. He is photographed here in Sydney's Botanic Gardens.

was something like: "I believe there is a woman leader in Melbourne. I have never had a woman leader and I don't intend to have one now." So I had been warned. Well, when he got to his first orchestral rehearsal he was introduced to all the other principals, who were all tallish men as it happened, and then he was introduced to me, and I'm about five foot nothing.

'He looked at me as if I was something you put your foot on, and he said, in front of the whole orchestra, "Where have you studied?". I said, as defiantly as I could, "Only in Australia". Then he said, "You have good ear? If you have a good ear it will be difficult."

'He was talking about Mahler 4, and the passage that calls for the leader to use two violins. Like most players in Australia at the time, I knew nothing about this piece, but he obviously liked my performance of it because we became quite friendly after that. In fact I think he was embarrassed by his initial attitude because he gave me a marcasite brooch when he left, "to remember me by". He was a real old devil, a wonderful personality. That Mahler 4 was my introduction to that repertoire, and I'll never forget those concerts. He was the greatest.'

Word had got out that Klemperer was something of a tyrant, and Neville Amadio remembers that the SSO was scared of him before he had even rehearsed them. Werner Baer was the ABC's Music Supervisor for NSW during the second Klemperer tour, and was asked to be his 'minder' while the conductor was in Sydney.

'Klemperer's English was not so good, so James asked me to go about with him. I also conducted some of the early choir rehearsals for the *Resurrection* symphony. He was my god, and I was very much in awe of him, but he did some frightful things while he was here. He was a very difficult man.'

Barry Tuckwell says that Klemperer could terrorise players with a word or a gesture. 'He was very tall—about six foot four [1.9 metres]—and very blunt. He used to walk around the orchestra during rehearsals to hear details he felt he might miss from the podium, and he once stood at the back desks of the second violins, watching the two women there coming to grips with a difficult part of the Mahler score. On seeing them struggling he suddenly thrust his hand at the music in front of them and bellowed "Play!" He really put the fear of God into them.

'He also became quite violent when he felt details were not falling into place as they should. The orchestra's harpist at the time was a very softly spoken woman called Elizabeth Vidler, and at an early rehearsal for this symphony she was accidentally given the second harp part instead of the first. During a play-through Klemperer stopped and told her she was phrasing a particular passage incorrectly. She was genuinely confused by this, because she thought she had the right part in front of her. Anyway, before she could say "But Maestro . . ." he had moved on to the next thing. At the rehearsal break she decided she was going to sort this out, so she took her music up to Klemperer, and said "You see, Maestro, in my part . . ." and he took the music from her, flung it away with great drama, and yelled "I do not understand!".'

The popular press loved Klemperer's ogre-like image, and in a particularly silly review of his Brahms 1 with the SSO, headlined '6ft. Conductor brings drama into Concert', the *Sunday Sun* referred to him as 'an intellectual Boris Karloff'. Lindsey Browne thought the concert in which the Brahms was given—Klemperer's first in Australia—offered music-making 'as profoundly musical and powerfully exciting as any that audiences have yet heard in Australia'. He wrote that:

The Brahms was played with astonishing breadth of vision and dramatic concentration: the force of its tragic ideas was communicated with a driving directness that shunned the plausible superficialities of swelling theatrical tragedy just as surely as it shunned monkish humilities and dull ashen melancholy.

Humility was certainly not one of Klemperer's abiding traits. As Neville Amadio recalls, 'I was in the conductor's room when Ken Lawson and Klemperer were having an argument about Brahms 4. Ken was trying to explain to Klemperer that this symphony had been broadcast from Brisbane the week before with another conductor, and that as the ABC was also going to broadcast Klemperer's next concert, he could not have Brahms 4 in that program, as much as Ken respected Klemperer's wish to do so. Klemperer listened to this then took a revolver out of his briefcase and put it on the table. He said, "No matter about Brisbane, I *will* conduct it". That was the end of that discussion!'.

Clarrie Mellor also remembers Klemperer brandishing his gun

at William James to get an extra rehearsal out of a reluctant SSO, asking rhetorically, 'Do you think this will persuade them?'.

Although one women's magazine called a Klemperer profile 'His Glare is not meant to Scare you' it did scare quite a few people, including Ray Price, the jazzman who was then playing double bass in the SSO. Nadine Amadio, who was married to Price at the time, says that he fell asleep during one of Klemperer's rehearsals, 'in one of his thousand-bar rests, I think, and Klemperer cast a very disapproving eye over him. After the rehearsal break, Ray, who was very short, was coming up the stairs, and suddenly saw Klemperer, who was immensely tall, coming down. Ray was petrified and didn't know what to do, so he saluted Klemperer, who was so amazed he burst out laughing.'

He was not always terrifying, and at times could relieve tension with surprising grace and good humour. In *Facing the Music*, Helen Bainton recalled that at one Kings Cross rehearsal someone began hammering persistently and audibly in the building next door to the studio. This was obviously interfering with Klemperer's concentration. After the hammering had gone on for an apparent eternity, Klemperer said to the violins, 'Don't play so loudly, I can't hear the hammering!'.

'The first of Schwarzkopf's Sydney concerts with Klemperer was a good example of his strange manner', says Peter Sainthill. 'She preceded him onto the stage, wearing an incredible off-the-shoulder blue frock. She went into a deep, slow curtsey to the audience and as she rose Klemperer gripped her by the shoulders and put her in her place very firmly, as if to say "That's where you are to stand, I'm the boss". He found it difficult to forgive her for staying in Germany during the war.' Klemperer had been forced to leave Germany for the United States in 1933 when, as a Jew, his contract with the Berlin State Opera was cancelled.

For all his eccentricities, there was no denying the brilliance of his best performances, which in Sydney included a Bruckner 7 (September 1949) described as 'truly magnificent and deeply moving' by Wolfgang Wagner, and a Brahms 4 (August 1950) which, in the words of Lindsey Browne, 'comprehended fully the immense and patient tragedy of the work, and the stateliness of its monumental design'.

But the concerts that live most vividly in the memory of Sydney

The SSO in the Botanic Gardens, conducted by Klemperer in September 1950.

people who went to Klemperer's SSO performances are those that took place on 19, 20, 23 and 25 September 1950 in which he conducted Mahler's *Resurrection* symphony, with soloists Valda Bagnall and Florence Taylor, and the Hurlstone Choral Society. Helen Bainton has described these concerts as 'one of those rare experiences when the players transcend all earthbound thoughts and reach a level of performance quite beyond their normal powers'. Linda Vogt says that 'when it was all over you did not remember being an individual playing in it. You were so inspired during the performance'.

Lindsey Browne wrote simply that the 19 September performance was 'the experience of a lifetime—a wholly wonderful pilgrimage through the teeming imagery and demon lore, and fevered romantic tragedy of a composer who, of all, is music's most nervously convulsed intellect'. The *Daily Mirror's* response was more earthbound: 'One found it difficult to believe that this was the same orchestra one has heard under lesser conductors'.

The Saturday night performance was one of the first concerts in the SSO's history where the audience would not let the players or the conductor go. There were many people in the hall who had heard Klemperer's performances in the vanished Europe of the 1920s and 1930s, and his appearances here brought back for them what must have been emotionally charged memories. On that Saturday night in 1950 he was recalled time after time, long after the house lights had gone up. Finally, he appeared on the stage in his street clothes—overcoat and hat—silenced the applause, and yelled out commandingly 'Go home!'.

The number of SSO performances from this period that survive on disc or tape is scandalously small, but a surprisingly good copy of that 1950 *Resurrection* Symphony exists due to the fact that special discs were pressed of it for presentation to Klemperer. Most ABC 'house' records of the period were made of a soft material called acetate. Such discs were made for regional radio stations that did not regularly receive live concert broadcasts. After about five playings the acetate had usually worn through. But these Klemperer discs were given to Columbia for pressing on vinyl and, luckily, multiple copies were made.

'Even though only one of the four concerts was broadcast, the ABC and the PMG recorded all four performances of the work.

Klemperer then listened through each one, and chose which movements from which nights would go onto those records', Neville Amadio recalls. 'So the discs actually represent several evenings' playing.'

The performance that survives on these records is pretty remarkable. It is not surprising to find that it contains some glaring technical errors and slips in ensemble. In 1950 few orchestras in the world were familiar with this music, and the SSO had never performed the work before. Yet they play assuredly and often magnificently, despite what would now be regarded as some hectoring tempi on Klemperer's part. The soloists sing their music vividly and intensely.

'I might have missed out on playing under Klemperer but I used to feel that his influence had stayed around for years', says Ron Cragg. 'During rehearsals of pieces he had conducted here some players would say, "remember how Klemperer used to do this?" He was burned into their memories.'

The Sydney debut of another great guest conductor in these years was burned into the memory of the SSO, too, but not entirely for musical reasons. Although the orchestra enjoyed working with Sir John Barbirolli on his two visits here (1950 and 1955), his name will always be associated in Sydney with an incident that has come to be known as The Night They Stole the Music.

Barbirolli's debut concert in Sydney took place on 28 December, 1950, and was to have comprised Rossini's overture *The Thieving Magpie* (oh exquisite irony!), Sibelius' *The Swan of Tuonela*, Vaughan Williams' sixth symphony and Brahms' second. The scores had been left on their music stands in the Town Hall after the morning rehearsal, but when Harold Welford, the music librarian, arrived at 7 pm, all the music had gone. The ABC staff present started searching the Town Hall, but none of the parts could be found anywhere. The police were called in. At 7.45 Moses, Goossens, Barbirolli, SSO section leaders and broadcast technicians met and decided to find out if there were duplicate sets of parts in the Conservatorium library for any of the works programmed. The orchestral cellist Cedric Ashton bashfully admitted that he knew a way of getting into the Conservatorium after hours by sliding up a side gate.

Welford, Goossens, Llewellyn, Ashton, Robert Miller and horn

ABOVE: Two of the ABC's starry guests of the immediate post-war years, Ginette Neveu (left) and pianist Moura Lympany.

TOP LEFT: Goossens and Barbirolli photographed in Sydney in 1955.

Sir John Barbirolli in action during his first Australian tour.

player Claude Katz then sped to the Conservatorium. Ashton later recalled that this was the only occasion on which he ever heard Goossens, usually the most refined of men, swear. Llewellyn was driving at high speed, and caused Goossens to utter 'Jeesus Christ!' when he narrowly missed an old lady who was trying to cross Park Street.

Once at the Conservatorium, Ashton broke in as promised and let the others in through the main door. Inside the library they found a full set of parts for Brahms 2 and then began looking for anything that might be suitable for performance without rehearsal. The rapid-fire repartee went something like this: 'Put it in.' 'It's unrehearsed.' 'Leave it out.' 'Get the *Oberon* overture. We can play that backwards. Get something we know.' 'What have you got there?' 'The *Oberon* overture.' 'Excellent. Bring it.' Eventually the librarians-for-a-night settled on the prelude to Wagner's *The Mastersingers of Nuremburg*.

Meanwhile at the Town Hall the eight o'clock starting time had come and gone, and the natives—sitting in the sticky warmth of a Sydney summer night—were getting restless. Moses decided that something had to be said which would sound tactful and plausible, and would not cause the entire house to run in fury to the box office demanding its money back. He wrote a statement that he wanted read out from the concert platform, and chose announcer Bruce Webber to do the deed. (Webber was scheduled to introduce the concert live on ABC radio.) It was with some trepidation that he approached the microphone on the Town Hall platform.

'Ladies and gentlemen, it is with great regret that we have to announce that an irresponsible person has removed all the music for tonight's concert from the stands. It is possible that we may be able to find a duplicate set of parts for the Brahms symphony and also parts for the *Mastersingers* prelude. Sir John Barbirolli is anxious to conduct these works rather than disappoint you.' This announcement was greeted with a mixture of laughter and applause.

The Conservatorium contingent finally reappeared, and Barbirolli walked to the podium at nine o'clock to conduct the Wagner prelude and the Brahms symphony. The orchestra played with enormous energy for the next hour, and received rapt applause from the audience and many compliments from Barbirolli on their unrehearsed Wagner.

At eleven o'clock that same evening a *Daily Telegraph* reporter received an anonymous phone call from a man who explained that the missing parts could be found in the Department of Health building, which at the time was about ten metres from the stage door. And there they were. When he was asked why he had stolen the scores, the man replied, 'I wanted to make John Barbirolli's first concert in Australia truly memorable. I am a fan of his'. He was never caught.

The music for Barbirolli's next concerts stayed on the music stands, and included the second suite from Roussel's ballet *Bacchus and Ariadne*, receiving its first Australian performance, and Elgar's second symphony. Martin Long wrote of the Elgar in the *Sydney Morning Herald* that

it was astonishing to hear so big and complex a work handled with such microscopic subtlety of detail without any loss in the essential spirit and design . . . The response of the orchestra to the conductor's meticulous demands was triumphant. The strings of the orchestra have not achieved a finer pianissimo than they have found in these [Barbirolli] concerts.

Amazingly, the concert in which the Elgar was performed also featured the first Australian performance of Haydn's Symphony No 83.

Barbirolli's three SSO concerts were given as a special summer series, and such events became a regular part of the musical year in the 1940s and 1950s. Brahms festivals under Heinze, a Beethoven festival under Kurt Woess, a British Music festival under Code and Bainton—they were all great box office successes. But one of these was also controversial, and gave its organiser, Heinze, more to think about than he had bargained for: the 1952 Festival of Contemporary Music, held in the main hall of the Conservatorium.

The festival was controversial for several reasons. First, the programs were either cautious or eccentric. In none of the four concerts was there a note of Stravinsky, Prokofiev (then still living) or Martinu, and no American music was played. Some critics were also puzzled by the inclusion of such works as Schoenberg's

Transfigured Night (1899) and Rachmaninov's *The Isle of the Dead* (1907)[1] when there was nothing of late Sibelius or Ravel programmed.

Lindsey Browne believed that the ABC had been 'too wary for its own good. Because of Goossens' liberal but by no means revolutionary policy as an eclectic program-maker, hardly an item in the festival would be considered daring, or even out of place, in the orchestra's regular concert series'. Perhaps Heinze's bravest act was giving the first Australian performance of Schoenberg's *Ode to Napoleon* during the festival.

It was very un-brave, though, to include not one note of new Australian music. The only Australian piece in the Festival was octogenarian Alfred Hill's *Green Water*. As Max Keogh noted in *Tempo* magazine:

I suppose this surprised Mr Hill as much as anyone else. For his music is neither modern nor contemporary: he himself would not claim that it is . . . a lot of music has passed under the bridge since Mr Hill's style was modern.

The ABC has no interest in the Australian composer, unless he be the manufacturer of ballads, bush songs or 'pop' numbers. And the Commission cannot bring forward recent competitions for composers as defence, for it is little use feeding our composers an annual goblet of burgundy if their regular diet be buckets of brine.

(Indeed, works written for such competitions never seem to have had any sort of life in the Australian orchestral repertoire, probably because, in Lindsey Browne's words, such works have a 'cautious eclecticism—the desire to back the greatest possible number of safe stylistic horses—that inevitably associates itself with composers' competitions'.)

Another question asked of the Festival of Contemporary Music was why, with so much new music yet to be played in Sydney, each concert ended with a baroque or classical work. One program finished with the Khachaturian piano concerto, followed by the third of Bach's *Brandenburg* concertos. On the one hand, the *Bulletin* described the tactic as one akin to seeing 'Professor

---

[1] Although it may be hard to believe, this was the occasion of the first performance of the Rachmaninov work in Australia.

Einstein consorting with bodgies in a fun parlour'. On the other, many people felt it reinforced the timidity of the whole exercise. The *Telegraph* said that the programs had been 'well designed to save listeners any touch of mental indigestion'.

It is easy to be smug about these concerts, for they do now seem to be coy and unduly selective in their approach to 'contemporary' music, but they were the first instance of an SSO series based on the premise that the bulk of the music to be played in it would be new. The vigour of the debate that surrounded the Festival says much for the changes that had occurred in Australian musical culture since the war. As Eunice Gardiner wrote in the *Telegraph*: 'It isn't many years since such programs would have been given to a near-empty hall, [but] audiences have overflowed the Conservatorium into the surrounding gardens, where they have heard the music through loud-speakers'.

※

Despite Goossens' reluctance to share the SSO with many other conductors, it was not physically possible for him to conduct even half of the orchestra's concerts. By 1953 they were giving 148 performances a year, or on average one concert every three days of the year. This huge increase in activity from the pre-war years introduced the SSO to a lot of conductors, with some of whom the orchestra would form lasting relationships.

One of the most enduring partnerships was with the Czech conductor Walter Susskind, who first appeared with them in 1946 and made his final tour in 1974, the year of his death. He was also, briefly, the MSO's chief conductor in the 1950s. A talented and versatile musician, Susskind was one of the first people to appear with the SSO conducting from the keyboard (in Mozart's D minor concerto, in 1953).

Juan José Castro was another notable figure of the period. A conductor and composer, he was a naturally shy man and a most underrated figure in our musical history. Lindsey Browne thought Castro's SSO concerts of 1953 provided some of the best music-making of the year, including 'some quite unforgettable Mozart performances'. In *Tempo* magazine, Max Keogh called him 'an original, vital intelligence'. His piano concerto was played with enormous success in Sydney by Hepzibah Menuhin. Castro too became chief conductor of the MSO, in 1952, but the Melbourne orchestra was chewing up its chief conductors quickly at this time in its history, and Castro was gone, from Melbourne and from Australia, by 1955. In the words of the Melbourne *Herald's* John Sinclair: 'He was a better conductor than we deserved—unpretentious, genuinely modest and a colossal musician'.

Another short-lived Melbourne chief who gave Sydney concerts was Alceo Galliera. Kenneth Hince has described him as 'brusque, authoritarian and fiery', and although he struck some exciting chemistry with the MSO, the Sydney orchestra never seemed to play at their best for him. As well, his conservative musical tastes brought out a smug streak in Goossens-mad Sydney. As one critic wrote, 'I prefer not to rush to any conclusions now about Signor Galliera's considerable abilities until we hear him under more favourable circumstances, and in programs that are less hackneyed. If he had studied Goossens' programs he would have realised that we are used to slightly more interesting fare'.

Galliera's quick temper and uneven grasp of English did not always endear him to players. During one rehearsal he shouted 'Basta!' to bass trombone player William Waterer, meaning, in this case, that Waterer was playing in the wrong place. Those around the trombone section then heard 'No one's going to call me "bastard"!' and, Barry Tuckwell recalls, Waterer had to be physically restrained from marching straight to the podium and knocking the maestro over.

Eva Kelly: 'This was a time when individual players could be monstered during rehearsals, and Galliera often just stared along the line of violins if the intonation was bad. Then he would point and say "You, play that!".'

And then there was Heinze. He had a difficult enough time of it with the Sydney orchestra, but it was also hard for him to get a good review out of Lindsey Browne. About a Heinze performance (1955) of Berlioz's *Symphonie fantastique*, Browne wrote that 'the witches' sabbath was, in places, suspiciously like a Melbourne Sunday'. Nor did he think much of a Heinze concert of Beethoven symphonies 1 and 9 given in 1950:

The performances under Heinze's energetic and complaisant leadership quite blunted the astonishing musical and ideological contrast between these works. A rather heavy, unspringy treatment of the first and a lack of real depth and of ranging imaginative vitality and will in the ninth naturally tended to shrink the gap that separates these symphonies.

Although the relationship between Heinze and the SSO was never honestly friendly, there were a number of conductors the SSO found it hard to get along with at all. One of these was the Hungarian Tibor Paul, who appeared with the orchestra through the 1950s and 1960s. 'He had a fine memory and could be a good conductor, but he was a martinet', Clarrie Mellor recalls. 'One day Robert Pikler told him, in front of the orchestra, that we would not play for him. unless his attitude changed.' Werner Baer is less circumspect: 'Paul was a fascist, a dictatorial bastard. The players rightly named him Two Bar Paul, because he stopped so often in rehearsal.'

A conductor the orchestra saw a lot of in the mid-1950s was the Austrian Kurt Woess, who became another short-lived chief conductor in Melbourne. Clarrie Mellor: 'We used to call him the storm trooper. If you got on the wrong side of him he was a horror.' Only a few players have positive memories of him and John Matthews says simply, 'as far as he was concerned things went from Woess to Woess'. Of one Woess/SSO concert, Eunice Gardiner wrote that it was 'mediocre in every way, [and] one of the lowest points in some seasons'. Several Lindsey Browne Specials were aimed in Woess' direction too, the following, from 1956, being perhaps the most pointed: 'It was not an interesting concert...Harems full and bulging of 20-stone beauties were amply suggested by the inexcusably coarse and heavy account of Mozart's *Seraglio* overture'.

The performance of Beethoven 5 in the same concert caused the *Sun's* Julian Russell to remark that 'the finale sounded as if it was being used as an accompaniment to pursuit in an old silent film'. The only remotely friendly Sydney remark this writer could find about the conductor was a limerick printed in the *Sun-Herald* under the headline 'Pronounced *Vurse*':

An orchestral conductor named Woess
Went riding one day on a hoess
When he saw that the driver
Was Lady Godiva
He said, 'Well it might have been Woess!"

Among the many soloists who made ABC tours during the Goossens period, some were outstanding, some were merely good, and at least one was downright embarrassing. The tenor Gino Mattera was recommendable to audiences chiefly because of his good looks, which might be described as 'Italian matinee idol'. Lindsey Browne thought his singing 'sloppy, undisciplined and naive' while Julian Russell wrote (under the misleading headline 'Tenor's manner pleases') that he was 'not nearly so easy on the ear as he [was] on the eye. Throughout his performance he used his hands, arms and eyes much more effectively than he did his voice'. Mattera so disliked the reviews of his performances here that he refused to finish his tour. He was not invited back.

Hans Schmidt-Isserstedt, like Klemperer, came here at a time when the uncertainties of European life were creating a lacuna in his career. It was only a few years before his first ABC tour of 1953 that auditions for his Hamburg radio orchestra had to be held in barracks, schools, and even in the open-air, as so many of the city's buildings had been destroyed during the war. His first Sydney concerts were a great success, with Lindsey Browne praising particularly his reading of Mozart's *Prague* symphony:

This was a vintage performance, warm in affection and laughter, long in pedigree, uncommonly gracious in design. It was drawn, as it needed to be, on small and elegant lines, yet without fussy miniaturishness, and without any caricaturist's supposition that Mozart is a kind of fancy-dress ball where 'chic' period characters never stop flirting fans or taking snuff. The life of this playing was deep and intense; there was no room for pretences.

But Schmidt-Isserstedt really raised the roof on his second tour in 1956, when he gave the first Australian performance of Orff's *Carmina Burana*. The *Mirror* described the audience response as 'tumultuous', and the *Sun* rather patronisingly remarked that 'Orff's music, though truly contemporary in spirit and technique, is simple enough to be enjoyed without pondering at a first performance'.

For all its success, Schmidt-Isserstedt felt that the women of the Hurlstone Choral Society did not get into the spirit of the work's fleshy ribaldry. Werner Baer conducted some of the early choral rehearsals, and Schmidt-Isserstedt told him: 'These women in their white frocks, they have never been with a man in their lives. They have no idea what this is all about'.

A permanent souvenir of Schmidt-Isserstedt's SSO concerts is a disc of Haydn's *Oxford* symphony, recorded at a live performance given during subscription concerts in 1953.

Perhaps the most controversial guest artist in the early 1950s was the American pianist William Kapell. He had performed here, to great acclaim, in 1945, when he was still a discovery. By the time of his second tour in 1953, when he was thirty-one, he was widely considered one of the finest young pianists in the world. Around this time he recorded some of Chopin's piano music— a collection of mazurkas and the third sonata—with such command that they are still regarded as some of the most stimulating recorded performances of the repertoire.

Between 1945 and 1953 the ABC brought to Australia such pianists as Solomon, Claudio Arrau, Lili Kraus, Moura Lympany, Witold Malcużyński, Eileen Joyce (her second tour), Noel Mewton-Wood, Richard Farrell, Pnina Salzman, Paul Badura-Skoda, Louis Kentner and Walter Gieseking. Hephzibah Menuhin lived in Melbourne and gave regular public performances, and such important Australian pianists as Muriel Cohen and Isador Goodman were active, too. So by the time of Kapell's 1953 ABC tour Sydney audiences and critics had heard a lot of great piano playing. Yet the notices he received from Sydney critics—great praise tempered with some reservations about coolness of style—made him howl.

In writing of the success of Kapell's performance of Schubert's A major sonata, Lindsey Browne described it as 'an outstanding success, in [a work] one would have thought less suited to the rather hard-edged, black-and-white style he revealed at his first recital. Kapell commanded attention . . . with the breadth of his design and the surprising warmth of his sympathy'. In the *Telegraph*, John Moses wrote: 'Kapell's way of looking at music as a problem in patterns of dynamics, phrasing, and the construction of a work's sentences and paragraphs was eminently suited to the dry brilliance of Prokofiev's seventh sonata'.

Kapell was furious at such notices, and told the *Telegraph* that Australian critics were ignorant and self-serving. Browne's reviews, in particular, were in the main 'uninformed, false and malicious . . . They say my Schubert sonata had "surprising warmth". Why surprising? It doesn't surprise me'. He vowed that when he left Australia 'it will be goodbye forever. I shall never return'.

The *Sydney Morning Herald*'s response to this broadside was one of the most mature statements about Australian culture yet printed in a newspaper. An editorial published on the day of Kapell's departure said, in part: 'It is hard to resist the conclusion that Mr Kapell and some other artists come to Australia in the mistaken belief that they are conferring great honour on the rude colonials whose duty is to be grateful and applaud . . . In a homely phrase, we are not so green as we are cabbage-looking'.

Kapell had left Australia on a DC6 airliner, headed for San Francisco. Near the end of its journey, the plane crashed and burned on a mountain, killing nineteen people, including Kapell. His final concert in Australia, a recital in Geelong, had included Chopin's 'Funeral March' sonata.

❧

The tragedy of Kapell's death, and the rancour that preceded it, was a bittersweet episode in the death of the cultural cringe. It is an illustration of how far we had come since Beecham had put on his 'illiterate, unpleasant and even vicious' act for us thirteen years beforehand, when we kicked and screamed in an appropriately crude and insular manner.

But how much of the cringe was there in the very system that had brought Kapell here? The ABC was not giving resident Australian artists much exposure in mainstream subscription series, and it was still using the term 'Celebrity Concert' for performances featuring an overseas soloist or conductor. The young performing talent brought to light by the Instrumental and Vocal Competition and in ABC radio's 'Young Australia' program was rarely nurtured beyond the 'discovery' stage. Young conductors were even less encouraged. The 'big bow-wow effect' was part of the system. Roger Covell wrote in 1963 that, 'as the arbiter of orchestral destinies in this country, the ABC must accept blame for its lack of foresight in not taking much more active steps to encourage and develop new conductors in Australia itself'. By the mid-1950s Heinze, Post and Clive Douglas were about the only three home-grown conductors working regularly with the orchestras, and chief conductor posts in smaller States always went to foreign-born conductors, as with Henri Krips in Adelaide.

In a 1953 article summarising the state of music in Australia, the British critic Arthur Jacobs noted that too many types of musical performance—opera and chamber music particularly— were underdeveloped, and that the ABC 'might have pushed too far the cult of the symphony orchestra'. Now a kind of musical monolith, the ABC was of course an easy target for criticism, partly because its well-controlled, broadcast-connected concert-giving mechanism was so successful. Writing about the ABC's twenty-first birthday in 1953, Martin Long thought this success was part of the problem:

The ABC has laid such stress on big orchestral music and on big names that, probably unconsciously, it has created the attitude that nothing that happens outside the big concert halls is musically 'the thing'. [It is time] for the ABC to turn to those less spectacular aspects of music which many regard as indicative of artistic maturity.

Was the ABC interested only in the glamorous end of concert life? Did it intend taking Australian music seriously? Serious long-term answers to questions of this kind would have demanded of the ABC's concert-giving managements an energy that was already beginning to fade. The brand of success Martin Long wrote about would soon turn into a slow, sinking complacency, so that much of the criticism of the 1950s would only be addressed as audiences began falling away in the 1960s. This is one of the reasons why the thinking of the ABC's music and concert managements in this period has been called middle aged. Another powerful reason, though, is the way in which the Commission responded to Goossens' run-in with the Vice Squad in 1956.

≈

It is now hard to understand why a conductor who had so dramatically altered the destiny of one of Australia's great musical organisations should have been hounded out of the country so ruthlessly and with so much self-satisfaction. One moment he was the great Sir Eugene (he was knighted, to much acclaim from the Australian press, in 1955). The next the scenario had changed utterly. It was not unlike the disappearance of Leon Trotsky from official Soviet photographs: perhaps he was not important, or maybe he did not exist at all. For all Australia's sudden, recent interest in the new diversity of culture there still lingered 'the conscience of the wowser', as Donald Horne has put it. Dame Edna Everage was not far off the mark when recently she recalled the 1950s in Australia as being characterised, not by rock and roll or beat poetry, but by the wooden salad bowl and original cast recordings of *My Fair Lady* and *South Pacific*.

The facts of the matter are plain enough. On 9 March 1956, Goossens arrived back in Australia by plane from five months' work in Europe. At the bottom of the aircraft's stairway he was greeted by two Vice Squad detectives who walked with him through Customs and took him into a nearby room. There, Goossens was asked to open his bags, and it was found that they contained 1166 obscene items—films, photographs, masks and books. These were immediately confiscated, and Goossens was taken to CIB headquarters for questioning. These incidents hit newspaper headlines that afternoon.

Within days, Goossens had conferred with ABC Chairman Sir Richard Boyer; the Minister for Education, R.J. Heffron; and representatives of the Public Service Board and the Sydney City Council. He then resigned from the Conservatorium and the SSO, and a public welcome organised by the SSO subscribers' committee was cancelled. Goossens was too ill to appear in court but pleaded guilty to importing prohibited goods. Charles Moses appeared as a character witness. It was during this hearing that Goossens' barrister, J.W. Shand, spoke of threats and menaces, and the possibility that 'those really responsible for these most pornographic exhibits coming to Australia are persons who . . . feel that the name of the person in the position of the defendant would not receive the keenest scrutiny, [otherwise] this was constituted as an attempt to destroy a world figure'. These other parties were never mentioned again publicly.

The day after the court case, the Vice Squad revealed that Goossens had been under investigation for six months.

The ABC commissioners officially accepted Goossens' resignation on 11 April, and ruled that, if any public farewell were organised for him, the ABC would take no part in it.[2] Then, at the end of May, Goossens left Sydney for good, on a KLM flight under the pseudonym of E. Gray. He had tried to slip out quietly, but the press were there. He issued a statement through his solicitor in which he said: 'It is my misfortune that I allowed myself to be used to bring prohibited matter into this country as a result of persistent menaces I could not ignore involving others'.

It is a depressing tale, and made more so by the number of loose ends. On what information was the Vice Squad acting that Goossens was met by them at the airport? Why were the commissioners so keen to distance themselves from him? What became of Shand's veiled threat to expose people who had threatened Goossens? Why was no investigation undertaken into Goossens' own remarks about 'persistent menaces'?

It is these loose ends that have led to the mountain of speculation about how and why Goossens was arrested. Opinion has ranged from theories that the conductor was simply being careless about his private affairs to allegations about his involvement in a national security scandal. To make sense of these conflicting scenarios we need to go back one step further and look briefly at aspects of his personality, his chief conductorship and his running of the Conservatorium.

One thing Goossens was never afraid to do, albeit in a gentlemanly manner, was kick heads. He felt he had been brought here with a clear mandate to improve standards, and this meant to him weeding out poor players from the SSO and failing poor students from the Conservatorium. Helen Bainton wrote of Goossens' dismissal methods:

'He used to write a letter thanking the person in question for his work over the years; this would be followed by an official document informing him his services were no longer required.' In 1947, Goossens inherited an orchestra that was essentially a war-time one, and it had many more women in it than he was used to. Cellist Colleen McMeekan remembers:

'He had a purge of the women in the orchestra through 1948,

---

[2] These were largely the same commissioners who had in 1952 banned from broadcast four songs from Cole Porter's *Kiss me Kate* on the grounds that they were 'objectionable'.

which I did not survive. He thought this was the way to begin rebuilding the orchestra after the war had brought so many more women into it.' About fifteen women were left afterwards, from a 1947 total of thirty-two.

Goossens undertook a purge of another kind at the Conservatorium. Richard Bonynge: 'He lifted standards there enormously in the time I was there, and I believe he turned it into a world-class institution. He was a real shock to the place after the relatively easy reign of Bainton, because for the first couple of years of his directorship Goossens failed almost everyone in the diploma course. In 1950 I was the only person to pass. I took my scholarship to the Royal College of Music, and I can tell you standards there were much lower then than they were in Sydney. This was all Goossens' doing. He attracted better instrumental teachers and opened our ears up to new repertoire. I played a lot of Debussy and Ravel piano music at his suggestion, at a time when the chamber music course the Conservatorium offered was terribly restricted. I remember doing Haydn in first year, Mozart in second year and Mendelssohn and Beethoven in third year. I don't remember ever being given a twentieth-century chamber work as an official part of my study.'

One of Goossens' innovations at the Conservatorium was to widen dramatically the scope of the repertoire the Conservtorium's opera school performed. Under his direction performances were given of such works as *Pelléas et Mélisande, Boris Godunov, Die Walküre, Falstaff,* Charpentier's *Louise* and (with the young Joan Sutherland in the lead) his own opera *Judith.* By his own admission these productions, 'while serving the dual purpose of instruction and entertainment, do not lay claim (because of limitations of stage space and available talent) to Metropolitan, Paris Opera, Covent Garden and Berlin Opera House standards . . . but . . . three-quarters of a fresh loaf in Sydney's empty operatic larder is better than no bread at all'.[3]

The Conservatorium operas were terrific training ground for the young singers and instrumentalists who took part in them, but many people privately criticised Goossens' policy of augmenting

---

[3] This was in 1950, a year before the first Sydney season given by Clarice Lorenz's National Opera of Australia.

the cast and orchestra with professional musicians (including SSO players) to make the productions appear better than they otherwise might have been.

There was also some ill-feeling within the Conservatorium when Goossens disbanded some of the institution's performance groups—choirs and chamber music ensembles—because he felt they did not reach a high enough standard. Ken Tribe:

'The standard of training at the Conservatorium before the war was very uneven, and Bainton certainly began to improve the quality of the teaching staff. But Goossens got us used to the idea that the second-rate was not acceptable, and I remember that when he wound up the Conservatorium choir a lot of people were very angry, but he was right in a way because it was not of a standard. Similarly, the Hurlstone Choral Society was trained at the time by a man called Albert Keats, and Goossens would not accept the work he'd done on Beethoven's *Missa Solemnis*, so the performance had to be held over to the following year. Once the war was over there were more records available here, too, and this also helped us get a feeling for the international standard.'

Goossens' available time did not always stretch as far as the Conservatorium's senior staff would have liked. That he could not keep his hand in everything with equal success was illustrated in his 1951 SSO performances of Mahler's massive eighth symphony, which he undertook very much in reply to the overwhelming success of Klemperer's Mahler 2 the previous year. Where the orchestra and soloists shone, it would seem that the choirs let the side down badly. Wolfgang Wagner wrote of the 'artistic gap between orchestra and the main body of the two choirs'. Lindsey Browne's review also heaped most of its praise on the orchestral playing:

It was often brilliant, always resourceful and vital, [and] provided the one strong, dependable thread through a performance of many aberrations, many doubts, many bad guesses, many loose ends. [But] if the adult choirs in these performances cannot behave more artistically than this after many months of preparation under their own leaders, then there is something drastically wrong with the choirs or the leadership.

Similar problems affected Goossens' own massive choral work, *The Apocalypse*, which was given its world premiere by the SSO and various Sydney choirs in 1954. And while there was general agreement that Mahler 8 was worth doing (and it was a completely unfamiliar score in Sydney at the time) *The Apocalypse* met with a mixed reception. The sheer size of the work, and its many special effects (including speakers installed in the Town Hall ceiling for the Voice of God) were impressive, and the first night audience responded enthusiastically, but it was too uneven to warrant the critical hosannas Goossens had expected. This was the most spectacular of his own works that he had conducted in Sydney—he had previously given his two symphonies, his oboe concerto (with his brother Leon the soloist) and other shorter pieces, but he did not make a fuss about them. Indeed, for all his very public achievements, Goossens generally went out of his way to play down his work as a composer. He was a naturally shy man, and somewhat distant. 'He was very nice to us, but about five levels above us, too', Richard Bonynge says. 'For me he was like a god, partly I suppose because he was so dignified and aloof.'

'There was not much warmth from him', Bertha Jorgensen recalls of his concerts with the MSO. 'He would say to the strings 'warm it up', and I used to think to myself, 'Well, why don't you do something about it?' It was this quality that led some SSO players to refer to him as 'that stately bag of bullshit' as he strode imposingly into the Town Hall in his big overcoat.

'He had an aura, there is no question', says his friend of many years Gretel Feher. 'I recall my husband and I driving back from the country with him, and Gene decided to buy some fruit from a stall by the side of the road. So he got out of the car and came back with the things he'd bought. Then I went to buy something, and the woman behind the counter leaned over to me and asked "Who was that great man?". She had no idea who he was, but she felt that presence and wanted me to explain it for her.'

John Matthews: 'He was a most fastidious man. He would not let anyone see him at interval because he did a complete change of clothing and wiped himself down with eau-de-Cologne. He would be wringing wet at the end of the first half of a concert, but would return to the podium always looking absolutely immaculate. The same routine at the end of a concert—he always wanted ten minutes to change into street clothes before greeting anyone.'

Maintaining formality: Goossens at Bondi Beach in the 1950s.

A rare informal snap of Goossens and his wife relaxing at Palm Beach.

Goossens had moved to Australia with his third wife Marjorie and his daughters (her stepdaughters) Sidonie and Renee. Marjorie was a very glamorous American who proved to be a real social asset and something of a fashion plate. Some twenty years younger than her husband, she eased Goossens' settling-in enormously.

'I think at the beginning Father felt very strange culturally and climatically in Sydney, and Stepmother, who was very beautiful and a real socialite, was a great help in creating friendships for them both', Renee says. 'Father's aloofness extended to his children as well, and it was very much a privilege to spend time with him, very much like a Victorian household. We were to be seen and not heard. He never hugged us, for it was not done. He was very correct and had beautiful manners. Father was there to be respected and obeyed. He was also quite naive and absent-minded in some ways. We had lived in our house at Wahroonga for several years when he came downstairs in his dressing gown one night and asked us where the kitchen was.'

Part of the shock of Goossens' being caught at the airport was that the nature of the scandal did not match the gentlemanly discretion and distance that seemed so integral to his personality. But it was known to sections of musical Sydney that he was consorting with the artist Rosaleen Norton, sometimes called the Witch of the Cross, and her offsider Gavin Greenlees. He was also rumoured to be linked through doctor and sometime SSO violinist Michael Bialoguski to ASIO circles. What was the attraction? The key lies perhaps in this sentence from Helen Bainton's book:

When I remarked to Goossens' wife Marjorie that he must be exhausted with all his work, she merely replied, 'Gene is never tired, only bored.'

'I think you could say that it was cultural boredom that led him to dabble in all that "Cross" stuff', Renee says. 'The Sydney of the fifties did not offer much on the cultural front to a man of his background.'

Peter Sainthill: 'Ken Lawson loved Goossens very much, as you know, but his one criticism of him was that he once left an indiscreet note at the box office saying that if Gavin Greenlees arrived at a concert he was always to be given house seats. Goossens had a background of interest in the occult, after all, from his student days with Peter Warlock and Cyril Scott.'

The reality of why Goossens was caught that day in March 1956 remains a riddle. John Matthews believes that on his fateful journey back to Australia Goossens was told in Darwin, when the plane was refuelling, that his luggage was going to be searched in Sydney. 'That a number of people had been tipped off is virtually certain', says Peter Sainthill. 'Jim MacDougall used to have a column in the *Mirror*, and about a week before all this happened he ran a piece hinting that a sensation surrounding a conductor was about to occur.'

Was Goossens simply careless? Someone who knew him well at the time puts the scandal down to the conductor's mixture of naivety and loftiness. 'During that 1955-56 period when he was overseas Rosaleen Norton had been in jail, and Gene had been corresponding with her. Well, the police were opening her mail, and all they had to do was read a letter that said "I am bringing back to Australia X number of books, X number of masks" and so on. I saw him late on the day he was arrested, and when I asked him why he was carrying all this material in his bags he said simply, loftily, as a Great Man would: "No one has ever inspected my luggage".

But Renee believes it is more complex than that. 'He really was involved in a national security scandal of some kind, and so was Stepmother, which is why she is now living a reclusive life in a French convent, and has been for many years. It was to do with Father's naivety; I think he got himself involved in things unwittingly, even the Petrov affair.'

Betty Barnett, Charles Moses' secretary in the mid-1950s, believes the entire matter was a frame-up. 'Goossens was framed at the airport, because I'm sure he did not have that stuff in his luggage. The security people admitted that they had a tip-off. I was really furious about the hypocrisy of the press and the commissioners. I mean, he could hardly corrupt a grown up 82-piece orchestra, could he? Yet all Goossens said to me about it was: "Things are not as you have heard them. The whole story will be told one day".'

Werner Baer had doubts about that. 'It was all too long ago, and we will never know the complete ins and outs because, no doubt, much of the information has been suppressed or destroyed by now. "I have been very foolish, Werner" he said to me at the time. Now it would not make a bit of difference.'

Goossens died in London in 1962, and players from the SSO approached ABC management about a memorial concert. Nothing doing. Eva Kelly recalls: 'A group of us took it in hand to put a concert on at the Con, and we played some of Goossens' chamber music, his piano quintet, the cello sonata. It was sponsored by the Bartok Society, and was a great success. But there was a lot of opposition to it'.

Whatever the reasons for Goossens' arrest, the ABC commissioners wanted no more to do with him, and Moses had the greatest difficulty persuading them to pay his airfare back to the United Kingdom. Moses remained a loyal friend to the conductor, and sincerely believed that once the scandal had blown over Goossens could return and take up the chief conductor post again. It was not to be. Richard Bonynge recalls that when he and Joan Sutherland called on Goossens in London in 1957 he was 'old and frail and ill. He had really been broken by the scandal'.

'He was broke too, because he had to pay so much alimony to his previous wives', said Werner Baer, who also visited Goossens that year. 'He talked about "his" SSO, and what a great love it had been for him. But thank God all this scandal is long ago and forgotten. Time has taken care of that. When we are gone only the memory of his achievements will remain, and that is good because what he achieved here was absolutely tremendous.'[4]

And suddenly Goossens was gone. There had been no gentle handing over to an anointed successor, no fond farewells, no tributes. Now there was no SSO chief conductor, either, and the main concert season was just beginning. Luckily, Joseph Post again took over some of the concerts Goossens had been scheduled to do, as did Heinze and Tibor Paul, and many of the Goossens-chosen programs were retained. But 1956 was a bad year for the orchestra. Demoralised by Goossens' disappearance, the

[4] It is not as forgotten as it seems. Inez Baranay's recent novel *Pagan* is a fictionalised version of the Goossens/Norton relationship, and at time of writing ABC TV is considering the production of a mini-series about Goossens' years in Sydney.

Commission's attitude to it, and rumours that Heinze was to be appointed chief conductor, their standard of playing see-sawed all year. As well, Ernest Llewellyn was in the United States, part-way through year-long studies he was undertaking at Juilliard and other US musical institutions. Although the SSO was ably led by British violinist Maurice Clare (a former leader of the Boyd Neel String Orchestra), Llewellyn's absence in this time of crisis did nothing to raise morale.

Already in 1952 Wolfgang Wagner could point to 'the orchestra's only shortcoming: it will play really well only if inspired by an authoritative and sympathetically guiding conductor. A first-rate orchestra, however, ought to play even better when left more or less to its own resources'.

The SSO of the day could not do that, not because there were not marvellous players in it, but because, Roger Covell suggests, 'Goossens did not have every player he wanted sitting in every seat. There were some people in the orchestra who encouraged this feeling that "if the conductor's no good we will not play well", which meant that in order to give a good performance the SSO required to be inspired'.

Lindsey Browne described the SSO's 1956 career as 'Jekyll and Hyde', and suggested that 'many an uncharitable listener might suppose that this orchestra is using performance as a way of "voting" for and against various conductors'. The best concerts of the year were probably those under Post and the visiting French conductor Jean Martinon, who was very popular with players but was given very cool notices. He did not return.

All year the press speculated on who would be appointed as the next chief conductor. One certain thing was that the SSO and the Conservatorium could not be run by one person at the same time. Moses and senior Conservatorium staff recognised that the two appointments were demanding of too various a range of skills. So when Heinze was appointed the new director of the Conservatorium in July the SSO was relieved. As Cliff Goodchild remembers, 'they used to say 1956 was the year Melbourne got the Olympic Games and got rid of Heinze'.

In fact, the Olympic Games got the SSO, for the Sydney *Telegraph* and Melbourne *Argus* helped pay for the orchestra to give three concerts during the Olympic Arts Festival, the third

It's Gold for the orchestra! The combined Sydney and Victorian Symphonies playing beside the Olympic Swimming Pool during the 1956 Olympic Games in Melbourne. The conductor is Sir Bernard Heinze.

being a combined SSO/MSO concert under Heinze. The orchestras played on a special stage erected over the Olympic Pool while the audience sat in tiers around it. Although this epic event was considered a success, the obbligato contributions by the pool's fans, pumps and water purifiers apparently did little to enhance the shining hour.

Schmidt-Isserstedt's successful return visit in July started fresh rumours that he was to be appointed chief conductor, but Moses had already begun negotiations with Sir John Barbirolli to take up the position. All the while the press continued to run stories headlined 'Pessimism on Sydney Post' and 'Sydney's orchestra suffers'. Professor Peart told the *Telegraph* that 'the standard of the orchestra will slip a lot further until it gets a first-class resident conductor'. The Barbirolli negotiations fell over.

Another SSO crisis boiled up in the meantime just to make the year more eventful. In August double bass player Ray Price, who also ran the Port Jackson Jazz Band, was told that his playing of jazz in addition to his work with the SSO was affecting his orchestral performance. A letter from Ken Lawson indicated that he would therefore have to stop playing jazz, but that 'such [outside] engagements as are comparable with normal orchestral symphonic work will at all times be given every consideration'.

Price was eager to tell the press about the ABC's anti-jazz attitude, and even more eager to talk to them when he was sacked later in the year. Charles Gray by this time had said plainly that Price was a disgrace to his section, but as neither James nor Moses was interested in discussing the matter Price had the argument all his own way, which was, in short: the stuffed shirts at the ABC have done me in. It was not one of the ABC's public relations triumphs. Clarrie Mellor: 'Ray was a bit of a lurk merchant, you know. He used to do outside gigs after concerts and, at afternoon rehearsals, there he would be on the end of the basses, with his arm around his bass, fast asleep, snoring!'

In October Moses ended months of speculation when he announced that, as of April 1957, Dr Nicolai Malko would be the next chief conductor of the Sydney Symphony Orchestra. Malko was immensely distinguished, a living link to near-vanishing Russian traditions. He had studied with Rimsky-Korsakov and Glazunov and had given the world premiere performances of

Shostakovich's first and second symphonies. But his was a controversial appointment even before he got here. For one thing he had never conducted the SSO before, and for another 'he was seventy-three, which was too old', Werner Baer recalled. 'We were aghast at the announcement that he was taking the orchestra over.'

As we will see, Malko gave some inspiring performances with the SSO, at least in his first two seasons. To an extent, he surprised his critics and brought with him unique insights into the Russian and Soviet repertoire. But Goossens had changed Sydney and had helped its thinking about music mature. Malko was not able to take advantage of that.

CHAPTER SIX

The path broadens,
the summit recedes

In 1957 the 'new' SSO was eleven years old, and was no longer the impressionable infant it had been when Goossens came to conduct it for the first time. The players now had their own Benevolent Fund; they had made a series of internationally acclaimed recordings; and their country audiences were well established, and seemed as devoted and sometimes more enthusiastic than their city counterparts. The SSO players were also used to performing a diverse and demanding range of repertoire. The 1957 orchestra was a very sophisticated eleven-year-old, but the Malko years would bring a number of important adolescent experiences.

The Benevolent Fund was Goossens' idea. When it began, in 1947, the period of paid sick leave for salaried musicians was one week a year, which was obviously not sufficient for players who developed complicated illnesses. Nor were there any superannuation schemes retiring players could rely on. The orchestra already had a 'sick' fund, which had been running informally since 1936, but when the 'new' SSO got under way Goossens suggested an annual fund-raising concert for which players and conductor would donate their services. The Fund continues to operate successfully, and the 1991 Benevolent Fund concert, conducted by Carlo Felice Cillario, was the forty-fifth such event.

Country touring was by this time a regular fixture in the SSO calendar (although it usually involved a reduced orchestra of 65 to 70 players). In 1956 the orchestra had spent 20-23 February in Bathurst, Parkes, Dubbo and Orange; 9-18 April in Cessnock, Newcastle, Moree, Inverell, Glen Innes, Armidale and Tamworth; 15-26 October in Wollongong, Maitland, Newcastle, Casino, Murwillumbah, Lismore and Grafton; and finally, 19-22 December in Canberra, Albury and Wagga. The trains the musicians took on such journeys, the halls they played in, and the hotels they stayed in, often demanded a terrific sense of humour.[1] In *Facing the Music*, Helen Bainton recalled one of the many country cinemas in which special stage extensions had been built for the orchestra:

One winter's night in Orange it was so cold that we all wore flannel pyjamas under our evening clothes so that we would be warm enough to move our frozen fingers. Fierce draughts blew up from below us throughout the concert because the extension to the platform was built over oil drums!

Rattly trains with old engines that turned hair and clothes black were common, too. Clarrie Mellor: 'We became very good at keeping ourselves amused through all these things. We divided ourselves up into "steerage" (the drinkers) and the "tea and bickies". The steerage used to assemble in the bars after concerts for a jam session while the locals made up the audience.'

Neville Amadio says the country schools concerts are some of his fondest memories. 'For one concert in Casino Hans George played *The Swan* as his cello demonstration piece. So as this lovely, serene music began a rubber chicken I'd strung up across the proscenium slowly made its way across the stage. The kids loved it!'

Ron Cragg: 'We thought of the country schools concerts as great fun, and some of the personality players really brought something special to them. Our percussionist Lou Tutscka would go to the back of the hall during the tuba demonstration, and when Cliff has finished played his ghostly tune Lou would let

---

[1] Sometimes the response of the locals did, too. In an editorial written before the SSO's very first country tour, in 1938, the *Western Times* (Bathurst) wrote that 'money spent by the State in the encouragement of musical proficiency does not merely add to public enjoyment; it is also an agency for the prevention of low-living and for the fostering of lofty thoughts and desirable habits'.

out a kind of slow devilish "ha . . . ha . . . ha."

Goossens could be very charming on country tours, silencing the audience applause in preparation for the encore by saying 'Good evening, ladies and gentlemen, it is nice to be back in Bathurst (or whatever town was appropriate). We have had an awful lot of music tonight, but we have just one more piece to play'. Although he usually made a fine speech during the post-concert reception, his patience sometimes ran out when faced with poor rustic manners. Rex Ellis: 'At a post-concert supper in Armidale the mayor made a speech in which he kept referring to "Eugene Goossens and the boys in the band", and he must have said this ten times. Goossens just couldn't bring himself to respond, and he whispered to me, "If he does not know the difference between an orchestra and a band I will not be the one to tell him". There was a terrible hush until I stepped forward and made a brief speech.'

Joseph Post did not have the right temperament for schools concerts. There were always two songs on the program for the young audience to sing, and Post would get short with the children if he felt they did not sing with sufficient gusto. John Matthews recalls that Post was once sternly pointing out the instruments of the orchestra to a country schools audience. 'When referring to the more exotic instruments he would habitually talk about "the cor anglais which we have not got today", or "the alto flute which we have not got". So one day we found this chair leg and an old bed post, and painted them up, so that when Post said "and the contrabassoon which we have not got" the bass trombone played its lowest note and we waved this thing at the kids. That routine became part of the show.'

During one country schools concert conducted by Post a dog wandered in through the back door of the hall. One of the players then said quietly, 'that dog is looking for the post'.

Post's brusqueness could reveal itself at the most unexpected moments. During one Post-led country tour of the 1960s one of the SSO's principal players was the soloist in the tour program's concerto. As soloist and conductor were coming off stage together, one of the ABC's tour staff remarked to the soloist that he had given a good performance. 'You must have cloth ears', Post retorted. 'It was bloody terrible!'

As stages in country halls are usually smaller than those in capital cities, the full SSO rarely goes to the bush. This means that Strauss tone poems or excerpts from Wagner's *Ring* cycle cannot be played in these venues, but John Matthews found that the Music Department's programming staff did not always understand that.

'We were to do a concert in Wollongong, for example, which required two harpsichords in the first piece, then there was to be a piano concerto, and after interval the Mussorgsky/Ravel *Pictures at an Exhibition*, which calls for an orchestra that includes alto saxophone, two harps, a lot of extra percussion instruments and so on. Anyway, if you know Wollongong Town Hall you'd know you just couldn't stage a concert like that in there. So I went straight to Rex Ellis and suggested that the orchestra play in the hall and the audience sit on the stage. He saw my point and we ended up doing an all-Beethoven program.'

Despite the passing of the steam train, country tours still bring their share of hairy stories. The SSO now travels to regional centres by aeroplane, and on one journey by DC3 a player spent most of his time keeping the plane's faulty back door from flying open by holding the door handle in one hand and an air hostess in the other.

❧

The first fresh challenge of 1957 hit the SSO right at the beginning of the year: playing in an opera pit for the opera seasons staged by the Australian Elizabethan Theatre Trust. The Trust had been founded in 1954 as a memorial to the previous year's Royal tour, with the purpose of fostering the indigenous performance of theatre, opera and ballet. The Trust grew out of the Arts Committee for the Jubilee Year,[2] and was the brainchild of H.C. Coombs, Chairman of the Commonwealth Bank; John Douglas Pringle, editor of the *Sydney Morning Herald*; and Charles Moses. Coombs persuaded the Prime Minister, (then Mr) R.G. Menzies, and the Treasurer Sir Arthur Fadden to allow the Trust to offer tax deductibility for donations, a revolutionary concept in its day.

The Trust was determined to give the administration of operatic

---

[2] The jubilee, celebrated in 1951, being that of Federation.

performance in Australia a national shape. In order to do so it needed the co-operation of two formidable women, Gertrude Johnson and Clarice Lorenz, who in 1954 were running opera companies—the National Theatre Company and the National Opera of Australia—in Melbourne and Sydney respectively. The Melbourne organisation had been performing regularly since 1939 while Lorenz was a relative newcomer, her first season being staged in 1951.

The two companies had collaborated in one joint season in 1952 that represented one of the peaks of indigenous operatic performance this century. Such singers as Marie Collier, Ronald Dowd, John Shaw and Phyllis Rogers were featured, in productions designed by William Constable, Robyn Lovejoy and Louis Kahan. Joseph Post conducted.

For all the companies' considerable successes over the years, neither of them was consistently well managed and their finances were often precarious. It was Coombs' hope that if the two companies worked with the Trust a well-run national opera company might be born.

The Trust did have access to some of the Johnson and Lorenz talent for its first opera season in 1956, notably Post as musical director, stage director Stefan Haag and some fine singers, but it did not receive much personal help from the women themselves, even though they were on the Trust's first board. John Cargher has summarised the attitude of Johnson and Lorenz to the Trust as follows: 'In a joint success there is less personal glory than in a separate failure. And personal glory was the name of the game!'. This also explains why they did not collaborate on a joint season more than once.

One of the things that attracted some of the other companies' singers over to the Trust was the national exposure they would receive, for the Trust's first operas were to be performed in all State capitals. It should be noted that such an enterprise would be considered formidable in the 1990s, and when train travel was the norm it was even more audacious. Given the logistical complications of moving sets, costumes, singers and technicians around the country, one of the greatest gifts to this first Trust opera season was the one bestowed by Moses and Boyer (who was vice-president of the Trust's Board of Directors as well as

ABC chairman): the use of ABC orchestras in each city for the entire season. As Roger Covell has written, this may have brought the problems of creating pit/stage ensemble afresh in each centre, but it also saved the Trust a great deal of money. Dr Coombs suggested, before the first season got under way, that the free provision of orchestras was the equivalent to a subsidy of £50 000 per year.

The touring opera companies that had visited Australia from time to time in the first half of this century had brought with them mostly French and Italian repertory. But 1956 was the bicentenary of Mozart's birth, and although Australians were not, on the whole, familiar with his operas, the Trust took the enlightened decision of making its first season an all-Mozart one: *Don Giovanni, The Marriage of Figaro, The Magic Flute* and *Così fan tutte*. All the operas were performed in English.

The productions did not reach Sydney until January 1957, and were given in the Elizabethan Theatre, Newtown. In the *Sunday Sun*, Julian Russell wrote of *The Marriage of Figaro* that the SSO offered 'the best orchestral playing I have ever heard in an Australian opera house'.

The SSO (or part of it) continued to play for the Trust opera seasons until the Trust formed its own orchestra in 1967, and if it did not always reach the standards praised by Julian Russell in that first season, that is not surprising, for most of the players did not enjoy the pit experience at all. As early as the Trust's second Sydney season, in September 1957, Ernest Llewellyn told the *ABC Weekly* that in the context of the SSO's already tight annual schedule, the operas were just too much. 'Such activities are in excess of what can be expected of any musician. Do you realise that by the end of this year we will have given 183 performances, including those for the opera? Sydney needs an opera orchestra of its own.'

The pit in the Elizabethan Theatre was, to put it mildly, small. In the Trust's first season it was able to hold a Mozart-sized orchestra of thirty-six players. With such operas in the second season as Puccini's *La Bohéme* and Verdi's *Otello*, the pit was enlarged, so that the SSO contingent which filled it numbered fifty-one. But this was not the total orchestral complement. Even with the ends of the pit pushed out bigger instruments could not fit inside it, so the double basses and percussion were installed inside stalls boxes.

Ron Cragg does not remember the Trust seasons with any fondness. 'The hazards of that pit were just diabolical. The ensemble problems when you have double basses in one box and percussion in another are just incredible. It was so frustratingly unmusical.'

Neville Amadio's memories of the theatre are not happy, either. 'Apart from the conditions in the pit the facilities for singers and players were appalling. You even had to go next door to go the loo!'

'I felt like a mole', says harpist June Loney, who joined the SSO in 1961. 'I even had to have a light on the harp strings, because it was so hard to see in that pit.'

The other problem the Trust seasons brought was that the orchestra was split in two while the operas were being performed. Sometimes the Trust performances coincided with country tours, which was fine, but more often they did not. Later in this chapter we will see how the orchestra's time was used in the new circumstances the opera seasons created.

⁂

If the opera experience provided a damp start to 1957, better things were to come in April, when Malko arrived to take up his chief conductor appointment. This was to be the last major achievement of his long and varied career.

As a young man he had been one of the leading Russian musicians of his generation. He had studied with Liadov, Rimsky-Korsakov and Glazunov; had been a professor at the Leningrad Conservatory; and had been an early champion of Shostakovich and Miaskovsky. But the restrictive artistic atmosphere that had begun to prevail in the Soviet Union during the late 1920s led him to leave the country for good, and he settled for a time in Denmark, where a conducting competition is still held in his honour every three years. In 1940 he moved to the United States, where he divided his time between lecturing and conducting. He came back to Europe after the Second World War and quickly re-established his career there as a guest conductor.

By 1957 he had a reputation as a prolific recording artist and an expert in Russian repertory, but he had not secured a major

A pause for the cameras during Nicolai Malko's first rehearsal with the SSO. On his left, violinist Eva Kelly, and on his right, concertmaster Ernest Llewellyn.

Malko conducting the SSO in the Sydney Town Hall.

chief conductor's job until he came to Sydney. Donald Hazelwood remembers the orchestra's first rehearsal with him:

'At the initial downbeat you knew exactly what he was going to do, because he was so set in his ways. He would stop you even in passages that were right because that was where he had always stopped. He could be very authoritarian. We were rehearsing the Prelude to Act Three of *Lohengrin* with him, and he went through parts of the piece with the violins, methodically, desk by desk. It was a terrifying experience for some players, and I remember some of the women in tears after that.'

His firm sense of discipline—which became less frightening during his first year with the orchestra—contributed to a swift raising of standards that critics did not fail to notice. Malko conducting pupil, and now ABC Concerts planning co-ordinator, Michael Corban describes the nature of the SSO/Malko relationship.

'It was based on mutual respect, I would say. The players realised that Malko was very experienced and almost uniquely well versed in the Russian style. He was also a great gentleman, and came to treat the orchestra as such, but there was a pretty formidable bunch of first-desk players in the SSO at the time, and they knew that Malko's personal style was also his conducting style—an old-world one. I think that some people in the audience regarded him as old-fashioned, too.'

Reviewing one of Malko's first concerts with the SSO, Lindsey Browne noted that it was 'a most happy signpost to this city's orchestral future':

The orchestra at all times seemed happy under his leadership, and its constant readiness to respond affectionately to the demands of his mellow and sensitive mind produced one of the vintage concerts of recent seasons. Fine tone, fine sentiment, fine scruple in matters of balance, lucid textures—what more could you ask?

Only a month after these first performances with the SSO, critic Max Keogh wrote that

the orchestra's long, upward trek to its former eminent position of world rank has commenced. It could well be that these concerts have been the turning point in a critical situation. No one could forget the deterioration almost to the point of disintegration which followed upon Goossens' departure. The road ahead is long and steep but, on the evidence of these first concerts, it is not without the bounds of possibility that Malko will reach his goal.

Malko and his wife had moved to Sydney, and spent almost half of each year here. The conductor took a diplomatic, never forceful, interest in the work of the orchestra under other conductors, and would often attend regular subscription performances and even schools concerts. 'We were very surprised that he took such a great interest in all the things we were doing', says Clarrie Mellor.

There were some magnificent performances under his direction. His strengths and his interests lay unequivocally in Russian and Soviet music (and in the symphonies of Sibelius), and it was in this repertoire that the orchestra played at its best for him. 'Shostakovich with Malko was amazing!' Cliff Goodchild recalls. 'Visiting soloists would sometimes say to you, in awe, "listen to the Master".'

Indeed, many players believe the finest SSO/Malko performances to have been those of Shostakovich's fifth symphony, a work the combination performed together in Sydney and on tour. A private recording exists of a performance of the work given during Town Hall subscription concerts in April 1959. It is a terrific reading in every way, full of drama, precisely and intelligently played, and intensely atmospheric. It would be considered a great achievement in the life of any orchestra.

Unfortunately, where Malko could bring enormous panache to the music of Shostakovich, he was not always at home in the central German or French repertoire. Even some of the romantic Russian music he conducted was unfamiliar to him, as Robert Miller remembers:

'There were many standard works which he had not performed. For example, we were quite amazed at the enormous amount of time he spent over rehearsals for Tchaikovsky's *Romeo and Juliet* overture. In the end he apologised for taking so long over a work that the orchestra knew so well—I must have played it about 200 times by then—and said "but the plain fact is that I have never performed it before". So he was getting a thorough knowledge of the piece by tiring us out!'

Ron Cragg: 'Malko's first couple of years with us were wonderful. I think many players really enjoyed working with him. But he had not really had his own orchestra since leaving the Soviet Union, so he had the repertoire of a guest conductor, in other words of the pieces he liked and had grown up conducting.'

The orchestra's relationship with Malko began to sour irrevocably when his health began to affect his behaviour. He had the first of his two heart attacks early in 1961, during a rehearsal of Mahler's *Resurrection* symphony.

Michael Corban: 'I was conducting the off-stage brass, and we could not get the entry right. After about the third attempt he had an attack and fell off his chair. That was really the end for him, although he kept conducting for a few months.'

One very public sign that Malko was losing his grip came in the April subscription concerts of 1961, when Isaac Stern was soloist in the Bartok violin concerto. During one performance Malko's beat became smaller and smaller as his head slowly inclined down toward his music stand. When his head had touched his score, some players thought that he had died then and there. But then the conductor began to lift his head, and as gradually as it had descended it ascended, and he began to conduct again as normal. Orchestra and soloist had valiantly continued playing throughout this disturbing episode.

Ron Cragg remembers other strange changes in Malko's behaviour that followed his heart attack. 'He became very peculiar, blithely offering people's jobs to other people from other States . . . it got so bad we had a meeting at the Musicians' Union asking the ABC to take away from Malko the right of hiring and firing, because his illness was affecting his thinking so profoundly. Anyway, the ABC responded by telling us that, as far as they were concerned, there was nothing wrong with Dr Malko's health. Two weeks later he died.' It was June, 1961.

In a review of one of Malko's first concerts in Sydney, Lindsey Browne asked whether the conservative nature of the program (Prokofiev's *Classical* symphony, Sibelius' violin concerto and Rimsky-Korsakov's *Scheherazade*) held any special significance. 'Does it mean that Malko does not much care for the urgencies and challenges of the world of now?' The answer was to be 'yes', as Michael Corban explains. 'I don't think he was very interested

ABOVE: Ernest Llewellyn's widow, Ruth, has described this picture as 'a rogues gallery'. Captured during an SSO country tour are (from left) Joseph Post, associate concertmaster Robert Miller, orchestra manager Ken Lawson and Ernest Llewellyn.

The first ABC concert recorded for television: Malko and pianist Claudio Arrau acknowledge the applause with the SSO after a performance of Beethoven's Emperor Concerto *on 20 June 1957.*

in new music, but he realised he had to do some. He did his bit, you might say.'

He was not a complete conservative, by any means, for his concerts included some unusual music, although little of it was new—Samuel Barber's Second Essay for Orchestra, pieces from Copland's ballet *Rodeo*, Prokofiev's *Scythian Suite*, the suite from Alban Berg's opera *Lulu*, the fifth symphony of the Estonian composer Eduard Tubin, Stravinsky's *Oedipus Rex* (the first Australian performance), Orff's *Carmina Burana*[3] and Honegger's *King David* were some of the pieces he conducted in Sydney. He also gave world premiere performances of such Australian pieces as David Morgan's fourth symphony, Malcolm Williamson's first piano concerto (with Igor Hmelnitsky the soloist) and a suite, *Sydney Pictures*, by George Kraus, a member of the SSO's double bass section. (Most of this Australian music was done at the ABC's request.)

So the crucial question about Malko is not, was he a good conductor? but, rather, was he a good choice for chief conductor of a young Australian symphony orchestra? Roger Covell believes he was not. 'He came here at the end of his career, and was not at his most vigorous. I recall some fine performances under him, but he was not a forward-looking programmer, and he was under-energised for an orchestra that clearly needed some dynamic and innovative leadership. There was no sense of musical adventure. He was probably a good person to have for a short visit.'

Lindsey Browne feels that, in retrospect, the Malko years were not that satisfactory for the audience, either. 'I thought he was terribly well informed, but I never got much excitement out of him. It reminded me a bit of the last tours here by the pianist Benno Moiseiwitsch. You know, it was all over and he was just doing it by memory. He'd forgotten what the basic urges were.'

Helen Bainton seems to sum up the Malko years most vividly of all in *Facing the Music*:

---

[3] It says much about the moral temper of the times that in this 1958 performance of the Orff, No 19 in the score—*When a Boy and a Maiden are alone together*— was omitted entirely. Perhaps the Schmidt-Isserstedt/SSO *Carmina Burana* three years beforehand had been too steamy.

It was a difficult time for everyone, for Malko, because his mind worked slowly, saturated as it was with things of the past; for the orchestra, because they were too young to want the past as for them the present and future were what mattered. The seeds sown by Goossens had developed roots; Malko kept the plant alive, but could not provide the stimulus necessary for new growth.

❧

The period in which Malko was the SSO's chief conductor were problematic for the orchestra in other respects, too. Most obviously to the players, the quality of the guest conductors was declining, and, less obviously in immediate effect, the first generation of ABC concert and music managers had retired or were nearing the end of their careers.

The Europe of the early 1950s was still recovering from the devastations of war. Many artists had no place of residence, as they had moved from country to country through the years of the Second World War. Germany had only recently been divided into four zones; some basic goods remained rationed in Britain until July 1954; concert halls and opera houses that had been hit by war-time bombs had not yet been rebuilt or replaced; and of course there were fewer of the arts festivals in existence that now take place in the European summer. Under these circumstances Australia was a relative haven, with its good weather, political stability and large and enthusiastic audiences.

But our deficiencies to performers as an artistic destination seemed to increase as the 1950s progressed. The lure of the high fees North American concert managements could offer, the gradual resumption of normal concert life in many European countries and the flourishing recording industry (now gaining momentum due to the success of the long-playing record) had the expected effect on Australian concert life. As the *Sydney Morning Herald* reported in September, 1957:

Australia in the next few years will find it increasingly difficult to get famous concert artists for long engagements, and tours will certainly have to be shortened . . . Many of those artists who have already been to Australia, and those who would like to go, can no longer afford an

Australian season. In terms of hard cash and sheer physical strain it is no longer worth their while.

From the late 1950s, then, the ABC has had two major difficulties to contend with in bringing artists to Australia. One is that of distance. It is not simply that Australia is a long way from Europe and North America, but that Adelaide is a long way from Sydney. A national tour involving subscription concerts in each capital city can take six weeks to two months, even travelling by air. A second difficulty is that of money. With the gradual decline in the ABC's concert-giving spending power from 1956, the competition from concert managements in other countries and, over the last decade, the weakening value of the Australian dollar, it has been difficult and sometimes impossible to attract some of the art music stars here for national tours.[4]

A third difficulty, which ceased to exist after 1980, was caused by the inclusion in the ABC Act of the requirement to broadcast all or part of any concert for which a charge was made. The Act had been amended to incorporate this requirement as a result of the Tait case of the late 1930s. It meant that a soloist touring five States would have to bring with him or her five concertos and four or five recital programs so that the same works were not broadcast repeatedly within a short space of time. (For example, over his two tours Klemperer conducted twenty-three different programs. None was identical to another.)

The 1938 amendment caused problems almost as soon as it was enacted. In an attempt to lessen the impact it would have, Moses made sure that visiting artists gave the least possible number of performances to avoid repeating concert repertoire on air. But this did not help much. As early as 1941 Roy Lamb told the ABC commissioners that 'the continuous broadcasting of Celebrity Artists materially affects box office returns after such artists had been in the country for some weeks'.

By April 1946 concert activity had increased markedly and the commissioners were concerned that this development would mean putting even more concerts to air, resulting in less room for other

---

[4] These problems are not uniquely the ABC's of course. They affect Musica Viva, the Australian Chamber Orchestra and many other performing arts companies. I am discussing them here in the context of the ABC's concert-giving operations.

programs. In June of that year Boyer wrote to the Postmaster-General that 'it is becoming increasingly difficult to reconcile the demands of the thousands of concert-goers in the capital cities with the demands of listeners for a reasonable balance between broadcasts from concerts and other programs'.

This plea did not move the PMG's department at all, and soon Moses had no recourse but to encourage a bending of the rules. When in 1952 a Perth listener complained to Dame Enid Lyons, then an ABC commissioner, that not all of Walter Gieseking's Perth recital had been broadcast, Moses explained that Gieseking had only (!) brought five recital programs with him to Australia, and that 'all of these had been broadcast in Perth at some time during his Australian tour'.

Supply outstripped demand (or available air time) to such an extent that some recordings of live concerts were broadcast only by regional stations, and some were even heard only on domestic short-wave services where, in the words of Clement Semmler, 'they wasted their sweetness on the central Australian desert air'.

Another, frequently employed, method of broadcasting concert material while causing minimum dislocation to other programs was 'mining'. Once magnetic tape became available to Australian broadcasters in the late 1940s it was possible to pre-record concerts, re-package them in the studio with scripted announcements and perhaps broadcast only one piece at a time from them. While this was a convenient method of using live material, it also drained performances of their sense of occasion. Fortunately, after 1983, most concerts have been broadcast as complete programs, whether they are relayed live-to-air or not.

But in the Malko years and beyond, while the amendment was still in force, artists touring for the ABC were asked to travel great distances for relatively small fees, and to bring a large repertoire for concert tours that took place over a period of weeks in which it would have been possible to secure a greater number of engagements for bigger fees in other major concert centres.

There were some outstanding guest conductors between 1957 and 1961, and they were a returning Rafael Kubelik, the Romanian Constantin Silvestri, Igor Markevich, Sargent (again!), the young Charles Mackerras, the even younger Lorin Maazel and Karel Ančerl. That is the complete list of first-rate conductors from those years. A decade earlier Klemperer and Kubelik had both toured here twice, Barbirolli and Paul Kletzki had appeared, Castro and Susskind were working here regularly, and Schmidt-Isserstedt's first tour was being negotiated.

The times they were a-changing.

The lesser availability of international concert artists for ABC tours was compounded by the changes that were taking place within the ABC. William James completed nearly thirty years of ABC life when he retired in August 1957. He had started his life of musical administration in the days of the Australian Broadcasting Company, and was absolutely crucial to the establishment and success of the ABC as an entrepreneur. He was also a perceptive talent-spotter. We have already seen how he arranged Paul Badura-Skoda's first tours here. On his return from the 1951 European trip during which Badura-Skoda had auditioned for him, he told reporters at a press conference of some of the other artists who had impressed him: Victoria de Los Angeles, Friedrich Gulda, Aldo Ciccolini, Horst Stein and Ferenc Fricsay were among them. All at the beginning of their careers, all to become significant international musicians.

He also used this conference to suggest that Australian cities should begin to run arts festivals along the lines of those run during the European summer. 'But it is no use just leaving the festival to the musicians, and running the rest of our affairs as we run them now. For one thing, we must do something about our licensing laws. We must be able to offer visitors to an Australian festival all of the amenities of pleasant, civilised living.' Two major predictions appear in this quote alone.

James' retirement came at a time when his energy and vision were needed most. Apart from the changing international concert scene of the late 1950s, there were also the new challenges of television: how it would affect the ABC's spending priorities, and how the orchestras would be presented by the new medium.

The ABC began its television operations in November 1956.[5] One of the first guest artists on the first night of ABC TV was the violinist Christian Ferras (appearing in ABC concerts that

---

[5] It is not appropriate here to relate the history of the ABC's entry into television. For a good short account see Inglis, pp 193-200.

year), who played a piece of unaccompanied Bach. Unfortunately viewers at home could see him playing, but due to a technical mishap could hear no music emanating from his instrument. In fact the first sound heard during the item was the voice of a technician exclaiming (in desperate tones) 'I can't find the bloody sound!'.

This incident should have been regarded as an omen for the Music Department's early relationship with ABC TV, for there was much soul-searching and variation in opinion about whether, how best and how often the ABC orchestras should be seen on television. Perhaps James would have had the plasticity of mind to have been able to come up with some novel solutions to these problems, and it is tantalising to wonder how Goossens would have approached the opportunity.

As it was, James' successor as Director of Music was Herbert Cannon. In him the ABC had, in Ken Tribe's view, a 'safe' appointment. Charles Buttrose has described Cannon as 'sober-sided'. An organist by training, he had worked with James for many years, and certainly knew how the ABC operated. But, as with Malko, the times called for energies different to his, and while Cannon kept the motor running, he did not take the vehicle into new fields.

The first televised ABC concert was relayed direct from the Sydney Town Hall in June 1957, when Claudio Arrau played Beethoven's *Emperor* concerto with the SSO under Malko. The following year the SSO went to ABC TV's Gore Hill studios for the first time to give a special 45-minute concert under Heinze. This included Alfred Hill's work for narrator and orchestra, *Green Water*, which was based on a poem by John Wheeler. The TV producer Arthur Wyndham explained to the *Daily Telegraph* that he would be trying to show, as part of the performance, film of the scenes which inspired Wheeler's poem.

'Problems are involved in synchronising the film sequences with the narration, because this has to be done more or less in the transmission.' Such were the perils of early television. And yet all this effort did not convince the critics that orchestral music was at home on the small screen. One reviewer wondered if his pleasure would have been impaired if he had shut his eyes for the duration of the telecast.

More studio work followed for the SSO, and for some of the chamber groups that had recently sprung up from within its ranks. Oboist Ian Wilson (soon to die tragically of cancer), principal clarinet Gabor Reeves, Colin Evans, bassoonist Ray Maling (brother of the orchestra's timpanist Alard) and Alan Mann had formed a wind quintet which, as well as performing for Musica Viva, appeared before the television cameras. Charles Gray also formed a string ensemble that got together during the orchestra's country tours (as these did not require all the string players) and pit appearances, and this group also worked for television. Most players found the conditions of the television studio pretty sterile, but such performances made for better results on screen than straight concert reportage.

Partly for this reason, it was apparent by the early 1960s that regular transmission of live concerts was not going to occur. With the exception of special events like the Stravinsky concerts in 1961, time allotted to concerts on television was meagre. Some senior managers, such as Clement Semmler who was working to Moses on television programming in the late 1950s, felt that 'viewing a concert under normal home conditions . . . may actually detract from appreciation by providing distracting and irrelevant visual detail'.

To televise live concerts effectively demanded (and still demands) a lot of rehearsal time[6] and a specialist director; one who could read a score, who could tell the difference between an oboe and a clarinet, who knew something of the orchestral repertoire. In an industry where versatility was the byword, such talent was hard to find. Moreover, television producers had begun to stage opera in the studio with some success, and although the results of their efforts look somewhat stilted today, opera-for-television was an inherently visual and dramatic idea, and met with sufficient audience interest to make it the dominant music idiom of ABC TV's first decade.

Ken Inglis has suggested that people within the organisation could 'feel the ABC change character' because of television, and the gradually diminishing status of concert-giving as a corporate

---

[6] In Europe, some broadcasting organisations have up to eight camera rehearsals per concert. In Australia it is usual to have one.

activity was one of these character changes. Television was not only new and expensive for the ABC, demanding special skills and new kinds of creative thinking; it was also an incredibly popular medium: by 1960 more than half the households of Sydney and Melbourne had a television set.

'TV changed everything for the orchestras', Donald Hazelwood believes. 'Before it came on the scene, we were the ABC's bright star. But then audiences became less and less willing to come out at night when they could be entertained so easily at home. TV has ruined the concentration spans of at least two generations in Australia.'

James' departure was not the only big change to the ABC's management of orchestral music-making in the late 1950s. Roy Lamb retired as Federal Concert Manager in 1958. In Alan Ziegler's estimation, it was a great achievement that he had lasted that long. 'He outlived Eric Burnett by several years, and was one of the few senior concert staff who survived long enough in his job to retire. You know, most of them were pensioned off with heart trouble, blood pressure . . . it was that kind of work.'

The vacancy caused by Lamb's departure was not immediately filled in any official way, but some delicate concert negotiations had already been undertaken a year before Lamb's retirement by a new face at the ABC, Charles Buttrose.

In May 1957 Buttrose left Sir Frank Packer's Consolidated Press, where he had been a leader writer on the *Daily Telegraph*, to become Federal Supervisor of Publicity at the ABC. He had been in journalism a long time, and had known Moses for many years. Buttrose makes no bones about that being an advantage when he applied for the ABC job. And we can see from the tasks Buttrose was given that Moses had now decided that concerts were no longer promoted with sufficient nous or vigour, and that there was not the talent in-house to get the ABC involved in special entrepreneurial opportunities. In other words, the business of concert giving was losing profile.

Moses immediately gave Buttrose the Concert Department as one of his watching briefs. Buttrose was decidedly unimpressed with its publicity performance. 'They [Concerts] did their own publicity, which meant it was usually handled by some clerk better equipped for doing long-tots than designing and writing an acceptable brochure, poster or newspaper advertisement', he has written. Nor did he have much confidence in Roy Lamb's abilities. 'Lamb was charming and very gentlemanly, but he didn't know one end of a grand piano from the other. I was sorry when he left, but it was definitely for the best', he says.

Buttrose's first test piece was negotiating a national tour with violinist David Oistrakh that was to be a joint venture between J.C. Williamson (in the person of Sir Frank Tait) and the ABC. Williamson's had signed Oistrakh, but needed the orchestras so that the soloist could play concertos on the proposed tour. Despite the long history of animosity between the two organisations, Buttrose came away with a solid and amicable arrangement that worked: Williamson's even agreed to allow complete broadcasts of the performances. Neither Herbert Cannon nor Roy Lamb had been asked to take part in this negotiating process.

Buttrose soon became Director of Publicity and not long after Moses made him Director of Publicity and Concerts, a seemingly strange combination of posts that can only be explained by Buttrose's idiosyncratic range of interests and the successful Moses/Buttrose chemistry. They had great rapport as colleagues. (Buttrose was to discover how different things could be when Duckmanton became general manager in 1965.) And by 1960, when Concerts officially became part of his bailiwick, Buttrose had scored some spectacular successes, notably the tours of the Czech Philharmonic Orchestra under chief conductor Karel Ančerl (a joint venture with Musica Viva) and the Boston Symphony under its chief Charles Munch. Buttrose had worked closely on both visits.

The Czech orchestra was the first symphony orchestra from overseas to play in Australia. Their concerts are indelible memories for many people, and were equally exciting (and important, as an illustration of corporate standards) for local players. The tour resulted in Ančerl being asked back for a national tour with the ABC orchestras for the following year. And as we shall see, he might have come to stay.

Much to everyone's delight, the Czechs' tour made money. The Boston Symphony tour, which the ABC ran on its own, was not profitable but it made as big a splash, and was marked by Munch's repeated (and usually failed) attempts to seduce women much

ABOVE: A gathering of conductors in 1959: Sir Bernard Heinze (left) with Tibor Paul, Malko and Post.

A conductorial grimace of approval as Malko congratulates the orchestra during one of his rare open air appearances, at Sydney's Cooper Park in December 1959. The orchestra's principal cellist, John Painter, is at the right of the picture.

younger than his sixty-nine years. 'The maestro is old, but he is very strong', he told Buttrose.

These orchestral tours symbolise Buttrose's attitude and interests: he wanted concerts again to be spectacular and newsworthy elements in the life of the capital cities, and felt the ABC's concert-giving process had to be streamlined for this to happen. To this end, his long experience in private enterprise was invaluable. He did not have the cultural predispositions of some of his colleagues who had grown up in the ABC, and under his leadership publicity became more aggressive; overseas artists' tours became perhaps the best organised in the world, and he felt no compunction in folding up concert series in country centres when they were not doing well. He also argued for and got extra staff for the Concert Department so that not everyone was overworked all the time. (Unfortunately, in making the department more powerful, Buttrose contributed to the structural inequalities that came to make the ABC's concert-giving process so unweildy.)

The Czech and Boston orchestra tours represent a more widely felt occurrence that even Buttrose, for all his energy, could not quite address: in the world of the arts and ideas, Sydney was beginning to take its role as a world city seriously. By 1960 the first obviously modernist office buildings, such as Anzac House in College Street, had been built, and work had begun on the Sydney Opera House and on Sydney's first skyscraper, the AMP building; such avowedly intellectual journals as Tom Fitzgerald's *Nation* and Donald Horne's *Observer* had been going for two years; the National Institute of Dramatic Art (NIDA) had been established in 1958 on the campus of the University of NSW; and Hal Missingham had, with some difficulty, turned the Art Gallery of NSW into an institution that looked forward and out to the contemporary world.

One of Missingham's bravest and most successful acts was also a turning point in the mainstream acceptance of avant-garde idioms: he organised the historic French exhibition of 1953, much against the will of his conservative trustees. The 119 paintings on show included works by Léger, Miró, Chagall and Dufy, and the event was as great a public success as Keith Murdoch's pre-war show, but, unlike that exhibition, was the work of a major Australian public gallery. There was even faint praise from the President of the NSW Progressive Housewives Association, a lady with the glorious name of Miss Portia Geach. She was quoted as saying of the exhibition: 'Everyone to his taste, I say. But it's bright and modern'. (It is for another author to speculate on the extent to which Goossens' advocacy of new music had made the display of new or unseen idioms in other established art forms publicly acceptable.)

These changes and events all had a big effect on how Sydney saw itself. 'Old Sydney' was slowly disappearing and the streetscapes were changing. By the late 1950s Australians were more articulate about art than they had been a decade earlier, and had finally caught up with some of the old and new European and North American avant-garde thinking that had been held up by a depression, a war and a powerful old guard. And I have already discussed in the previous two chapters how much more art, in the broadest sense, there was on offer. It had become part of the business of living in Sydney.

And yet the world of new music had grown smaller and smaller on the stage of the Town Hall since Goossens' departure. Under Malko the works of younger composers, and even those of figures who were well established in international concert halls, such as Tippett, Lutoslawski and Messiaen, were almost invisible. If the critics of the 1930s were zealously hostile toward works like Mahler 5 or Sibelius 4, their successors a generation on were leading the charge in the opposite direction.

Thus, unsurprisingly, the attitude towards Sydney's oldest performing arts body, the SSO, was changing. In 1963 Roger Covell described the orchestra's previous season as 'destitute of important new music' and argued that the ABC's standards as a concert-giver 'are now too limited to meet all the demands of the present musical situation . . . It is probably inevitable that the paternalistic zeal of the ABC's early years should have weakened into complacency and caution'.

Had the art of orchestral music in Sydney lost its sense of adventure because the ABC's musical managers had allowed themselves to be led by audiences' lack of interest in change? Martin Long, by this time writing for the *Telegraph*, found most of the SSO's audiences chronically apathetic and complained that the ABC was not interested in encouraging new audiences to its orchestral series in the Town Hall. He questioned whether older subscribers really valued their ability to renew their seats each year as much as the ABC made out:

As witness: the number of empty seats when the weather is at all discouraging or there is something more modern than Debussy on the program; . . . and the general air of apathy that hangs over some of the audiences.

If a few of the old subscribers stayed home with the television and passed their tickets over to graduates from the Youth Concerts the atmosphere might grow a little livelier.

More aggressive Buttrose's publicity may have been, but the best-publicised concerts were the prestigious 'Celebrity' specials: two-concerto evenings with Claudio Arrau and Alfred Brendel; orchestral songs with Elisabeth Schwarzkopf. The Concert Department was in charge of all publicity, but no one in it seemed to be interested in where tomorrow's audience for the major orchestral series was going to come from. How entrenched the audience had become can be gauged by the programs printed for the last subscription concert of each season in the 1960s. In these, the following years' 'Celebrity Artists' (that word again) were announced, but that is all. With one exception—November 1965 for the 1966 season—no advice was given about how, where or when to book tickets. None was needed. Even that 1965 copy is hardly couched in the language of persuasion:

Renewals—Current subscribers to the Red, Blue and White series are advised that 1966 renewal of season concert tickets will take place in the period from Monday, January 24 to Saturday, Feburary 12.

Exchanges—Exchanges, which must be undertaken personally, will be effected on one day only, i.e. Saturday, February 19 from 8 a.m. to 12 noon.

And on the rare occasions when the Youth Concerts were advertised in concert programs, they were not so much sold as discussed. 'Subscriptions available to those under the age of 29', one advertisement admitted in the mid-1960s. 'Brochures, booking details etc., available at ABC Concert Department.'[7]

And yet subscriptions to Youth Concerts had begun to fall away, so that the just-on 6000 people who had taken out Youth subscriptions right through the 1950s dwindled gradually into the low 5000s through the 1960s until in 1976 the third evening was abolished altogether. The atmosphere they generated was no longer one of newness and adventure. In short, they had become routine. As Roger Covell recalls:

'They became gradually more fusty, because the ABC had somehow developed the attitude "this is good for you" rather than "this is exciting".' This change was matched by an irrevocable shift in the priorities of young people. Some senior members of ABC staff must have blinked in disbelief at the scenes of adulation and mass hysteria generated by the Beatles' Australian tour of 1964. But the Beatles phenomenon was only one example of the many new diversions the just-dawned age of television and mass marketing offered people in their teens and twenties. These diversions spoke a young language far more directly than the art music on offer at the Town Hall. (The Proms, the one successful attempt to bring a fresh audience to the Town Hall, would fail as soon as the ABC lost the will to promote it properly. See next chapter.)

So young audiences—those who might have graduated from their own series to become the subscribers to tomorrow's eight o'clock concerts, if there had been any seats for them—were not as easy to capture now as they had been in the cosily homogenous atmosphere of the Goossens era.

Indeed, such a critique as Martin Long's would have been inconceivable ten years earlier, when SSO concerts offered some of Sydney's greatest artistic experiences. The gap left by Malko's death meant that the orchestra was in no position to provide such experiences, either. For in truth, by the time of his demise, the SSO was badly demoralised.

---

[7] The *Bulletin* no doubt had this kind of approach in mind when it suggested, in July 1966, that most Australian theatrical managements 'tend to make you feel that an actual performance is really only something rather unpleasant under their noses'.

CHAPTER SEVEN

Vital signs

Malko had been conducting an increasingly unhappy orchestra. It was unhappy partly because of him. From mid-1960, when Malko's health problems began, he became increasingly unpredictable, and adopted what one musician described as a 'tsarist, off-with-your-head' policy of dismissing players he did not favour. 'Towards the end of his life he took such a set on players that we gave a vote of no-confidence in him,' Cliff Goodchild remembers. 'In 1961 we did not ask him to conduct our Benevolent Fund concert. We asked Post instead, but he refused because he felt we should have asked Malko. So we asked Georg Tintner and he did it.'

If Malko had caused orchestral unhappiness, most SSO musicians were also far from pleased about having to play in the pit for opera seasons when they already had a full concert year. And they did not enjoy having to make studio recordings simply because all their spare 'calls' had to be used up.

In its correspondence of the 1950s and 1960s, the Music Department frequently referred to the 'primary broadcasting function' of the orchestras[1], and studio work was still a regular part of life in the SSO during these years. But the orchestra was not always called the SSO in studio broadcasts. Frequently two

---

[1] See also the section concerned with the continuing repercussions of the 'Tait Amendment' in Chapters 2 and 6.

groups were created for studio performances, the group with wind and brass instruments now called the Sydney Concert Orchestra, and the one without, the Sydney String Orchestra.[2] Michael Corban explains how some of these recordings were made:

'There was an attitude in the Music Department that if the orchestras were paid to work eight or ten calls a week, then that was what they were going to do. Sometimes there was one call left over in a week when, say, the conductor of the subscription concert rehearsed the concert program in one [rehearsal] call less than allotted. In that case you would get a not-very-good studio conductor to do a thirty-minute recording, usually of an Australian piece or what used to be called light music, for later broadcast. All rehearsed and recorded in one call. It was time-filling.

'Here's another example: when the SSO went on a country tour there might be fifteen of the string players left in Sydney. They were not allowed to do their own thing. Instead they became the group called the Sydney String Orchestra[3], and had to perform in the studio so that inexperienced conductors like me could be given some sessions. Werner Baer would be told that there was a thirty-minute spot to fill on a Thursday night and I would be invited to put together a program to plug the hole.'

The decline in Malko's health during the last eighteen months of his tenure only heightened his tendency to zero in ruthlessly on players whose work he disliked. The changes to orchestra personnel after Malko's first three years were dramatic. At the beginning of the 1959 season horn player Alf Hooper had left due to, in Richard Montz's estimation, 'a personality conflict with the chief conductor'. Hans George left, for the same reason, to become first cello in the Utrecht orchestra. At the end of the

---

[2] Arriving at the new nomenclature involved a classic piece of bureaucratic process. A.C. Jowett, the Assistant Director of Programs (NSW), wrote to the State music department in November, 1955:
Historically, if memory serves us, 'Symphony' was first dropped from the title of the [Sydney] studio combination to differentiate between the standard orchestra and the orchestra as augmented for public concerts. Later, when the full symphony orchestra was engaged full time, the 'Symphony' orchestra again played for studio broadcasts but the title 'Symphony' was subsequently dropped for varying reasons. This has led to the present doubts or ambiguities.

[3] Most of this group were also in Charles Gray's string ensemble, referred to previously.

year principal oboe Ian Wilson also left, under pressure from Malko to do so, and principal trombone Stan Brown was fired a few months later. The rank-and-file string players found out about depositions or dismissals by looking at the orchestral notice board! Helen Bainton notes that 'if you were lucky your name did not appear'.

In the early 1960s the SSO's concert workload approached its natural physical limit of 160 performances. The schedules of the principal players could be particularly heavy. Some—Ernest Llewellyn, John Robertson, Neville Amadio, Robert Pikler, Hans George and his successor John Painter, Ian Wilson and his successor David Woolley—appeared frequently as soloists with the orchestra. Amadio recalls many occasions when he was invited to play a flute concerto but had also been expected to play in his first flute chair for all the other works on the program. This practice was maintained until the mid-1960s, when the SSO and MSO became the first Australian orchestras for which associate principal positions were created.

'After Malko's death I think the SSO felt it was on the bottom of the heap', says Roger Covell. 'The players were perhaps over-ready to assume that, but they certainly felt that the ABC did not take them seriously, and I don't think that perception lifted until the restructuring of the orchestral management in the mid-1980s.' John Hopkins, the ABC's Director of Music from 1963 to 1973, agrees.

Some happenings could temporarily dispel the gloom. Joseph Post devised a creative method of using the time of those players 'left over' from the opera seasons, and conducted some significant performances in the process. He formed the Sydney Little Symphony Orchestra, which gave concerts annually from 1963 until the early 1970s at the Cell Block Theatre. The programs Post devised for the SLSO were frequently adventurous, reflecting Post's musical inquisitiveness and the interests of the players, for many of these concerts featured soloists from the orchestra.[4]

---

[4] In terms of the exploration of the chamber orchestra repertoire, they were far more daring than any recent seasons by the Australian Chamber Orchestra. Post relinquished artistic control of the programs after the 1967 season, after which the repertoire selection became more cautious.

The world premiere of an important Australian work was programmed as follows in a 1964 concert:

Violin Concerto in B flat, K 207 ....Mozart

Transfigured Night ....Schoenberg

Interval

Homage to Garcia Lorca ....Meale

Symphony No 97 ....Haydn

'The remarkable thing about the Little Symphony concerts was the breadth of repertoire you got in them', says critic Fred Blanks. 'There would be everything from a *Brandenburg* concerto to Sculthorpe's *Irkanda IV*. The repertoire the SLSO used to play is now left to full-sized orchestras or specialist groups—usually contemporary ensembles or early music orchestras.'

1961 had brought a history-creating event, when Stravinsky came to Australia to conduct his music with his assistant Robert Craft. The concert they gave with the SSO (Craft conducting the first half, Stravinsky the second) is fondly remembered by players who took part. The SSO gave its all for the composer, although an off-the-air recording of the second half of the concert reveals some slips in ensemble that probably resulted from Stravinsky's gentle and slightly unclear movements and the players' unfamiliarity with some of the musical idioms. The capacity Town Hall audience applauded the seventy-nine-year-old composer fervently until the house lights had been turned up and the orchestra had begun to leave the stage.[5]

But the problems of morale were indelibly there, and Stravinsky could hardly influence them. On a world scale, the SSO was poorly paid. Most players, except the few on contract, were not paid salaries that would lure the best freelance musicians into the orchestra. A busy freelancer of 1963 might earn £50 a week compared to a rank-and-file SSO salary of £33.

The Malko-driven resignations of the late 1950s would seem small beer in 1967, by which time around twelve of the SSO's most important players of the decade had willingly left the orchestra, mostly for better-paid jobs in teaching institutions. And

---

[5] The concert was filmed for ABC TV, but all footage has been lost.

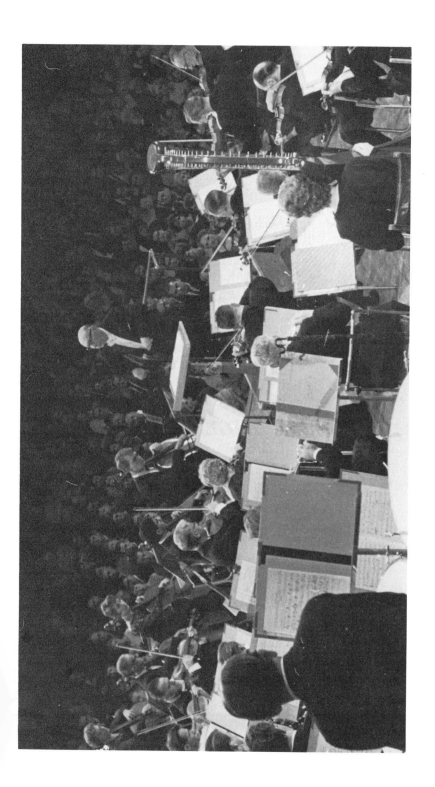

The composer conducts: The SSO with Igor Stravinsky in 1961.

the players who stayed knew that it was getting more and more difficult to attract players to the orchestra. For by the early 1960s the shortage of classical musicians, particularly string players, had reached crisis point in Australia.

The opportunities in Australia for freelance players had expanded rapidly since the war, so that the combination of ad hoc pit bands for musicals or ballet, radio and then television, variety show orchestras, and sessions for television commercials and recordings were keeping busy what good players there were. The shortage of string players was particularly vexatious: it was blamed on everything from an increase in the number of families living in flats (and therefore not wanting to disturb the neighbours with instrumental noises) to the extermination of the European Jews in the Second World War.

A more immediate reason for the musician shortage within the SSO was that many of its players were also instrumental teachers, and were not recommending that their pupils join the orchestra. For the younger players, particularly, life in the SSO had become too frustrating, as John Painter told the *Sun-Herald* in 1967, eighteen months after leaving the principal cello chair he occupied for six years. 'Only twice have I recommended youngsters to take up a career in the SSO. One was very, very talented. The other was talented and had no other vocation. It was either that or being a factory worker.'

Another part of the equation was that many fine Australian musicians were playing in foreign orchestras. Painter believed at the time that 'a first-class orchestra could be formed out of Australians who have gone overseas'.

The ABC's inability to import the appropriate number of players for its needs had been at issue since the 1940s, but solving this problem was now more urgent because each State had an ABC orchestra of reasonable strength, and each was finding it difficult to fill vacancies.

The most likely short-term solution at the time was considered to be the easing of Musicians Union restrictions on the importation of overseas players. As we've seen, the ABC had been negotiating with the union over this issue since the war years, but progress had been slow. By the mid-1950s no more than twenty per cent of the players in any ABC orchestra could be foreign-born, and the union was charging recently emigrated European musicians a £21 joining fee, as opposed to the joining fee for locally born players of £5.5s. Restrictions were finally eased in the 1960s, partly because the union agreed that there were more orchestral vacancies than there were local players of a high enough standard to fill them. In any case, Moses was not in a frame of mind to give the union much choice. In July 1960, clearly exasperated by the decades of discussion and the ABC's own dithering, he told the union's federal secretary that

. . . henceforth we shall not feel obliged to limit the number of foreign-born musicians employed in our orchestras in the terms of our previous agreement. This will in no way affect our intention to maintain the essential Australian character of our orchestras. We feel, however, that discrimination against foreign-born musicians, particularly those who have become naturalised Australians, is not in the national interest and cannot be supported.

Unfortunately, the player shortage coincided with a need, recognised by players, critics and managers, to make the orchestra bigger. At a platform strength of eighty-two, the SSO was small by international standards. The string section comprised sixteen first and twelve second violins, nine each of violas and cellos, and seven double basses. The lower string strengths, in particular, were too small for the bigger romantic works, and a player's absence could leave sections badly exposed. Each of the wind sections was one person short of ideal: instead of four flutes (or three flutes, plus one piccolo doubling on fourth flute) there were three, instead of three oboes (plus cor anglais) there were two, instead of three bassoons (plus contrabassoon) there were two. As Roger Covell noted in 1961: 'The sickness of a leading wind player could put a whole program in jeopardy'.

The first move to enlarge the SSO from its 1946 establishment strength was made in 1964, when ten extra string positions were created. This brought the sectional strengths up to eighteen firsts, fourteen seconds, and twelve each of violas and cellos. Appropriate to the difficult times—difficult in terms of instrumental recruitment—the positions went to young, promising players with little professional orchestral experience.

Although this expansion was a rare piece of good news for the

SSO, it was accomplished with great financial difficulty because the ABC had lobbied its orchestral funding partners so poorly. In 1946 the ABC's contribution to the SSO's upkeep was £30 000. In 1949 it was £48 000. In 1952 it was £85 000. In 1962 it was £174 000. In the same period the City Council's contribution to the orchestra's upkeep remained fixed at its 1946 level of £10 000. The NSW government had increased its 1946 investment of £20 000 to £25 000 in 1952, but was still contributing this same amount ten years later.

When the ABC's musical management decided that the SSO needed to grow, it also saw that the ABC could not afford to pay for such growth itself. Moses was thought privately by some of the ABC commissioners to have become an increasingly erratic manager since the mid-1950s, and there is something too relaxed in the fact that in ten years nobody from the ABC had persuaded the SSO's other investors to part with any more money. But he could still pull strings when he wanted to. In late 1963 the State government increased its annual subsidy to the SSO from £25 000 to £37 000. At the same time the newly appointed Director of Music, John Hopkins, went to great pains to persuade the Sydney City Council to vote another £2500 per year to the orchestra. These increases paid for the extra players.

❧

Between June 1961 and June 1964 the SSO did not have a chief conductor. This is a long time for a major cultural unit to be without artistic leadership, and the lack of a guiding spirit was a major contributor to the SSO's declining spirits. It was also a preview of the instability that would plague the orchestra's fortunes through the 1960s.

In choosing the chief conductor for any of its six orchestras, the ABC has usually paid close attention to the quality of the work the orchestra achieves with guest conductors, with a view to appointing one of these 'guests' as chief conductor. Such was the case in the early 1960s.

The front runners for the position were few and well defined. There was Karel Ančerl, whose 1961 tour (*sans* the Czech orchestra) was a great success. Buttrose asked him if he would like to become the SSO's next chief, but he was not free to leave Czechoslovakia.

There was Willem van Otterloo, for whom the orchestra had played extremely well during his 1962 tour. His long-standing commitments in the Netherlands meant that he was not free immediately. (As it eventuated, he would first become chief conductor in Melbourne, in 1967.) The 32-year-old Lorin Maazel had conducted a spectacularly good Mahler 9 in Sydney during his 1961 tour. Helen Bainton remembers that 'his virtuosity was astounding and his memory faultless', but in Neville Amadio's eyes he was 'unbelievably arrogant'. In the course of a speech to the audience during one Youth Concert he demonstrated a passage from a violin concerto by borrowing the soloist's instrument and playing a few bars himself!

Most SSO players had fairly well-defined views about who they did not want as chief conductor. During his 1959 tour, the Romanian conductor Constantin Silvestri had an unfortunate run-in with the orchestra, possibly due to his poor command of English. Silvestri was not at his most ebullient during his Sydney visit, and, after poor reviews for his first concerts, appeared fairly morose at the first (10 a.m.) rehearsal for his next program. When he inadvertently continued rehearsing past the traditional 11.30 'smoko' time, Llewellyn reminded him at 11.45 that the orchestra customarily had a rehearsal break. Silvestri then walked out and did not return. He did not bother to come back for the concerts, either, and a valiant Joseph Post once more stepped into the breach. 'The SSO is a good orchestra, but it is asleep', Silvestri told the press. 'Its players are too conceited, too uppish. Melbourne's orchestra is weaker than Sydney's, but is more enthusiastic, more warm, more human.'

Jascha Horenstein's 1962 concerts were great musical successes, but he was very stern and the orchestra did not enjoy working with him. It could be that he was simply too forcefully intolerant of the SSO's working methods. 'Play it at the point! I don't care whether you have played it in the middle of the bow for twenty years, *I* want it played at the point!' was one of his rehearsal instructions to the string section. Dean Dixon, too, would be suspicious of such traditions.

Someone who was never considered for the job was Joseph Post. He may not have wanted it, and it certainly was not offered to him. It is indicative of his temperament that after William James' retirement he happily became Assistant Director of Music to Herbert Cannon, a job in which he stayed until taking over the Conservatorium from Heinze in 1966.

Then there was Charles Mackerras.

The non-appointment of Mackerras in the early 1960s, when he was ready and willing to take up the post, points up two characteristics of the era. One is that, under a management to which it was becoming increasingly hostile, the orchestra's opinion of itself gradually rose, so that such feelings as 'we are better than the ABC treats us' were frequently expressed. The question of who should succeed Malko was not, then, solely about getting the 'best' conductor in musical terms—as the 'best' might not be the most famous—but one with a sufficiently high international profile. Such an appointment would confirm the orchestra's opinion of itself as being worthy of attracting the most highly regarded international talent.

This opinion also formed part of the second characteristic, one ABC management shared, that an 'illustrious name' (in the *Sunday Mirror's* phrase) was needed to become the SSO's musical director. Maazel was a popular choice with management because of his youth, flamboyance and rising international reputation. During the last months of Malko's tenure, Roger Covell asked him, 'purely hypothetically', how he would respond if asked to take up a permanent appointment in Australia. Maazel said it would only be possible if 'it would be on terms that allowed him at least seven months of the year free for conducting in other centres', Covell wrote in the *Sydney Morning Herald.* 'I take this to be true of many of his colleagues who, like him, are in the process of building an international reputation.'

Yet both orchestra and management wanted someone, of Maazel's calibre, who would stay here for half the year, and ideally more than that. In moving to Sydney to live at his advanced age, Malko had been a buffer between the ABC and the reality of the new international conducting order. For the ABC's expectations now were deeply unrealistic when the organisation was no longer able to offer the fees of the James era; when Australia itself represented a huge detour from the main concert circuits; when there was an international shortage of good conductors, and when Australia was not on the career paths of many of these;

and when the SSO's high opinion of itself was not always justified. A week after Malko's death, a *Herald* editorial noted soberly that none of the great conductors of the day 'is likely to be tempted by a post demanding nine months' residence in Australia'.

Mackerras was interested in taking the job as seriously as the ABC wanted it taken. But he was considered too inexperienced and not sufficiently starry a choice. Buttrose kept at Moses about a Mackerras appointment, but received a dismissive response. 'Tell him to go away and prove himself. The Sydney Symphony still regards him as a second oboe player.'[6] Of the thirty-six-year-old conductor, who was then beginning to make his name in Europe, the *Sunday Mirror* could only say: 'The boy from Turramurra doesn't qualify'. As opposed to Maazel, the boy from Pittsburgh, who did.

This spectacular, if unsurprising, example of superciliousness and cultural cringe would cost the orchestra and the ABC dearly. Mackerras may not have been famous enough in 1962 for the ABC or the SSO, but he might have had the time and the willingness to be a real orchestra builder, raising morale and standards after the patchiness of the Malko years. With help from management, he might also have had an impact on the creation of new and younger audiences.

'I think they felt I wasn't ready', Mackerras recalls. 'But, as Stuart Challender did later, I think I would have grown with the orchestra. I wanted to stay, because it would have given me the chance to take up a position with a good orchestra in my own country. I felt that this was something I could make a real contribution to.'

As it was, black, American-born, German-resident Dean Dixon made his first Australian tour (at Herbert Cannon's invitation) towards the end of 1962, and conducted a Mozart festival in Sydney. The SSO enjoyed the experience enormously as did audiences and critics, and only a few months later Dixon was announced as the orchestra's next chief conductor, as of July 1964. The appointment proved to be a frustrating one for the orchestra,

---

[6] Moses was not speaking for the SSO out of turn. He attended Town Hall concerts often, and knew many of the SSO's principal players well. Neville Amadio remembers him as a frequent backstage visitor.

for Dixon and for ABC management. It began as a period full of promise, but ended in bitterness and regret only three years later. John Hopkins became Director of Music shortly after the decision about Dixon had been taken, and came to think that Dixon with the SSO was just the wrong combination.

'The orchestra was longing for a chief conductor, and the temptation always is to appoint someone who has been good on a short visit and hope they will be consistently good over an extended period. But Dixon was not the right person for this orchestra. Gradually, he made it sound dull.'

He was also to turn himself into a martyr, seemingly on its behalf.

If I have spent some time on these various options for SSO chief conductor, it is because of the potency of The Lost Moments of History, Hugh Trevor-Roper's notion that the 'alternatives that were on offer at any time were real in the minds of those who rejected them, or could not grasp them: they were an intangible but real element in the total historical situation'. For the years 1961-63 were years of crisis for the SSO. The first half of 1961 was spent under the directorship of an increasingly eccentric old man, and until late 1962 no clear choice for the orchestra's future artistic leader had emerged. And even though his appointment was announced in 1963, Dixon would not be present until mid-1964.

During this time the orchestra's playing was erratic: committed and world class under the right conductors, undisciplined under the wrong ones. As Covell noted shortly before Malko's death: 'Its day-to-day standard has tended to be below that of some American and European orchestras'.

※

Dean Dixon was a fighter. As a teenager he joined his school orchestra in New York and became its concertmaster. The 'inside' player in most orchestral string desks—the player farther from the audience—turns the pages of the music during a concert, but the white 'inside' player next to Dixon, a boy called Brown, refused to turn pages for a Negro. Both players took their music home to practise after their first rehearsal together, and the next

Dean Dixon rehearsing the SSO in its then new Chatswood studio.

day Brown again refused to turn the page. Both Brown and Dixon kept playing.

'After five minutes Brown began to slow down', Dixon recalled many years later. 'His memory had failed him. Thank God mine stayed. That was one of the first battles and the first victories.'

One of his other victories was becoming the first black conductor to achieve international recognition. But he laid the foundations for his career outside North America. After conducting many of the leading United States orchestras in the 1940s, he went to France in 1949 (he gave the French premiere of Mahler 9 in 1960) and spent most of his working life from then on in Europe. 'I kicked myself out of America', he said later, 'because helping a Negro in *my field*, a field which requires a certain intellectual background, which requires a *leadership* ability, goes against what America says we Negroes don't possess'.

He worked with the Israel Philharmonic for a few years, then became musical director for the Gothenburg Symphony during the 1950s and was holding the same post with the Hesse Radio Orchestra in Germany when he came to Australia for the first time. He would remain the chief conductor in Hesse until 1974, and worked with increasing frequency in the United States after 1970. He died in 1976.

The first months of Dixon's SSO leadership were a honeymoon with audiences and critics. Even though he had injured his right arm in one of his early rehearsals, he still conducted his first concerts with sufficient authority to draw some of the best notices the orchestra had been given since Malko's first year in Sydney. In the *Sun*, Julian Russell wrote of the partnership's very first performance together that 'the playing came closer to perfection in the first half than any I've heard from the orchestra for many a long day'. In the *Telegraph*, Martin Long wrote that 'Dixon is an even finer conductor than we thought . . . There was a vibrancy about every bar of music'. Covell felt that the concert was 'an occasion of profound artistic and technical significance . . . music-making here has no better news than the return of Dixon.'[7]

---

[7] The main works on the program were Beethoven's C minor piano concerto with John Ogdon, and Tchaikovsky's *Pathetique* symphony. The concert opened with Haydn's still rarely heard Symphony No 46.

The performance of Mahler's first symphony which followed a few days later was even more rapturously received. 'This was a performance of memorable clarity of outline, precision of balance, and almost complete freedom from those minor vexatious mishaps that can occur at any time in any orchestra', wrote Julian Russell. 'The improvement in all departments of the orchestra since Dixon's week-old return is as marked as it is astonishing.'

Covell, his prose dressed in full Lindsey Browne regalia,[8] averred that 'not many altitudes short of paradise could be expected to yield a reading more fully endowed with brimming wonder or noonday sensuousness . . . This was playing of an order sufficient to leave no doubt that Dixon is the man we have been waiting for to establish Mahler in this country in the full pride of his achievement.'

In the first months of his directorship Dixon also staged the first of the events that for many people remain the most striking feature of his time here: the concerts for three- and four-year olds. They represented a completely new concept in the 1960s, and were much more involving for children than even the successful Heinze-based children's concerts that the orchestra had given for so long. Dixon explained to an education conference in 1965 how his young children's concerts worked:

There is no stage/floor relationship but a level relationship, so that there are the children in the middle and the symphony orchestra completely surrounding them, which makes the orchestra as close as it can possibly get to the child at a performance.

In the first half of the concert we introduce the instruments; first by asking each player to stand, say a few words about the instrument and then play it; then by playing [orchestral] pieces chosen with the idea of their opening focal point. The part of Schoenberg's Variations Opus 31 we play happens to begin with isolated woodwinds, the opening of Tchaikovsky 4 features the big brass. Each piece starts after [the children] have looked at me or whoever is conducting to hear what it is that is to be played. The only thing we do when the piece is announced is to ask the children 'And now have you heard of Mr Schoenberg?'.

[8] Browne had retired from full-time concert reviewing for the *Sydney Morning Herald* in 1960.

An Infants' concert at the Chatswood studio in June 1965. Dixon and the SSO are performing Beethoven's Symphony No 1 while children from Manly, West Manly and Dee Why Infants schools use the music as inspiration for their painting.

Dean Dixon

'Oh, yes.' 'And who have you heard of?' We get all kinds of answers to that.

Then the children are invited to go over with their chairs and sit next to or underneath or on top of—as close as they can get—their favourite instrument for the final number. If possible, with the big instruments, they will touch them during this part of the performance.

Of the first such Sydney concert, at which a gallery of critical observers (psychologists, music teachers, journalists and parents) and film cameras were in attendance, Covell wrote that 'it was easily the most important musical experiment conducted in this country since the introduction of youth and schools concerts . . . No one is ever likely to persuade the children who attended that a symphony orchestra is a remote or intimidating mystery'.

For the five-to-nine age group, whose SSO concerts were given in the main hall at the Conservatorium, Dixon devised a questionnaire they were to fill out. During the performance of a complete work a large numbered placard was held up, and the children filled in answers against correspondingly numbered questions in the printed program. Robert Miller recalls another of Dixon's novel ideas for these concerts.

'Dixon felt that the children of the audience should be given more than just music, that some sort of action on stage was important, particularly if it could be justified in program music. Well, for this five-to-nines concert we were playing the *Danse Macabre* of Saint-Saëns, which has a big solo part for the concertmaster. I was leading the orchestra on this occasion, and Dixon asked me if I would take the part of the devil, while the percussionist, Lou Tutschka, played the xylophone while dressed as a skeleton.

'We both agreed to this, not knowing the significance of the whole thing until we were confronted with a mask and costume that we each had to wear while we were performing. My papier mache devil mask had two holes for the eyes, and one each for the nose and mouth. I had to walk on stage wearing this while the orchestra played the first bars of the piece, and arrive at the leader's seat in time to begin my solo. So I stepped it all out—the number of yards I would have to walk in how many seconds and so on—but didn't realise that when I put my violin up to play, it completely altered the position of the mask, whereby the eye holes were up in the top of my head and I couldn't see anything at all. It was a dreadful experience, and one I will certainly never get involved in again. From the children's point of view, of course, it was a great success.'

Other successful (and less hazardous) Dixon experiments included an art competition for school children, with the best pictures being hung in the Conservatorium foyer, and a concert for blind children, given in the Kings Cross studios.

As far as the SSO was concerned, Dixon was not the only important figure interested in experiment. Before he began his term as chief conductor, one other important ABC appointment had been made. Herbert Cannon had retired and in November 1963 John Hopkins became the ABC's Director of Music.

Hopkins had conducted the SSO on several Australian visits, beginning in 1960. Although born in Yorkshire, his base until succeeding Cannon was New Zealand. There he had been musical director of its National Orchestra for six years, the director of its opera company, and founder of its national youth orchestra— in short, 'the leader of music-making' in the country. His appointment as Director of Music began an era of new adventure. He had many bold ideas, and many of them became reality: he created the Proms, a uniquely relaxed forum for courageous concert-giving; allowed his programming staff, which then included Richard Meale and Nigel Butterley, greater freedom in scheduling new and neglected repertoire for broadcast; introduced much new music to Australian audiences as a conductor; helped create radio programs that demonstrated and explained the work of the international avant-garde; and made the programming of music on ABC radio less haphazard and more thematic. But, like many of Australia's musical administrators, he was not good at thinking in television terms, nor did he have the staff who could solve the problem of how the orchestras could best be represented on television.

Perhaps his greatest weakness in the eyes of his colleagues was the mixture of ambitions he attempted to satisfy, for throughout his directorship he conducted many of the orchestras he was largely responsible for administratively.[9] He was seen to be, at best, a

---

[9] This was now true of Post, also, but he had been a regular conductor of ABC orchestras for more than twenty years before he became Assistant Director of Music.

workmanlike conductor. As one regular concertgoer of the day has put it, 'of all the resident conductors, the SSO still gave of its best in the 1960s under Post'. Yet, as we shall see, Hopkins had his successes on the podium as well.

In New Zealand he enjoyed a high level of day-to-day involvement with players. This had given him an understanding of orchestral life that made his working relationship with Dixon guarded and uncertain. For Dixon had plainly expressed and sometimes eccentric ideas about how the SSO should be run. These ideas and those of Hopkins did not always coincide. Indeed, Dixon's dazzling performance with the critics was looked upon with active scorn by some ABC music staff.

That he became friendly with Covell and Curt Prerauer does not mean that these critics suddenly lost their objectivity. (Cardus' friendship with Heinze did not prevent him writing bad reviews of Heinze's conducting.) But it began to cause bad feeling among those ABC people who had been close to Goossens and Malko. On 27 July 1964, just over a month after Dixon's arrival, Covell wrote in the *Sydney Morning Herald* that Dixon was 'a complete conductor, the first permanent director of the Sydney orchestra to be thoroughly at home in the full spectrum of the repertoire'.

Werner Baer was incensed. He wrote to Hopkins that

such an utterance should not remain unchallenged . . . The musical equipment and intellectual status of the late Sir Eugene Goossens, was as least as formidable as that of Mr Dixon, who is now hailed as the Messiah of Sydney music . . . It is inconceivable that Sydney's music lovers would accept certain of Mr Covell's statements without feeling embarrassed, or at least disquietened. Are we really to believe that Sydney has never heard certain and quite conventional works of the orchestral literature correctly interpreted until Mr Dixon's advent on the Australian musical scene? I feel that [Covell] has not taken sufficient trouble to acquaint himself with the history of the SSO which, in this context, must be fully taken into account.

Baer wanted to publish an official statement praising Dixon's work in the context of 'grateful comments about the role of earlier makers of fine music who . . . gave Sydney and indeed Australia the basis for its present and now much maligned standards'. But Buttrose and Hopkins decided that there would be nothing to gain from doing so.

This was the first example of a strange doubleness that developed during Dixon's chiefdom. As his reputation with the critics and public became resolutely radiant, his relationship with the orchestra and ABC management became increasingly troubled.

The first major conflict Dixon had with ABC management was over the SSO's proposed visit to the Commonwealth Arts Festival, which was to be held in London in September 1965.

꙳

Since the Olympic Games concerts in Melbourne, the SSO had played there again in 1959, in combination with the MSO, for the opening of the Myer Music Bowl; and twice at the Adelaide Festival, in 1960 and 1964, but it had never performed outside Australia. These interstate tours were usually a refreshing musical experience for the players and, in Robert Miller's words, 'invaluable experience for the management and planners'. They were in many ways dry runs for the 1965 spectacular.

This Commonwealth tour brought important firsts: the first overseas tour by the SSO, and the first time an Australian orchestra would play in the United Kingdom or Asia. As such, it was a prestigious endeavour: the second of the three planned London concerts would be given in the presence of Queen Elizabeth and Prince Phillip. Less prestigiously, from the players point of view, the orchestra would also play for the Australian Ballet's performances during the festival. The ABC also planned an extensive tour around the two London concerts, with performances to be given in Cardiff, Liverpool, Glasgow, Birmingham, Manila, Tokyo, Hong Kong and Bombay.

Moses had been the chief architect of the tour, and had it pencilled in the SSO's schedule in 1963. Once the concert dates had been firmed up, Moses wrote to Dixon in May, 1964, a month before he was to arrive in Sydney as chief conductor, telling him of the tour and asking him to conduct the major concerts. Dixon replied that the tour dates clashed with his commitments in Frankfurt and that 'September 1966 would be better . . . from the standpoint of allowing me to fix my own individual stamp on the Sydney Symphony Orchestra and really have time to smooth out some of the uneven elements'.

But after two months as chief conductor Dixon said simply that the orchestra was 'not ready' for the tour, 'from purely artistic considerations'. Moses put a brave face on the issue and said simply that there had been a misunderstanding, but he was clearly upset to see the trip so threatened. Due to retire in early 1965, Moses regarded the tour as an appropriate parting gesture to the orchestra in which he had taken such a huge interest over his thirty-one years as general manager. It would allow the ABC to present one of its two major orchestras in London before the Queen, in a fitting 'showcase' concert for the SSO's first overseas tour, and it would create a prestige orchestral connection with Asia. It was also timely from the point of view of the expectations of the orchestra's Sydney audience. Between 1960 and 1965 Sydney would receive visits by the Czech Philharmonic, Boston Symphony, Berlin Chamber, London Philharmonic, Polish National Radio and NHK (Japan) Symphony orchestras, and the London Symphony and Israel Philharmonic would perform around Australia in 1966. The SSO was expected to return the favour sooner rather than later.

Moses was not one to linger over his misfortune, and after Dixon's rebuff asked the SSO which conductor it would like on the tour if Dixon would not come. The players' committee suggested van Otterloo. Moses booked the Dutch conductor for a number of tour dates, then rang Hopkins, who was conducting in New Zealand at the time, to tell him the news. 'I'll be back in a couple of days, and we'd better discuss it then', he told Moses.

'So we had a meeting, and I said that it was imperative that we get Dixon for at least one concert, because it would be absurd if the orchestra did such an important tour without the chief conductor', Hopkins recalls. 'Van Otterloo had no official association with the SSO at that time, and I told Moses that favouring van Otterloo over Heinze and Post was in any case very poor. Moses was taken aback but he agreed. So I went to Hamburg on my next European trip and secured the release of Dixon from one of his concerts there. Of course I also had to tell van Otterloo that he was no longer booked for the tour, and that was very hard to do.'

Dixon eventually conducted the SSO's 'Royal' London concert. The remainder of the tour schedule was to be shared by Heinze,

The Commonwealth tour: John Hopkins and the SSO rehearsing in London's Royal Festival Hall.

Post, and Sargent but Heinze became ill and had to cancel all his concerts. Hopkins took his place.

Some preliminary window-dressing occurred. Until this trip the SSO had played its concerts in dinner clothes, but all the musicians were re-fitted for their overseas debut: in Asia, white tuxedos for the men and white blouses and black skirts for the women; in the United Kingdom tails for the men and black gowns for the women. From now on, tails and black gowns would also become the norm for concerts at home.

A different kind of display was provided by the Commonwealth Film Unit (now Film Australia), which in 1964 made a short documentary about the SSO and Dixon called *Concerto for Orchestra*. Made to be shown in cinemas in the countries in which the SSO was about to appear, it was essentially a record of the orchestra preparing Bartok's work with Dixon, culminating in excerpts from the final performances at subscription concerts. There were also interviews with players and a portion of one of the 'babies' concerts. It was well reviewed by local critics and remains an absorbing and intelligent film about music-making.[10]

The tour was successful but arduous. The pre-London concerts in Asia went well, but the Bombay leg of the tour was cancelled because of fighting between India and Pakistan. According to the *Telegraph's* tour correspondent, Martin Long, this was just as well. 'The pace [one concert each in Manila, Tokyo and Hong Kong in four days] has been telling on the players, and it seemed inevitable that exhaustion, coupled with minor illnesses, would bring casualties in the orchestra's ranks if the tour had gone on as planned.'

Violinist Jennifer James remembers many orchestral illnesses before the travel began, as a result of the injections the orchestra had to have for the Asian stops. 'One night when Dorati was conducting in the Town Hall [during his 1965 tour] there were seventeen players off sick. Dorati walked on to the platform, bowed, looked at the orchestra, and walked off again.'

The first London concert in the Commonwealth tour included

---

[10] *Concerto for Orchestra* was directed by Robert Parker, who in the 1980s was better known as the producer of a series of digitally re-mastered records featuring vintage jazz performances.

works the orchestra could not rehearse sufficiently before it left Australia, including Malcolm Williamson's new violin concerto; and which involved a chorus—the Christchurch Harmonic Choir— it had never worked with before and with which it could not rehearse until the day before the concert in which the two groups were to perform together.[11] Initially, Hopkins asked Dixon if he would conduct the Williamson in his 'Royal' concert. Dixon refused to do so. In February 1965 he wrote:

. . . Given that we have only nine hours rehearsal for the work, in London, this is one of the classic SUICIDE PROPOSALS! As you know, I am doing modern works each week of my life here in Europe, and therefore for myself I can say a definitive yes.

However with the SSO it is another story. They are not used to reading and performing 'fresh-off-the-press' modern works every week, week after week on end, as the German radio orchestras are. Therefore I think that in all responsible aspects [*sic*] we cannot artistically afford to commit the SSO to such a deal unless someone, preferably me, has a chance to see the score well in advance of the performance date.

But the score of the Williamson would not be ready for some months. And to complicate matters further this first London concert had two conductors—Hopkins for the first half and Sargent for the second. Not surprisingly, Martin Long described the evening as 'a curious hotch-potch'.[12] Roger Covell was tour reporter for the *Sydney Morning Herald* and remembers the concert well.

'It was an indifferent performance, really. The orchestra sounded under-rehearsed, as if they were playing in a municipal band stand. I thought then that there was not much point in the SSO going abroad if that was the sound it was going to make.'

The reviews for this concert were, predictably, lukewarm or dismissive. *The Times'* critic noted that the orchestra 'is a virile group . . . The tone quality, if not of the sleekest, was always

---

[11] Much of the music the orchestra was to play in the pit for the Australian Ballet was also rehearsed in the United Kingdom sight unseen.

[12] Apart from the Williamson concerto, with Hopkins conducting and Yehudi Menuhin as soloist, the program included Beethoven's first symphony, Parry's *Blest Pair of Sirens* and Brahms' *Academic Festival Overture* 'with choral ending by Sir Malcolm Sargent'.

generous and intense, and the players managed to convey enthusiasm without loss of discipline'. But in the Sydney *Sun*, Julian Russell (also covering the tour) described the first half of the evening as 'embarrassingly inept'. Hopkins received better reviews when he conducted the third London concert a fortnight later. This included the world premiere performance of Peter Sculthorpe's *Sun Music I*, a work Heinze had commissioned, and which *The Times* called 'a strikingly imaginative aural achievement'.

Dixon's concert, given two nights after the Hopkins/Sargent one, was a marked success. The main work was Brahms 1, which the orchestra had played under Dixon twelve times in 1965. Dixon also bravely included Richard Meale's challenging new work for strings, *Homage to Garcia Lorca*. The (London) *Telegraph* found the playing in the Brahms achieved 'the kind of perfection that has almost fallen into oblivion in the metropolitan bustle of our concert life . . . the Australians have completely assimilated the ideas of their conductor-in-chief'. Helen Bainton wrote of this performance that it was 'uplifting beyond anything I remember'.

The concert's success was a typical example of Dixon's working methods. He was almost painfully systematic, and believed in building up the orchestra's repertoire gradually and with plentiful rehearsal. 'He had the view that certain works were to become the foundation of a repertoire', Covell recalls, 'and the Brahms is a good example. That was thoroughly played in before it was taken to London'.

After the 1964 *Lorca* performances by the Little Symphony under Post, the SSO had also played it with Dixon in 1965 subscription concerts. A month before the Commonwealth tour, Dixon wrote an open letter to the players who would perform the work with him in London and noted that he would be taking the score with him to Frankfurt so that he could refresh his memory of the work before the London concert.

Could I ask you to do the same? That is, take the individual part with you into your luggage, and from the beginning of the tour go through at least one movement per day, by which I mean tapping out the correct rhythms in some semblance of the correct tempo . . . For artists of our calibre any London reaction [to this piece] except a tremendous success will be begging the question, a thing that we don't want to do.

The orchestra's success on the tour was a great morale booster. It also taught the SSO players how much energy was needed in order to keep the standard of playing consistent over a period in which constant travel was added to regular repertoire changes. This was a particularly valuable lesson: the orchestra's next major international tour, in 1974, would be more extensive and would offer more dramatic successes and failures.

$$\maltese$$

Dixon's initial reluctance to take part in the tour was long-lived. His first letter about the tour to Moses, suggesting September 1966 as a more appropriate tour date, was written in June 1964. He did not finally agree to conduct the 'Royal' London concert until January 1965. The reversal was due to one major change to the orchestra's personnel: In September 1964 Ernest Llewellyn resigned from the SSO.

Llewellyn was leaving, he said, to concentrate on teaching, although it was rumoured at the time that it was because he could not tolerate Dixon's working methods. 'I am concerned that there is a shortage of good players and teachers. I believe I can make my contribution to alleviating these shortages. I expect to be able to help bring about a higher standard in teaching and also, through the development of chamber music groups and string ensembles in centres outside the State capitals to develop players fit to take their places in the Sydney and [Melbourne] Symphony Orchestras.'

Since returning from his Kapell scholarship studies in 1957, Llewellyn had been increasingly busy. Under Malko, he became assistant conductor as well as leader,[13] and increased his teaching commitments, for the Kapell scholarship required the recipient (and Llewellyn was the first and only one) to apply his experience to the raising of teaching standards. Llewellyn was, in any event, a committed instrumental teacher and when, in 1964, his doctors told him he had to reduce his workload, he and his wife Ruth saw this as an opportunity to leave the stresses of orchestral life behind. Yet he would become hardly less active. He had recently taken up an offer made by Musica Viva's founder, Richard Goldner,

---

[13] This appointment coincided with Joseph Post's relinquishing his associate conductor position for his new job in the Music Department.

to set up a summer school at Mittagong (which subsequently became the Musica Viva Easter Festival), and he wanted more time to teach his students there. And within months of his retirement he would become the founding director of the Canberra School of Music.

Moses, Hopkins and Dixon tried to induce Llewellyn to stay as leader, at least until the Commonwealth tour was over, but he would not do so. He said he would lead the SSO on the tour, but only if a permanent replacement could not be found for him in the meantime.

The search for a new concertmaster was complicated by Dixon's belief that the success of the 1965 tour depended on having a leader who had become 'acquainted with the orchestra', not one who was new to it. One potential concertmaster surfaced in December 1964, an Italian violinist called Angelo Stefanato, who at that time was leader of the RAI orchestra in Rome. He was married to the Australian-born pianist Margaret Barton, who had been living in Europe since the early 1950s. She had written to Post explaining that her husband was interested in the possibility of becoming SSO concertmaster. 'He appears to have splendid credentials', Post wrote to Dixon. Dixon agreed to travel to Rome to hear him play, but there are no further records of Stefanato being considered for the job.

In January 1965 Robert Miller and Donald Hazelwood were appointed joint concertmasters, a move Dixon declared himself very happy with. Miller was one of the most distinguished string players of his time (he has been retired for many years). A founding member of the original Sydney String Quartet, he had been in the SSO since 1936, and assistant concertmaster since Goossens' time. Hazelwood was a comparative newcomer. He had played in the first and second violins for two years under Goossens before spending some time in Europe studying with, among others, Nathan Milstein. On his return in 1956 he rejoined the SSO first violin section and a few years later joined one of the major new chamber groups to emerge from the orchestra, the Austral String Quartet.

This group comprised Hazelwood (succeeding fellow SSO violinist and Austral founding member Alwyn Elliott) as first violin; leader of the SSO's second violins, Ron Ryder, as second; Ron Cragg as viola and SSO cellist Gregory Elmaloglou. The

Australs performed an enormous amount of new Australian music, and made a number of records. They also gave two concerts in the United Kingdom during the Commonwealth tour. Covell has noted that the group had to 'struggle gamely against the disabilities of having to combine its quartet schedule with a full program of orchestral work', and critic John Carmody believes that 'Sydney's music in the sixties was unthinkable without them'.

Another important group to emerge from the SSO in the 1960s was the New Sydney Woodwind Quintet, which, like the Australs, frequently toured other State capitals and regional centres for Musica Viva. When it began, in 1965, its members were Neville Amadio; Donald Westlake, who joined the SSO as principal clarinet in 1960; Clarrie Mellor; oboist David Woolley; and bassoonist John Cran.[14]

Dixon and Hopkins supported chamber music performance by SSO members, and believed firmly in giving orchestral principals as many solo opportunities as possible. From the 1966 season all the soloists on Dixon's country tour concerts were drawn from the ranks of the SSO. But like Goossens, Dixon knew that as much as chamber music performance and solo opportunities were good for corporate playing standards, the greatest difficulty the orchestra faced was its huge workload. The Miller/Hazelwood appointment, in which the leadership was shared equally by the two players, was the first in the SSO to recognise this as the central problem in the orchestra's life. Robert Miller explains how the concept of co-principals began in the SSO.

'It was at the request of the members of the orchestra. We felt that we should be brought into line with overseas groups, and Dixon and Hopkins agreed. The first section to be affected was the first violins, and it meant that Don and I took it in turns, three weeks at a time, to lead the orchestra. Not at any time did we play on the first desk together. This seemed to be a very happy arrangement, but it did mean that the player who was not performing had to learn the program as a kind of understudy.

'This did not prevent the scheme from being a success, though, and in 1966 co-principal leaders were subsequently appointed to

---

[14] Cran joined the SSO as second bassoon in 1957, and became principal in 1963. He is still leading the section at time of writing.

the flute, oboe, clarinet, bassoon and trumpet sections. This did not work quite so well. True to the nature of musicians, they could see an advantage in the three-weeks-on, three-weeks-off system, and would make arrangements with their offsiders to perhaps carry on in their place for another two weeks, making a five-week break. This meant that, although they were theoretically supposed to be on call, they might be out of Sydney altogether and would be completely out of touch with the orchestra's general technique when they did rejoin.

'Dixon decided that this was not the way he had meant the co-principal system to work, so he insisted that the two principals instead should share concerts. This was really an Associate Principal system, similar to the one the SSO now has. One player would take the first half of the concert and the second player would relieve him in the second half. In the next concert the players would swap halves, so that the major works were shared about. This was of course a much better arrangement.'

The creation of Associate Principals is a major reform in the life of any orchestra, and for the SSO it was made more difficult by the number and quality of the musicians who were leaving. Neville Amadio remarks of this period that 'players were dropping off like flies. It was very destabilising'. Moreover, major changes in ABC management were taking place that would affect the orchestra's future irrevocably.

The Canadian trombonist Peter Ash had replaced Stan Brown in 1961, but he left in 1964 to return to Canada. Llewellyn resigned in the same year. In 1965 violist Robert Pikler and cellist John Painter, both principals, resigned to take up teaching positions at the Conservatorium. Violinists Harry Curby and Robert Ingram resigned a short while later. Alan Mann had left as principal horn in 1963, and spent a year teaching. He returned to the SSO in 1964, by which time Clarrie Mellor was principal horn. The conflicts within the section were sometimes immense, and Mann resigned again in 1968 prompted, he wrote, 'by health grounds arising out of my personal attitudes to work in the orchestra'. The fourth horn, Patrick Brislan, resigned in early 1967 because, Hopkins told Dixon, 'he is dissatisfied with his position'. Principal oboe David Woolley left at the same time to work overseas.

The mid-1960s was also a period of retirements. Double bass

principal Charles Gray, second clarinet Douglas Williamson and timpanist Alard Maling all reached retirement age during the Dixon years. And in 1967 Robert Miller left the orchestra after thirty-one years. He was to become the musical director of the National Training Orchestra, which the ABC had formed as a way of solving the player shortage. It existed to prepare young players for life in the ABC's adult orchestras, and did so until, as the ABC Sinfonia, it was disbanded in 1986.

Audiences were not blind to these departures. Early in 1967 Robert Sturgess, a correspondent to the *Sydney Morning Herald*, noted that in a recent SSO performance

string strength had dropped alarmingly from the optimum 16, 14, 12, 10, 8 to the haphazard proportions of 13, 7, 8, 9, 6—43 strings instead of 60. And this for Elgar's first symphony!

It is perhaps only two years since widespread publicity was given to an increase of ten string players in the Sydney orchestra; a curious silence pervades its recent savage decimation.

All this orchestral leave-taking occurred over a four-year period that coincided almost exactly with Dixon's time as chief conductor. And it is tempting to suggest straight-forwardly that it was because of Dixon that many of these players resigned. For, despite his reforming zeal and his concern for the orchestra's welfare, many players found that, as his tenure progressed, he became increasingly difficult to work with. Colin Evans:

'His first season with us was wonderful, and I thought we gave him everything. But something went wrong, and I remember feeling that a lot of pieces came out sounding too like one another. He was very meticulous and would not let himself go. Even in the most unbuttoned moments of Shostakovich symphonies he would rein himself in. This made it very difficult to play solos for him with any freedom.'

'He was very conscious of internal balance and the exact obeyance of dynamic markings, and that was very good for us', Donald Hazelwood recalls. 'But he used to ride the principal players and suppress their musical personalities. Everything we played had to be done his way.'

Neville Amadio agrees. 'I was onto him. If he was conducting anything with an extended solo he would always ask me to play it in the opposite manner to the way I had played it for him first. So in order to play a passage as I wanted I would say to him, in rehearsal, "You would like this played very strictly, maestro?", and he would say "No, with great freedom". Or I would say, "You would like me to use rubato here" and he would say, "No, play that passage in very strict rhythm". It was ridiculous to have to do that, but I felt so straight-jacketed.'

Ron Cragg also recalls that Dixon could be equally strict with soloists. 'He did not really like conducting concertos, and he would beat time right through solo passages, so that soloists were locked into a steady beat. Very silly. He also brought this attitude to works of the classical period. In terms of the style of playing, we did some of our best Mozart ever with him, but he would insist on doing every repeat, which made the pieces interminable to us.'

Robert Miller admits that Dixon had a higher regard for the players' welfare than perhaps any of his predecessors, but that this did not make him any more engaging a conductor.

'There were some situations that were really intolerable. He would demand that the orchestra, at a particular point in the work, should not look at the music, but watch him, regardless of whether there was a difficult passage to play. In his desire to keep the orchestra together he would be very insistent about this—"I must have your eye" was one of his favourite phrases— to the extent that the orchestra sometimes became overly nervous. It didn't seem to matter whether you played the right notes or not, as long as you were watching his beat. I'm afraid the feeling between conductor and orchestra was more strained at the end of his period here than it had been at the beginning.'

To some players, Dixon's interest in experiment caused some of these 'intolerable' situations. He might ask string players to swap desks, or to have principal players sit at the back of their section rather than the front. He explained that he was concerned 'not with the relative distance a player sits from the front desk, but the total homogeneity of the section. I would rather distribute experienced players evenly through a section than have it tail off suddenly after the first few desks'. Putting such ideas into practice demanded great diplomatic skill, but he failed to convince

many of the musicians that such explorations were worth while.
'He was always coming up with weird plans,' one player explained wearily.

'I liked Dixon, but he bored the orchestra to death', Cliff
Goodchild recalls. 'He became infamous with us for all the talking
he did at rehearsal. He would finish each call by giving us notes,
so that we could mark our parts with things he wanted done,
and these pencil sessions could be very long. At the end of one
Mahler symphony rehearsal he talked for thirty minutes!'

'I remember one of the cleaners at the studios asking me once
why there were so many more cigarette butts on the floor after
some rehearsals than after others', says Neville Amadio. 'I realised
then that it was only during Dixon's pencil sessions that some
players smoked so much.'

How justified was the orchestra's irritation with Dixon? Roger
Covell believes it was unjust but inevitable. 'Dixon was an excellent
thing for them. The orchestra often played more rhythmically
for him than it did for anyone else, because he had a wonderful
sense of orchestral texture. He was also able to attract the right
sort of attention from the public and the press. In the end the
players got thoroughly tired of Dixon just as they have got tired
of every other conductor they have ever had. The complaints
that he talked too much have to be put down to impatience, to
the limited musical culture as well as general culture of some
of the people involved. Some of them were essentially musical
tradesmen.'

'It was very difficult dealing with Dixon's deficiencies when
he had such great support from the critics', says John Hopkins.
'But the problems were the same each year. When he came for
his first concerts there was high expectation from the orchestra
and audiences, and there was a lot of excitement in the playing.
But by the end of his months here, the orchestra sounded neat,
very well-balanced, but boring, and audiences would wonder why
they weren't enjoying Dixon concerts, when they felt that they
should be enjoying them. Where the MSO had developed a central
European sound by this time, the SSO was a chromium-plated
American car. Under really outstanding guest conductors like
Cluytens and Kubelik[15] they made a very vibrant sound. Well, Dixon

[15] Both conductors toured for the ABC in 1964.

was taking the chrome off and not replacing it with very much. For example, John Robertson could be a very exciting player, but Dixon would put his hand up to quiet him, and suddenly you got this subdued, very dull trumpet sound.'

Through all these experiences, Dixon continued to impress the critics with his breadth of musical interests and his patient building of a central repertoire. The perception that overall standards were improving under his direction was widespread. But he was not liked by the SSO. Nor was the ABC's new general manager.

In 1965, the year Talbot Duckmanton took over as the ABC's general manager, the organisation was moving quickly through a series of transformations. Television and radio activities were becoming increasingly complex and diverse. In 1960 ABC TV began transmission in Brisbane, Perth, Adelaide and Hobart. 'University of the Air' began the following year, as did 'Four Corners'. Work on establishing thirteen new ABC TV channels in country centres began in 1962 and in 1964 the ABC took over all the technical services (including the recording of concerts) from the PMG's department. Throughout this period, the entire radio division was being restructured under a system called NEWRAD.

The ABC was a much larger and more versatile beast than it had been when Cleary announced in 1935 that the Commission's Sydney orchestra would be increased from thirty-five to forty-five members. The new chairman, James Darling, had taken over after Boyer's death in 1961, and came to think that the ABC had become too big for Moses' sometimes grand methods. He would write later of the ABC during his chairmanship that 'it was no longer possible to administer the organisation in the old paternalistic way, and it may be that it was the failure of Sir Charles[16] to adjust himself to the size of the change.'

Yet for orchestral players it was Moses' retirement in 1965 that dealt them the greatest blow. The ABC's headquarters in Pitt Street were sometimes jokingly called Commonwealth Ministry for Musical Culture, and Moses was glad to foster this perception. He went to as many concerts as he could, knew many orchestral players well, and would often listen to concert broadcasts from his office. One of his secretaries, Betty Barnett, remembers him

[16] Moses was knighted in 1961.

conducting many performances from behind his desk!

In musical terms, Moses' successor represented the forces of disinterest. Talbot Duckmanton had worked his way up through the ABC since 1939, when he joined as a sports announcer. As general manager he was far calmer than Moses and not at all prone to the epic heartiness that characterised Moses' more expansive moments, but he was also more aloof, more ponderous, more formal and less accessible. He was not inclined to be musical. 'He was never interested in what we were doing', says one SSO veteran. 'I never saw him at a concert and any time you met him he was insufferably stilted.'

He could be astonishingly ignorant of the needs of musicians. John Hopkins: 'I tried to explain to him once how valuable it was to have the members of the SSO playing in chamber groups, because the exposure to different kinds of ensemble playing was an investment that got ploughed back into the orchestra in the form of high playing standards. Also of course because such activities helped show how crucial the symphony orchestras were to our musical well-being in general. He sucked on his pipe for a while and then he said, "Why couldn't they just rehearse together and not give performances?".'

One of Duckmanton's first changes to the ABC's musical administration was to give Buttrose, the major source of the ABC's concert-giving energy, the job of running the Commission's New York office.

Buttrose was flattered at the time, but later realised that New York was probably a glamorous form of punishment for behaviour the ABC regarded as scandalous. It says much about the moral uptightness of Australia in 1962 that when Buttrose's wife began divorce proceedings against him that year it made front-page news ('ABC Chief Divorced'). Darling asked him to resign, telling him: 'Buttrose, you know the decent thing for you to do would be to give us your resignation and we can act on it if we wish. That's the way this kind of thing would be done in Britain'.

If Buttrose was being pushed out of the way, he did not mind too much. 'A lot of the savour had gone out of working for the ABC after Moses went', he wrote later. Buttrose's leaving was made more sinister for the orchestras by the way in which his vacuum was filled. Duckmanton did not replace him as Director of Publicity and Concerts, but left concerts under the care of his deputy, the neat-minded Rex Ellis, who was called Federal Concert Manager. Publicity was separated altogether. But Ellis's position was still a powerful one: he had better access to Duckmanton than did Hopkins.

Not long after these changes, Joseph Post resigned from the Music Department to run the Conservatorium, for Heinze retired in 1966. It was Hopkins' third year as Director of Music.

In terms of orchestra and management, then, the mid-1960s could hardly be described as stable. Apart from its effect on the SSO's self-perception, this instability had a fatal impact on Dixon's future.

Like most conductors, Dixon was interested in power, but he was not a tyrant. He pursued power to the point where he felt able to implement his musical vision. Like most conductors of his era, he held more than one chief conductor post, and made many guest appearances. He spent an average of four months a year with the SSO, but tried to find ways to keep in contact with the performances the orchestra gave in his absence. His methods of doing this were typically thorough and sometimes excessively so.

In mid-1965 he told Hopkins that he 'should like to have made available for me a tape of each public concert that the SSO performs, while not under my direction, together with the names of the wind players specifically saying who was playing what in each number. And, of course, also a percussion list stating the same'. He wanted these tapes to include the tuning-up before each half of the concert.

This was done, but not with any enthusiasm. Hopkins told his colleagues: 'Whilst the SSO was on its overseas tour several other aspects of this matter were investigated and it would seem that we are now in a position to meet Mr Dixon's wishes'.

'In 1966 we had the conductor Michael Gielen here on his first Australian tour', Hopkins says, 'and Dixon stayed on after his usual few months of concerts here had finished to watch the rehearsals. During the final rehearsal for Gielen's first concert he sat in the Eastern Gallery of the Town Hall peering at each of the players in turn through a pair of binoculars. That really freaked some of them out'.

Dixon knew that the SSO did not play consistently well. 'It will be a couple of years before we have a world class orchestra', he had said during his first season. He was convinced that the erratic quality of the SSO's playing could be attributed to their overwork. There was little he could do about the opera commitments (which in any case would soon come to an end with the formation of the 'Trust' orchestra), but for his 1966 and 1967 seasons he succeeded in having half of each major subscription program repeated in all series. So when Mahler 5 was the major work in the Red series, it stayed as the major work in the Blue. A first half comprising Haydn's Symphony No 93 and the world premiere of Richard Meale's *Nocturnes* was also given five times. This was a major breakthrough in an organisation that still saw its first musical priority as finding enough live concert material to meet its broadcast commitments.

Goossens had been the last conductor to have real freedom in putting concert programs together. Writing to the ABC's London representative in October 1956, a few months before Malko became the SSO's chief conductor, William James noted that 'Dr Malko has the utmost freedom in his programming and general planning of the orchestra's activities . . . he will find the co-operation of the ABC's Music Department in no way restrictive and in many respects decidedly helpful'. James then included a list of guidelines Malko would need to keep in mind when planning works for his concerts. The following is among them.

Timing of Programmes: Unless otherwise stated, the first half of each programme occupies 59 minutes of broadcasting time, including the National Anthem at the opening. This means that the actual performing time of the items should be 48-50 minutes. The second half occupies 44 minutes—actual playing time 37-40 minutes. Special arrangements can generally be made to extend the second half by up to 15 minutes to accommodate longer works.

Malko's programming freedom then, was akin to the freedom enjoyed under a benevolent dictatorship.

James also remarked in this letter that 'the engagement of soloists for public concerts is basically the Commission's responsibility'. Malko later came to feel he was not being consulted sufficiently about the soloists he was slotted to work with. Dixon also wanted greater control over this, and over the choice of conductors who were to appear with the SSO in his absence. The need to adhere to the conditions of the 'Tait amendment' and the rigid attitude of the Concert Department towards scheduling complicated the wishes of both men.

As part of every ABC concert performed before a paying audience had to be broadcast, the Music Department had little room to manoeuvre when it came to soloists' repertoire. If a pianist could only bring four concertos and not five, or if a conductor objected to the inclusion of a particular concerto in one of his programs, the national repertoire balance could be thrown seriously awry. And the national schedule of concerts and recitals had become so comprehensive by the mid-1960s (about 800 performances per year by 1968) that the Concert Department managers felt it was irresponsible for them not to act of their own volition when it came to filling performance slots.

The engagement of soloists and conductors was further complicated by the workings of the Artists' Tours Committee, which was established shortly after James' retirement. The group comprised representatives from the Music, Concert and (Radio) Program departments, with the general manager acting as chairman. It was the regular, official and only forum for the discussion of artists to be booked for ABC tours. Following ATC meetings, an official letter would be written over the general manager's signature to the ABC's London and New York offices, instructing them officially to approach the artists' agents with an offer. (ABC staff in Sydney were not to approach agents direct unless they were on business overseas.) Naturally enough, this gave the New York and London office managers a great deal of power, and created an enormous amount of extra work. But it did not always bring the desired results. John Hopkins:

'To give you just one of many such examples, we had been trying to get the pianist Annie Fischer here for some years, and her answer to our London office had always been "no". So on one of my European trips I went to see her in Hungary. We had a meal together, at the end of which she said, "I will come to Australia, but only for you". You couldn't get people of her calibre to work here by dealing with them at one remove.'

Traditionally, chief conductors had been told of artists who were to appear with them only as a matter of courtesy, but Dixon wanted more authority, the kind enjoyed by other chief conductors around the world. In July 1966 he went straight to Duckmanton with the following request:

In 1962, 1964, 1965 and 1966 I accepted the soloists with their details as given for playing with me in Sydney with the SSO . . . However, after 1967 it will not be possible for me to continue this way of work.

I should, therefore, like to say that for 1968 and future years after that it is necessary for me to give my personal OK for any soloists projected to perform with me, and as head conductor of the SSO I should like (as done internationally) to have a voice in the choice of our guest conductors.

This was not answered immediately, but Dixon raised the subject again in a long letter to Harold Hort, who had become Assistant Director of Music after Post's departure. Hort had written to Dixon around the time Dixon had written to Duckmanton, explaining that the 'repeat one half' formula Dixon now applied to his concerts had 'caused a number of problems, as the arrangements you've proposed affect the way in which we have worked in the past a good deal'. Hort went on:

I have consulted with the various departments concerned and I am sure you will realise that we are all very anxious to do everything we can to put your ideas into effect. There is no lack of goodwill on our part— still we have definite commitments with artists in 1967. It therefore seems to me that if we are to be really effective in 1968, it would be a good idea to let us have some thoughts about the actual programs you have in mind even now, so that in arranging soloists, dates of bookings and so on (which in fact is already well in hand) *we may be able* to take your views into account. [my italics]

Dixon was clearly shocked that he should be approached as if his ideas were simply troublesome to an orderly system. His reply to Hort (September 1966) and the events that followed it are a testament to the inflexibility the ABC's methods of concert management had come to by 1966:

I am fully aware that my programs [for 1967] are capable of giving 'a number of problems', especially as held up against the background of the way things have been working in the past. However . . . I can only remind [you] that progress is sometimes a little painful; and I, for one, cannot subscribe to tradition for tradition's sake. As well, my so-called 'new' ways have been tried and are proving successful in many of the modern international cities, are used by the most modern radio networks and are, in the final analysis, for the good of symphonic music in Australia, and especially for the good of the musically growing and expanding SSO.

That 'the various departments concerned are very anxious to do everything they can do to put "my" ideas into effect' is true beyond any doubt— and I both know and believe this. Too, [*sic*] I know there is no lack of goodwill on your and their parts. But the way it is now set up it can't possibly work artistically. Also, the suggestion that I let you [now] have 'some thoughts about the actual programs I have in mind for 1968 even now' so that you *may* be able to take my views concerning soloists is not a possible solution, mainly because:

1. Making the programs so far in advance is not taking into account the 'how' and 'where' of the orchestra. By that I mean where our strings have gone stylistically and in bowing knowhow, where our woodwinds have gone in intonation and tone colour-blending, where our brass have gone in ensemble and attack etc.
2. The Head Conductor *must* be asked to give his agreement as to which soloists he can and will accept and those he will not and cannot accept.
3. The aspect of which instruments and which voices have available repertoire to go with which symphonies on which programs.

. . . The main point of the above three is, of course, No 2. For the Head Conductor has *the* responsibility of seeing that *his* concerts not only have a logical line in the overall picture of the season, but also for seeing that his programs have a musical and logical progression in themselves.

Toward an effective solution of the above problems I would herewith ask, in my role as Head Conductor of the SSO, that I be kept abreast of the progress of the negotiations with soloists who are being considered for *my* Sydney periods so that I have a chance to say—before they are thrust into my arms—whether I can or cannot accept them . . . After having accepted known and unknown, great and near-great, and also quite mediocre artists in 1962, 1964, 1965 and 1966, and having already

accepted known and unknown artists for 1967, and believing, if I am
told it, that 1968 is already set (I do sincerely hope not), I am therefore
forced to *insist* that I am in the picture regarding *my* potential soloists
for 1969! I do hope that I have made myself absolutely clear about
the above.

Rex Ellis found Dixon's letter very disturbing, as it implied an
undermining of the primacy of the ABC's traditional artist-
procurement procedures. 'The degree of uncertainty about
scheduling artists on this basis will seriously inhibit our planning',
Ellis told Hopkins. 'Perhaps more importantly it could complicate
our negotiations with artists who, in the early stages of negotiation
have to be offered a guaranteed number of concerts in a given
period.'

Finally, Duckmanton took the matter up, and responded by
writing, in a note which seems appallingly severe, that 'it is not
proposed that Mr Dixon should be given the right to determine
which soloists shall appear at concerts which he conducts, and
he is being informed accordingly'.

Denied this potentially vital component of his authority as chief
conductor, Dixon nonetheless maintained a fairly full program
of reform in other areas. He wanted to involve players in this
process more fully than they had been used to. At the end of
his series of 1966 concerts he interviewed individually every player
in the orchestra, asking them about 'their hopes, intentions, fears
and capabilities', Roger Covell reported. 'He has already startled
them by inviting their suggestions for music to be played in the
future.'

He had many other plans in place for his 1967 season. The
printed program for his first concerts that year included this
sentence in his biography: 'On this visit Dixon hopes to put into
effect ideas which will, he hopes, take the Sydney Symphony
Orchestra into the first rank of world music-makers'. These ideas
included the establishment of regular sectional rehearsals between
full orchestral rehearsals; an appointment of a permanent assistant
conductor; and the commissioning of a portable acoustic shell
which could be adjusted for use in different country centres.

He had also wanted to repeat an experiment that had worked
well the previous year. The ABC custom for many years had been

to introduce the chief conductor at the very beginning of the season, in an important Sydney concert. But this was not Dixon's style. He preferred working up to things gradually because, after several months' absence (in Frankfurt) 'a head conductor has to work doubly hard to get an orchestra comfortable with him again'. So in 1966 he had taken the SSO on a country tour before conducting it in Sydney. His request to repeat this in 1967 came too late to alter the concert schedules.

All these ideas came undone as John Hopkins' conviction grew that Dixon's term of office should not be extended. 'His contract was up for renewal at the end of 1968, and by the end of his season here in 1966 I realised that we just couldn't renew with him, because the SSO's playing standards were deteriorating so markedly in the course of his months here. He was so repressive of the orchestra's personality, so musically stubborn with the players. This is why some of them resigned. He had become meticulous to the point of being boring.

'On my European trip in 1966 I went to see him—this was after he'd gone back to Frankfurt—and I told him as gently as I could what problems there were and what areas he needed to attend to with the SSO. He told me he was glad we'd discussed these things, and we parted amicably.'

Dixon came back to Sydney in April 1967 and, for the second year running, gave concerts in which 'halves' were repeated right through the Red, Blue and White series. Hopkins: 'I respected Dixon's musical reasons for doing this, because he felt that by giving these works right through a run of performances the orchestra would really get the music played in. But it was hell for the broadcast schedules, and more importantly the performance of the relevant works was not any better, as the players were still losing their enthusiasm for the music under him.'

In May Duckmanton came back from an overseas trip, during which he had had discussions with a young Jewish-Hungarian conductor called Moshe Atzmon. He had received good notices on his first visit here as a guest conductor and had since made a successful Salzburg Festival debut with the Vienna Philharmonic. Duckmanton had established that, if offered the job of SSO chief conductor, Atzmon was prepared to spend six months here each year. Dixon had never been able to spend more than four in Sydney.

Duckmanton wanted Atzmon up his sleeve before he told Dixon finally of the ABC's decision not to renew. He had a meeting with Dixon on 22 June, and on receiving the news of his forthcoming non-renewal Dixon said that he would resign 'in protest over the ABC's industrial relations with the SSO'. Hopkins remembers that many of the issues Dixon raised were already the subject of on-going negotiations between the Musicians' Union and the ABC.

Dixon then badly overplayed his hand. He told Duckmanton on 5 July that he planned to make a press statement containing a 'protest resignation' the following Sunday. Duckmanton told him that nothing would be gained by this—discussing industrial matters that were already on the official agenda would do little for SSO musicians, and a possible press discussion would embarrass Dixon and the ABC.

But Dixon knew that any press coverage was likely to favour him, as indeed it did. The 'protest resignation' occurred the following Sunday evening. He said ABC officials were 'impossible to work with' and described his 'resignation' as 'a gesture on behalf of the welfare of the orchestra'. He issued a list of twenty-three reforms he said were needed, as 'working conditions were hampering the orchestra's artistic development'. These included a suitable pension scheme, longer holidays, better travelling conditions, higher quality promotion of SSO activities and fewer public concerts. Rather pathetically, No 16 was that 'improvements and innovations made by the Musical Director should be continued in his absence'. He said he would return to finish the term of his current contract in 1968.

The issue dragged itself through the media for days, with such press headlines as 'I Won't Renew My Contract—Dixon', 'Cancer Eating Into Sydney Orchestra', and 'Dean Dixon in shock—"I can't go on".' In some stories, Dixon's wife claimed that her husband had been 'crucified'.

The episode might have been avoided altogether if Dixon had been told about his non-renewal earlier and more openly, but would he then have conducted the SSO with any commitment in 1967? Would he have responded to his dismissal this fiercely in any case? To Hopkins and Duckmanton it was simple: Dixon had been fired, but had chosen to announce his resignation instead.

In response to Dixon's public accusations, Duckmanton said little that was retaliatory, except for one typically cool remark. 'I am puzzled that Mr Dixon should find conditions so impossible for him and yet want to return next year.'

Dixon left Australia, as scheduled, the day after his press statement, even though some players had begged him to stay. He would have none of it. He seemed convinced that the bigness of his gesture would ensure that 'heads would roll'.

'I believe that the ABC genuinely intends to do something constructive about at least some of the points of reform I have listed', he had told the press. 'But the discussions have also convinced me that the ABC is not going to move far enough and fast enough in this direction.

'Therefore, I feel it is consistent with my deep concern for the welfare of the orchestra to make a gesture designed to draw urgent attention to the orchestra's needs.'

But within a week of his departure the Musicians' Union publicly attacked him, accusing him of latching onto claims already under negotiation to explain his resignation. The union's federal secretary said that 'what [Dixon] used as reasons were matters that have already been under consideration and discussion for several months'. And soon the ABC commissioners decided to view Dixon's public airing of his grievances as an outrage, and sought and found legal advice from the Crown Solicitor which allowed Dixon's contract to be terminated immediately. It was apparent that Dixon had breached a clause in his contract which forbade him to bring discredit to the ABC.

'I think the head he really wanted to see rolling was mine', says Hopkins. 'The way in which he went to the press showed us that, in his typically methodical way, he had collected all the complaints the orchestra had as a way of showing his solidarity with them. But the players soon saw that there was more to the issue than Dixon simply taking their side.'

Shortly before Dixon held his 'resignation' press conference, he threw a party for the orchestra to cement his show of sympathy for many of their industrial claims. This had made him something of a hero to his supporters within the SSO, but by the time he flew out of the country he had become a martyr to them, having publicly suffered for their cause.

A few days after he left, these players, with representatives of the union, met with Hopkins and Duckmanton. Hopkins spent much time explaining the artistic reasons behind the decision not to renew Dixon's contract, when one of the players said, 'But he's been so good to us. He threw us that wonderful party'. At this point Duckmanton took a piece of paper out of his jacket pocket, unfolded it, and laid it out on his desk. Then he drawled, 'Yes, and here's the bill. It was sent to the ABC'. There was a moment's silence. As John Hopkins recalls, 'I've never seen a meeting change so quickly'.

※

No 8 of Dixon's twenty-three points was that 'the SSO should have a longer period of warming up after its return from vacation'. This was a none too subtle reference to one of John Hopkins' innovations, a summer concert series known simply as the Proms. It was the ABC's one major initiative in the presentation of concerts in the 1960s, a tacit recognition that life, after all, was not the way it had always been, that Australia could house radical musical spirits, and that they need not be regarded simply as bogies to the existing adult audience.

Like Buttrose, Hopkins had come to ABC culture fresh from a mixture of endeavours, and was shocked at the level of resistance in the major subscription series to the programming of new or 'difficult' music.

'When Gielen came here in 1966 we asked him to do Stravinsky's ballet score *Agon*. This was the first performance of the piece in Australia. Well, the Battleship, as she was called, not only had her hands in her ears the whole way through but stared at me accusingly all the time. I could see her thinking "this is your fault". So I couldn't enjoy the piece! And when Ferdinand Leitner conducted Webern's Passacaglia in the same year, many people stayed out of the hall until it was over. There wasn't enough applause to see him off the platform. And this is early Webern, very romantic. I was amazed at how unwilling people were to give such music a fair hearing.'

In part, the Proms were begun in response. But Hopkins was also concerned at the public's waning interest in the SSO's summer concerts. The Brahms and Beethoven festivals that had once packed the Town Hall every January and February were now playing to small houses, and he felt a more spirited series would attract a new audience.

Hopkins had run a Proms series in New Zealand, but they were intended as family-oriented summer concerts. In Sydney, he saw them from the beginning as forums for adventurous programming, both in the choice of works and the context in which works were performed.[17] Basing the format of the concerts on that of the Henry Wood proms given in London's Royal Albert Hall, the seats in the stalls of the Town Hall were removed, and the audience sat on the floor (there was never much room to promenade about). People were invited to bring cushions and mats. Gallery seats were available in the usual way. The Town Hall was festooned with ferns and flowers, and a dribbling fountain.

During his period as Director of Music, Hopkins retained 'architect' status over all Proms programs, but from the beginning had as collaborators two programmers whom he had plucked out of the NSW Music Department, where they had produced programs for radio: Nigel Butterley and Richard Meale.

'These two were the ones with ideas', Hopkins recalls. 'We would each keep a list of pieces we wanted to do, including new pieces we'd heard from overseas radio tapes, and we would pool these ideas and turn them into programs. We went through an incredible sifting process to keep the programs sharp. But we had to be a bit cautious to start with, because the Proms was a risky idea. Some critics were convinced it would be a disaster, and of course, unlike the major subscription series, every seat was available, so the Proms had to sell well if they were to continue.'

Dixon was one of the nay-sayers. 'This aspect of informality is a most important vehicle for a great part of the public', he told the *Australian*. 'It is the converse for another section of the public, including those who are musically educated. The European so-called 'stuffiness', the cathedral-like approach, has become necessary for the opening of our mental, emotional and spiritual avenues. The Prom idea, psychologically, is generally to share feelings of the happenings of the night with other members of

[17] The same philosophy was applied to the Melbourne Proms, which began a few years later, along with Proms in Adelaide, Brisbane and Perth.

the audience. When we come to this higher point of involvement, and deeper concentration, then the Prom idea becomes *passé*.'

The first Proms were given in 1965, and although the programs were not as adventurous as they would become, they nevertheless contain such then-unusual items as Messiaen's *Oiseaux Exotiques* for piano and orchestra, with Richard Meale as soloist. This was an Australian premiere. The following year, the first half of one concert comprised excerpts from Monteverdi's *Vespers* and Peter Maxwell Davies' *Fantasia on an In Nomine of John Taverner*. Critics agreed that the atmosphere was refreshingly informal, and the audiences younger, more responsive and less stuffy than their elders who attended the regular subscription concerts. But they also found the playing to be of a variable standard. As the programs became more inquisitive, some players resented having to learn so many new scores straight after their holidays (*pace* Dixon's Point No 8), and there was not always enough time to rehearse such complex programs fully. By 1968 the Proms were offering an extraordinary range of music. Two of the five programs that year were:

Concerto for Orchestra ....Lutoslawski
Clarinet Concerto ....Mozart
Soloist: Donald Westlake

Interval

Mass (sections) ....Machaut
with the Orianna Singers and Renaissance Players
Et Exspecto Resurrectionem Mortuorum ....Messiaen
(first performance in Australia)

❧

Overture: *Rosamunde*....................................Schubert
Four Essays for Orchestra ....Tadeusz Baird
(first performance in Australia)
Concerto for Seven Wind Instruments, Strings
and Percussion ....Martin
(first performance in Australia)
Soloists: SSO wind principals
Ned Kelly Music....................................David Ahern
(world premiere)

Interval

Symphony No 1 (*Winter Dreams*) ....Tchaikovsky

The following year saw some of the most complex and risk-laden programming ever attempted in Australia. Two of the 1969 concerts were structured this way:

Concerto for four pianos ....Bach
  Soloists: Donald Hollier, Larry Sitsky, Nigel Butterley
         and Richard Meale
Fifteen Prints (Pages) after Durer's Apocalypse ....Fiser
                 (first performance in Australia)
Symphony No 6..............................Vaughan Williams

Interval

Tower Concerto ....Felix Werder
                 (world premiere)
The Wedding ....Stravinsky
                 (first performance in Australia)
  with Philharmonia Choir, the four composer-pianists
  and Marilyn Richardson, Florence Taylor, Robert Gard
         and John Pringle

❧

Symphony No 6, *Le Matin* ....Haydn
Tapiola..Sibelius
Forty-part motet: *Spem in alium* ....Tallis
         with nine Sydney choirs

Interval

Three Places in New England ....Ives
                 (first performance in Australia)
Ketjak...Peter Sculthorpe
                 (world premiere)
Apotheose from *Grand Symphonie Funebre*
  et Triomphale ....Berlioz
                 (first performance in Australia)

Such programs reflect an attitude of unconditional embrace toward the body of Western art music, and, appropriately, the series

There was nothing quite like the Proms. Fans of John Hopkins and cellist Lois Simpson give their all for their idols.

became enormously popular with young people. The more conservative players were astonished to see capacity crowds in the hall for concerts which contained music they did not regard highly. Already by 1967 the only people who could buy tickets were those who stood in the queue on the first day the Proms sales opened. As under Goossens, some people camped overnight to buy tickets. The line of people could stretch a block or more from the ABC building. As Maria Prerauer would later write of this spectacle:

The long queues at 3 a.m., the pavement camping, the mounds of coloured cushions, rugs and thermos-flasks, the hammocks slung enterprisingly between handy poles, the overwhelming air of excitement that amounted almost to hysteria as the youngsters gathered for their annual tribal corroboree.

People who tried to book by mail usually got their money back.

John Hopkins admits that the Proms were as much a marketing exercise as a musical one, and that the queuing system was an important part of its success. 'It helped create a camaraderie among the Prommers, a special sense of occasion.' But it was in any case a much better publicised series than the Red, Blue or White. The brochure was informative and well designed; Hopkins gave special press lunches each year at which the series was launched, explaining each program in detail and inviting as speakers local composers whose work was going to be performed that year; and the sense of freedom implied by the creation within the hallowed precincts of the Town Hall of a promenade area—in which you could basically do as you pleased as long as you behaved yourself— found common cause with the young spirit of the 1960s. As well, the Proms were cheap to attend. In 1968 a promenade area ticket to all five concerts cost $3.15, which was about half the price of a C Reserve subscription to an 'adult' series.

The concerts had an energy of their own, and for all their musical importance, sometimes the point of being at the Proms was not to hear the music but to be at the Proms. They were the SSO's first and, so far last, Happening. Roger Covell:

'The Proms attracted young people who would not have gone to other concerts anyway. They appealed to the 'flower-power' ethos, and for the most part, in their best years, they were enjoyable as concerts, too.'

They highlighted many works that are remembered as seminal events of the day. The collaborative piece by Nigel Butterley and painter John Peart was one. Called *Interaction—Music and Painting*, it involved Peart painting while Butterley improvised at the piano and gave Hopkins cues for the orchestra to play one of a series of pre-composed fragments, in an improvised order. Another was the re-discovery of Grainger's magnum opus, *The Warriors*, in 1968, the Prom performance of which Covell described as 'one of the year's major musical events'. Peter Sculthorpe's *Love 200*, written for the SSO, singer Jeannie Lewis and a rock group called Tully for the bicentennial of Cook's landing at Farm Cove, was another unrepeatable experience. So was *First Day Covers*, a philatelogical piece for narrator and orchestra which Butterley wrote with a pre-Damed Edna Everage. One movement was called 'Morceau en form de "meat pie"' and another 'March of the Gladdyators'.

Hopkins left the ABC in 1973 to become Dean of Music at the Victorian College of the Arts, and in a way the Proms left the ABC as well. (Meale and Butterley by this time had also gone.) Their demise was caused by many factors. Hopkins' successor, Harold Hort, knew that part of the Proms' success lay in the overall vision of Hopkins, and, although he was invited to conduct many Prom concerts around the country, Hopkins no longer had planning control over them.

'One year I conducted the last two of the five Sydney proms, and for the first three nights the Prommers had had Johann Strauss under Willi Boskovsky. I came out on the fourth night to conduct *Hi-Lo* by David Ahern. Well, I don't know how you could confuse an audience more than by that kind of programming! It was bizarre, as if there were no planning.'

Hort and Rex Ellis decided to abandon the annual press conference, and instituted a mail-only booking system. The queue vanished. The promotion of the series became dutiful. Conductors like Boskovsky, Morton Gould and Charles Groves conducted and planned more than half the concerts in each series. One long-time arts administrator and one-time Prommer says simply that 'Boskovsky killed the Proms. You could see it happening. It was

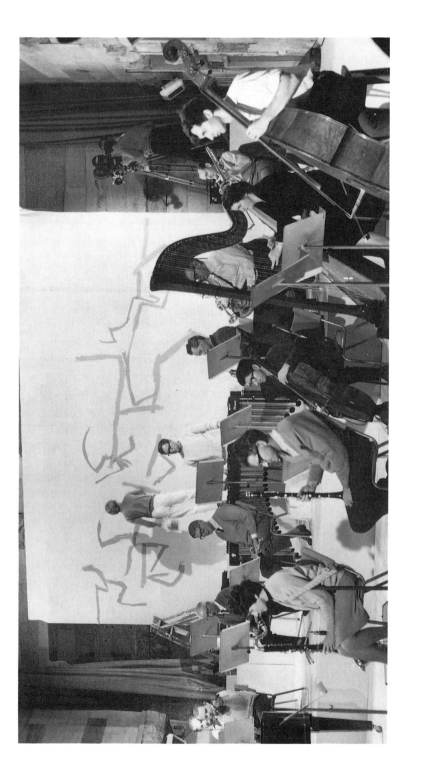

Nigel Butterley's Interaction—Music and Painting was performed at a Prom Concert in 1967. The picture is of a subsequent filming of the work at the Cell Block Theatre. The painter is John Peart.

as if the ABC was determined to "get" Hopkins for making them a success'.

Did Hopkins use his job to promote himself as a conductor? Were the Proms too expensive to put on, demanding as they did plentiful rehearsal and large and exotic forces? Were too many performances under Hopkins ordinary rather than outstanding? His successors seemed to think so, and as Hopkins himself says, 'It is hard to believe that they did not set out to destroy the Proms. They were, I think, trying to remove my image from them. It was a very damaging marketing exercise, and very damaging for music in this country. I mean, is Morton Gould an important composer in the context of what we'd been doing?'.

Hopkins had in some ways dug his own grave with the Proms' success. The rehearsal time he commanded for them, the praise he garnered, the firm control he kept over their content, all gave rise to bitter feelings in some of his colleagues, as did his determination to pursue his conducting career as well as his administrative one. Hopkins travelled overseas as a performer regularly during his period as Director of Music.

Once Hopkins had left the ABC, the newly ensconced Hort decided that his predecessor's frequent absences abroad, and his administrative load at the Victorian College of the Arts, made it impossible to contemplate his retention as Proms guru. There was also a degree of personal animosity between the two men that could not help but colour Hort's decision.

Under Hort, there was no vision of the Proms that seemed integral and appealing, as Hopkins' had been. The end of the queuing system meant that the audience was now an older one—radical spirits in 1974 did not believe in booking by mail—and therefore the programs became less radical to suit. As well as being older, the audience was smaller. The more orthodox post-1973 programs seemed not to be special enough. Hort, although of the belief that one option was to make the Proms more appealing to families, was unwilling to turn them into Pops concerts, as this was thought to be too restrictive musically. In 1976 Hort write to Ellis:

When John Hopkins left you will remember my own view that we could no longer rely on him to run the whole of the Proms season; that, in any case, his inspiration and the type of programming he had advocated was wearing thin and there was no way in which this kind of Prom could be continued . . . I feel we should persist in the [new] pattern, which has not yet been disproved.

It was in this year that the whole issue of the Proms began to be re-examined. Duckmanton felt they were no longer working, and the Music Department conducted its own research into the methods that might be used to revive the series. This research was not conclusive, and included such observations as: 'The festive spirit must be introduced and this can only be done by providing programs à la Viennese night or whatever', forgetting how festive the best years of the Proms had been.

By 1977 the Sydney and Melbourne press saw how tired the Proms formula had become. In the *Age*, composer and critic Felix Werder wrote a piece about the Proms predicament called 'The Day of Wrath Arrives', while in the *Australian* Maria Prerauer asked 'Where Have all the Promenaders Gone?'. Predictably, their solutions to the malaise reflected their personal tastes rather than an understanding of the box office, but the Music Department could do little better. Prompted by Prerauer's critique, Hort told Duckmanton that 'the attendances at Prom concerts have given us concern over a number of years . . . it seems that the efforts we've made to pick up the lag have not really been successful'. He admitted that he had no ready answers, and that he did not know how to find them:

An opportunity for the audience to express its views might be worthwhile—but how? Our research questionnaire type of enquiry is not likely to help. Committees have proved of little use. It seems to me experimentation is the answer.

The composer festivals began again in 1978 and continued until the mid-1980s, by which time the rationale for the Proms seemed far away indeed. There would be no more Proms in Sydney after 1977. They were, it seems, of their age in more ways than one.

Interlude:
Moving experiences

The move out of Kings Cross had been a long time coming. While an improvement over conditions in Burwood, the studio was a little too small physically and acoustically for the SSO, particularly in works which required large forces. It was also in a fairly unsalubrious location, above the Woolworths store in Darlinghurst Road, and looked very shabby. John Hopkins remembers feeling ashamed when bringing guest conductors there to work.

At one time it was thought the orchestra's salvation might be found in a church. The opera-for-television discussed earlier involved the SSO in pre-recording the music with the soloists before the final filming took place in the television studios. As the Kings Cross facilities were too small for this pre-recording, it invariably took place in a Methodist church in Bourke Street, Taylor Square, which was known simply as Studio 226. Moses hoped that this might have possibilties as the orchestra's post-Kings Cross home, but those who worked in the church found it at best dilapidated and at worst dangerous.

One of the most vocal urgers for the abandonment of this building was Bert Read, one-time pianist with the dance bands of Jack Hylton and Ambrose, from 1959 the ABC's Director of Light Entertainment and *ergo* supervisor of the ABC Dance Band, which shared the church with the SSO. 'Apart from its acoustical deficiencies I am honestly ashamed of such anachronistic surroundings. What a shocking advertisement this studio really is for the ABC!' he wrote in March 1961. 'Is it hoping too much for us to "give away" these ecclesiastical relics and have proper music studios in their place? . . . How any artist can be expected to produce their best in these depressing surroundings is beyond my comprehension.'

A few months later, Read noted that 'the ceiling is slowly falling apart, the upstairs woodwork is rotting, rain is constantly seeping through and a Health Inspector has already expressed his dissatisfaction with the inadequate and insanitary toilet accommodation'. The ABC's building supervisor also found himself having to juggle orchestral needs against the demands of church groups, who wanted to use the building for jumble sales and the storage of clothing. In wet weather, a drooping gutter on the building's north side sent a stream of water onto the outside toilet of the next door property. The church also became unbearably hot in summer because, the ABC's assistant general manager Walter Hamilton noted, 'its natural ventilation does not cope with the large numbers of the orchestra'.

By late 1962 Moses had approved the purchase of a disused cinema in Chatswood, the Arcadia, for conversion to a rehearsal and recording studio for the SSO. Although it was on the wrong side of the harbour in relation to the orchestra's Radio colleagues, its advantages included a dry but not confining acoustic, proximity to Chatswood railway station, off-street parking, and room in a side lane to park an Outside Broadcast van for television filming. The continuing stream of television operas made this an important consideration, and after some test rehearsals and a soundtrack recording of Humperdinck's opera *Hansel and Gretel*, the ABC took a lease on the building in early 1964.

※

The Arcadia was not Arcadian, but it was relative luxury compared to the Kings Cross studio. The accommodation for the orchestra management was cramped, and alterations to the acoustic and the air-conditioning would go on for some years. But the SSO learned to like it, and many of its members came to live near it. Apart from one notable hiccup, the Arcadia was to be its rehearsal home until the end of 1989.[1]

❧

Another move of a more profound and public nature was allegedly imminent. Since 1959, when construction had begun on Jorn Utzon's design for the Sydney Opera House, journalists had been writing about the building being finished 'next year'. Next year was always a long way off, and in 1966 seemed further away than ever when Duckmanton and the ABC commissioners finally realised what the term 'multi-purpose hall' meant.

Goossens had made it clear that the main hall in the building of his dreams was to allow for the presentation of opera and ballet performances but 'will be chiefly concerned with housing the SSO'. Goossens had left Australia before Utzon's design was selected, and was thus not around to ensure that his ideas came into being. But his successor as director of the Conservatorium, Sir Bernard Heinze, was on the Opera House Executive Committee[2] (this was the body of which Goossens had been a member when it was called the Sydney Opera House Committee), and like Goossens, believed that the orchestra's priorities came first in the design of the main hall.

This is not the place for a blow-by-blow description of the machinations behind Utzon's resignation from the Opera House in 1966. The numerous strikes and cost blow-outs, and the defeat of the State Labor government in the 1965 election are well known and have been much discussed. It is sufficient to note here that Heinze worked long and hard from his place on the Opera House committee for the SSO's needs, against what seems to have been Utzon's belief that the needs of the Elizabethan Trust Opera Company were paramount. When Heinze explained to Utzon that the orchestra pit had to accommodate a maximum of 110 players, that it had to be of particular dimensions for communication between conductor and orchestra to be best established, and that

---

[1] In July 1965 most of the ABC's concert management and box office also moved, from 264 Pitt Street to a building (since demolished) in 145 Elizabeth Street, near Market Street, that became known simply as Broadcast House.

[2] Heinze was knighted in 1950.

about a third of the orchestra should be positioned under the stage to ensure an adequate balance between pit and stage, Utzon replied that the building of a revolving platform and concomitant concrete support made it impossible to provide a pit that met these specifications.

The inclusion of the revolve, which Utzon had added to his Opera House plans after he had won the design competition for the building, meant that the pit would be too small and the wrong shape. It also altered the shape of the stage for concert presentation. Heinze noted that 'we must not lose sight of the primary purpose of the Large Hall—orchestral concerts, and choral concerts with or without orchestral support. The arrangements for these concerts since the amendment of the original plans to provide for a revolving stage are totally inadequate'.

While it was the primary purpose in Heinze's view, it was not in Utzon's. He had been given the task, after all, of designing a multi-purpose hall. Nor were orchestral concerts the major concern of the Opera House Trust or the Elizabethan Trust.

Duckmanton discovered other problems, among them that the main hall was going to be smaller than envisaged (2500 seats at most compared to the 3000 the ABC wanted) and its acoustic reverberation period too short for orchestral performances. After Utzon's resignation in 1966, Duckmanton and the ABC's chairman James Darling[3] began lobbying the panel of architects who had been appointed to finish the building, and they in turn told the NSW Department of Works that the main hall should be converted to a concert hall. A public tug-of-war ensued in which the ABC and the Askin government's Minister for Public Works, Davis Hughes, were on one side and the Opera House and Elizabethan trusts were on the other.

The ABC won, partly because it was able to book the hall for many more nights per year than the Trust Opera. The changes to the main hall had a domino effect on the rest of the building. The Drama Theatre became the Opera Theatre, in which both revolve and pit are inadequate; the housing for the main hall's stage machinery became the Recording Hall, which subsequently served the people of Sydney as a site office for Opera House

---

[3] Darling was appointed chairman after Boyer's death in 1961.

renovations; and the hall for conventions, amateur theatrical societies and chamber music became the Drama Theatre, with too small an auditorium and a low-proscenium, Cinemascope-shaped stage that has become the Curse of the Theatre Designers. The SSO's gain has proved to be the source of much pain to the other main hirers of the Opera House, and the ABC's victory was, in the short-term, pyrrhic. The Commission was soundly vilified by the press as a bastion of meddling fuddy-duddyism. At the time Roger Covell was particularly vehement in his criticism:

There is, I believe, a real analogy between the experience of concert-going for many people and certain kinds of puritanism. The halls usually have a Low Church bareness; the seats have a minimum of comfort; the accepted manners of concerts demand persistence in attitudes of Sunday-best solemnity and the sort of pharisaical self-righteousness that finds pleasure in shushing someone who innocently or spontaneously claps between movements of a symphony.

. . . As I happen to be of the opinion that the future (like the past) is on the side of musical theatre and that the orchestral concert in its present form is already ossified and likely to disintegrate or disappear at a time not very distant from now, I find it a cause for dejection that the main hall of the Opera House should be committed so completely to existing models of concert-giving.

Sydney's consolation, and it is quite a handsome one, is that it has one of the finest modern concert halls in the world. But it is one of the few consolations in a building that became a playground for politics instead of a first-rate performing arts centre.[4]

The SSO gave its first performance in the Opera House—a concert for construction workers and their families conducted, appropriately, by Heinze—in 1972. The Concert Hall became the orchestra's major performance venue from October 1973, by which

---

[4] Yet the consequences of the building being opened as it was originally planned have not been considered widely. It seems likely that, given the explosion in Sydney's performing arts activity in the 1970s, demand for the main hall would have outstripped available dates by a large margin. The minor hall, as it was called, would have had a seating capacity of only 1100 compared to the current 1450. This would have made it unattractively small for opera and ballet promoters.

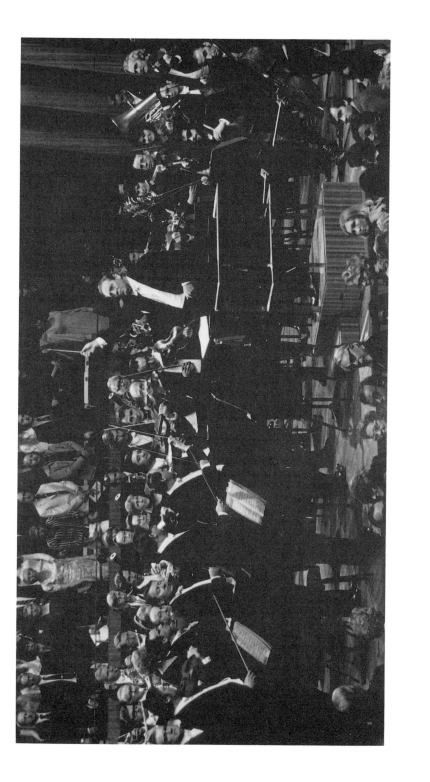

Suspense: Audience and orchestra alike await the arrival of the Vice-regal party at the official opening concert of the Sydney Opera House Concert Hall on September 29, 1973. The conductor is Sir Charles Mackerras. Concertmaster is Donald Hazelwood.

time the SSO had left the Arcadia with the intention of making the Recording Hall its permanent rehearsal venue. But it was not to be. The SSO rehearsed there for just over a year.

The apparent reason why the Recording Hall was not an improvement on the Arcadia was its acoustic, which many SSO musicians considered unworkable for orchestral rehearsal: too reverberant, too loud, too 'bathroomy'. In short, the space was the wrong shape. It had been designed originally as a scenery store, after all, and was very tall and very square, so that the sound went straight up and away from the players. In heavily textured music, the front half of the orchestra could not hear the back half.

But John Matthews, then SSO manager, believes that, bad as these deficiencies seemed at the time, they were not immovable. 'With a bit of patience, the players might have stayed there, allowed adjustments to be made to the hall, and gradually made it work. But it was the ever-present human problem of being completely averse to change. They had become comfortable in Chatswood, and many of them had moved to the Northern suburbs to be near their work. There was a shopping centre near the Arcadia, which they badly missed in the relative isolation of Bennelong Point, and they could meet their children at the theatre after school.' The SSO was back in the Arcadia in November 1974.

There was less dissension about the acoustics of the Concert Hall. Some of the more senior members of the orchestra found it too clinical, but most agreed with the critics that, where the Town Hall had cast a sometimes smudgy halo over everything, the Concert Hall acoustics clarified textures and gave the music more air. The official opening concert was held on 29 September 1973 with soprano Birgit Nilsson, and featured music entirely by 'that famous Australian composer, Richard Wagner', as the conductor on that occasion, Sir Charles Mackerras, remembers. Covell noted that the opening of the prelude to *Tristan and Isolde* 'resonated . . . as if the hall itself were one large cello'.

'There had been so many strikes on the site of the Opera House that it was not certain early in 1973 that the building would be ready on time', says Mackerras. 'So while it might seem strange now that the opening concert contained nothing but Wagner— that there wasn't more 'ceremonial' repertoire—it was arranged in this way so that, if the Opera House were not ready, the concert could have been given as a 'special' in the Town Hall. The one really ceremonial piece was 'Dich Teure Halle' from *Tannhäuser*, which was most appropriate, given that 'Teure' can mean 'dear' or 'expensive'.

By the time the Opera House opened, the SSO was two chief conductors on from Dixon. Indeed, enough history had passed for Dixon to be invited back to conduct some of the first concerts in the building. But Moshe Atzmon, the conductor who succeeded Dixon in 1968, was nowhere to be seen.

CHAPTER EIGHT

The Atzmon blip and the Dutch Renaissance

Moshe Atzmon is in many ways the most problematic of the SSO's chief conductors. He was well liked by audiences, conducted some outstanding concerts and caused no crises. Yet he left no imprint of his personality on the orchestra, and is rarely discussed when SSO musicians remember their favourite conductors. He stayed in Sydney as chief conductor for three years, but they were less eventful and less stimulating years than the three in which Dixon had been Musical Director. And Atzmon has caused no major ripples internationally since his time in Australia.

He was already known to be available and interested in a Sydney appointment when Duckmanton had his fateful meeting with Dixon in June 1967. In March of that year, Atzmon was spotted as potential chief conductor material in the same way Dixon had been; he made his first guest appearance here and had impressed everyone. He was thirty-five, and had been a horn player, an instrument he learned after he and his family moved to Israel (or Palestine as it then was) in 1944. In the early 1960s he had been conductor of the Israeli Broadcasting Light Music Orchestra, and at Antal Dorati's urging entered a number of conducting competitions. He won many of these, and went on to study at the Guildhall School of Music in London.

By the time his period as chief conductor began in 1969 he had gathered good notices from appearances with the Berlin Philharmonic, Vienna Philharmonic, Royal Philharmonic and

Halle orchestras. But many of these reviews were for his first performances with these ensembles. He was not 'there' yet, not a young star of the conducting firmament. Atzmon's appointment to Sydney traded fame for time, and signalled that reality had dawned in the minds of the orchestra and its management. The SSO was assured, and Hopkins believed, that Atzmon was being caught at the beginning of what would be a great career. 'After Dixon, we realised that there were no big names who would spend half the year here', Donald Hazelwood recalls. 'We felt Atzmon would take an interest in the orchestra over a long period each season.'

And yet one of the first moves Atzmon made in Sydney was to remove the title Musical Director, which Malko and Dixon had held, and to replace it with Chief Conductor, which, he said, 'more accurately reflected' the role he planned to take in the orchestra's affairs.

The honeymoon period lasted for most of his time in Sydney in 1968, when he spent some months as 'Chief Conductor Designate', and for his first year as Chief, 1969.[1] 'It was hugely enjoyable to sense at last night's concert . . . how the SSO's new conductor revelled in his work', Covell noted in the *Sydney Morning Herald* of Atzmon's first 1968 concert. In the *Telegraph*, Julian Russell concurred. 'From the way the orchestra responded to Atzmon's clear directions he seemed to be as welcome to them as he obviously was to his enthusiastic audience.' He soon exploited the orchestra's naturally brilliant and 'flashy' sound in exciting interpretations of such works as Tchaikovsky 4, Berlioz's *Symphonie Fantastique* and Stravinsky's *The Rite of Spring*.

'He doesn't talk half as much as Dixon', one player was quoted as saying after one of Atzmon's early rehearsals in 1969, but soon the more experienced musicians in the orchestra knew why: he was learning much of his repertoire as he went.

'I have to admit that once it became clear that Dixon was not going to return in 1968 we were grasping at straws to replace him', John Hopkins says. 'Atzmon was available for the time we wanted, and people in Europe were talking about him as a rising

---

[1] He also took the orchestra to New Zealand in 1968, where he conducted successful performances in Christchurch as part of the Pan Pacific Arts Festival.

star. We took a chance on him, but it didn't work out at all. I think the bottom line is that he did not contribute enough to the orchestra's musical growth. He was full of promise, but he did not have enough depth, was not clear enough in his concept of many of the pieces he was doing.'

One of his other attractions was his youth and good looks, and the hope that these things might further raise the orchestra's profile. But there were too many factors working against this. The major subscription series (Red, Blue and White) were still for the most part fully subscribed. There was therefore little room in them for audience growth. The Proms were a freak activity held at a time of the year when Atzmon worked overseas, and which in any case Hopkins controlled; and the Youth Concerts needed a huge overhaul if they were to reclaim relevance. Atzmon's energies were directed solely towards his conducting career. Unlike Dixon, he was neither a visionary nor a reformer, and although he did make decisions about the hiring and positioning of players, he took little interest in the structural elements of the orchestra's life.

'The less said the better' is one SSO veteran's estimation of Atzmon's period with the orchestra. Others are more specific. After many years of working in the United Kingdom (where he was for a time second oboe at Sadler's Wells) and in his own country, New-Zealand born Guy Henderson became principal oboe in 1967, after David Woolley's departure, and Atzmon was the first chief conductor he worked with. 'I tried to have as little to do with him as possible, frankly, because he annoyed me intensely. I was late for rehearsal one day, which I rarely am, and apologised to him. He just looked at me and said: "Yes, why?" To be fair, he did sometimes try to foster better feelings outside rehearsals with little soirees and the like.

'I think the major problem was his patchiness. Some repertoire went very well under him and with other things he seemed poorly prepared. His was not a period of great development for us, frankly, and my overriding impression of his time here is that, as with Frémaux later, we were coasting.'

Colin Piper, after two years in the National Training Orchestra, joined the SSO percussion section in the middle of Atzmon's tenure, in 1970. He remembers that at first he was greatly impressed

Moshe Atzmon and pianist Daniel Barenboim acknowledge the applause at a 1969 concert in the Sydney Town Hall.

with Atzmon's conducting. 'I thought he was pretty good, but when he came back as a guest conductor in 1977 I would not have liked him to have been our Chief. When Stuart [Challender] became our main conductor he was about the same age Atzmon was in 1970, and, like Atzmon, Stuart was learning a lot of music as he went. But he was doing his "first pieces" much more convincingly than Atzmon did his.'

Some critics noticed in Atzmon a tendency to increase the volume in moments of textual uncertainty, and a short-sighted, detail-obsessed view of complex works he was conducting for the first time. Nor was he an adventurous programmer. At one point the *Sydney Morning Herald* described him as 'one of the most conservative of the SSO's resident conductors'. Nonetheless, he did conduct such unusual works as Kodaly's *Psalmus Hungaricus*, Ligeti's *Lontano* and Takemitsu's *Music of Tree*, and he tackled such epic Berlioz pieces as *Romeo and Juliet* and *The Damnation of Faust*. Some of the Australian works he directed include Clive Douglas' *Three Frescoes*, George Dreyfus' first symphony, Felix Werder's *Sound Canvas*, Nigel Butterley's *Meditations of Thomas Traherne*[2] and *Pentad* (world premieres), and Meale's *Soon it will Die* (world premiere). He also gave some fine performances of works from the central repertoire, notably of Brahms 3 and Mahler 4. He was a considerate and skilful concerto accompanist.[3]

In March 1971 Atzmon announced that he would not renew his ABC contract, as he had been offered musical directorships in Europe. One was with the North German Radio Orchestra in Frankfurt, and the other was with the Basle Symphony Orchestra in Switzerland. Covell remarked that 'one of the noteworthy aspects

---

[2] A performance the composer did not like. Atzmon had asked him to write drum rolls through the opening bars, because he felt the silences Butterley had written in would disturb the audience. 'He seemed to be unfamiliar with the idiom', Butterley recalls.

[3] He conducted the 1970 Royal concert given in the presence of the Queen, the Duke of Edinburgh and Princess Anne during their visit to mark the bicentenary of Cook's landing. This concert included the world premiere of Nigel Butterley's appropriately titled *Explorations for Piano and Orchestra*, with soloist Ian Farr. The opening of this work, a series of five-note chords repeated on the piano, prompted the Duke to whisper jocularly to an unresponsive Her Majesty, 'Edward', referring apparently to the latest results of their younger son's piano lessons.

of Atzmon's new appointments is that they make relatively limited demands on his time in comparison with his six-month stay in Australia each year'.

These two appointments also took Atzmon securely back to Europe, and many SSO principals saw his departure as the logical extension of his attitude to his Sydney job. As one player puts it: 'He was very musical, and he put together many well balanced programs, but he could be arrogant in his dealings with us and created a sense of war between himself and the orchestra by moving players around. I understand he perpetuated the 'move the players' problem in Europe, too. In any case, we felt somewhat let down when he just left the way he did. It was as if he'd got what he wanted and that was the end of Sydney.'

This time, at least, there was no public bitterness, no hard feelings. The SSO chief conductor left the ABC on cordial terms, even though Hopkins and his colleagues and many of the SSO's section principals were clearly disappointed with him. But if it had not been a period of growth or diversity for the orchestra this was partly because the massive changes to Australian culture that had taken place through the last half of the 1960s had left the ABC's concert-givers some way behind.

It was not until the late 1970s that two public reports and one of the organisation's more vigorous groups of commissioners forced the Music and Concert departments to look thoroughly at methods of concert presentation that had been taken as given. But in the year of Atzmon's departure there were weaknesses enough. Sydney Youth Concert attendances continued to fall through the 1960s, but so did concert attendances around the country, from 644534 in 1962 to 492107 in 1967. By 1971 there had been a small increase on this last figure, but it would not have been realistic to suggest this represented growth. In 1980 the figure of 644,534 had yet to be regained.

What then was the future of the Red, Blue and White concerts in the early 1970s, when the audience and its taste was ossifying? Given that no audience growth was taking place, the only possible movement was a continued audience shrinkage. Would young people eventually take their place in these series? Were younger audiences interested in the annual commitment of a concert subscription? The critic Kenneth Robins thought this unlikely.

Writing in the *Bulletin*, he complained that 'far too much orchestral concert-going in this country has developed into a rather dreary ritual'. He referred to 'the tyranny of the subscription system' and noted that 'the average age of our concert subscribers precludes any rapture, careless or otherwise'.

Such comments could now be made based on the experience of a wide range of other performing activities. Where, in the early 1950s, the SSO was Sydney's major regular established performing body, the late 1960s was a relative feast of theatre, chamber music, opera and ballet. The SSO's major adult subscription series seemed definitively sedate compared to some of the more involved and responsive audiences these art forms were attracting. It was also a more political age, in which a play like *Fortune and Men's Eyes*, which dealt realistically and brutally with prison life, could be produced in Sydney (by the Ensemble Theatre) without incurring the wrath of the Vice Squad. The 'mainstreaming' of new music had become a fact of life in many European centres, including London, where Sir William Glock had renovated the Proms in characteristically inquiring 1960s fashion. In 1966 the *Financial Times* praised the way in which the Proms had developed from 'the complacent, tradition-bound institution they had dwindled into in the late 1950s to the wonderfully enterprising, flexible and comprehensive music festival we now delight in.' But no shake-up was in sight for the major orchestral series in Sydney.

The creation of the Sydney Proms had brought to light an unexpected new orchestral audience, for these concerts clearly attracted a wide range of age groups which continued to be shut out from the major subscription series. But where the London Proms ran virtually every night for three months, and formed one of London's major concert attractions, the Sydney ones comprised five performances over two months in the off- season. Much of the most unusual Prom repertoire was never heard in a Red, White or Blue concert. New Australian works were sometimes played in Youth Concerts, but very rarely anywhere else. It was almost as if Sculthorpe would 'frighten the horses'.

'Australian composers had to bear the brunt of audience intolerance', Covell recalls. 'Since not a lot of other new music was being played outside the Proms and the Cell Block Theatre, a new Australian piece meant "not another of those horrible works", because the major series subscribers did not get that sort of work from anyone else. In an ideal world the audience should have understood that this was par for the course, that if you did not like the work of Australian composers you were not going to like other composers in those styles either.'

Not that orchestral musicians were much interested in new pieces. In the 1960s, when serialism had made a decisive change in the language of new music, there were players who responded well to its challenges. Donald Hazelwood, Ron Cragg, harpist June Loney and orchestral pianist Joyce Hutchinson were among them, but they were exceptions. Nigel Butterley: 'I have a feeling that the SSO was largely antagonistic to new works through that period. The musicians were apprehensive and, to composers, not really encouraging. I always felt on the outer. Some players would always look for wrong notes, or would relish finding something you'd written which was not suitable for their instrument.'

In 1965, in his thorough way, Dixon had created a questionnaire for SSO musicians to fill in after the first performance of a new piece. This asked them twenty questions in all, including whether, in their view, the length of the piece was justified by its material, how playable the work was technically and whether there was a high degree of harmonic and rhythmic inventiveness. There was also a section for Other Comments, to which some players responded considerately and advisedly, but in which many others vented their spleen. One prominent player's response to *Garcia Lorca* is only unusual in its degree of calm:

It is my opinion that the professional musicians, program committees and music critics have failed miserably in their duty to the concert-going public and also to the contemporary composers firstly by including this work in a program of orchestral music over which the subscriber has no control or choice and secondly by reviewing it in the daily press in the same terms (in fact on the same page) as the music of Berg and Brahms. By taking the trouble to put pen to paper I feel I am attaching too much importance to Mr Meale's 'Homage,' but as I was asked to fill out this set of questions, I feel I should explain that I do not consider the work as a musical composition and have furnished the above answers in the hope that they may help in some way if Mr Meale ever decided to try his hand at musical composition.

As a conductor, Hopkins knew that players' attitudes to new works were changeable, but he was not so certain about the audience. Realising that the major series subscribers were a kind of impenetrable fortress against the new, Hopkins and his programming colleagues (which now included the pianist Ian Farr) devised a new concert series which was fired by the same adventurous spirit that distinguished the Proms.

The Gold Series began in 1971, and ran concurrently through the year alongside the Red, Blue and White concerts. Like the Proms, it was a quick sell-out. As John Hopkins recalls: 'The idea was to create a flexible series that presented different groups through the year—choirs, chamber ensembles, the Sydney Little Symphony and the SSO—in a wider range of music than we had on offer in the other major subscription series.'

The first year of Gold concerts offered a complete concert performance of Handel's *Semele* under Mackerras; the SSO with the Percussions of Strasbourg in works by Stravinsky, Messiaen, Varese and Barry Conyngham;[4] Atzmon conducting Roberto Gerhard's Concerto for Orchestra, a concert of choral music by Machaut and Ockeghem; 'Music of Bach and Jazz Improvisations' that featured the Don Burrows Quartet; and Isaac Stern, fellow violinist Jean-Pierre Wallez and the SLSO in a concert that included Spohr's *Duo Concertante* for two violins.

The Machaut/Ockeghem concert also included the first Australian performance of Harrison Birtwistle's *Medusa*, which caused exactly the kind of stir it was supposed to. After noting that controversy over new music was A Good Thing, *Mirror* critic Frank Harris remarked that the work was 'inordinately long,' and that 'when, towards the end, a string player burped a couple of monotonous notes interminably the inevitable happened—first laughter, then slow-clapping and finally amusing cries of encouragement to the solitary strummer'. The work was soundly hissed and booed.

One of the big strengths of the Gold Series in its early years lay in the way the SSO was featured in the series—in the context of a whole range of music-makers, in avowedly exploratory repertoire. But as the 1970s progressed, the series became firmly

---

4 This was Post's last concert.

SSO-centred, more predictable, and more fussily promoted. Where the brochure for the 1971 series promised 'evenings of stimulating listening to a cross-section of the Sydney public,' that for the 1974 series promised 'stimulating listening for the connoisseur.' By 1979 audiences had declined, in Hort's words, 'to the point of embarrassment both to themselves and the artists.' When the series was closed down at the end of that year there were 567 subscribers. The Gold Series died the death of the Proms.

Hopkins' theories about the Proms' demise apply equally to the Gold concerts. Whatever his colleagues thought about Hopkins as an administrator, his strong point was that he had not grown up as part of the ABC culture. His ideas and methods were, like Buttrose's, inherently unfussy, and for the brief time the two men worked together they got on well.[5] But in the end the bureaucracy and Hopkins did not mix. Hopkins and Rex Ellis, Buttrose's successor and now Director of Concerts, were not natural colleagues. 'Rex was a very gentle man but had a very cool and precise mind, which often made it difficult to argue artistic imperatives with him,' he recalls. Hopkins was, perhaps, also making it hard for himself by trying to maintain a conducting career as well. When he was offered the position of Dean of Music at the Victorian College of the Arts he accepted it quickly.

On his departure he gave Duckmanton two important pieces of advice. One was to mount a thorough international search for the next Director of Music, and the other was to combine the Music and Concert departments, as Hopkins had become convinced of the unwieldiness of the existing structure. Both pieces of advice were ignored.

Duckmanton instead swiftly appointed Hort as director. Assistant director to Hopkins since 1966, Hort had worked at the ABC since 1941, when he joined as a general cadet. He had also studied piano with Laurence Godfrey Smith, and at one point thought he might become a concert pianist. 'But I decided it was not to be.' He worked in many different parts of the ABC, and at one time was the assistant program director for radio and

---

[5] This was before Buttrose was sent to New York and after his return in 1971, when he was given a position that had the wonderful ABC title Assistant General Manager (General).

television in Victoria. He spent many years in the Music Department, in a variety of jobs including music supervisor in Tasmania and music producer in New South Wales. He was also a Buddhist, a vegetarian, a conscientious objector and Duckmanton's brother-in-law. As Director of Music he was too much the dreamer to grasp the range of complex issues that now affected the ABC as a presenter of music, and he seemed rarely to be in touch with the feelings and desires of concert-goers. He was slow to act, and prone to ponder. These were dangerous times for a man of such temperament.

🦋

John Hopkins and Willem van Otterloo became firm friends under the most testing circumstances. When Hopkins went to Holland in 1964 to explain to Otterloo that he would not, after all, be taking the SSO on its Commonwealth tour the following year, the Director of Music feared that this might be the end of the Dutchman's relationship with Australia. But somehow their meeting was more than amicable. Hopkins explained the circumstances as best he could, and promised to compensate Otterloo for this disappointment. The two men parted on warm terms.

Although Otterloo had been chief conductor in Melbourne since 1967, his love affair with the Sydney orchestra—and with Sydney—began during his first Australian tour of 1962, and was clearly reciprocated. So when Otterloo was announced as Atzmon's successor in the same month as Atzmon's resignation there was general rejoicing amongst critics and orchestral musicians. But he was in some ways the least likely conductor to appeal to Sydney audiences. They traditionally liked a bit of platform dash to their maestri, some gratuitous emotional semaphoring. Goossens was master of the wide, luscious beat and Atzmon used full-body showman's gestures constantly, whereas Dixon's directorial sobriety was probably a factor in Sydney audiences' slow fade to disinterest in him. But never was an SSO chief conductor less flashy than Otterloo. In 1973 Lindsey Browne made an elegant summing-up of his platform style:

He thinks with balance, breeding, lucidity and unimpeachable integrity—

which means, among other things that he never drives hard to force his points across, never seeks to pump up his music with rhetorician tricks of bombast, fist-shaking and exaggeration, never forgets in his concern for precision in even the most intricately geared 'clever' music that his commitment is to human nobility and warmth, not to stunting mechanics.

Always with taste and wisdom he generates the illusion that his music is dictating the terms of its own growth pretty much as a tree will grow whether the forester is about or not...All is invitation and persuasion. Compulsion and the whip are banished.

In his own country Otterloo was regarded with a mixture of respect and irritation. He was born (in 1907) in Winterswijk, a small town in one of the eastern provinces of the Netherlands, and Holland's main orchestra, the Concertgebouw, seems always to have regarded him as a provincial. A little too passive, not sufficiently glamorous. Some of the SSO musicians who had worked in the better European and North American orchestras also found him a bit ponderous. But his gentlemanly ways, his apparent disinterest in the higher peaks of fame, his intense musicality, were considered by most of his Australian colleagues as ample compensation.

He had not intended to become a musician, and first studied medicine, but later enrolled at the Amsterdam conservatory, where he studied cello and composition. After playing cello in the Utrecht orchestra for a few years, his Third Suite won a competition organised by the Concertgebouw orchestra.[6] The prize also included a performance of his work under the Concertgebouw's legendary musical director, Willem Mengelberg. Otterloo's conducting career began when Mengelberg fell ill and invited Otterloo to conduct his own piece. His first major appointment came a few years later, in 1949, when he became first conductor of the Residency Orchestra in The Hague. He and the orchestra struck up a great chemistry, and he stayed principal there until 1973. Their records together were well known in Australia when Otterloo made his 1962 tour.

---

[6] He was modest about his compositions, and only conducted one—his Symphonietta— in Sydney, in 1972.

Despite his old-world manner, his repertoire interests were determinedly idiosyncratic, and he gave Sydney's Red, Blue and White series subscribers more ear-opening repertoire than they had bargained for. Otterloo was naturally drawn to the romantic literature, but not always to the expected parts of it. He was Australia's first consistently fine Bruckner conductor, and was able to steer the SSO through the crooked chromatic byways of Max Reger. He was also a fine central interpreter of Beethoven and Brahms. In the realms of his own century, he had great success in the music of Debussy and Ravel, and was a Mahlerian of noble and confident instincts. He was also a champion of the Swiss composer Frank Martin, and with the SSO made one of the finest recordings of Martin's *Petite Symphonie Concertante*.

Otterloo's very first concert with the SSO, in 1962, gave a good indication of his areas of strength:

Suite no 3 ....Bach
Nocturnes: Nuages et Fetes...................Debussy
Suite: *Electra*.........................Diepenbrock

Interval

Symphony No. 5........................Beethoven

Bach's orchestral suites were a Mengelberg speciality for decades, so that Otterloo would have grown up with 'big-band' Bach. Alphons Diepenbrock (1862-1921) was that rare thing, a Dutch composer, whose music is still well regarded in Holland. His pointillistic, late romantic idiom earned Mahler's approval, and Otterloo was as assured within it as he was amongst Mahler's scores.

He also conducted a lot of Australian music in Sydney, and while he did not enjoy every score he was given to conduct, he brought a composer's care and interest to many of them. When he performed, and subsequently recorded *Fire in the Heavens*, the composer, Nigel Butterley recalls that Otterloo was 'really meticulous, and gave great attention to detail'. In Colin Piper's view: 'he was committed to whatever he was doing.'

In 1972 Otterloo conducted twenty-one SSO concerts, which were in effect warm-ups for the following year, when his period as SSO chief began.[7] His first 1973 concert, given in late March, included Reger's *Romantic Suite*, Opus 125, and did not set pulses racing. In the *Sydney Morning Herald* Fred Blanks referred to Otterloo's direction as 'eminently clear and never fussy,' which does not constitute a rave review. David Gyger, now editor of *Opera Australia* but then writing in the *Australian*, said simply that 'Otterloo is not a particularly interesting conductor to watch.' In the *Sun-Herald*, Lindsey Browne went so far as to say that the concert 'confirmed my unhappy suspicion that the institution of the old-style symphony concert is now in its dying years'.

Browne's review was not an omen for Otterloo's tenure. As the year progressed a number of big works gave vivid proof of the Dutchman's strengths. In particular, the performance of Mahler 3, which took place in May during the 1973 Gold Series, marked the real beginning of the Otterloo period.

Sydney had been a Mahler town since Goossens' time, but the orchestra had worked with only a few outstanding Mahler conductors—Goossens, Klemperer, Maazel and Dixon. With the 1973 performance of Mahler 3, Otterloo placed himself in their company. Fred Blanks referred to the performance as 'an ennobling experience...[Otterloo] might have lost a battle or two in particular climaxes or showy outbursts, but he won the war with a reading that was consistent and logically continuous from the first to the last note.' Ironically, one of Otterloo's last triumphs as SSO chief, in 1978, was a performance of Mahler 6, a tougher, more severe work than the third symphony, and more testing of a conductor's feeling for musical architecture. Again, Blanks was full of praise. 'No doubt it will have been a performance of the year, perhaps of the decade, searing the memory with a permanent imprint.' Of a Mahler 5 given in 1976, Covell wrote that he would always remember it as 'one of the major experiences of concert going.' Otterloo had grown up in a country which maintained a Mahler tradition when most of the world's major music centres had abandoned the composer altogether. His interpretations spoke of such a tradition: of patience and vision, an understanding of the landscape of the idiom. He was the only conductor the orchestra

---

[7] They were also testing ground for repertoire Otterloo wanted to take on the 1974 European tour.

Watch the hands: pianist Joerg Demus in conversation with Heinze and Otterloo at a 1972 function.

had worked with who had come from a school of Mahler conducting. As a tape of this performance of the 6th reveals, he was scrupulous about dynamic shading and internal balance, nor did he overplay the big moments that came early in the piece. The SSO's collective memory of working with him on these scores would be of great benefit to Sydney's next great Mahler conductor, Stuart Challender.

And yet none of Otterloo's Mahler performances reached a level of technical excellence that might have been expected from, say, one of the middle-ranking European orchestras. In particular, some of the longer works tended to droop in their finales. This was less to do with the SSO's corporate skill—although that was a factor—than with the orchestra's schedule. Ideally, the big Mahler symphonies need lavish rehearsal time and few distractions, such as surrounding concerts. Until very recently, the SSO was not in a position where either requirement could be met consistently.

In addition to Mahler 3, another 1973 performance that placed the Otterloo stamp on the orchestra was that of Bruckner 7. Again, this was admired for its authority and sense of purpose, and Otterloo would later give notable performances with the SSO of Bruckner 3 and 6 and the F minor mass.

The first year of Otterloo's tenure gave the signal that a personality was clearly in charge, and audiences, although not always fired up by the Otterloo style, noticed that the orchestra again displayed a will to do well that had not been seen since the beginning of the Atzmon years. This will would face its greatest test the following year, when the SSO embarked on what Charles Buttrose has described as 'the bravest concert venture ever likely to be essayed by an Australian orchestra', an intense eight-week tour of Great Britain and continental Europe.

※

'*Sehr interessant!* We have heard of the kangaroo. But an orchestra!' So a Viennese taxi driver remarked to Roger Covell during the SSO's European tour of September and October 1974. Indeed, one of the orchestra's great achievements was to make middle Europe aware that the Sydney Opera House was not a piece of sculpture, but that a fine orchestra played in it.

No Australian orchestra had ever been to continental Europe

before and, as if to emphasise the fact, the SSO was given a particularly demanding tour schedule: thirty-three concerts in seven countries in eight weeks. The impetus for the tour came from one Rene Klopfenstein, who was music director of the Montreux-Vevey Musical Festival in Switzerland. From this event, all else sprang, and there was a lot of 'else.' Unlike the 1965 tour, this one took advantage of the European festival season. The orchestra would play during the final week of the Edinburgh Festival; in Lincoln Cathedral, concluding the celebrations surrounding the bicentenary of the birth of Australia's circumnavigator, Lincolnshire's own Matthew Flinders; at the Proms; in Otterloo's heartland of Amsterdam and the Hague; and, audaciously, at the end of the annual Bruckner Festival in Linz. There were also concerts in Scandinavia, Germany and Portugal.

Concerts in virtually every centre were conducted by either Otterloo or Mackerras, with the one exception of Braunschweig, where the then chief conductor of the Queensland Symphony, Patrick Thomas, conducted. The soloists were John Williams (Edinburgh), Roger Woodward (Edinburgh and London), the flautist Aurele Nicolet (Regensburg), cellist Pierre Fournier and violinist Ulf Hoelscher (Brahms double concerto in Hannover), and two young pianists then at the beginning of their careers: Mitsuko Uchida (Montreux) and Maria Joao Pires (Lisbon, an appropriate date for a Portuguese soloist).[8] All these soloists joined the SSO on tour. The orchestra's principal clarinettist, Donald Westlake, also gave some well-reviewed performances of Mozart's clarinet concerto.

As in 1965, Australian repertoire was a feature of the tour. Don Banks' new work, *Prospects*; Richard Meale's *Clouds Now and Then*; and Peter Sculthorpe's *Sun Music IV* were played throughout the eight weeks, but some concerts featured no Australian music at all. This was inevitable, given that most of the programs were compiled jointly by the ABC and each of the European concert promoters. At the time, Klopfenstein said that 'if I put in an Australian work, 500 people stay away— not because it is Australian, but because it is modern and unknown'. He might

---

[8] Pires was listed in the repertoire itinerary as 'Mario'. She must have given the orchestra quite a surprise.

have been speaking for Sydney concert audiences.

Despite the heavy demands the tour made on both players and organisers, there were very few organisational mishaps and only a few bad nights musically. Of course luggage went missing and planes were late, and, in echoes of the Commonwealth Festival scenario, the orchestra could not rehearse with Mackerras until they arrived at their first stop, Edinburgh. Fortunately, Otterloo's presence in Sydney for most of the 1974 season meant that his programs were thoroughly rehearsed in. He had already test-driven two of the big tour pieces, Bruckner 6 and Ravel's complete *Daphnis and Chloe*, in 1972, and conducted two others, the *Symphonie fantastique* and R. Strauss' *A Hero's Life*, several times each in 1974. The Banks and Sculthorpe pieces were also played frequently in the months leading up to the tour. By the time of the last Sydney performance of the Berlioz, David Gyger wrote that 'the interpretation now conveys a real sense of macabre excitement'. European critics would not always agree.

The two Edinburgh concerts were a fantastic beginning and at once gave SSO players some idea of what their international reputation might be if they played in full-adrenalin mode at all times. Of the first concert, under Mackerras, the *Glasgow Herald* noted that 'the final week of the Festival, which began with mediocre performances by the Vienna Symphony Orchestra, ended on a much higher plane, with the Sydney Symphony Orchestra on Friday showing itself to be an ensemble of distinction'. In the second Edinburgh performance, the orchestra joined the Edinburgh Festival Chorus under Otterloo for *Daphnis and Chloe*. Covell, the only Australian journalist on tour, wrote that this ranked 'as one of [the SSO's] most zealous and masterly achievements'. The Edinburgh critics were also impressed, but more with the playing than Otterloo's interpretation.

After Lincoln Cathedral, in which the capacity audience gave the orchestra a standing ovation, the Proms concert began tentatively but finished blazingly with an acclaimed performance of the Berlioz. Again, the critics were uncertain about Otterloo's interpretation. In *The Times*, Stanley Sadie wrote that 'the *Symphonie fantastique* . . . needs a certain verve, a hint of the sensuous in its phrasing . . . Otterloo's reading was careful and respectful but never sounded really convinced about the music'.

This view was echoed by Felix Aprahamian in the *Sunday Times*: 'Otterloo is an estimable, careful rather than impassioned musician and certainly no fire-eater, so that in [this piece] the letter rather than the spirit was observed'. The Prommers loved the concert, though, and called Otterloo back to the podium seven times.

The rigours of this tour were vividly illustrated the following day when the orchestra had a full day's rehearsal at the BBC's Maida Vale studios, working on repertoire for the next concerts. In the morning they spent four hours with Mackerras on *Clouds Now and Then* and Brahms 4, and in the afternoon three hours with Otterloo on Bruckner 6. The concerts in Sweden went quite well, the highlight perhaps being a wonderfully vivid reading of Brahms 4 in Stockholm, which was broadcast live to Australia and is preserved on tape. But the most testing concerts were to follow, in Austria and the Netherlands.

For the orchestra and Otterloo, Linz was the greatest challenge and perhaps the greatest disappointment. Playing Bruckner in a festival devoted to his music in his home town was typical Australian cheek, and a classic case of 'coals to Newcastle'. The players and the conductor were well pleased with their performance of Bruckner 6 until they saw the reviews, one of which opined that Otterloo gave 'an interpretation of cool sobriety'. Another Linz paper headlined its review 'Exactly the Average Reached'.

Linz at least provided some comedy relief. After a rehearsal Otterloo told the orchestra that Bruckner was buried there. 'You will all want to see his grave?' he asked, half serious. There was a long pause. 'Is there a bar there, maestro?' one of the players remarked.

Such banter could be hard-won. Rex Ellis recalls occasions on tour when Otterloo was primarily a stern disciplinarian. 'On the 1974 tour he held extra rehearsals when he thought standards were dropping. I remember him having a separate brass rehearsal after a concert at which he thought the players had let him down. The wonderful thing was that most of those players grumbled about it at the time, but would later admit how necessary the extra work had been.'

In contrast to Linz, the response in Graz was ecstatic. In the final movement of the Berlioz, Covell reported, 'Otterloo unleashed the orchestra's energies with rare abandon. The result was thrilling

An august moment: The SSO with its Dutch chief conductor Willem van Otterloo performing in the Amsterdam Concertgebouw during the 1974 European tour.

in the extreme and the audience responded with a sustained demonstration of applause and cheers such as I have never witnessed in any other concert hall.' One local critic found that the SSO created 'a transparency not frequently found in local orchestras'. The Vienna concert also went well, despite the tiredness that was now beginning to set in. The players had travelled to Vienna from Graz on the same day, which apparently told in the last moment of Dvořák 8, one of Mackerras' tour pieces. (This was one of Mackerras' last stops on the tour. He bade farewell to the orchestra at Stuttgart.) Otterloo was unhappy that he was not conducting in Vienna, which was one of the most prestigious dates on the tour, and where he wanted to conduct the Bruckner, but the organisation promoting the concert, the Jeunesses Musicales, knew the Mackerras name better than they did the Otterloo. More disappointments were to follow.

The Munich concert, under Otterloo, was the low point of the endeavour. The players were clearly tired, and made too many mistakes to escape the wrath of the local press. The first savage review of the tour appeared the following morning, in the *Suddeutche Zeitung*: 'It was the worst, coarsest, most unnecessary concert in a long time . . . the number of more or less conspicuously wrong notes was not noteworthy, but rather the insipidity and lacklustre roughness of the right ones.'

Disappointments vanished with the concerts that followed. Regensburg offered, in Covell's opinion, 'the cleanest, most dashing performance of the tour', and a young, enthusiastic audience. The concerts in Amsterdam's Concertgebouw and The Hague's Congresgebouw were enormous successes. The players knew this was a special homecoming for their chief conductor, and wanted to give their best for him. The audience response on both occasions was a sign of their achievement.

The showpiece in the Hague concert was *A Hero's Life*, which the critic of the *Haagsche Courant* thought was performed 'more or less perfectly . . . van Otterloo . . . gave the entire piece enormous drive and excitement without missing the moments of relaxation and lyricism, [yet] it was not just because of seeing him again that The Hague audience reacted so enthusiastically . . . something special was going on'. Covell reported that 'the entire body of listeners in the sold-out house rose as one for the final bars of the work'.

The Concertgebouw concert was broadcast direct to Australia, and contained the most confident and finished performance of Bruckner 6 given during the tour. The cheers at its conclusion were tumultuous.

That this was a successful tour is beyond doubt. The players who were part of it remember it with excitement and gratitude, and it was made more memorable for them by the brilliant logistics. These were a tribute to the organisational skills of the Concert Department, in particular to Rex Ellis; Daryl Miley, who was Controller of Radio Programs but acted as tour manager; John Matthews, who did not go on the tour but did much of the spadework; his successor Colin Dunton; and Ken Neville and Bob Rowlings, who set the orchestral stage on thirty different platforms of various shapes and sizes. Charles Buttrose oversaw preparations for the vast operation until his retirement in June 1974.[9]

Great as it was, a number of important negatives emerged in the post-mortems. Above all, eight weeks was considered too long to sustain such an intense schedule. It meant that it was necessary to take a lot of different programs, perhaps too many. In the eight weeks the SSO played twenty-four different works, some of which they had not performed in the months before September. There were also possibly too many different soloists who had to be rehearsed with along the way. And for all the importance attached to press reviews, many players and administrators learned to take them with a small grain of salt. It is hard to take seriously such divergent opinions as '[the SSO] possess a string section of exceptional quality, unequalled by any other orchestra appearing at this year's Festival' (Edinburgh) and 'the violin group in particular seemed to be the weak spot in this unquestionably fine orchestra' (The Hague). Yet one happy aspect of the critical coverage was the attention given to the Australian works.

For the players, the behaviour of the European audiences was the greatest revelation. Even if they did not always cheer, they were at all times attentive and courteous. There were none of the walking ovations that are still so dismal a feature of Sydney

---

[9] Buttrose had also supervised the organisation of a successful two-week Asian tour the SSO had undertaken at the beginning of the year, to Manila and Hong Kong.

concert life. Cliff Goodchild was not shy in saying so on the orchestra's return. 'Sydney audiences always seem to be half asleep—some of them don't even take their gloves off and they leave before the conductor. They should be more appreciative of the orchestra they have.'

⁂

Compared to 1965, it was not necessarily a better orchestra that toured in 1974, but it was a more stable one. The appointment of associate principal positions had been completed in 1972, so that the SSO's establishment strength was now a respectable ninety-six, and it was in this shape (more or less, as extra players were needed for most of the big pieces) that the orchestra played in Europe. It was also a different-sounding orchestra to its 1965 self. The Goossens-generation players were gradually being replaced, for the most part by younger musicians. In Buttrose's view, the new breed were 'more talented, better taught and more musical than those who preceded them'. Otterloo won their respect, and helped turn the orchestra from a naturally bright, and sometimes brash, instrument, into a mellower and more subtle one. The relationship with Otterloo had also had more time to work in 1974 than the Dixon/SSO combination had in 1965. It was apparent to players and administrators alike that Otterloo had taken the Australian temperament and lifestyle to his heart, and his enjoyment at working in Sydney gave his dealings with the SSO a natural shine.

But for all the success of the 1974 tour—which included a recognition of these qualities—Otterloo held some private reservations about its results.

Put simply, he was hoping to be hailed for his interpretative skills, for his qualities as a conductor, not just as the SSO's conductor. That this did not happen on a grand scale disappointed him. Reviewers here and abroad alluded to his sometimes dull platform manner, the flipside of his visionary patience as an interpreter. But while SSO players, and the people he worked with in the Concert and Music departments, knew this to be one of his faults, to many of them Otterloo was irreplaceable.

'Of all the conductors I have worked with, he was the one I admired the most', says Ron Cragg. 'He was not an audience conductor, but a musician's conductor. Even if you did not like him as a person he was an admirable musician, with the best ear I have known ever. Once a problem had been fixed, he would not brood or glare at anyone. He just got on with the job.' Cliff Goodchild: 'He was a giant.' Neville Amadio: 'Until Otterloo, we had not played as consistently well for anyone since Goossens. Now that is saying something.'

Michael Corban worked intensively with Otterloo on the creation of the concert programs he would conduct, and he remembers these sessions with great affection. 'Otterloo was one of God's brothers', Corban says. 'A tremendous, charming man, enormously accomplished. If he saw a good reason for doing a piece, he would do it and usually make a fine job of it. He refined the orchestra's sense of style, which is a great legacy.'

John Matthews believes Otterloo's major achievement was the improved playing standard the SSO reached under his direction. 'He was a great musician and a very human man, although it is true unfortunately that his greatness often came out at the final rehearsal.'

Some of the SSO's players felt this too. Covell is not alone in thinking, even now, that 'he could work up considerable excitement in the final rehearsal, but the resulting performance could be a let-down'. Gordon Webb, for example, agrees with this assessment. Webb joined the SSO as first trumpet in 1974, two years after John Robertson's retirement. Although, like Guy Henderson, he was originally from New Zealand, he had come to Sydney from the London Philharmonic, where Bernard Haitink was then chief conductor. Otterloo was his second Dutchman in a row, and he found many differences between the two.

'Haitink had an excellent rehearsal technique, trusted the musicians and preferred his performances to have another ten to fifteen per cent on top of what you'd achieved at the rehearsal. There was room for you to do something different in the performance. In other words, the LPO had some of the attitudes of a chamber ensemble. With Otterloo, the way you did it in rehearsal was the way he wanted it in performance. There was little freedom, and I think this is what stopped many of his performances from being first class.'

In recollection, Lindsey Browne feels the symptoms of plainness that manifested themselves in an Otterloo performance were tied closely to his integrity as a musician. 'There were borderline occasions when he seemed to be dull because of his refusal to be tasteless. He was fastidious. There were no cheap colour tricks, for example.'

Otterloo's frequent inability to 'let go' in performance was particularly apparent in music that demanded a degree of theatricality. His 1977 performance of Tchaikovsky 5 with the SSO, which has been kept for posterity, lacks a quality central to a successful performance of music by this composer: the ability to live for the moment. Works such as the Mussorgsky/Ravel *Pictures at an Exhibition* (which he conducted in Sydney in 1977) and Rimsky-Korsakov's *Schéhérazade* (1978) were similarly affected.

But for every work that suffered from the Otterloo approach, there was seemingly another which responded well. Before his time, the SSO would not have been thought of as a Bruckner orchestra, but his solid work on this composer meant that when, for example, Franz-Paul Decker conducted Bruckner 7 in 1978, it was widely regarded as one of the orchestra's finest performances of the decade. The Beethoven cycle Otterloo had started recording in Sydney for RCA in the same year is a fine example of his working methods at their best. *The Rite of the Spring* might have seemed a work unsuited to his temperament but it turned out to be one of the high points of his tenure, and surprised those critics who thought that there was not enough fire in his belly. The most concentrated run of performances he gave of the work in Sydney occurred in July 1978, when it occupied the last half of all five Red, Blue and White concerts. A recording followed. One of the great fortunes of Otterloo's reign was that the ABC's licensing agreement with record companies allowed so much of his best repertoire to be recorded. We are the poorer that such a system was not put in place earlier.

Those *Rite* concerts were Otterloo's last. In 1976 he signalled to the ABC that he wished to scale down his Australian commitments from 1978. He would by then be seventy-one, and wanted to spend more time in Holland, less time travelling, and fewer hours on the podium. Hort and Ellis worked out a package of concerts in 1979 that effectively reduced his Australian workload but allowed him to retain the title of Principal Guest Conductor of the Melbourne and Sydney orchestras. The SSO players farewelled him as Chief at a party given during the *Rite* rehearsals, and enjoyed recalling two of his pet sayings: 'What a Pity' when a player had made a mistake in rehearsal, and 'Dangerous Moments,' when a particularly difficult passage was approaching.

'Of course I am tough', Otterloo told Lenore Nicklin, for a profile that appeared in the *Sydney Morning Herald* to mark his departure. 'I don't like people reading newspapers even when they have a 178 bar rest . . . and there was even one of our dear ladies knitting. I was looking with great eyes at her. It didn't happen again.' Nicklin asked Otterloo if it was possible to sack a musician. 'We always say—in Holland and here—you can only sack a musician when he has murdered his father and his mother.'

A few days after the farewell party he was in Melbourne to rehearse Beethoven 9 with the MSO, and was riding in a car that was hit by a cattle truck on the corner of Dandenong and Williams Roads in Prahran. Otterloo was thrown through the car's back window by the force of the collision. He died instantly.

In the face of the numbing shock of his death, Maria Prerauer's obituary was an eloquent summary of his achievements:

The SSO recognised that in his own quiet way Otterloo had taught them that every concert was something to be approached with the greatest sense of beauty, perfectionism and attention to the smallest detail.

On the day of his last rehearsal he had said that when he became the SSO's chief conductor he had found the orchestra in a 'very well state'. At that rate, he had left it in the best shape it had been in for twenty years. His quiet inspiration would be sorely missed in the years to follow.

CHAPTER NINE

"*The sound of distant thunder . . .*"[1]

When he retired from his full-time SSO post, Otterloo had enjoyed a sixteen-year association with the orchestra. He had become their Grand Old Man.

But the orchestra already had a G.O.M. in its ranks, in Neville Amadio. He retired in the same year as Otterloo, after fifty-one years as the orchestra's principal flute. He had played for the ABC in many capacities—in dinner music ensembles, dance bands (he recalls in particular an assignment to play *Piccolo Pete* with the ABC Dance unit), chamber groups, and as concerto soloist, and in the earliest of those fifty-one years had been first and only flute before the |SSO|had its name. Toward the end of his time as principal he was known as Dr Amadio, because of the wisdom he had accumulated over the decades. Guy Henderson remembers him with great affection. 'I was always amazed at his enthusiasm. In the fifteen years in which I sat next to him he never seemed bored, and we never had a cross word. He's a marvellous person.' Sir Charles Mackerras has a long and abiding admiration for Amadio as a man and as a musician. 'Neville's playing was of a standard that truly epitomises that much-abused term, "world class". He was one of the most remarkable flute players I've ever known.'

By the time of Amadio's retirement a third G.O.M. had celebrated

---

[1] From Berlioz's description of the third movement of the *Symphonie fantastique*.

Neville Amadio
The Queen meets the orchestra. After the Royal concert, held in the Opera House Concert Hall in October 1973 to mark the Queen's visit to open the building, Her Majesty is introduced to, from left, Donald Hazelwood, Neville Amadio and violinist Jennifer James. Cliff Goodchild waits to be presented. On the Queen's left, Prince Phillip is meeting other members of the orchestra while at the extreme left of the picture is Charles Buttrose, making the presentations.

two landmarks: his eightieth birthday and his jubilee year as a conductor. In 1974 Sir Bernard Heinze marked both events by conducting youth concerts in every Australian capital. As Therese Radic has written, these were 'the beginning of a long series of farewells'. His Sydney youth concert, with bass-baritone Simon Estes, was an uneven affair, and David Gyger noted that 'the first half of this concert did justice neither to Sir Bernard nor the SSO'. Even in Melbourne, where critics and musicians have always been more respectful of him, Kenneth Hince has written that 'he was, at worst, an erratic conductor'. But his achievements off the podium were great and enduring. Covell provided the best epitaph when he wrote that Heinze would be remembered as 'the great innovator of Australian musical organisation'. He believed that a thriving musical culture was a major civilising force, and, whatever his weaknesses, his actions on music's behalf were always governed by this principle. He died, aged eighty-eight, in 1982.

Heinze's great legacies as an organisational innovator were the Australian symphony orchestras. With Cleary and Moses, he had fought for the establishment of a network of orchestras around the country, servicing the capital cities and the rural centres. But only two years after the euphoria occasioned by Heinze's eightieth birthday celebrations, the empire he had helped build was under threat on two fronts.

In November 1976 the contents of two publicly funded reports that directly concerned the ABC orchestras were made public. One was the *Report on the structure of the Australian broadcasting system and associated matters*, which was produced by F.J. Green, the secretary of the then Postal and Telecommunications Department; the other was a draft report, *Assistance to the Performing Arts*, by the Industries Assistance Commission. Both questioned whether it was appropriate for the ABC to subsidise the performance of orchestral music.

For the IAC, the availability of high-quality musical performance from other sources (discs, overseas tapes, etc.), and the high cost of maintaining the orchestras, meant that 'the justification for the ABC subsidising public performances to such an extent is limited and declining'.

The spartan cultural ideology of the IAC's report made its criticisms far less potent than those in Green's study, which was better focused and in any case carried more weight, since it had been commissioned by the Fraser government. In particular, one of Green's recommendations set the wheels of outrage and anguish resolutely in motion:

The inquiry believes that subsidising symphony orchestras is now a largely anachronistic and inappropriate activity for the ABC as a national broadcasting service. If the government intends that such subsidies should be made, they should more properly be administered through some other body such as the Australia Council which already subsidises the Elizabethan Trust and Western Australian Arts orchestras . . . it recommends that the number of orchestras employed by the ABC be held to that number required to undertake broadcasting functions and that the ABC initiate discussions with the Australia Council on the future of those orchestras which may be disbanded.[2]

When these reports appeared the orchestras were already seen to be in danger from the first wave of the Fraser government's Razor Gang cuts. Based on the Whitlam administration's funding, the ABC had projected that its budget allocation in 1976-77 would be around $139 million. Shortly after the Coalition was elected this was reduced to $128 million. Production cuts were put in place across Radio and TV. The ABC Sydney Show Band (the final mutation of the old ABC Dance Band) and the Adelaide Singers (the last of the original wireless choruses) had already been closed down; the Melbourne Showband was to meet its fate a few months later.

After Green's report had been published one of the commissioners leaked the information that the disbandment of the Tasmanian, Western Australian and Adelaide orchestras was being considered because of funding cuts. In such an atmosphere Green was bound to appear to numerous critics and musicians as the prophet of a dark age in Australian music. A Keep Music Alive campaign swung into action, petitions were signed, journalists wrote of 'anti-cultural bureaucratic thinking', and the SSO Musicians' Association issued a statement denouncing the Green

---

[2] It should be remembered that this report was written while the Tait amendment was still in force, so that Green's broadcast-oriented priorities can be seen as an interpretation of the ABC charter as it then stood.

and IAC reports as 'an attack on the creative, imaginative and spiritual life of Australia'.

Brutal as Green's remedy seemed, it raised an issue that was now being articulated for the first time by the Music Department, and that Hort knew was playing a part in the demise of the Proms. As Geoffrey Serle has put it in *The Creative Spirit in Australia:* 'Everyone's attention span was shortening'. Serle was referring to the crisis the novel suffered in the 1960s, when 'cinema and television were attracting away both talented writers and the potential audience'. But, as Donald Hazelwood has intimated, it also affected the fortunes of orchestral music in Australia. Green, coincidentally to his aims, had pinpointed the ABC's failure to determine what an audience which had grown up in an age of electronic diversion might want from a concert organisation.

Green was not calling for divestment, the term that came to be used in the 1980s whenever the removal of the orchestras from the ABC's control was discussed, but wholesale dismemberment. The idea caused great anguish when, however they might have played or been administered, the symphony orchestras had become precious cultural commodities to the cities in which they lived and performed. Green had ignored the community's interests. In so doing, he unwittingly created a climate of mistrust around all future reports into Australia's orchestral life, even those which were more considered and better informed. In the end, the Green recommendations were not adopted, whereas the two major reports that were to come had profound effects on the future of orchestral performance in Australia. They also caused huge tensions within the ABC, for the old would be forced to give way to the new.

After a few years the Green report was forgotten. It may seem surprising now to realise that, for Sydney, Neville Amadio's retirement in 1978 established more convincingly than the Green or IAC documents an atmosphere of uncertainty surrounding the ABC's abilities as an orchestral manager. For Amadio retired during a period when many fine players were leaving the SSO for professional reasons: Gordon Webb had resigned to take up a wider range of performing opportunities;[3] Richard McIntyre,

---

[3] He subsequently became Head of Brass at the Victorian College of the Arts, and is now holding the equivalent position at the NSW Conservatorium.

associate principal bassoon, left to join the teaching staff at the Canberra School of Music; Donald Westlake resigned; and the first horn, Anthony Buddle, left to teach at the New South Wales Conservatorium. He had been principal since Clarence Mellor stepped down as principal in 1976 to rejoin his section.

The departure of so many wind players at one time was unprecedented. Such an exodus meant a dramatic change in the colour and character of the SSO sound. Even the Dixon-era resignations and retirements were spread more evenly through the orchestral sections than this. What had led so many fine players to leave within a few months of one another?

The tangle of factors of which this situation was a symptom would begin to be explored in the process that led up to the publication of the Dix report in 1981, when orchestral players and managers from around the country were able to speak freely about their work to an independent body. In Sydney, some of the short-term issues were undoubtedly the ABC's inflexibility over its musicians playing 'outside' engagements;[4] the uneven quality of guest conductors; and the obvious decline in audiences, which manifested itself as 'no shows'—subscribers who chose not to come to concerts for which they had bought seats—in the sold-out major series, and plain poor houses for the Gold Series and Youth Concerts.[5] The attendance problem was tied closely to the musicians' frustration at having no say in how concert programs were put together. For Gordon Webb, one of the clinch issues was also the orchestra's attitude to its performance standards. He felt that the public service approach that hampered the orchestra's management had begun to affect the players' attitude to standards.

'When I went to London the London Philharmonic had no hesitation in asking me to do some trial concerts as an audition. They were prepared to hear anybody so long as they found someone they were happy with playing first trumpet. One of the reasons

---

[4] For many years ABC orchestral musicians had to make an official application before being allowed to perform for another organisation, and such applications were frequently refused. In this instance, Westlake was particularly angry at the Music Department's refusal to allow him to accept some solo engagements in New Zealand.

[5] The third series of Youth Concerts was abolished from the 1977 season because of falling attendances.

I eventually left the SSO was that at that time they did not follow that philosophy. The bottom line should have been "Are we going to get the right person for the job?".

'In my case, we were auditioning for a trumpet position, we'd heard all the SSO trumpet players, and I wanted to be 100 per cent convinced that we were not leaving out someone else who might have been suitable. I wasn't allowed to do that because the regulations did not allow it, nor was I allowed to audition anyone by asking them to play in a concert.

'It was strange, because in a way my honesty was being questioned. In the LPO—which earns money based on how much work it gets—a wrong player appointment can matter terribly. You might lose a recording session or even a conductor. The relative comfort of the SSO as a salaried ABC orchestra meant that the sort of work you got was not going to suffer because of a player decision. I really believe that some of the SSO players of my time took advantage of that. They were not visionary enough to see that these decisions can help make or break an orchestra's reputation.'

※

Otterloo had given the ABC plenty of notice for his impending semi-retirement, and Hort and Ellis had two full seasons before them until Otterloo's chiefdom came to an end. As far as the Artists' Tours Committee was concerned, Otterloo's successor could be one of three workable contenders: Kurt Sanderling, Franz-Paul Decker and Louis Frémaux.

Sanderling, one of the finest conductors in what was formerly East Germany, also had spent many years in the Soviet Union, as joint conductor of the Leningrad Philharmonic with Evgeny Mravinsky. A respected interpreter of Mahler and Shostakovich, he has a vivid sense of platform theatre. He had made his first Australian tour in 1976, when both critics and players liked him enormously. Decker is one of the great eccentrics of the conducting firmament, a fiery Wagnerian with a tremendous sense of architecture in big works. He has made three ABC tours, in 1967, 1975 and 1978, and his calling cards then included Beethoven's *Eroica* symphony, the *Grande Messe des Morts* of Berlioz, the aforementioned Bruckner 7, and R. Strauss' *An Alpine Symphony*.

By his side, Frémaux was a relative newcomer to Australia. His one visit, in 1975, had been a great success, with Covell remarking that his 'conducting lifts the SSO's playing out of the dour and heavy-footed routine in which it spends too much of its time. His way of making music has a youthful pliancy to it. It is fresh, vital, full of attack'. The SSO musicians enjoyed working with him as well.

1977 presented one other chief conductor possibility in Charles Dutoit, now the celebrated chief in Montreal. But Dutoit was not at all happy with the SSO's playing, and a tape of the performance the SSO gave with him of Stravinsky's *Petrushka* during that visit reveals a sense of struggle that does not become a fine orchestra.

Frémaux's appointment as chief in Sydney was confirmed unusually far ahead of time. In May 1977 it was announced that he would be taking over from the 1979 season. But the likelihood of his appointment was old news to some. In December 1975, in her *Sunday Telegraph* 'Musetta' column, Maria Prerauer was tipping that he would get the job. In doing so, she uttered some prophetic words of warning:

Before being hasty (as the ABC was with Moshe Atzmon) may I remind ABC bigwigs that we haven't heard Frémaux in Mozart, Beethoven, Brahms or Mahler. Surely he should make a return visit where he can be judged on the standard classics.

A chief conductor does not, of course, have to conduct Mahler regularly, but he should have a thorough knowledge of style in the basic repertoire. Frémaux's reputation had been made in French music, and before his appointment began in Sydney he was best known for the recordings he had made with the City of Birmingham Symphony Orchestra, whose musical director he was from 1971 to 1979. With the CBSO he recorded much French music, and their discs of Saint-Saëns' Organ symphony, the Poulenc *Gloria* and piano concerto (with Cristina Ortiz), and Massenet orchestral music were award winners and best sellers. Before Birmingham, Frémaux's life had a uniquely French insouciance that would have appealed to an E. Phillips Oppenheim or Georgette Heyer. He had worked with the French Resistance and joined the Foreign Legion, and was released from legionnaire's duty at the personal intervention of Prince Rainier of Monaco, to head the Monte Carlo Opera Orchestra. He later became a Chevalier of the Légion d'honneur.

The ABC's press release announcing Frémaux's chiefdom makes many references to his recordings, and the Music Department clearly hoped that he would also make records in Sydney, thus enhancing the orchestra's international reputation, and perhaps leading to another overseas tour. But he never expressed any interest in undertaking a program of recording with the SSO. This was one symptom of many that made his tenure disappointing for the musicians. But there were also aspects of his disposition that the ABC's Music and Concert administrators found difficult to handle.

The first sign that Frémaux's reign was not going to be consistently distinguished came, predictably, in concert. His 'calling card' program in the 1979 Red Series contained French works and Haydn's *Surprise* symphony, in all of which he conveyed a high style. But when he came to Beethoven and Tchaikovsky in later concerts the doubts emerged. Michael Corban:

'I thought he brought a wonderful lightness and clarity to the orchestra. But sadly, everything he did was like that—elegant and sophisticated, very French.' The SSO players also had difficulty relating to him on a personal level after the warmth of the Otterloo relationship. One principal player says that there was no chemistry.

'It appeared to me that he didn't care much about his relationship with us. Once a rehearsal was over, he would go straight to his dressing room. He wouldn't talk to us privately about the music, or how things were sounding . . . it was very detached. We didn't give many outstanding performances under him.' Guy Henderson remembers that he kept a clear distance between himself and the players. 'There was an aloofness, a feeling that in some ways we did not exist for him. I think there was the hope that he would repeat his Birmingham success here, but it did not happen.'

Many players remember vividly the performance they regard as the highlight of Frémaux's tenure. This was a live broadcast to Europe, on the stations of the European Broadcasting Union, of a 1981 concert that included the Saint-Saëns Organ symphony. The SSO's current principal trombone, Ron Prussing, joined the orchestra as associate principal a few months before this concert took place. 'It was really stunning. We'd had lots of preparation for it, he conducted with great fire and passion, and great precision, and we played like men possessed. But there were so few performances with him that generated that level of heat.'

In short, Frémaux's excellence in the French repertoire was not complemented by a corresponding level of accomplishment in works by German, Russian or Australian composers. His performances of central nineteenth century repertoire could be curiously perfunctory, to the extent that one critic could remark (although not in print) that it seemed as if, in the finale of Tchaikovsky 4, the conductor was 'late to catch a plane'. Some complex modern scores were conducted with little idiomatic feeling. During the rehearsals of his Symphony, Nigel Butterley remembers discussing with one of the SSO principals Frémaux's tempo decisions. 'There's no use talking to Frémaux about tempi', the player replied. 'He'll just do the piece all at the same speed anyway.'

His musical tastes presented the programmers in the Music Department with a challenge: the list of works he was prepared to conduct was very small. As one programming staffer recalls: 'The size of his repertoire list became a real thorn in our sides as his tenure progressed. It got harder and harder to construct programs with him that would be interesting for audiences'. Frémaux's was in some ways the list a concert managament might seek from a guest conductor for a season's French program.

Indeed, once his chief's contract ended, in 1981, he happily accepted the post of principal guest conductor, which reduced his Sydney commitments from four or five months to two. But his repertoire list was to remain an issue during the three years he was to stay in this new post. The Music Department had an unwritten policy (which its successor, Concert Music, continues to implement) not to repeat works in the same subscription series more than once every three years.

Frémaux's program preferences were making this policy increasingly difficult to maintain. In one meeting, a programmer, somewhat flummoxed by Frémaux's unchanging musical tastes, suggested: 'you might learn some works, maestro'.

❧

Frémaux's last year as chief saw the harsh winds of public inquiry blowing again on the ABC orchestras. *The ABC in Review. National Broadcasting in the 1980s* was the name of the report commissioned by the federal government in 1979, and written by a committee of which the chairman was Alex Dix. Dix was well known in business circles but not in the public sector. Many managers and creative people within the ABC feared that he might be a Fraser government stooge, but he stated honestly that he could best be regarded as a small L liberal who had many Labor-voting friends.

During the inquiry process he proved to be patient and tenacious. Through 1980 the committee held public hearings in cities and towns all over Australia and read 2200 written submissions. It was not intended that the orchestras should be a major focus, but Dix was determined that they should be discussed and advice given about their future. In particular, he was conscious that a 1977 report by a Senate Standing Committee on Education and the Arts had recommended a full inquiry into all aspects of Australian orchestral resources.

When Dix's report was published, the chapter on the orchestras contained sweeping proposals for change, in the context of a major reorganisation of the ABC. In short, the management of orchestras by the ABC was to be brought to an end. In reaching this conclusion, it needs to be remembered that the Dix discussions of the orchestras were conducted in the context of the report's central thesis that, in the 1980s, the ABC had to become more focused on its role as a broadcaster of information, and that therefore the orchestras needed to be administered in such a way that they could become more attentive to the needs of their communities. The following was Dix's major proposal for the future of the ABC orchestras:

We recommend that the existing Concert Department and activities of the existing Music Department which are . . . related to the orchestras and concerts . . . be brought together in a new unit, Music Australia, which is independent of the broadcasting organisation and is headed by a Managing Director responsible directly to the [Commission's] Board of Directors.

Dix (as the report will be called from this point) further proposed that, over three years, Music Australia was to become 'functionally and financially' independent of the ABC; and that this would prepare it to become the new co-ordinating body for music in

Australia. Over those three transitional years, the ABC and the Federal and State governments would discuss the nature of the new body and how the community's interests would best be served by it. They would, particularly, establish 'the funding arrangements needed to allow the management of ABC state orchestras to pass to individual states'. In addition, Music Australia was to 'vigorously pursue the possibilities for attracting private funds to assist in the maintenance of the orchestras, through subscribers' committees and any other means it considers appropriate'.[6]

In the longer term (three to six years), each State was to take on the management of its orchestra, incorporating, where possible, that State's Music Australia staff. After this had taken place, Music Australia would then be regarded as a fully independent body, channelling government funds to the orchestras, initiating co-operative projects with other presenters, and arranging interstate and overseas tours for the orchestras 'and other musical groups'. As Justin Macdonnell has written of this proposed new organisation: 'It was . . . to become a super music entrepreneur, with some of the functions of the current-day Confederation of Performing Arts Centres, while looking back to some of the touring and entrepreneurial responsibilities of the Elizabethan Trust'.

Dix supported its conclusions with a range of tables and submissions which comprised a large number of criticisms of the ABC in its role as concert presenter. Some of these can be summarised as follows:
* The primary function of the orchestras is no longer one of broadcasting.
* Given this, the orchestras spend too much time recording music in the studio for broadcast or for permanent retention on ABC 'house discs'.[7]
* The structure of concert presentation, containing Music and Concert departments, 'is no longer appropriate . . . much of the evidence put to the Committee casts doubts on both the efficiency and artistic results of the current system'.

[6] Dix had also proposed that the ABC accept corporate underwriting for some of its TV programs.

[7] These discs were pressed for the ABC to provide, in effect, a library of Australian music that could be broadcast when required. Such material was also occasionally licensed for commercial release.

* Audience growth is non-existent, 'despite the fact that other bodies—Musica Viva and The Australian Opera, for example—have shown that they can attract healthy and growing audiences'.
* Concert programming was 'seen to be over-conservative and lacking in variety' by a number of independent respondents. In a submission by the Cultural Activities division of the New South Wales Premier's Department, the ABC was criticised for relying too heavily 'on box office returns, [which] is perhaps hindering some important functions of the SSO—principally the promotion of new music and the ability to reach wider audiences'.
* A reported decline in the quality of touring artists 'may be at least partially the result of unsatisfactory methods of selecting and engaging artists to tour'.
* 'Promotion [of concert activity] is widely perceived as deficient . . . the ABC clearly needs to give consideration to more systematic and imaginative promotion on a local basis, and preferably through other outlets as well as its own stations.'
* The marked national declines in State government subsidies could be the result of a dissatisfaction on the part of the States with the ABC's level of interest and co-operation in non-ABC orchestral activities.

One of Dix's final conclusions is worth reprinting in full, as it encapsulates the nature of the snowball effect achieved by the document as a whole:

For every advantage of the current system of orchestral management, there would appear to be an equivalent disadvantage. We would naturally expect that at least some of these disadvantages would be mitigated by the amalgamation of orchestras and concerts . . . [but] the more serious question of increasing the orchestras' service and responsiveness to their communities is not one which seems likely to be adequately answered in the long term by a continuation of or improvement in the current system. Communities should have a choice as to the music activities available to them. The concentration of the control and funding of orchestras within the ABC appears to have made orchestral activities somewhat immune from the pressures of the market place; it is a form of subsidy which does not necessarily take into account the needs of individual communities or attitudes towards the value of such activities.

The orchestral section of the Dix report was a terrible indictment of the ABC's capabilities. In particular, it revealed that, as a presenter of public performances, the ABC had been unable to renew its energies or revive itself structurally. Submission after submission from would-be collaborative organisations, State arts ministries and players' committees detail an apathy, lack of artistic vision and a distance from both the marketplace and the musicians that points to a system in crisis, or at least in a perilous isolation. Michael Corban now wonders how the setup survived for so long:

'The touring artists were treated as goods to service our concerts. There were certain formulas worked out that we stuck to year after year—you want your chief conductor to open the season, you want a top conductor for the last two concerts of the series. And the States had no say at all in programming until the late 1970s. At that point we began to hold annual planning meetings in Sydney to discuss repertoire with a State's music supervisor and concert manager, and a player from the orchestra. They were not usually amicable sessions.'

When Dix was tabled, the orchestral section caused even bigger howls of dismay than had Green. The Coalition government adopted some of the report's recommendations, including the turning of the ABC from a Commission into a Corporation, but left the orchestras alone. It was only with the first Hawke ministry that the orchestral issues raised in Dix came to be examined more closely in a public forum. They certainly needed a closer look, for the Music Australia concept had many cumbersome features, not the least of which was the working-out of the relationship the wider arts community was to have with the new supremo in its midst. Given its brief, Dix was only in a position to examine the edges of the question. There was also the inescapable fact that independently run orchestras would cost a lot more than orchestras run by an organisation that provided legal and accounting services, and publicity on radio and television (such as it was) that did not have to be paid for out of the ABC's orchestral budgets.

In the meantime Dame Leonie Kramer, the last ABC chairman, was appointed in 1982. Like Ken Tribe, she had been a commissioner since the late 1970s, and once she became chair, she and Tribe looked to see if the issues raised in Dix could not be profitably dealt with internally.

❧

When an aspiring eighteen-year old composer burst into one of Eugene Ormandy's SSO rehearsals in 1944, William James considered it high cheek. If he had been a little more patient, the teenager would have seen Ormandy in time. But it was a successful gamble: the young Conservatorium graduate handed up to the conductor a full score of his symphonic suite based on 'Waltzing Matilda', which Ormandy agreed to run through at a later rehearsal. After playing through the piece, Ormandy said it was very skilfully written and that the composer was 'extremely talented, a youth with a big future'.

So Charles Mackerras did not make his debut with the SSO as a conductor. When he stormed the Town Hall, his composing ambitions were already well established. His 'Waltzing Matilda' had been commissioned by the Kirsova ballet company, which had the piece in rehearsal in 1944, just when financial difficulties closed the company for good. The Ormandy run-through was the first time Mackerras had heard the work. ('It contained a *Schwanda the Bagpiper*ish fugue I was very proud of.') By the time he joined the SSO a few months later as second (after which he became principal) oboe he was making a living as an instrumentalist.

He had played in the pit of the Theatre Royal for performances of Gilbert and Sullivan, and had been in the orchestra on 2GB's Colgate-Palmolive show. He already had many friends in the SSO, some of whom were deputised to help copy the 'Waltzing Matilda' parts in time for Ormandy. These copyists included SSO horn players William and Jack Lego (father and son) and Richard Merewether.

The young Mackerras' reputation as an oboist/composer was soon to be further enhanced. He had long badgered W.G. James about wanting to conduct, and had already been given his first conducting audition, in the Burwood studios. This had not gone as well as Mackerras had hoped, but he did direct the SSO in four studio broadcasts as a result of it. Then, like almost all good Australian musicians, he was off to study overseas.

Australians next heard of Mackerras the composer. In 1951

Sir Charles Mackerras

A sixteen-year-old Charles Mackerras in 1942.

Sir Arthur Sullivan's music went out of copyright, and Mackerras arranged a number of his pieces into *Pineapple Poll*, a ballet score choreographed by John Cranko for Sadler's Wells. The Borovansky company scored a huge success with the Australian premiere of the work in 1954.

Mackerras did not return to Australia to conduct until 1960, when he appeared at the first Adelaide Festival and on an all-States ABC tour which included the SSO's summer festival concerts. By then he was a rising star. While playing second oboe and cor anglais in the Sadler's Wells orchestra in 1947, he took some conducting lessons from one of the company's staff conductors, Michael Mudie. He then went to Prague on a British Council scholarship, where he studied with Vaclav Talich. Here also began his lifelong enthusiasm for and championship of Janáček's music. He returned to England in 1948, when he began his conducting career in earnest. He worked regularly at Sadler's Wells and for the BBC, and in 1951 gave the first performance in England of any opera by Janacek, *Kata Kabanová*.

The 1960 concerts he conducted for the SSO constituted a Festival of 20th Century Music, the first such event since Heinze's controversial festival of 1952. This was also the first time in fourteen years that Mackerras had faced the orchestra of which he had been a member, and he was very nervous at the prospect, as he now recalls.

'I had brought my family with me from England by boat. It had not been a good journey, so we got off in Adelaide and flew the rest of the way. This gave me two unexpected free weeks in Sydney, which I spent getting more and more nervous about the whole business. At least half of the players in the SSO of 1960 had been in the orchestra when I had played in it, and here was I coming back as a minor celebrity! And on top of all that the programs I was conducting were very difficult. Among other things, we did Schoenberg's *Five Orchestral Pieces*, the Bartok *Music for Strings, Percussion and Celeste*, a piece by Skalkottas, and in the first concert, if you please, *Petrushka*. And it was all rehearsed in that terrible Kings Cross studio. So I wasn't going to have an easy time of it.

'As it turned out, most of the orchestra treated me very well. I did sense some resentment from a couple of players, but no real opposition, even when I had to tell famous players like John Robertson when they were wrong. It was daunting for me, within the first few minutes of a rehearsal, to have to tell him that he wasn't playing something correctly.'

These were important concerts for Mackerras, for he hoped that they would impress upon Moses and Cannon that he had what it took to be the orchestra's chief conductor when the post became vacant. It did become vacant only eighteen months later, but Mackerras found himself out of the running. He was disappointed at the time.

'But in retrospect I'm rather glad it didn't happen. If it had worked out over a period of years I would have had the terrible dilemma of wondering whether to go away again and seek my fortunes elsewhere or become a big fish in a little pond. And as the pond gets bigger do you get smaller? As it was, I did well abroad, and I was offered other permanent orchestral positions in other countries. But I found myself increasingly attracted to opera, and was able to make my name with certain specialities, in opera and in concert, which have remained my specialities. So I can't complain about not becoming Chief in the early 1960s.'

As the decade wore on, he was also offered the chief conductor posts in Brisbane and Melbourne, but he refused them both. He was happy to come back to Australia to tour, but his work in Europe and North America was increasing rapidly. He became first conductor with the Hamburg State Opera in 1966 and musical director of Sadler's Wells (now the English National Opera) in 1970. His recording career had also taken off, beginning with the 78 rpm set he conducted of *Pineapple Poll* in 1951. By the late 1960s his interest in historic performance practice had resulted in a number of important recordings, including one of Basil Lam's edition of *Messiah*, with the English Chamber Orchestra, and a celebrated one of Handel's *Music for the Royal Fireworks* in the original wind scoring, with London's Pro Arte Orchestra. This disc had to be made late at night so that the twenty-four oboes and twelve bassoons Handel required would be available.

Mackerras was as good as his word when he said that he would happily return to Australia for guest appearances. He conducted here in 1963, 1971, 1973 (for the opening of the Sydney Opera House) and 1978, as well as sharing the 1974 European tour with

Otterloo. Then in 1980 he received a phone call at his holiday house on the island of Elba from his old friend Charles Buttrose, who, although retired, had been dispatched with the job of asking Mackerras if he would consider becoming the SSO's next chief conductor. He accepted. In February 1981 the ABC announced that, from the following year, he would take up the position of SSO chief conductor for an initial term of three years.

Mackerras was in Sydney later that year to conduct subscription concerts and a concert performance of Wagner's *Götterdämmerung*. (He planned to conduct the whole of the *Ring* cycle in concert during his period as chief, but only conducted this opera and *Siegfried*.)

Mackerras' appointment was part of a double celebration, for 1982 was also the ABC's fiftieth anniversary, and the fiftieth anniversary of the SSO and MSO, as the nucleus groups which were to become these orchestras were brought under the Commission's wing in 1932. Mackerras was the first Australian appointed to the chief's position in Sydney, and there was much self-congratulation within the ABC on the marvellous timing of the appointment. But to some critics, the arrival of Mackerras was ironic given that the ABC had done little to help foster the development of younger resident conductors, with the exception of Patrick Thomas, who had in any case been stranded by the Music Department's indecision about what to do with him. In Melbourne, Richard Divall had the force of personality to strike a path for himself largely independent of the ABC. Stuart Challender's return from Europe in 1980 marked the beginning of a turnaround in the fortunes of local conductors in which the ABC has begun to play a decisive part only in the last six years.

The ABC's Golden Jubilee year was also marked by Parliament's response to Dix. This was announced on 4 July, during the week in which, exactly fifty years before, the ABC began broadcasting. It was made clear that the orchestras were to be left out of any Dix-inspired reforms. So for many people at the ABC, 1982 was a triple celebration.

In the nine years since Mackerras had conducted the opening concert at the Sydney Opera House, the ABC had been through some organisational change. Buttrose's retirement as Assistant

General Manager (General) had also seen his position lapse, and the old Controller of Programs position that Keith Barry had once occupied was also abolished as, given the distinct operations of the Radio and TV divisions, the ABC had essentially outgrown it. Along with these changes to upper management in the 1970s Duckmanton gradually handed over the remains of the Moses-style personal relations with artists to Keith Mackriell, who had worked at the ABC since 1955 when, aged twenty-five, he had joined the Talks Department. In 1974 he became Assistant General Manager for Radio. In a management structure that might be described as Late Baroque, it appears that Hort largely worked through Mackriell to get to Duckmanton. At the same time, Ellis still retained the powerful vestiges of Buttrose's period as Director of Concerts and Publicity, and found it much easier than Hort to get Duckmanton's ear. It was with Mackriell that Mackerras (now Sir Charles) did many of his contract negotiations, and early in 1983 the two men agreed that Mackerras' appointment should be regarded, in principle, as a six-year one.

Mackerras' excellence as a musician was not doubted by Sydney audiences and critics, but his years as the SSO's chief conductor (he, too, did not call himself musical director) gave them a sustained taste of his skills as a program builder, for he was in Sydney for three or four months of each year. His programs really got into their stride in 1983, when they revealed his taste for the spectacular and the esoteric. Vorisek's Symphony in D and Martinů's *Fantaisies symphoniques* were on the same program; he gave the first performance in Australia of Wagner's Symphony in C, and he conducted this bracing program:

Very High Kings ....Meale
Ich habe genug (It is enough): Cantata BWV 82 ....Bach
Glagolitic Mass..Janáček

He also conducted a concert peformance of Berlioz's Dramatic Symphony *Romeo and Juliet*, gave an all Webern and Schoenberg program and conducted Mozart's *Haffner* Serenade on the same program as Shostakovich's fourteenth symphony.

These are ambitious and varied undertakings for a year's concert season, particularly when, in between, there were Brahms, Beethovens and Sibelius to get through, as well as such new

Australian pieces as Barry Conyngham's *Mirages* and Graeme Koehne's *Rainforest*. Mackerras' performances were almost always splendidly alive and well conceived, and the critical response to the Martinů and Janáček verged on the ecstatic. The most important thing was that Mackerras was usually able to take the SSO convincingly with him on these wide-ranging stylistic safaris. Of one of his early 1983 concerts, which included Debussy's *Jeux*, an elusive piece to bring off in concert, Fred Blanks wrote in the *Sydney Morning Herald* that Mackerras' 'unflagging empathy with the SSO is showing every sign of restoring that variable body to a zenith of achievement . . . from the first pages of *Jeux* on Saturday the advantages of keeping Sir Charles in his home city became cumulatively obvious'. If Mackerras had a fault in performance, Martin Long felt it was that 'occasionally he sacrifices some refinement for hard-driving vitality . . . [but] his interpretations are never stodgy or over-cautious'.

The great achievements of Mackerras' tenure tended to be works that demanded great logistical skills as well as interpretative ones. A tape of the Berlioz *Romeo and Juliet* performance reveals a willingness and enthusiasm on the part of the orchestra but also insufficient rehearsal to iron out the bumps in this notoriously complex score. Mackerras' feeling for the piece ensured an overwhelmingly supportive critical response. His 1984 performances of Berlioz's *The Trojans*, the first of the complete work in Australia, were significant events in the history of musical performance in this country. The decision to split the opera in two, with Part I being given in Red concerts and Part II in the Blue and White, was not a particularly musical one, but the performances carried enormous power, and the work gained greatly from being given three performances. One of the great boons of the exercise was that, with the exception of the British tenor Philip Langridge as Aeneas, the entire cast was drawn from singers resident in Australia.

Other works in the 1984 season to which Mackerras brought a distinctive expertise were Smetana's cycle of tone poems *Má Vlast*; Elgar's *Falstaff* and choral ode *The Music Makers*; Holst's *The Planets* and Delius' *Appalachia* and *Brigg Fair*.[8] He also

8 1984 was the fiftieth anniversary of the deaths of Elgar, Delius and Holst.

conducted Tippett's recently composed Triple Concerto in the presence of the composer, but Tippett found the performance merely 'interesting'.

While Mackerras' reign was much more stimulating than that of his predecessor, his programs were not necessarily more popular with audiences. Mackerras remembers a devoted music lover telling him that 'she did not enjoy all the choral works I did. With Tony Fogg, who was a programmer then in the Music Department,[9] I worked out some very interesting programs, but looking back I think a lot of them were not popular enough. Doing *Appalachia* and *The Music Makers* in the one concert is not conducive to great box office, unless you are going to sell them as a special event. And that did not happen. It couldn't happen in some cases because I was doing these works in subscription series. I got the impression from some subscribers I spoke to that they did not feel they were subscribing to hear *The Trojans*. They would say, "well that's opera, and I'm subscribing to an orchestral series".'

But Mackerras' biggest concern was that he did not have the time he wanted to devote to the SSO. His international commitments in any one year were enormous, and by the time he came to Sydney to conduct the opening subscription concerts in March 1983 he had, since the previous January, conducted his own edition of Handel's *Semele* at Covent Garden, Massenet's *Werther* for the English National Opera, *Rosenkavalier* and Janáček's *Jenufa* in Vienna, and concerts in Rome, Switzerland, London and Leeds. Part-way through his period in Australia he flew to Geneva to conduct Handel's *Julius Caesar* at the Grand Theatre, and at the end of his Sydney season in July flew to Vienna for *Il trovatore*. He then went to the United Kingdom for some concerts with the Welsh National Opera before taking off on a three-week tour of the United States with the English Chamber Orchestra.

'In a way the time I was here as chief conductor was a wonderful experience, but in other ways it was a terrible one, because I was tired the whole time. The jet lag got worse and worse each year. You see, when I came for the beginning of my SSO period I would fly in from Europe on the Sunday, have Monday off

---

[9] At the time of writing he is the head of programming in the ABC's Concert Music department.

and be into intensive rehearsals on Tuesday for a concert on Wednesday. When you come to conduct opera you begin with some quiet preliminary rehearsals with the singers and after a little while you can say "Excuse me, I feel a bit sleepy. I'm going to bed now, I'll see you tomorrow" '.

Mackerras found the SSO's rehearsal pattern particularly draining. The Red programs were of course different from the Blue and White ones, and one of the orchestra's constant complaints down the years had been the strain of rehearsing one program on top of another. For example, on the day of a Red II concert (Thursday) the SSO would have a morning rehearsal of the Blue program, which would be played first the following Saturday. On one notable occasion, under Zdenek Macal, the orchestra rehearsed *Ein Heldenleben*, one of the blockbusters of the repertoire, in the morning, played Mahler 5 at night, and rehearsed *Heldenleben* again the following day.

'This is a very difficult way of working when you've got to get through so much repertoire', Mackerras says. 'It does not necessarily make an orchestra's playing any worse, but nor does it help to improve playing standards, and I have to say that the SSO's playing did not improve in the time I was here. Everything I did went well, but the orchestra needed someone with more time than me.'

Mackerras' frequent absences made it difficult for him to monitor personnel changes within the orchestra. There were players whose performance standard he was unhappy about, but he was not here for a sufficient time each year to force through change. Although he was powerful enough to do so, he had to leave many of these issues with Hort, who, he remembers, 'was a real stickler for the rules'. At that time the process for such dismissals was slower and more painful than it now is, and was affected almost to the point of petrification by the regulatory thinking Gordon Webb has discussed. SSO first horn Robert Johnson remembers how players were notified of unsatisfactory performance before the regulations changed in the late 1980s.

'There was a loadings committee made up usually of the concertmaster, the chief conductor if he was available, and a couple of management people, and they'd look through the list of players and say, "well XYZ have been playing well this year, so we'll give them another $3 a week." This was called a proficiency loading. It was rarely enough money to be meaningful, but people always felt left out if they didn't get it. Part of the reasoning behind this rather strange bonus was that, if the loading were removed when it came up for review the following year, you were in effect put on notice that your playing was not up to standard. But the regulations were set up so that there was very little else you could do if a player was not pulling their weight. It could take years to remove someone who might be very bad.'

(The proficiency loading was abolished in 1988, and a trial system for players on notice began in the same year.)

The pace of Mackerras' life also meant that he did not always have enough contact with ABC decisions about soloists and other conductors' repertoire, and he was not sure that consultations with him about programs and artists would have an effect. Like Macal after him, he felt that the ABC beast moved slowly when it often needed to move quickly.

But the problems Mackerras had in working with the ABC were not the reason his period as SSO chief conductor ended earlier than he had wanted. After his enormous 1983, he had simply changed his mind about how much work he could take on.

'I feel that working in two hemispheres every season is beginning to exhaust me to such an extent that I doubt if I can keep it up much longer', Mackerras wrote to his agent just before the Christmas of 1983. '. . . I love being in Australia, and have enjoyed my association with the SSO so much that I encouraged the ABC to extend my contract up till 1988. However, I don't really think I can continue in the position of Chief Conductor beyond 1985.'

1985 was indeed Mackerras' last year as chief, and it was marred for him by a bout of hepatitis he contracted in Paris. It struck him after his first three Sydney subscription concerts, and he was unable to conduct any of the other twenty-two concerts planned for him in Australia that year. He told the *Sydney Morning Herald* that the illness 'has rather spoiled my plans', which included, with the SSO, Handel's *Saul* and Berlioz's *The Damnation of Faust*.

As far as the orchestra's players were concerned, Mackerras was hard working, energetic and a fine technician, but they wished he had devoted more time to them. In the words of one musician: 'I don't think Mackerras is a great orchestral trainer, but he is a great organiser of music and musicians'. This opinion does not do justice to the many fine performances he and the SSO gave together, but it is true that the memory of his high musical demands faded quickly in his absence, and under some of the lesser guest conductors of the Mackerras years, standards were variable. By his own admission, he did not raise the day-to-day standards as much as he would have liked.

Once he regretfully gave up the remainder of his 1985 concerts, replacements for Mackerras needed to be found quickly. Miraculously, all four replacement conductors were in Australia, and one of these would soon become one of the most warmly regarded of any of the orchestra's major conductors. On 14 August 1985, Stuart Challender conducted his first performance with the SSO of Shostakovich 5. Shortly thereafter, Roger Covell wrote that 'with reasonable luck, Challender could be Australia's next major figure as an international conductor'.

≼

Much as Challender is now regarded as the greatest star of the SSO's recent history, this was not the opinion held in 1985. Challender was then considered an opera conductor who was beginning to make his way in concert, first with the Sydney Youth Orchestra and then, gradually, with the ABC. The great name in Sydney in the mid-1980s was Zdenek Macal.

Macal had first appeared as a guest conductor with the SSO in 1983, when his performance of the two suites from *Daphnis and Chloe* had blown everyone away. In the *Sydney Morning Herald*, he was praised for 'using his baton as a fencer handles his sword. He lunged, feinted, cut and thrust . . . challenging the whole SSO which . . . produced its most vivid response'. He was quickly booked for another guest slot in 1985.

The orchestra had enjoyed working with him so much, and audiences responded to him with such enthusiasm that, within days of Mackerras' decision of Christmas 1983, Ellis was asking the ABC's London office about Macal's availability for 1986 and beyond. It soon became clear that he was interested in a Sydney commitment and in June 1984 his appointment was announced as the SSO's next chief conductor, for an initial three-year period, from 1986.

Brilliant but troublesome: Zdenek Macal photographed in Sydney in 1983 (Photo Gordon Clarke).

Louis Fremaux

The concerts Macal returned for in September 1985 were as spectacular as those of two years before. After a concert featuring Tchaikovsky 5, Covell wrote that 'in Macal, the SSO has a musical leader burning to do great things with it and consumed by a passion for high standards of playing. For such zeal, and the talent to go with it, Sydney concertgoers can only be grateful and cheer him on to his objectives'. Martin Long was equally enthusiastic about a concert of music by Martinů and Bruckner given the week before. 'Macal conducts with passion and with an enthusiasm that communicates readily to the players. His passion is made visible in gestures that might seem extravagant and even irritating in a conductor who was not so obviously and sincerely absorbed in his task. What is more to the point, it comes through strongly in the musical result.'

Many of the players were more enthusiastic about him than they had been about anyone who had stood in front of them since Otterloo. Guy Henderson recalls that Macal made an overwhelming impression. 'I thought that, with him, magic time had arrived. It really felt as if the orchestra was going to be right on track again. He had a knack of turning it all into theatre— the way he walked on; how he could almost command silence from the audience before he began; the big, sweeping movements. He could extract from people more than they thought they could give.'

But what agonies lay ahead, and not just because of Macal. By the time the conductor had shaken the orchestra upside down in July of 1986, the world of the SSO had changed in a way that also seemed to be—painfully and irrevocably—earth-shaking.

CHAPTER TEN

The light on the hill?

The Dix report gave forth offspring. In 1984 the recently formed
Cultural Ministers' Council, a body which represented the arts
ministeries of each Australian State, created a study group to
examine *The future development of orchestras in Australia*. This was
to look not just at the ABC orchestras, but at regional groups,
the orchestras then being administered by the Elizabethan Trust,
and the various chamber orchestras dotted around the country.

When Kenneth Tribe was appointed its chairman in April of
that year, fear and loathing became bywords in large sections of
the media. 'Should a leading representative of one "rival" concert-
giving organisation be invited to sit in judgement on another?'
snorted one writer. Solicitor, chairman of Musica Viva, former
chairman of the Australia Council's Music Board, a softly spoken
and respected figure in Australian music, Tribe is an inherently
prudent and patient man who tends to have the big picture in
any argument well contextualised. At the inquiry's outset, he found
himself defending his appointment on several fronts at once. Asked
if his chairmanship involved a conflict of interest because of his
Musica Viva involvement he replied: 'There is room for both and
no conflict. Musica Viva puts me in touch with the music scene
and therefore qualifies rather than disqualifies me'.[1]

---

[1] The Study Group included representatives from each State and nominees from the
Minister for Communications and the Australia Council.

But conspiracy theories abounded, and flourished with the help of ABC 'moles'. The ABC was managing the orchestras badly on purpose so that it could get rid of them; the States as one wanted the orchestras to perform exclusively in the numerous new performing arts centres that were being built; divestment was a foregone conclusion and in the process some of the orchestras would be closed down; the Study Group itself wanted to control the orchestras. The committee of which Tribe was chairman had not yet taken one submission. The shadow of Green was long indeed.

In any case, the press were inclined to think that no further reports on the future of Australian orchestras were necessary. Yet Dix had been the only report written up to that time to have been of any lasting value. How many journalists had read it, or at least the orchestral section of it? If they had done so they would have seen that it was not sufficiently detailed properly to support its recommendations.

Tribe himself is unequivocal. 'The achievement of Dix from the orchestral angle was that it created a certain climate whereby people had to think about the reasons for the ABC's retention of the orchestras and what might be the alternative', he now says. 'Dix had given a blueprint for the future, but a lot more information was needed.' And the committee noted in its report that, if the Tribe process were purported to be unnecessary, '. . . why was the great weight of submissions to the Study Group from the musical and general community so heavily critical of the [existing] system?'.

As an ABC commissioner, Tribe had already begun some internal investigations into the problems of the Concert and Music departments' structure, and some of the reports he received do not make encouraging reading. In a document written in late 1979, entitled *Presentation and Content of ABC Concerts*, much is left unsaid in the following remarks about subscription levels:

Subscriptions reached a peak in 1975, reflecting the recent opening of new concert halls in Sydney, Adelaide and Perth. The subsequent decline reflects some waning of the novelty of those venues.

And the impression that some important national marketing

strategies were simply 'too hard' is reflected in the following analysis:

Various factors have prevented full 'in-depth' surveying of concert audiences in recent years . . . the proposition that ABC concert attendances may be static and aging implies that the concerts may be failing to attract newcomers, and it is impossible without undertaking further surveys to answer this with more than the results of subjective observation . . . while Head Office [is best equipped to comment on] the Sydney experience, it should be noted that findings could vary between different cities.

To an independent observer, the years immediately before Tribe's report was published seem to be marked by ABC orchestral management's reluctance to acknowledge external change. In 1981 the clause requiring the ABC to broadcast a whole or a part of all its concerts for which attendance is charged was removed from its Act. This 'Tait' clause had been the reason given for the high frequency in the change of orchestral programs, and thus also the reason touring artists had been made to bring so much repertoire with them. Yet until 1988 the SSO was still presented in its Red, Blue and White concerts as before, with no reduction in its workload. The important issue of how the cessation of this format would have improved morale and playing standards seems not to have been addressed.

Similarly, Dix had called for a national reduction in the amount of time used for studio calls, particularly as this affected an orchestra's ability to give suburban, regional, outdoor and schools concerts. Players had often complained that they were not certain whether the music they were recording was ever broadcast or released on disc. Two years after Dix, the SSO recorded Wagner's Symphony in C with Sir Charles Mackerras, after they had performed the work together in concert, for release on disc. The opportunities for such a record on the international market were good, as only one, much older, disc of the work was available. Yet the tapes remain unissued almost a decade later.

But from 1983, when the ABC became a corporation, it began to reform itself. In May 1984, just as the Tribe committee's investigations were beginning, the ABC's new chairman, Ken Myer, and new managing director, Geoffrey Whitehead, announced the formation of a Concert Music division, which was, in effect, an attempt to implement Dix's Music Australia from the inside. The idea was to remove from the Music Department all of its concert-giving elements and bring these and the Concert Department together, thus providing a tighter concert-giving focus within the Corporation. The new division's Statement of Purpose, for example, included the following commitment:

In accordance with the overall principles of the ABC's restructuring, there will be a strengthening of local branch delegation, so that orchestral and other activities can be responsive to local needs.

These developments were noted by the Tribe committee, but it came as no surprise to the cynics that when Tribe handed down his committee's report in March 1985 it contained a call for the kind of drastic action that had been foreshadowed in Dix. The major Tribe[2] recommendation for the ABC orchestras called for a severing of the ties that had bound:

All symphony orchestras now owned by the Australian Broadcasting Corporation . . . should be divested to independent local ownership; all funds now provided by the ABC to cover the deficit incurred in the operation of these orchestras should be withdrawn from the ABC, apportioned among the orchestras according to principles described in this paper, and channelled to them through the Australia Council or a Federal statutory authority established for the purpose, either authority to maintain an arms-length relationship with the orchestras, and not to enter into the management or co-ordination of their programs . . . divestment should be completed by 31 December 1988.

The core of the argument behind this conclusion is that an orchestra should be seen to belong to its community, and that as much as there is a broad national community of interest that is served through an orchestra's appearances on radio and television, it is the audience that pays to hear an orchestra which remains its major basis of community support. Tribe considered that the ABC had failed in this respect.

The report provoked outrage at the ABC and among ABC

---

[2] This term will from this point be used for the report in general.

supporters in the press. On the ABC itself little was heard about Tribe suggestions regarding orchestras it did not manage (as if this were not important), but there was much prophesying of the dismal times to come should the ABC orchestras be controlled by another body. But in the *Bulletin*, Brian Hoad would have none of this doomsday calling. 'The criticism of the ABC documented in this report is truly appalling . . . All great orchestras in the world are independent organisations. The ABC . . . is really only a dinosaur, a lumbering anachronism.'

The ABC's critics, including Hoad, had dismissed the creation of the new Concert Music division as cosmetic, but in July 1985, after more than a year of having a division that nobody ran, Whitehead appointed Trevor Green as its head. A bluff and voluble Lancastrian with seemingly unlimited supplies of energy, Green had been an orchestral trumpet player and went on to manage the BBC Scottish Symphony Orchestra and the Scottish Chamber Orchestra. He was immediately criticised for not being Australian. It was not appreciated at the time that, like Hopkins, Green had not been part of the ABC culture and could look at the ABC's orchestral woes with fresh eyes. Once here, he was eager to make changes and bruised many a head in the process. His first year was enormously challenging and confronting, but by the end of 1986 it seemed that the orchestras were going to be harder to remove from the ABC's embrace than had been the case in the bloodthirsty days of early 1985.

The change had come during the Federal government's negotiations with the Cultural Ministers' Council to give the orchestras to the States on the basis of maintained funding (this would be for three years, after which the levels of State and Federal subsidy would be looked at afresh). The Council decided that it liked the look of the ABC's Concert Music setup, and put divestment aside temporarily in exchange for regular progress reports from Green. This also gave the States time to look at a number of difficult issues affecting maintenance of the orchestras. As arts administrator Justin MacDonnell has written, these included:

How to maintain genuine co-ordination among the orchestras to affect economies of scale, and reasonable touring patterns for guest artists; maximise the value of the broadcasting network as a marketing and promotional tool, and maintain the nexus for concert broadcasting and studio recording purposes.

The answer to these questions, and the reforms Green began to put into place, would bring the value of divestment into question.

❧

The early 1980s had not been a happy time for the SSO. Following the 1977-78 player exodus, there were more departures through the early 1980s, and in 1984 the orchestra was, at various times, without a permanent principal viola, harp, clarinet or flute. In the numerous player submissions to his committee, Tribe says he felt an overwhelming lack of respect among orchestral musicians for ABC management.

'Artistic policy was one problem. There was a lot of criticism about the choice of guest conductors. Musicians are not always worldly, and individual players said they felt isolated and uncared for. That seemed to me to be a management defect. It did not surprise me that so many players were critical of the system, because I knew that the ABC was losing many people. This may sound an odd thing for me to say, but I believe that you have to love the thing you are selling, that which is the product of your efforts. It should be the impelling motive. I believe the people who ran the relevant ABC departments had lost that love.'

Colin Piper agrees that the period during which Mackerras was chief conductor was a bad one administratively. 'As far as marketing was concerned, it was just a disaster, and the orchestra overall was run very badly. Players were not treated like human beings— you were slots in the grid. It was not all gloom and doom, of course. I have very fond memories, for example, of John Matthews. He was very fatherly, full of good advice, and he did not play favourites with the players. But the way we are managed now is so much better than anything I experienced under the old system.'

'There was a terrible remoteness about management then', says Robert Johnson. 'And of course there was this desire to use absolutely every call, even if it meant doing, say, a Vivaldi flute concerto in an insufficient time to get the sound together properly. It encouraged you to think, "well, it's another 4500 notes to play, nobody's trying to make them sound beautiful. We've got to survive this call because the piece has been put there". You were there to play, as designated by ABC management.'

※

Macal was going to be one of the dynamos that brought this period to an end. By the time he came back to Australia in June 1986 to begin this period as chief conductor, Green had appointed Mary Vallentine as the SSO's first-ever general manager. Vallentine was one of Australia's most experienced young arts administrators, having worked in many different capacities for many different organisations: the Australia Council, Musica Viva, the Adelaide Festival, the State Theatre Company of South Australia, the Sydney Opera House and the Australian Chamber Orchestra. But she had never run an orchestra before.

'I'd had some contact with the ABC's Music Department through the Adelaide Festival', she says. 'I planned some orchestral concerts of contemporary music for the 1982 festival, and we wanted the SSO to do them. So I came to Sydney and had a meeting with some Music people, and we got round to talking about which conductor we'd use for these concerts. One of the people present said, "Bruno Maderna would be good". I'm not sure if this person was serious or not, because Maderna would've been terrific, but he'd died in 1974.

'It was Trevor who persuaded me to take the job on. I was impressed with his ideas and the force of his will to make changes. He was concerned above all with the musical problems, and believed management should be reformed to be more responsive to orchestral needs. Before this the idea of working for the ABC was frankly depressing, because it seemed like a large, inflexible structure. That was my perspective from working in organisations that had tried to collaborate with the ABC. To some extent that impression was reinforced when I started in the job. I found it very hard to figure out how the place worked.'

It had been clear to Vallentine's predecessors that Macal was something of an unguided missile. In 1985 he reduced his term as chief conductor from three years to one because of high taxes on his salary and the seesawing value of the Australian dollar. He also adopted guerilla tactics when things did not go as he wanted. A concert program he had approved for performance in late 1985 was, he felt, once he had conducted it, too long, so in one repeat performance he shortened the first item, Mozart's Symphony No 29, by omitting the slow movement and cutting the trio from the third movement. He was angry at the poor houses that had greeted his double-bill of Martinů's first symphony and Bruckner's fourth. The program, he said, was too unpopular, although he had played a major part in constructing it.

He wanted results quickly, and told anyone who would listen that he expected Sydney to respond to his presence. 'I'm ready to put a lot of energy into organising and managing . . . I think I can do that very well', he said on his arrival as chief conductor. 'But if I am going to invest that energy, I must see the results of my investment. If those results look like coming too slowly, then I must say, I am sorry but this place is not for me—I can get quicker results elsewhere.'

Macal's 1986 concerts received the usual rave reviews, Covell describing his return to Sydney as 'a major event in the 1986 concert calendar'. His sudden exit, then, was a major event of a less savoury kind. On the afternoon of Friday 25 July 1986, Trevor Green received a call from an ABC driver, asking if Macal was expected at work over the next few days. Green replied in the affirmative—Macal had two more subscription programs to conduct—whereupon the driver explained that he was taking the conductor, at his instruction, to the international terminal at Sydney airport. Macal was about to leave the country.

The principal and given reason for his departure was the money problem. But it was also well known that he and his wife did not enjoy Sydney as much as Sydney enjoyed them. He found the ABC administration larger than those he was used to working with overseas. 'It is more difficult to affect things', he told *Time* magazine. 'Too many people have a say.'

His leaving was a terrible blow to the orchestra. Whatever his antics with management, he never behaved badly with them. In rehearsal, it was always down to business. It hurt the players that he had not farewelled them in person. For Green and Vallentine, it was devastating. As the ABC's then head of marketing and publicity, Margaret Carter, told the *Sydney Morning Herald*, 'Trevor Green has been re-negotiating his contract, and I can promise you we have bent over backwards'. She regarded his behaviour as 'very unprofessional'.

According to one player, 'Macal saw himself on a much bigger stage'. For another, Macal's comet-like appearance left mixed feelings. 'He was to his core a musician, and we did some marvellous things with him. But he'd had no time to do anything developmental with us. I don't think he would have been interested in sitting in on auditions, frankly, even though he would make it clear that there were certain players he wanted for his concerts and others not. He was a very mercenary person, and I'm not sure that he handled people well enough to be our chief conductor. I doubt that he's a great strategist as far as his career is concerned, either, because you'd think we'd have heard of him in another context by now. You hear more about conductors who are far lesser talented.'

Green was unforgiving. When Macal's tax refund arrived at the ABC in June 1987, Green telexed his agent with the news. 'Due to Mr Macal's generous nature', he wrote, 'we have decided to donate his refund to the Musicians' Benevolent Fund'. He was joking, of course, but the memory of Macal's departure still burned brightly.

A calmer observer of the saga was veteran SSO subscriber Tempe Merewether, who enjoyed Macal's concerts enormously and watched his leaving from the distance of press reports. Her regrets are those of an informed admirer. 'It would have been interesting if he had stayed long enough to have run out of his repertoire', she says.

❧

Stuart Challender's arrival as a presence to be reckoned with in the life of the SSO came with the concert in August 1985 in which the major work was Shostakovich 5. He had conducted the orchestra before, in the two previous years, but here, replacing the ailing Mackerras, he turned 'a concert that aroused no particular feeling of expectation' into 'an exciting event', Martin Long wrote in the *Australian*. Covell was equally enthusiastic. 'This was one of the most auspicious appearances by a younger resident conductor at a major SSO concert . . . the orchestra members really played for Challender, played hard and well, played as they quite often don't do even for well-known visiting conductors.'

But Challender was not then principally known as an orchestral conductor. Through the 1970s he had been in Europe, like many young Australian musicians, learning his craft. He studied conducting with, among others, the legendary Romaninan Sergiu Celibidache, and worked in a number of opera houses as *répétiteur* and conductor. In the years after his return to Australia in 1980 he established himself primarily in opera, and as The Australian Opera's resident conductor tackled a wide range of repertoire from Mozart to Janáček. He also took a strong interest in contemporary music, and was the Seymour Group's artistic director between 1981 and 1983. By 1985 he had notched up some splendid achievements: powerful and authoritative performances of Janacek's *Jenufa* and Puccini's *Madame Butterfly*, a fully staged version of Schoenberg's *Pierrot Lunaire* with the Seymour Group, and a performance of Mahler 5 with the Sydney Youth Symphony Orchestra that was regarded as a major triumph.

Challender's appointment as the SSO's principal guest conductor in February 1986 was greeted with cheers by the orchestra and the music community. No such post had existed before and Green's plan in creating it was to provide a year-round continuity of artistic purpose. Macal, if he had stayed, would have been in Sydney for three months a year at most. Green felt strongly that someone needed to be present all year to discuss repertoire, examine the orchestra's strengths and weaknesses, and be a presence on audition panels for player vacancies. Challender accepted with cautious enthusiasm, as he explained to the author in July 1991.

'The orchestra was in a bad way, and was not the joy to conduct that it is now. One of the string sections was in total disarray and had no sound of its own. But with a lot of hard work you could get the odd good performance, in the sense that the overall sweep was there rather than the detail. The rest of the time it was pretty terrible, which was doubly embarrassing because the Melbourne orchestra was then on the top of its form. I agreed to spend a lot of time with the SSO, and when Trevor later told me that Mary was to be general manager I saw that there was a real chance to save the situation. I remember ringing Mary up and saying "we can save orchestral music in Sydney" and all of that caper.'

Challender took up his new duties when he was still busy with opera commitments and the re-establishment of his career overseas. He conducted Tchaikovsky's *Eugene Onegin* for San Diego opera in 1985 and was booked to work with a number of British orchestras in 1987. (Later, he would work with the orchestras of Boston and Chicago, with great success.) He did not conduct the SSO so often in 1986, and in many ways his calling card, in his new role, did not come until January 1987, when he conducted two performances of Mahler's *Resurrection* Symphony in the Sydney Town Hall during the Festival of Sydney.

'They offered it to me, and I thought, well, they must think I can do it', Challender said. 'So I went to Bali for three weeks and learned it.'

For the audiences present on those two sold-out evenings, it seemed clear after the last downbeat that they had witnessed an event of outstanding importance in the history of Australian musical performance. Here was an Australian conductor not yet forty, climbing one of the Everests of the orchestral repertoire, and giving a performance of astonishing confidence and conviction with the orchestra he was helping to re-build. Martin Long wrote that the concerts 'added up to an important event in any terms, and would have done so even if the attendance had been meagre or the response indifferent'. Recalling the event at three years' distance, Fred Blanks felt that it had 'added to our concert calendar one of those unforgettable landmarks which great Mahler readings leave behind as if by divine right'. He felt it surpassed every performance given of the work in Sydney since Klemperer.

A few months later, Challender was made the orchestra's chief conductor. 'When Mary asked me if I would accept the position I thought she was joking. But Trevor thought it was a good idea, so I told him that he needed to talk to all of the principals and see what they felt, because I would be a chief of a kind they had never had before. One who is to learn repertoire as he goes, and who will have much more day-to-day involvement with the life and problems of the orchestra. I did not have enough orchestral music under my belt and I did not know if the public would accept me. I felt unknown and very green, but later I realised that the appointment was going to break the cringe we'd had, of relying all the time of famous foreigners.'

'I didn't think Stuart's relative inexperience in concert was such a major concern', Vallentine says. 'I'd heard him conduct a lot in opera, and I thought it was so impressive that what might have been lacking in his knowledge of the repertoire would be made up for by the excitement of his ideas as an interpreter. And Trevor kept on making the point that Stuart was here, on the ground, that he could provide a link between the drafting of the concert schedules and the orchestra's interests. I mean, Trevor had worked in Britain and knew how hard it was to get that sort of time commitment from a major international conductor.'

Guy Henderson was at first sceptical about Stuart's ascendancy. 'It surprised me greatly. I was not immediately in favour because of his lack of experience, and because I felt we hadn't worked with him sufficiently. But I was quite wrong. Even on the day he started he seemed to forge ahead even more. It suddenly all came right again.'

Robert Johnson feels Challender rose to the new challenges presented to him with great speed. 'He suddenly had to take enormous steps and learn a staggering amount of new repertoire. In his first two years as chief there was a high percentage of music that was new to him. You can't hide that. The players are professionals and know where somebody is. But I'd say that within those two years he had won our respect.'

When Challender began as SSO chief conductor in August 1987 the divestment scenario had changed dramatically. Green had started his stewardship of Concert Music with uncertain aims. In May 1986 he told the *National Times* that 'I have the chance to take the orchestras away from the ABC. We may form a separate company at arms length—call it Music Australia or whatever you think—but it must become a part of the Australian people's cultural life'. By December of that year he was saying that his favoured option was 'a Music Australia model slightly divested from the ABC'. It was generally thought that Green was preparing the orchestras for divestment by streamlining their operations and making them more attractive to whatever body took them over.

But eighteen months later the process had stalled. In some ways the issues were swallowed up by the controversy surrounding David Hill's appointment as ABC managing director and the federal government's decisions about the future of the ABC as a whole. Then the State governments were not sure they could afford to run orchestras after the proposed three-year funding agreement with the federal government expired. And the Cultural Ministers' Council was genuinely impressed with the changes Green had pushed through. Local boards of advice had been appointed to each of the orchestras; general managers were in place across the country; the first piece of major corporate sponsorship was secured when Epson Computers and Printers became the SSO's major sponsor; the marketing of the orchestras had clearly improved and audiences were growing again[3]; fresh negotiations were begun with musicians to improve conditions; and the ABC seemed much more committed to the promotion of its orchestras on radio and television. By September 1988, the Council agreed that divestment was, in the short term at least, off the agenda. In the three years since Tribe, the ABC, it seemed, had got its act together.

Vallentine's aims, when she began, were clear enough: improve the orchestra's management, morale and day-to-day playing standards. The urgency with which these reforms needed to be brought about were put into focus by an event that was already in place for 1988: an invitation from the United Nations to play in the General Assembly in New York, to mark the bicentenary of white settlement in Australia. Clearly, if other concerts in the United States were to be put in place to make such a trip worthwhile, the orchestra would need to feel a lot better about itself than it did in mid-1986. Early in Challender's term as Principal Guest, he and Vallentine made one of the first moves towards improving the orchestra's self-perception by drastically cutting the number of studio calls in its schedule.

'We decided that if the SSO was to be primarily a concert orchestra, then studio broadcasts would have to go', Vallentine says. 'If we thought that audience development, regional touring

---

[3] Between 1987 and 1988, SSO subscriber numbers had grown by approximately 2000.

and an education program were important then we had to keep those activities going. I don't think a clear vision of the orchestras as concert orchestras was in place until Trevor arrived and then when Tony Fogg was appointed as head of programming a few months later.

'Another of our great early achievements—the general managers and Trevor, that is—was getting the ABC to place the full weight of its concert-giving promotion firmly on the orchestras. Regional concerts and recitals were being given in places where the audiences were really small, and even the recital series in Sydney was not popular. In the Seymour Centre we had something like 200 subscribers to the recital series in its final year. But a lot of energy and staff went into the organisation and promotion of these events.'

The appointment of young Australian violinist Dene Olding as the orchestra's co-concertmaster was also a product of the changes that were being put in place. Donald Hazelwood had been keen to again share the first desk with another player, and Olding's arrival in 1987 marked the first time the leader's position had been shared since Hazelwood and Robert Miller had shared it twenty years before. Players joining the orchestra were now mostly younger than those who had joined in the 1960s, and American audiences who saw the SSO on tour commented frequently on how young the orchestra looked. It certainly had, on average, a younger membership than some of the leading North American orchestras: in 1988 one-third of its members were under thirty and one-third were women.

Soon Vallentine began to gather around her a management team that was predominantly young and female. Ann Hoban became the new orchestra manager in October of 1987, and Merryn Carter the marketing manager—the orchestra's first—a few months later. Neither woman was yet thirty-five. Challender, meanwhile, had provided an immediate and visible young face for the SSO in the extensive press coverage he was receiving.

'This was the other sense in which Stuart's appointment was important', Vallentine says. 'He would have time to work with the orchestra intensively before any US tour we might plan, and he would be a young Australian conductor on tour with a newly energised Australian orchestra.'

A tour of the United States did indeed eventuate, the first overseas tour for the orchestra since 1974. Through the Harold Shaw concert agency in New York an itinerary of twelve cities was established—Orange County (south of Los Angeles), Las Vegas, Washington, New York, Amherst, Worcester, Hartford, Storrs, Urbana, Chicago, Lawrence (Kansas) and Manhattan (also in Kansas).

The major capital injection was provided by Epson, whose first $1 million sponsorship of the orchestra[4] went largely towards financing the tour. Another important source of finance was Valiant Office Furniture, whose chairman, Ed Sternberg, continues to be one of the SSO's most enthusiastic supporters. Controversially, the Australian Bicentennial Authority gave nothing, which placed its communications manager, Wendy McCarthy, in an awkward position. McCarthy was also the deputy chair of the ABC, and went on the tour as the orchestra's publicist.[5] Although the ABA decision not to fund the SSO tour was not hers, she made great efforts to compensate for it. She persuaded Hazel Hawke—wife of the then Prime Minister—to accompany the orchestra to the United States as a kind of ambassador-in-residence, and also put ABA funds towards the design of a striking tour logo that adorned T-shirts, advertisements, brochures and press releases.

For Challender, the heat was on. Three weeks, twelve cities, frequent changes of repertoire and two different soloists. And the big United States cities were no strangers to fine orchestras— the best European bands toured regularly, and if the hometown orchestra was the Chicago Symphony or the New York Philharmonic the everyday quality was not too bad, either.

'The tour was a very important carrot for everybody', Challender said. 'I wanted to use it as a catalyst so that I could say that this and this were not good enough for the US. I used to say, "this is not good enough for Carnegie Hall".'

Challender's 1988 concerts with the orchestra at home were to be a testing ground for the tour, and resulted in a much more

[4] Epson renewed its contract, for a second $1 million, in 1989.
[5] The orchestra did not yet have a publicist of its own. Another young woman, Jan Ross, would later become the orchestra's first full-time publicist.

consistently prepared series of pieces than had been the case in 1974. His championship of new Australian works made itself apparent in the choice of Carl Vine's new Symphony No 2 and Peter Sculthorpe's *Mangrove* as tour repertoire, in addition to the suite from Malcom Williamson's ballet *The Display*. Shostakovich 5 was taken and, perhaps less successfully, *Petrushka*. The Australian mezzo-soprano Elizabeth Campbell was soloist in many concerts, veteran Russian pianist Shura Cherkassky in others, and the partnership of Joan Sutherland and Richard Bonynge shared the bill with Challender in Washington and New York. Journalist and bon vivant Leo Schofield travelled as the tour correspondent. He answered some of the more difficult questions about the presence of the Sutherland/Bonynge due on the tour.

'The American promoters have said that one of the ways you will sell out a concert with the SSO is to put somebody like Sutherland with it', he told ABC broadcaster Margaret Throsby. '[Audiences] will be getting a chance to hear her but they will also be getting a chance, which wouldn't otherwise have occurred, of hearing our orchestra.'

In pre-tour Sydney concerts, the Vine symphony was played to great acclaim, as was another tour item, R. Strauss' *Till Eulenspiegel's Merry Pranks*. In the *Sun-Herald* Jill Sykes reported that 'on the eve of its departure, the SSO is playing with exciting assurance and verve'. The farewell concert which followed this report was not so secure, and revealed some last-minute nerves. Of the final Sydney performance of *Petrushka* before departure, Covell wrote that 'there were rough joins, some plain mistakes, a difficult brass solo that was potentially very good but was, as it happens, racing the beat, a general air of not being quite on target'.

Petruskha was, simply, not Challender's sort of piece. One of the SSO principals says most players came to realise that music which demanded a strong sense of rhythm did not usually suit him. 'He was not a great conductor of music where rhythm was the major impetus, and there were some very hairy moments in *Petruskha* on the United States tour, where changes of time signature were just not well signalled. But that is a relatively minor thing in the context of Stuart's achievements. We came to accept it as part of his personality.'

The SSO in Carnegie Hall during its tour of the United States in 1988. (Photo: Andrew Clarke)

The tour was intense and exhausting, but the good concerts outweighed the bad by a fair margin. One of the first rave reviews appeared in the *Washington Express*, where critic Octavio Roca described the SSO as 'one of the world's finest orchestras'. But as the tour progressed the rules about critics that had given the 1974 tour its schizophrenic moments applied here as well. Of one New York concert, the *New York Post* called the orchestra 'world-class', while the city's *Daily News* described the SSO's playing as 'a bad case of jet lag'. But Chicago, a city which hears a lot of good music, was warm in its praise. 'Shostakovich 5 is a standard showpiece for visiting orchestras', the *Chicago Tribune* wrote. 'But it is seldom played with such fervent conviction and controlled excitement as here.'

Invariably, the smaller centres were attentive and enthusiastic, and had better-behaved audiences than those in Sydney. Players recall with particular pleasure the concert given in the Mechanics Hall in Worcester, a venue which offered some of the best acoustics of the tour and perhaps the finest performance of the Shostakovich. The local critic described it as 'mesmerising'. And there were surprisingly few logistical glitches. In Las Vegas, Challender and Campbell were delivered to the wrong venue (luckily, with enough time left to get to the correct one); instruments were rarely sent to the wrong city; and New York's Omni Park Central hotel, chosen for its proximity to Carnegie Hall, proved to be the only out-and-out dive on the tour.

The major results of the United States trip were that it raised the SSO's stakes in its home base, and, more privately, Challender's stakes with the orchestra. Robert Johnson:

'That he survived the tour so well was fantastic. He was, you might say, under internal siege during it, because there were so many big dates, new venues, pieces he had only got to know over a few months. To his credit, he survived the experience very well, and I think many players respected him for that. 1989 was of course an even bigger year for him.'

The United States tour was one of a number of events that gave the SSO a better self-image. In the year of the tour the orchestra and the ABC struck an historic industrial agreement which boosted salaries, improved working conditions and established a firm and, it was hoped, dignified system for the retirement of musicians whose playing was no longer of a sufficient standard. In the same year the old Red, Blue and White pattern of concerts was abolished in favour of a four-concert run from Wednesday to Monday, the Epson Master Series; and with one change of piece the same concert, on Tuesday night, became the Epson Mozart Master Series.

Intrinsic to this process was the impression that Challender and Vallentine seemed, to the players, to be accountable.

Orchestral veterans began to feel that they had a real boss who, as often as possible, would ensure that the buck stopped with her, or Challender. Through their artistic committee, the SSO began to have more say in the repertoire they played. And, sadly, Challender's illness made him focus much more closely on issues important to him.

It was in 1989 and 1990 that Challender's relationship with the orchestra began to blossom into performances that were regularly outstanding. But ironically, by 1989, the AIDS virus Challender had contracted was beginning to tell on his energies. His conducting style, which had been very physical and full of vivid cueing gestures, became more restrained. Robert Johnson remembers how the change improved Challender's skills.

'He was forced to relax himself, to conserve his energy, and what came out of that was a more relaxed approach to the sheer beating of the pieces. Stuart had always been raw energy, which is exciting for sure, but it made it hard for him to bring off gentler works. You know, he was a big man, he had long arms . . . but in his last concert, when he was really not well at all, he conducted the *Hebrides* overture of Mendelssohn with such containment, and it worked beautifully.'

The landmarks of the Challender/SSO partnership rolled on. In 1989 there was Mahler 3, a new piece, *Bamaga Diptych*, by Richard Mills, and a concert for Peter Sculthorpe's sixtieth birthday that was as great an event as Mahler 2 had been. Sculthorpe later said that his *Kakadu* and *Irkanda IV* (with Hazelwood the soloist) might never be played as well again as they were on this occasion. The evening also provided a thrilling performance of Percy Grainger's magnum opus, *The Warriors*.

In this year Challender and the SSO began making records. For the ABC Classics label they made four discs together, of which

Stuart Challender rehearsing the SSO in its new Ultimo studio.

the most successful were those devoted respectively to the music of Sculthorpe and Carl Vine. Both won ARIA awards, and the Sculthorpe became one of the ABC's best-selling classical records.

1990 began with perhaps the most decisive triumph of the Challender years, Wagner's *Tristan and Isolde*. This was the first time since the recording of Richard Meale's opera *Voss* in 1986 that the SSO and The Australian Opera had collaborated on a project, and after performances in the Sydney Opera House Concert Hall the production, under Challender's baton, was taken to Adelaide. In Sydney, with the orchestra playing in an open pit— constructed by removing the first rows from the stalls—and the stage of Neil Armfield's production also open, with no proscenium, the experience of Challender's *Tristan* was engulfing. It was appropriate that the printed program, sold in conjunction with the performances, included an essay by Susan Sontag entitled *Wagner's Fluids*. The saddest thing about the experience was that it was all too clearly the kind of event Challender would have mastered repeatedly had he lived longer.

By 1990 Challender had ceased thinking about his conducting in the long term. He was less well and was now conducting music that was not the kind he might have programmed had he wanted to build up a guest conductor's repertoire, but rather the kind he loved. He knew that the massive eighth symphony of Bruckner was probably just beyond him, but he felt he had to do it, and he opened that year's Master Series with it. 'It is one of the pieces I love more than anything else in the world', he said. 'But I was too much in awe of it, and it was really only in the fourth performance that we were getting there. If I can put my feelings about the piece simply, I would say that in the first three movements it is as if someone is showing you around a great German cathedral with a hand-held torch. Then in the finale the floodlights are turned on.'

Critics had no doubts about his performance of Mahler's *The Song of the Earth*, which he conducted in July with soloists Elizabeth Campbell and Robert Tear. By now Fred Blanks was calling Challender 'Australia's most persuasive Mahlerian'. His repeat performances of Mahler 2 in the same month were also triumphantly successful, with Laurie Strachan declaring, in the *Australian*, that 'Challender's and the SSO's continued rise towards world class were emphatically confirmed with a performance . . . that might just have been the finest thing this team has ever done'. A few weeks later a second collaboration with The Australian Opera, this time a concert performance of Alban Berg's complete opera *Lulu*, which had been in rehearsal for more than a month, called forth similar praise. In the *Sun-Herald*, Ken Healey called it 'one of those nights of music drama that will remain forever etched on my memory'.

It is heartbreaking to write these lines so soon after Challender's death. During the SSO's 1990 season he cancelled an SSO concert for the first time, and after this conducted less frequently, as his condition deteriorated. He continued to involve himself in the daily life of the orchestra, but now had little energy left to conduct. 'The Great Mozart Concert', the SSO's commemoration of the bicentenary of Mozart's death, is perhaps the last Sydney concert by which he should be remembered. He gave his last orchestral concert in Hobart a few months later, and his last performances of any kind for The Australian Opera, in September, when he conducted the first four performances of R. Strauss' *Der Rosenkavalier*. He died on 13 December 1991, aged forty-four. In the words of record producer Christopher Lawrence, his long-time collaborator, Challender 'would have made a great old conductor'.

❧

Challender's own views on his legacy with the SSO were recorded for the purposes of this book only five months before his death.

'If I have achieved anything with the orchestra, it is that there is a flexibility there now. Their standard of playing on a daily basis is more polished and more stylish. In other words, they understand the difference between playing Brahms and Mozart and Debussy. I have always said that the great thing about Australia is that we are not bogged down in a particular tradition. We can learn them all. I don't think I am fooling myself when I say that I have managed to raise the morale of the orchestra to a point where they are now proud of anything they do. If they do not achieve the standard they want, they get terribly upset, which is most important.'

Ron Prussing: 'The big thing Stuart brought us was respect

June 1990: One of Stuart Challender's best remembered performances, Mahler's Resurrection Symphony, *given here in the Sydney Opera House Concert Hall. Dene Olding is the concertmaster. (Photo: Tracey Schramm).*

One of the portrait photographs of Stuart Challender in the Sydney Opera House taken by eminent New York photographer Arnold Newman in 1990.

for standards. He had a certain standard below which he would not sink, and as he matured that standard gradually went up and up, and we followed. There was always total commitment to whatever he was doing, both musically and as a director of people. That's his great legacy.'

Sir Charles Mackerras: 'What the SSO had with Stuart was someone who had a lot of time and a devotion to their welfare. This was a rare and wonderful thing, and gave the orchestra a huge advantage. His death is a tragedy for them in that respect, and I understand that he had really begun to grow as an interpreter, as well. In my darker moments, I do wonder who they will find now to match Stuart's level of involvement, to throw in their lot with the SSO, because Sydney is so much further from the centre of concert activity than anywhere else. And you see the important thing to remember is that the best orchestras in this country are the only orchestras of quality in the Southern Hemisphere. They may not be the greatest orchestras in the world, but they are discussable as great orchestras.'

❧

In early 1989 the SSO moved out of Chatswood to the Sydney Town Hall, which became its temporary home while its new permanent home, the Eugene Goossens Hall in the ABC Ultimo Centre, was being completed. The Arcadia Theatre had a spectacular demise when, during its demolition, part of its facade fell into, rather than away from, Victoria Avenue, Chatswood, crushing a car in the process.

By the time the SSO moved into Ultimo in April 1991, Trevor Green had long gone, exhausted from the fray, to run the BBC Philharmonic Orchestra in Manchester. In his place, in October 1988, Helen Mills was appointed as Concert Music's general manager. Mills had been the ABC's director of corporate policy, and was a polished and experienced manager with a great interest in music and the other arts.

❧

Despite its benefits, the ABC's post-Tribe system of concert-giving is not perfect. There has been some conflict between the ABC's resistance, as an independent broadcaster, to sponsorship and advertising for radio and television programs, and the orchestras' need (as defined by the ABC board) to seek corporate sponsorship. There is also the question of whether in a national, co-ordinated orchestral system, the orchestras which earn the greatest box office revenue must support, perhaps detrimentally, those which earn the least. In recent years ABC Radio has found it difficult to decide how best, and how frequently, the orchestras are to be featured on air, and attention has yet to be given to original and appealing ways of presenting the orchestras on television.

Yet clearly the system has fewer faults than the former one. Orchestral audiences are now bigger and represent a wider age group, there is more Australian music in subscription series (although, depending on which group is lobbying at the time, there is either too much or not enough), and special series devoted to contemporary music are marketed with enthusiasm. The orchestras belong to their cities far more clearly than they used to. As Tribe himself now says: 'I think the time will come when the orchestras will be independent entities, but unless the circumstances are right, and much better than they are now, I would feel much more secure for orchestral music if they stay with the ABC. When we wrote the report, we felt the orchestras were unlikely to best serve their communities while they were controlled by the ABC—a large organisation with other interests. The improvements that have been made in that regard, to some extent, refute that claim. Mind you, the right things or the wrong things could happen if the SSO were independent. I do believe that, in human affairs, none of us has enough wisdom to foresee all of the consequences of proposals we make.'

As the SSO turns sixty, many of its players mourn the recent death of their chief conductor, but they also acknowledge that the orchestra is in better shape than it was on its fiftieth birthday. It is playing at a higher standard, and the quality of this standard means more to its paying audience. Much depends, however, on the orchestra's next chief. For the moment, though, the SSO and the people of Sydney have much to celebrate.

Acknowledgments

I am indebted above all to my friend and researcher Denis Condon who interviewed, collated, foraged and allowed himself to be consulted for more than a year. His boundless sense of humour was a source of much comfort. In our numerous searches for press clippings and correspondence, we received the invaluable help of Pat Kelly and Geoff Harris at ABC Archives. They responded with understanding and good humour to some spectacularly obscure requests, and always made the task at hand seem pleasurable. I must also thank Pat for checking the early chapters for accuracy. Nina Riemer, the editor of this book, brought to the project an exhilarating mixture of enthusiasm, energy and devotion. I am very fortunate to have worked with her.

Of the many people who made time to be interviewed, the one I must thank most heartily is Neville Amadio. Initially, Denis and I spent one four-hour session with him, but after that he and I were on the 'phone regularly right through the writing of the book. He was an invaluable source of information and encouragement.

Interviews were also conducted with the following people: Donald Hazelwood, Lindsey Browne, Muriel Cohen, Eva Kelly, Isa Cohen, Kathleen Wall, Gretel Feher, Joyce Hutchinson, Rachel Valler, Osric Fyfe, Bertha Jorgensen, John Matthews, Robert Miller, Nadine Amadio, June Loney, Ron Cragg, Peter Sainthill, Renee Goossens, Clarence Mellor, Jennifer James and Russell

Mattocks (both of whom I quizzed before many a concert), Kathleen Tuohy, Nancy Post, George Fleischer, Tempe Merewether, Eve Jago, Betty Barnett, Hans George, Nigel Butterley, Fred Blanks, Alan Ziegler, the late Stuart Challender, John Hopkins, Rex Ellis (who also provided a lot of printed material), Ken Tribe (who was generous with his time and patient with my questions), Michael Corban, Gordon Webb, Robert Johnson, Colin Piper, Ron Prussing, Guy Henderson, Eunice Gardiner, Miriam Hyde, Paul Badura-Skoda, Mary Vallentine, Sir Charles Mackerras, Barry Tuckwell, Cliff Goodchild, Richard Bonynge, Roger Covell, the late Werner Baer, Colin Evans, Linda Vogt, Colleen McMeekan and Harold Hort.

Wilma Johnston kindly volunteered photos of and information about her father, Haydn Beck; other photos were kindly lent by Gretel Feher, Eve Jago, Eva Kelly and Clarence Mellor; Len Amadio allowed me to borrow original copies of the Goossens/EMI recordings; Mike Spencer of Film Australia arranged for me to see some important films featuring the SSO; Anise Vass, of the National Film and Sound Archive's Operation Newsreel project, unearthed some marvellous footage of Goossens and the SSO; Peter Spearrit gave me much information about Melbourne's centenary celebrations, as did Graham Code about the history of the Code family; John Spence and Neil Smith, of the ABC's Radio Archives, were patient and enthusiastic searchers for past SSO performances; Richard Montz generously allowed me access to his work on the history of the SSO brass section; and Ann Hoban and Tony Fogg answered pesky questions on an almost daily basis.

Many friends and colleagues were encouraging in their different ways. I value, in particular, the support and advice of Helen Mills (who made the circumstances of the book's writing possible), Mark McDonnell, Robyn and Anthony Clarke, Tim Bowden, Stephen Mould and Chris Lawrence. And I don't think I'd have written *Play On!* at all if it weren't for Brian Hodge and Graeme Harrison who, respectively, awakened and developed my historical imagination.

Bibliography

In addition to the books, booklets and articles listed below, during the preparation for *Play On!* I consulted a number of files located in the Australian Archives at Villawood, NSW, and press clippings and correspondence located in the ABC's Document Archives and in the ABC's Concert Music division.

ABC Booklet, 1965 *The Sydney Symphony Orchestra*.

Bainton, Helen 1967, *Facing the Music*. Currawong Publishing.

Blain, Ellis 1977, *Life with Aunty—Forty Years with the ABC*. Methuen Australia.

Brisbane, Catherine 1991, ed: *Entertaining Australia*. Currency Press, Sydney.

Buttrose, Charles 1982, *Playing for Australia*. Macmillan/ABC.

Buttrose, Charles 1984, *Words and Music*. Angus and Robertson

Cane, Anthony 1989, 'The Concert—Essential Radio'. *Symphony Australia* annual.

Cargher, John 1977, *Opera and Ballet in Australia*. Cassell Australia.

'Charles Moses Remembered'. *24 Hours* magazine, March 1989.

Code, Trevor 1988, *The Codes and music*. Paper, privately printed.

Covell, Roger 1967, *Australia's Music—Themes of a New Society*. Sun Books, Melbourne.

Covell, Roger 1963, *Music in Australia* (booklet). Current Affairs Bulletin, University of Sydney.

Daniel, Oliver 1982, *Stokowski—A Counterpoint of View*. Dodd, Mead and Company, New York.

Dorati, Antal 1979, *Notes of Seven Decades.* Hodder and Stoughton, London.

Dutton, Geoffrey 1986, *The Innovators.* Macmillan, Australia.

Exhibition catalogue 1984, *1934—a year in the life of Victoria.* Library Council of Victoria.

Hall, Barrie 1981, *The Proms.* Allen and Unwin, Sydney.

Hince, Kenneth 1966, *The Melbourne Symphony Orchestra—an appreciation.* ABC booklet.

Holford, Franz, ed *The Canon.* Magazine issues 1948–56.

Holmes, John L, 'Eugene Goossens in Sydney—His Rise and Fall'. *Quadrant*, July 1985. [This article is a useful impression of the period but contains many factual errors.]

Horne, Donald 1971, *The Lucky Country.* Revised edition, Penguin, Melbourne.

Hubble, Ava 1988, *The Strange Case of Eugene Goossens and other tales from the Operas House.* Collins Australia.

Inglis, K.S. 1983, *This is the ABC.* Melbourne University Press.

Lambert, Constant 1934, *Music Ho!* Faber and Faber, London.

Lebrecht, Norman 1991, *The Maestro Myth.* Simon and Schuster.

Llewellyn, Ruth 1990, 'A short history of Ernest Lllewellyn, CBE', 2MBS-FM Magazine. June issue.

Methuen-Campbell, James 1981, *Chopin Playing, from the Composer to the Present Day.* Victor Gollancz, London.

Montz, Richard 1986, *The Brass Section of the Sydney Symphony Orchestra— A survey of the most significant players from 1927 to 1986.* Masters Degree for NSW Conservatorium of Music. Privately printed.

Moresby, Elizabeth 1948, *Australia Makes Music.* Longman, Green & Co.

Moses, Charles 1957, 'The History of the ABC's Symphony Orchestras'. Concert Program, ABC.

Phelan, Nancy 1987, *Charles Mackerras—A Musician's Musician.* Oxford University Press.

Radic, Therese 1986, *Bernard Heinze.* Macmillan Australia.

Scholes, Percy 1967, *The Mirror of Music.* Novello/OUP (two volumes).

Schonberg, Harold C 1967, *The Great Conductors.* Simon and Schuster/Fireside, New York.

Schonberg, Harold C 1963, *The Great Pianists.* Simon and Schuster, New York.

Semmler, Clement 1981, *Aunt Sally and Sacred Cow.* Melbourne University Press.

Serle, Geoffrey 1987, *The Creative Spirit in Australia—A Cultural History*. Heinemann Australia.

Smith, Bernard 1987, *The Antipodean Manifesto—Essays in Art and History*. Oxford University Press.

Symons, Michael 1984, *One Continuous Picnic*. Penguin Australia.

Thomas, Alan 1980, *Broadcast and be Damned*. Melbourne University Press.

Wagner, Wolfgang 1950, 'Bruckner and Mahler in Australia'. Article published in *Chord and Discord*.

White, Mary 1990, 'Ernest Llewellyn remembered'. 2MBS-FM magazine, June issue.

Members of the Orchestra

1934
A.B.C. Symphony Orchestra

Conductor: Sir Hamilton Harty

1st Violins: Messrs. W. J. Grieves (Leader), J. Farnsworth Hall, Vic. Grieves, Lloyd Davies, Mischa Dobrinski, Cecil Berry, Ernest Long, Misses Dulcie Blair, Nora Williamson, Muriel Buchanan, A. De Rago, Daisy Richards.

2nd Violins: Messrs. H. Watts (Principal), Norman Deerson, J. De Rago, J. Hickey, Theo. Turner, W. Houston, R. Southworth, A. Hampton, E. Llewellyn, Les. Martin, Misses Phyllis McDonald, Inez Lang.

Violas: Messrs. W. Krasnik (Principal), R. Wood, J. Waud, A. Sorgato, G. Taylor, Misses R. Gumpertz, Orchard, Mrs. Fyffe.

'Cellos: Messrs. Bryce Carter (Principal), Jack Post, O. Fyffe, Cedric Ashton, Ivor Whittard, Misses R. Cornford, K. Touhy, M. Mankey.

Basses: Messrs. L. Blitz (Principal), W. Shephard, R. Simmons, E. Flack, G. Cleaver, J. Rannard, H. Jones, Jules Brinkman.

Flutes: Messrs. Neville Amadio (Principal), B. Anderson, A. Hole (Piccolo).

Oboes: Messrs. R. Waterfield (Principal), S. Ash.

Cor Anglaise: Mr. R. Elliott.

Clarinets: Messrs. G. Simpson (Principal), G. Paris.

Bass Clarinet: Mr. J. H. Antill.

Bassoons: Messrs. C. Sammull (Principal), G. Marr, J. Pemberton.

Contra Bassoon: Mr. C. Chamberlain.

French Horns: Messrs. H. Woolfe (Principal), E. Monk, A. C. Shaw, A. Strandberg.

Trumpets: Messrs. G. Walker (Principal), J. Tenukest, A. Stender.

Trombones: Messrs. H. Larsen (Principal), C. Prott, A. Mann.

Tuba: Mr. Les. Ryan.

Tympani: Mr. Alard Maling.

Drums and Percussion: Messrs. L. Tutschka, E. Lighton.

Harp: Miss Barnett.

Celeste: Miss R. Less.

Librarian: Mr. E. Pass.

4

SYMPHONY & CHORAL ORCHESTRAL CONCERT
SATURDAY, 13th JUNE, 1942

Personnel of Orchestra

Conductor · · · · · · · · ·	BERNARD HEINZE
Leader of Orchestra · · · · · · ·	LIONEL LAWSON

1st Violins:
Lawson, L.
Hall, J. F.
Grieves, W. J.
Miller, R.
Blair, Miss D.
Preston, A.
Williamson, Miss N.
Taberner, H.
Richards, Miss D.
Wareham, Miss V.
Wooderson, Miss E.
D'Hage, Miss C.
Carter, F. M.
Anschau, Miss D.

2nd Violins:
Grieves, V.
Solomons, S.
Ault, Miss B.
Buchanan, Miss M.
Frith, N.
Thorpe, C.
Finn, Miss E.
Cox, Miss N.
Price, Miss D.
Gibb, L. C.
O'Regan, Miss L.
Marsh, W.

Violas:
Wood, R.
Gumpertz, Miss R.
Hill, Miss B.
Napthine, R.
Sorgato, A.
Forshaw, Miss F.
Bainton, Miss H.
McLean, Miss G.
Wentzell, N.
Wentzell, C.

'Cellos:
Fyfe, O.
Marsh, N.
Cornford, Miss R.
Gotsch, C.
Tuohy, Miss K.
Lang, Miss M.
Van Der Klei, J.
Holmes, Miss C.
Paull, Miss F.
Mankey, Miss J.

Basses:
Waddington, R.
Shephard, W.
Ney, W.
Blitz, L.
Cleaver, G.
Turner, J.
Tranter, G.
Jones, H.

Flutes:
Anderson, B.
McMahon, V.
Hole, A.

Oboes:
Waterfield, M.
Brinkman, J.
Ash, S.

Cor Anglais:
Wolstenholme, S.

Clarinets:
Simson, E.
Paris, G.
Williamson, D.

Bass Clarinet:
Brockie, M.

Bassoons:
Sammul, C.
Black, W.
Pemberton, J.

Contrabassoon:
Maher, G.

Horns:
Woolfe, H.
Gervasoni, G.
Mann, A.
Lego, W.

Trumpets:
Mellor, T.
Walker, C.
Fellows, E.

Trombones:
Larsen, H.
Fellows, W.
Holley, J.

Tuba:
Ward, D.

Tympani:
Maling, A.

Drums and Effects:
Charlesworth, A.
Palmer, S.
Bowden, A. R.

Harp:
Gibson, Miss U.
Bendall, A.

Librarian:
McKenzie, W. H.

Next Concert:
TOWN HALL, SYDNEY
SATURDAY, 11th JULY, at 2.15 p.m.
Conductor: PERCY CODE.
Soloist: ISADOR GOODMAN.

SYDNEY SYMPHONY ORCHESTRA
(SEASON OF 1953)

EUGENE GOOSSENS, Conductor
JOSEPH POST, Associate Conductor

Violins (1):
Ernest Llewellyn
(Concertmaster)
Robert Miller
(Asst. Concertmaster)
Harold Taberner
Samuel Helfgott
Bela Dekany
Donald Blair
Peter Abraham
Gordon Bennett
Nora Williamson
Dulcie Blair
Heather Sumner
Veta Wareham
Eva Kelly
Barbara Kearns
Klara Korda
Yvonne Gannoni

Violins (2):
Victor Grieves
(Principal)
Ronald Ryder
Robert Acheson
Bernard Donnelly
Claude McGlynn
Clyde Thorpe
Muriel Buchanan
Gwynneth Brooks
Cliff. Hanney
Fred Kramer
Donald Hazelwood
Craig Coomer

Violas:
Robert Pikler
(Principal)
Robert Wood
Blodwen Hill
Reginald Napthine
Helen Bainton
Nathan Beresniakoff
Cliff. Gibbs
Max Cooke
Doreen Price

'Cellos:
Hans George
(Principal)
Niel Marsh
Jessie Mankey
Lois Simpson
Edward Engel
Cyril Schulvater
Gwen Prockter
Rosamund Cornford
Barbara Woolley

Basses:
Charles H. Gray
(Principal)
William J. Shepherd
Horace Bissell
George Kraus
Gerald Tranter
John McPherson
Raymond Price
Ernest Howard

Harp:
Elizabeth Vidler

Flutes:
Neville Amadio
John Freeland

Piccolo:
Colin Evans

Oboes:
Horace Green
Frank Challen

Cor Anglais:
Ian Wilson

Clarinets:
Douglas Williamson
Henry Barlow

Bass Clarinet:
Mason Brockie

Bassoons:
Walter Black
Ray Maling

Contrabassoon:
George Maher

French Horns:
Alan Mann
Clarence Mellor
Alfred H. Hooper
Stan Fry
Guido Gervasoni

Trumpets:
John Robertson
David Price
Arthur Stender

Trombones:
Stan Browne
Frank Locke
William Waterer

Tuba:
Cliff. Goodchild

Timpani:
Alard Maling

Percussion:
Arthur Charlesworth
Lou Tutschka.
Joseph Mike

Piano:
Nancy Salas

Celeste:
Eva Kelly

Organ:
Maynard Wilkinson

Librarian:
H. P. Welford

ORCHESTRAL MANAGER - - - C. K. LAWSON

Page Eighteen

1967

SYDNEY SYMPHONY
ORCHESTRA

Musical Director:

DEAN DIXON

Concert Master:
DONALD HAZELWOOD

Violins (1)

Donald Hazelwood
Harold Taberner
(*Asst. Concert Master*)
Alwyn Elliott
Arthur Leech
Samuel Helfgott
Albert Preston
Donald Blair
Andrew Hoffman
Mascot Blake
Margaret Wilbow
Jennifer James
Nerida Ritchie
Errol Russell

Violins (2)

Ronald Ryder
(Principal)
Antoni Bonetti
Bernard Donnelly
Joseph Costa
Dan Scully
Gary Andrews
Ferenc Gyors
Frank Ellery
Clyde Thorpe

Violas

Ronald Cragg
(Principal)
John Gould
David Jackson
Cliff Gibbs
Max Cooke
Blodwen Hill
Robert Wood
Reginald Napthine
Helen Bainton
Margaret Berriman

Basses

Walter Sutcliffe
(Principal)
Horace Bissell
Donald Wrighter
Tibor Nappholz
Winston Sterling
Ken McLure
Max Claxton

Harp

June Loney

Flutes

Neville Amadio
Paul Curtis
William Frater

Piccolo

Colin Evans

Oboes

Pauline Strait
Claire Fox

Cor Anglais

Peter Newbury

Clarinets

Donald Westlake
Kevin Murphy
Anne Menzies

Cellos

Lois Simpson
(Principal)
Gregory Elmaloglou
Juris Muiznieks
Peggy Leech
Neil Marsh
Brian Duke
Rosamund Cornford
Alex Pogodin
Edward Engel

Bass Clarinet

Peter Kyng

Bassoons

John Cran
Glen Spicer
Walter Black

Contrabassoon

Ray Maling

French Horns

Clarence Mellor
Douglas Trengove
Edwin Lorentsen
Napier Dunn
Alan Mann

Trumpets

John Robertson
John Wood
David Price

Trombones

Russell Mattocks
Baden McCarron

Bass Trombone

William Waterer

Tuba

Cliff Goodchild

Timpani

Barry Heywood

Percussion

Lou Tutschka
David Kember
Miloslav Penicka

Librarian

Miloslav Penicka

ORCHESTRA MANAGER - - ERNEST GIBB

1977

SYDNEY SYMPHONY ORCHESTRA
Chief Conductor: WILLEM VAN OTTERLOO
Concertmaster: DONALD HAZELWOOD, O.B.E.

First Violins
Donald Hazelwood, OBE
(Concertmaster)
Alwyn Elliott
(Dep. Concertmaster)
Antoni Bonetti
(Repetiteur)
Donald Blair
Mascot Blake
Joseph Costa
Noelene Gower
Andrew Hoffman
Jennifer James
Gisela Kopsch
Arthur Leech
Kek Tjiang Lim
Errol Russell
Heather Sumner
Harold Taberner
Margaret Wilbow

Second Violins
Gary Andrews
(Principal)
Peter Ashley
(Assoc. Princ.)
Edna Beech
Susan Dobbie
Bernard Donnelly
Ruth Micheli
Anton Nevistich
Janet Piper
Janos Rac
Janet Sapritchian
Boris Warton
Virginia Weekes
Warren Reid
Mark Singer

Violas
Ronald Cragg
(Principal)
Laszlo Vidak
(Assoc. Princ.)
Margaret Berriman
Linda Cale
Max Cooke
Cliff Gibbs
Joyce Horwood
Robert Humes
David Jackson
Catherine O'Flynn
Keith Steele
Waldemar Wolski

Celli
Algimantas Motiekaitis
(Principal)
Gregory Elmaloglou
(Assoc. Princ.)
Brian Duke
Robert W. Miller
Anthony Morgan
Juris Muiznieks
Joyce Murphy
Maureen O'Carroll
Alex Pogodin
Leslie Strait

Basses
Walter Sutcliffe
(Principal)
David McBride
(Assoc. Princ.)
Neil Brawley
Maxwell Claxton
Kenneth McLure
David Potts
John Shields
Winston Sterling

Harp
June Loney

Flutes
Neville Amadio, MBE
(Principal)
Paul Curtis
(Assoc. Princ.)
Geoffrey Collins

Piccolo
Colin Evans

Oboes
Guy Henderson
(Principal)
Kathryn Martin
(Assoc. Princ.)
Claire Fox

Cor Anglais
Peter Newbury

Clarinets
Donald Westlake
(Principal)
Kevin Murphy
(Assoc. Princ.)
Anne Menzies

Bass Clarinet
Peter Kyng

Bassoons
John Cran
(Principal)
Richard McIntyre
(Assoc. Princ.)
John Noble

Contrabassoon
Martin Foster

French Horns
Anthony Buddle
(Principal)
Clarence Mellor
(A. Assoc. Princ.)
Bernard Hillman
Douglas Trengove
(Principal)
Edwin Lorentsen

Trumpets
Gordon Webb
(Principal)
John Wood
(Assoc. Princ.)
Peter Walmsley
Geoff Payne

Trombones
Russell Mattocks
(Principal)
Baden McCarron

Bass Trombone
Alan Mewett

Tuba
Cliff Goodchild

Timpani
Barry Heywood

Percussion
Michael Askill
(Principal)
Colin Piper
Ian Bloxsom
Richard Miller

Asst. Orchestra Manager
Robert Rowling

Librarian
Walter Owen

Orchestra Manager — COLIN DUNTON

Permanent string players are listed in alphabetical order

1983
SYDNEY SYMPHONY ORCHESTRA

Chief Conductor: SIR CHARLES MACKERRAS
Concertmaster: DONALD HAZELWOOD, OBE

First Violins
Donald Hazelwood, OBE
(Concertmaster)
Alwyn Elliott
(Dep. Concertmaster)
Antoni Bonetti
(Principal)
Mascot Blake
Joseph Costa
Noelene Gower
Margaret Heywood
Jennifer James
Natalia Koloskova
Warren Reid
Janet Sapritchian
Deborah Scholem
Alexander Vinokurov
Léone Ziegler
Fiona Ziegler
Martin Lass

Second Violins
Gary Andrews
(Principal)
Peter Ashley
(Assoc. Princ.)
Karl Bloom
Christine Cottle
Susan Dobbie
Christine Forstat
Faina Krel
Ruth Micheli
Anton Nevistich
Janos Rac
Robert Tepper
Boris Warton
Christine Hill
Philippa Paige

Violas
Laszlo Vidak
(A/Princ.)
David Jackson
(A/Assoc. Princ.)
Margaret Berriman

Max Cooke
Cliff Gibbs
Robert Humes
Mary McVarish
Dittany Morgan
Keith Steele
Waldemar Wolski
Jane Hazelwood
Janet Syke

Cellos
Algimantas Motiekaitis
(Principal)
Gregory Elmaloglou
(Assoc. Princ.)
Detlev Deubach
Brian Duke
Mayor Gorbatov
Robert W. Miller
Juris Muiznieks
Joyce Murphy
Wendy Reid
Leslie Strait

Basses
Walter Sutcliffe
(Principal)
Neil Brawley
(Assoc. Princ.)
Brett Berthold
Maxwell Claxton
David Potts
Ross Radford
John Shields
Winston Sterling

Harp
Ulpia Erdos
(A/Princ.)

Flutes
Geofrey Collins
(Guest Principal)
Susan West
(Assoc. Princ.)
Christine Draegar

Piccolo
Jenny Andrews

Oboes
Guy Henderson
(Principal)
Kathryn Martin
(Assoc. Princ.)
Carol Hellmers

Cor Anglais
Karel Lang

Clarinets
Alan Vivian
(Principal)
Lawrence Dobell
(Assoc. Princ.)
Anne Menzies

Bass Clarinets
Craig Wernicke

Bassoons
John Cran
(Principal)
Roger Brooke
(Assoc. Princ.)
Keith Robinson

Contrabassoon
Martin Foster

French Horns
Kazimierz Machala
(Principal)
Lee Bracegirdle
(Assoc. Princ.)
Bernard Hillman
Douglas Trengove
(Principal 3rd)
Clarence Mellor
Chris Harrison

Trumpets
Daniel Mendelow
(Principal)
John Wood
(Assoc. Princ.)
Peter Walmsley
Paul Goodchild

Trombones
Russell Mattocks
(Principal)
Ronald Prussing
(Assoc. Princ.)
Baden McCarron

Bass Trombone
Alan Mewett

Tuba
Cameron Brook

Timpani
Barry Heywood

Percussion
Michael Askill
(Principal)
Colin Piper
Richard Miller

Continuo
Peter Watcham

Celeste
Anthony Baldwin

A/Librarian
David White

A/Asst. Orchestra Manager
Mary Jo Capps

Orchestra Manager — COLIN DUNTON

Permanent string players are listed in alphabetical order

SYDNEY SYMPHONY ORCHESTRA
1992

Donald Hazelwood AO, OBE, Dene Olding *Co-Concertmasters*

FIRST VIOLINS
Donald Hazelwood
(*Concertmaster*)
Dene Olding (*Concertmaster*)
Goetz Richter
Antoni Bonetti (*Principal*)
Julie Batty
Jennifer Booth
Joseph Costa
Alwyn Elliott
Jennifer James
Rosalind Maud
Warren Reid
Janet Sapritchian
Alexander Vinokurov
Fiona Ziegler
Leone Ziegler

SECOND VIOLINS
Gary Andrews (*Principal*)
Sue Dobbie (*Assoc. Principal*)
Pieter Bersee
Maria Durek
Shuti Huang
Stanislaw Kornel
Faina Krel
Georges Lentz
Nicola Lewis
Benjamin Li
Elizabeth Lockwood
Philippa Paige
Biyana Rozenblit
Karl Titchener-Bloom
Boris Warton
Maja Verunica

VIOLAS
Peter Pfuhl (*Principal*)
Anne-louise Comerford
(*Assoc. Principal*)
Robyn Brookfield
Graham Hennings
Robert Humes
David Jackson
Rodney Lovenfosse
Justine Marsden-Wickham
Mary McVarish
Catherine O'Flynn
Leonid Volovelsky
Waldemar Wolski

CELLOS
Catherine Hewgill
(*Principal*)
Gregory Elmaloglou (*Assoc. Principal*)
Mayor Gorbatov
Frederick McKay
Patricia Mendelow
Antony Morgan
Peter Morrison
Juris Muiznieks
Wendy Reid
David Wickham

DOUBLE BASS
Kees Boersma (*Principal*)
Neil Brawley (*Assoc. Principal*)
Maxwell Claxton
David Potts
Ross Radford
John Shields
Winston Sterling
Walter Sutcliffe

HARP
Louise Johnson (*Principal*)

FLUTES
Janet Webb (*Principal*)
James Kortum

PICCOLO
Rosamund Plummer
(*Principal*)

OBOES
Guy Henderson (*Principal*)
Simon Blount
Carol Hellmers

COR ANGLAIS
Karel Lang (*Principal*)

CLARINETS
Lawrence Dobell (*Principal*)
Margery Smith (*Assoc. Principal*)
Anne Menzies

BASS CLARINET
Craig Wernicke (*Principal*)

BASSOONS
John Cran (*Principal*)
Roger Brooke (*Assoc. Principal*)
Lorelei Dowling

CONTRABASSOON
Martin Foster (*Principal*)

HORNS
Robert Johnson (*Principal*)
Lee Bracegirdle (*Assoc. Principal*)
Bernard Hillman
Douglas Trengrove
(*Principal 3rd*)
Clarence Mellor
Chris Harrison

TRUMPETS
Daniel Mendelow (*Principal*)
Paul Goodchild (*Assoc. Principal*)
Peter Walmsley
John Wood

TROMBONES
Ronald Prussing (*Principal*)
Scott Kinmont (*Assoc. Principal*)
Russell Mattocks

BASS TROMBONE
Alan Mewett (*Principal*)

TUBA
Steve Rosse (*Principal*)

TIMPANI
Richard Miller (*Principal*)

PERCUSSION
Ian Cleworth (*Principal*)
Rebecca Lagos
Colin Piper

Some world premieres and first Australian performances given by the Sydney Symphony Orchestra

1937 Mahler: Symphony No 5. *Conductor*: Schneevoigt.*

1938 Prokofiev: Violin Concerto No 1. *Soloist*: Llewellyn. *Conductor*: Szell.*

1939 Sibelius: Symphony No 5. *Conductor*: Bainton.* Walton: Symphony No 1. *Conductor*: Szell.*

1940 Copland: El Salon Mexico. *Conductor*: Heinze.* Delius: Appalachia. *Soloist*: Harold Williams. *Conductor*: Beecham.* Holst: Somerset Rhapsody. *Conductor*: Heinze.* Mahler: Symphony No 4. *Conductor*: Dorati.* Weinberger: Variations and Fugue on an Old English Folk Tune (Under the Spreading Chestnut Tree). *Conductor*: Dorati.*

1941 Bainton: Symphony in D minor. *Conductor*: Bainton.+ Hyde: Fantasy Romantic for Piano and Orchestra. *Soloist*: Hyde. *Conductor*: Heinze.+ Agnew: The Breaking of the Drought—Poem for Orchestra and Voice. *Soloist*: Helmrich. *Conductor*: Heinze.+

1943 Shostakovich: Symphony No 7, Leningrad. *Conductor*: Heinze.*

1944 Respighi: Concerto Gregoriano. *Soloist*: Beck. *Conductor*: Edwin McArthur.* Bach-Ormandy: Toccata, Intermezzo and Fugue in C. *Conductor*: Ormandy.* Shostakovich: Symphony No 5. *Conductor*: Ormandy.*

1945 Moeran: Symphony. *Conductor*: Code.* Vaughan-Williams: Symphony No 5. *Conductor*: Code.* Britten: Serenade for Tenor, Horn and Strings. *Soloists*: John Fullard and Roy White. *Conductor*: Code.* Bax: Violin Concerto. *Soloist*: Llewellyn. *Conductor*: Code.* Bliss: Piano Concerto. *Soloist*: Alan McCristal. *Conductor*: Code.* Busoni: Violin Concerto. *Soloist*: Beck. *Conductor*: MacMillan.*

1946 Britten: Sinfonia da Requiem. *Conductor*: Susskind.* Stravinsky: The Rite of Spring. *Conductor*: Goossens.* Piston: The Incredible Flutist—Suite. *Conductor*: Goossens.* Antill: Corroboree—Suite.+ Britten: Four Sea Interludes from Peter Grimes. *Conductor*: J.F. Hall.*

1947 (all conducted by Goossens) Smetana: Richard III.* R. Strauss: Rosenkavalier Suite.* Franck, orch. Pierne: Prelude, Chorale and Fugue.* Bloch: Schelomo. *Soloist*: Lauri Kennedy.*

1948 (all conducted by Goossens unless noted) Ravel: Valses Nobles et Sentimentales.* Schoenberg: Transfigured Night (orchestral version).* Mahler: Symphony No 1.* Walton: Violin Concerto. *Soloist*: Llewellyn. *Conductor*: Paul Kletzki.* Bax: Symphony No 4.* R. Harris: Symphony No 3.* Prokofiev: Symphony No 5.* Berners: Fantasie Espagnole.* Gerhard: Six Spanish Songs. *Soloist*: S. Wyss. *Conductor*: Heinze.+ Ravel: Rapsodie Espagnole.* Tchaikovsky: Manfred.*

1949 Britten: Violin Concerto. *Soloist*: Thomas Matthews. *Conductor*: Heinze.* R. Strauss: Symphonia Domestica. *Conductor*: Goossens.* Martinu: Concerto for double string orchestra, piano and timpani. *Conductor*: Kubelik.* Mahler: Symphony No 7. *Conductor*: Goossens.* Stravinsky: Apollo. *Conductor*: Goossens.* Shostakovich: Symphony No 9. *Conductor*: Klemperer.*

1950 (all conducted by Goossens unless noted) Liszt: A Faust Symphony.* Martin: Petite Symphonie Concertante.* Bruckner: Symphony No 1.* Bartok: Music for Strings, Percussion and Celeste.* Schoenberg: Theme and Variations for Orchestra. *Conductor*: Klemperer.* Benjamin: Piano Concerto. *Soloist*: Benjamin.+

1951 (all conducted by Goossens unless noted) R. Strauss: An Alpine Symphony.* Salome (concert performance).* Elektra (concert performance).* Villa-Lobos: Bachianas Brasileiras No 2.* Scriabin: Prometheus. *Soloist*: Muriel Cohen.* Stravinsky: Symphony in Three Movements.* Bloch: Concerto symphonique. *Soloist*: Jascha Spivakovsky.* Vaughan-Williams: Symphony No 4.* Mahler: Symphony No 8. M. Sutherland: Haunted Hills.+ Debussy: Jeux.* Copland: Billy the Kid.* Roussel: Bacchus and Ariadne—Suite No 2. *Conductor*: Barbirolli.

1952 Shostakovich: Symphony No 6. *Conductor*: Goossens. Honegger: Symphony No 3. *Conductor*: Heinze. Symphony No 4. *Conductor*: Heinze. R. Strauss: Metamorphosen. *Conductor*: Goossens. David Moule-Evans: Symphony. Goossens.+ Stravinsky: Song of the Nightingale. *Conductor*: Goossens.* Berg: Wozzeck—fragments. *Soloist*: Haas. *Conductor*: Goossens.* Nielsen: Symphony No 4 (Inextinguishable). *Conductor*: Post.* Bartok: Two Portraits. *Conductor*: Paul.* Britten: Piano Concerto. *Soloist*: Spivakovsky. *Conductor*: Paul.* R. Hanson: Trumpet Concerto. *Soloist*: Robertson. *Conductor*: Heinze.+ Schoenberg: Ode to Napoleon. *Soloist*: Malcolm Williamson. *Conductor*: Heinze.* Rachmaninov: The Isle of the Dead. *Conductor*: Heinze.*

1953 (all conducted by Goossens unless noted) Kabalevsky: Symphony No 2.* Hindemith: Philharmonic Concerto.* Prokofiev: Romeo and Juliet—Suite.* Scythian Suite.* Vaughan-Williams: Sinfonia Antartica. *Soloist*: Margaret Moore.* Martinu: Symphony No 5.* Bruckner: Symphony No 9.* C. Douglas: Essay for Strings. *Conductor*: Susskind.+

1954 (all conducted by Goossens) Gliere: Symphony No 3 (Ilya Mourometz).* Rawsthorne: Violin Concerto. *Soloist*: Maurice Clare. Hindemith: Symphony in E flat.* Tippett: Concerto for Double String Orchestra.* Mahler: The Song of the Earth. *Soloists*: Florence Taylor and Max Worthley.* Goossens: The Apocalypse.+ Don Banks: Four Pieces.+

1955 (all conducted by Goossens unless noted) Nielsen: Symphony No 5.* Sibelius: The Tempest—Prelude. *Conductor*: Susskind.* Bloch: Concerto Grosso

No 2.* Rachmaninov: Symphony No 3.* Stravinsky: Symphony in C.* Prokofiev: Symphony No 7. *Conductor*: Heinze.* Britten: Gloriana—Suite.* Rubbra: Symphony No 6. *Conductor*: Barbirolli.*

1956   Roussel: Symphony No 3. *Conductor*: Post.* R. Strauss: Le Bourgeois Gentilhomme. *Conductor*: Heinze.* Martinu: Oboe concerto. *Soloist*: Tancibudek. *Conductor*: Schmidt-Isserstedt.+ Shostakovich: Symphony No 10. *Conductor*: Heinze.* Kodaly: Peacock Variations. *Conductor*: Post.* Orff: Carmina Burana. *Conductor*: Schmidt-Isserstedt.*

1957   Bainton: Symphony No 3. *Conductor*: Heinze.+ Copland: Rodeo—Four Dances. *Conductor*: Malko.*

1958   Falla: Homenajes—Suite. *Conductor*: Malko.* Milhaud: Piano Concerto No 3. *Soloist*: Gordon Watson. *Conductor*: Heinze.* Tubin: Symphony No 5. *Conductor*: Malko.* Berg: Lulu—Suite. *Conductor*: Malko.* Villa Lobos: Bachianas Brasileiras No 4.* Creston: Symphony No 2. *Conductor*: Edouard van Remoortel. David Morgan: Symphony No 4 (Classical). *Conductor*: Malko.+

1959   Walton: Partita. *Conductor*: Heinze.* Shostakovich: Symphony No 11. *Conductor*: Heinze.* Stravinsky: Oedipus Rex. *Conductor*: Malko. Yves de la Casiniere: Improvised Concerto for Organ and Orchestra. *Soloist*: Pierre Cochereau. *Conductor*: Malko.* Glazunov: Les Ruses d'Amour. *Conductor*: Malko.* J.C. Bach: Harpsichord Concerto in B flat. *Soloist*: Dallas Haslam. *Conductor*: Woess.* Bartok: Rhapsody for piano and orchestra. *Soloist*: Andor Foldes. *Conductor*: Heinze.* Williamson: Piano concerto No 1. *Soloist*: Igor Hmelnitsky. *Conductor*: Malko.*

1960   Prokofiev: Sinfonie Concertante. *Soloist*: Mstislav Rostropovich. *Conductor*: George Tzipine.* Berwald: Symphonie Singuliere. *Conductor*: Markevitch.*

1961   Walton: Symphony No 2. *Conductor*: Heinze.* W. Schuman: Judith—Choreographic Poem. *Conductor*: Post.* Martinu: Symphony No. 6. *Conductor*: Karel Ancerl.* Villa Lobos: Bachianas Brasileiras No 8. *Conductor*: Alberto Bolet.

1962   Shostakovich: Violin Concerto. *Soloist*: Leonid Kogan. *Conductor*: Horenstein.* Chausson: Poeme de l'Amour et de la Mer. *Soloist*: Maureen Forrester. *Conductor*: Francesco Mander.*

1963   Bartok: Bluebeard's Castle. *Soloists*: Lauris Elms and Alan Light. *Conductor*: Hopkins.* Goossens: Divertissment. *Conductor*: Post.+ Haydn: Symphony No 58. *Conductor*: Massimo Freccia.* Henze: Three Dithyrambs for chamber orchestra. *Conductor*: Post.*

1964   Stravinsky: The Rake's Progress—Anna's Scene. *Soloist*: Elsie Morison. *Conductor*: Kubelik.* Mahler: Symphony No 10—adagio. *Conductor*: Heinze.* Bliss: A Knot of Riddles. *Soloist*: John Shirley-Quirk. *Conductor*: Bliss.* Richard Meale: Homage to Garcia Lorca. *Conductor*: Post.+ M. Williamson: Piano Concerto No 3. *Soloist*: John Ogdon. *Conductor*: Dixon.* Ravel: Tzigane (arr for cimbalon). *Soloist*: Hmelnitsky. *Conductor*: Llewellyn.*

1965   Prokofiev: Alexander Nevsky. *Soloist*: Heather Harper. *Conductor*: Dixon.* Messiaen: Oiseaux Exotiques. *Soloist*: Richard Meale. *Conductor*: Hopkins.*

1966   Stravinsky: Agon. *Conductor*: Gielen.* Rieger: Study in Sonority for Ten Violins. *Conductor*: Dixon.* Seiber/Dankworth: Improvisation for Jazz Band and Orchestra. *Conductor*: Dixon.* Lutoslawski: Three Poems of Henri Michaux. *Conductor*: Hopkins.* Webern: Five Pieces for String Orchestra. *Conductor*: Post.*

1967   Meale: Nocturnes. *Conductor*: Dixon.+ Henze: Symphony No 1. *Conductor*: Dixon.* Penderecki Threnody for Victims of Hiroshima. *Conductor*: Hopkins.*

Takemitsu: Textures. *Conductor*: Hopkins.* Berlioz: Te Deum. *Soloist*: Raymond McDonald. *Conductor*: Hopkins.* Xenakis: Pithoprakta.* Nigel Butterley: Interaction—Music and Painting. With John Peart. *Conductor*: Hopkins.+ W. Lovelock: Divertimento for Strings. *Conductor*: Heinze.*

1968 Butterley: Meditations of Thomas Traherne. *Conductor*: Atzmon.+ Prokofiev: Symphony No 3. *Conductor*: Stanford Robinson.* Meale: Very High Kings. *Conductor*: Post.+ Szymanowski: Violin Concerto No 1. *Soloist*: Ladislav Jasek. *Conductor*: Hopkins.* Lutoslawski: Concerto for Orchestra. *Conductor*: Hopkins.* Messiaen: Et Exspecto Resurrectionem Mortuorum. *Conductor*: Hopkins.* David Ahern: Ned Kelly Music. *Conductor*: Hopkins.+

1969 Butterley: Pentad. *Conductor*: Atzmon.+ Varese: Deserts. *Conductor*: Gary Bertini.* Stravinsky: Les Noces (The Wedding). *Conductor*: Hopkins.* Felix Werder: Tower Concerto. *Conductor*: Hopkins.+ Ives: Three Places in New England. *Conductor*: Hopkins.* Sculthorpe: Ketjak (Sun Music II). *Conductor*: Hopkins.+ Messiaen: Reveil des oiseaux. *Soloist*: David Miller. *Conductor*: Atzmon.* Takemitsu: Music of Tree. *Conductor*: Atzmon.* Meale: Soon It Will Die. *Conductor*: Atzmon.+

1970 Ligeti: Atmospheres. *Conductor*: Charles Bruck.* Tippett: Piano Concerto. *Soloist*: Ogden. *Conductor*: Bruck.* Sculthorpe: Music of Rain. Conductor: Janos Ferencsik.+ Werder: Sound Canvas. *Conductor*: Atzmon.+ Haydn: Symphony No 39. *Conductor*: Paul.* Sculthorpe: Love 200. *Conductor*: Hopkins.+ Mahler: Symphony No 10 (ed. Cooke/Goldschmidt). *Conductor*: Hopkins.* Lutoslawski: Symphony No 2. *Conductor*: Hopkins.* Ligeti: Lontano. *Conductor*: Hopkins.*

1971 Douglas: Three Frescoes. *Conductor*: Atzmon.+ Larry Sitsky: Concerto for Woodwind Quintet and Orchestra. *Conductor*: Mackerras.+ Gerhard: Concerto for Orchestra. *Conductor*: Atzmon.* Messiaen: Colours of the Celestial City. *Soloist*: Miller. *Conductor*: Post.* Barry Conyngham: Six. *Soloists*: The Percussions of Strasbourg. *Conductor*: Post.+ Varese: Ionisation. *Conductor*: Post.* Ross Edwards: Etude for Orchestra. *Conductor*: Mackerras.+ Mahler: Symphony No 6. *Conductor*: Hopkins.*

1972 Prokofiev: Violin concerto No 2. *Soloist*: Sylvia Rosenberg. *Conductor*: Otterloo.* R.R. Bennett: Piano Concerto. *Soloist*: Stephen Bishop. *Conductor*: Elyakum Shapirra.* Copland: Symphony No 3. *Conductor*: Shapirra.* Shostakovich: Symphony No 4. *Conductor*: Hopkins.* Butterley: First Day Covers. *Soloist*: Gordon Chater. *Conductor*: Hopkins.+ R. Hanson: Piano Concerto. *Soloist*: Albert Landa. *Conductor*: Patrick Thomas.+

1973 Berlioz: Beatrice et Benedict. *Conductor*: Hopkins.* Banks: Nexus. *Conductor*: Hopkins.+ Webern: Five Orchestral Pieces. *Conductor*: Otterloo.* Prokofiev: Symphony No 6. *Conductor*: Comissiona.*

1974 Shostakovich: Symphony No 14. *Soloists*: Marilyn Richardson and Simon Estes. *Conductor*: Susskind.* Banks: Prospects. *Conductor*: Otterloo.+ Stravinsky: Danses Concertantes. *Conductor*: Otterloo.* Williamson: Symphony No 3. *Conductor*: Hopkins.* Shostakovich: Symphony No 15. *Conductor*: Hopkins.*

1976 Martin Wesley-Smith: Sh. *Conductors*: Hopkins and Peter Seymour.+

1977 William Schuman: Violin Concerto. *Soloist*: Zvi Zeitlin. *Conductor*: Otterloo.* Poulenc: Flute Concerto. *Soloist*: James Galway. *Conductor*: Hiroyuki Iwaki.* Haydn: Symphony No 89. *Conductor*: Iwaki.*

1978 Ives: Decoration Day. *Conductor*: Aaron Copland.* Hoddinott: Clarinet Concerto. *Soloist*: Jack Brymer. *Conductor*: Otterloo.* Martin: Maria Triptychon. *Soloists*: Elly Ameling and Donald Hazelwood. *Conductor*: Otterloo.* Lutoslawski:

Cello Concerto. *Soloist*: Heinrich Schiff. *Conductor*: Michi Inoue.* Bloch: Sacred Service, *Soloist*: Raymond Myers. *Conductor*: Shapirra.* Busoni: Piano concerto. *Soloist*: Larry Sitsky. *Conductor*: Mackerras.*

1979   Sculthorpe: Mangrove. *Conductor*: Fremaux.+

1980   Sculthorpe: Visions of Captain Quiros. *Soloist*: John Williams. *Conductor*: Niklaus Wyss.+

1981   Butterley: Symphony. *Conductor*: Fremaux.+ Williamson: Symphony No 5. *Conductor*: Thomas.* Berio: Sinfonia. *Soloists*: New Swingle Singers. *Conductor*: Dalia Atlas.* Szymanowski: Stabat Mater. *Conductor*: Skrowaczewski.*

1982   Haydn: Overture—Le Pescatrice. *Conductor*: Werner Andreas Albert.* Tippett: Concerto for violin, viola, cello and orchestra. *Conductor*: Thomas.* Graham Koehne: Rain forest. *Conductor*: Ronald Zollman.+

1983   Wagner: Symphony in C. *Conductor*: Mackerras.* John McCabe: Notturni ed Alba. *Soloist*: Beverley Bergen. *Conductor*: Fremaux.* Webern: Im Sommerwind. *Conductor*: Mackerras.*

1984   Lutoslawski: Symphony No 3. *Conductor*: Elgar Howarth.* Berlioz: The Trojans. *Conductor*: Mackerras.* (First complete performance.) Sitsky: Songs and Dances from The Golem. *Conductor*: James Loughran.+ Koechlin: Les Bandar-Log. *Conductor*: David Zinman.*

1985   Bach-Stravinsky: Variations on Von Himmel Hoch. *Conductor*: Tintner.* Kokkonen: Symphony No 4. *Conductor*: Okko Kamu.* Shostakovich: Symphony No 8. *Conductor*: Nicholas Braithwaite.* Martinu: Symphony No 1. *Conductor*: Zdenek Macal.*

1986   John Adams: Shaker Loops. *Conductor*: Thomas.* Harmonium. *Conductor*: Iwaki.* H. Hanson: Symphony No 2, Romantic. *Conductor*: Antonio de Almeida.* Moya Henderson: Six Urban Songs. *Soloist*: Elizabeth Harwood. *Conductor*: Almeida.+ Vincent Plush: Pacifica. *Conductor*: Macal.+ Penderecki: Cello Concerto No 2. *Soloist*: Schiff. *Conductor*: Challender.* Part: Cantus in memory of Benjamin Britten. *Conductor*: Hopkins.*

1987   Lutoslawski: Chain 2. *Soloist*: Dene Olding. *Conductor*: Lutoslawski.* Conyngham: Ice Carving. *Soloist*: Hazelwood. *Conductor*: Hopkins.+

1988   Richard Mills: Voyages and Visions. *Conductor*: Mills.+ R. Edwards: Maninyas. *Soloist*: Olding. *Conductor*: David Porcelijn.+ Boulez: Rituel—In Memoriam Maderna. *Conductor*: Porcelijn.*

1989   David Lumsdaine: Mandala 5. *Conductor*: Challender.+ Colin Bright: Earth Spirit. *Conductor*: Braithwaite.+ Bitwistle: Endless Parade. *Soloist*: Hakan Hardenberger. *Conductor*: Challender.* Varese: Arcana. *Conductor*: Challender.* R. Edwards: Yarrageh—Nocturne for solo percussion and orchestra. *Soloist*: Ian Cleworth. *Conductor*: Hopkins.+ Corigliano: Clarinet concerto. *Soloist*: Lawrence Dobell. *Conductor*: Jorge Mester.*

Index